M000220874

TEMPLAR GOLD

"Mr. Byrne is perhaps the first to crack the enigma and mystery of the Masonic oral tradition and put to rest a 3500-year-old mystery. A must-read book for any Freemason and most especially for any royal Arch Mason."

—Stephen Dafoe, Grand Historian for
the Sovereign Great Priory of Canada Knights Templar

TEMPLAR GOLD

GOLD

Discovering the
Ark of the Covenant

Patrick Byrne, M.A.

SYMPOSIUM

Copyright © 2001 Patrick Byrne
All rights reserved.

Published by Symposium Publishing,
an imprint of Blue Dolphin Publishing, Inc.

For inquiries or orders, address
Blue Dolphin Publishing, Inc.
P.O. Box 8, Nevada City, CA 95959
1-800-643-0765
www.bluedolphinpublishing.com

ISBN: 1-57733-099-4

Library of Congress Cataloging-in-Publication Data

Byrne, Patrick, 1940–
    Templar gold : discovering the Ark of the Covenant / Patrick Byrne.
        p. cm.
    Includes bibliographical references and index.
    ISBN 1-57733-099-4
        1. Ark of the Covenant—Miscellanea. 2. Templars—Miscellanea.
    3. Freemasonry—Miscellanea. 4. Rennes-le-Château (France)—
    Miscellanea. 5. Royal Arch Masons—Rituals—Miscellanea. I. Title.

BM657.A8 B97 2001
271'.7913—dc21

                                                                00-067976

Cover art, "The Ark of the Covenant," by Chester Comstock,
Comstock Sculpture Studio
http://www.artsales.com/comstock / email: chester@edgecity.com
Used with permission.

Printed in the United States of America

10   9   8   7   6   5   4   3   2

The following illustrations are printed with permission:

Figures 12, 13, 14, 15, 19, 20. Copyright © 2000 Leen Ritmeyer. Reconstruction by Dr. Leen Ritmeyer.

Figure 27. The First Degree Tracing Board. Photo by Anne Strachan.

Figures 31, 34, 35. IGN Map No. 72 © IGN Paris 1998, Authorization No. 90-0069.

Figures 43, 44, 48, 60. Drawings by Nicola Byrne.

Figure 46, 49, 50. IGN Map No. 2347OT © IGN Paris 1994, Authorization No. 90-0069.

Figure 52. *Circular map of Jerusalem.* Royal Library at The Hague.

Figure 58. *Chapter candles layout at Pech Cardou with the hexagram from Figure 57 superimposed.* IGN Map No. 72 © IGN Paris 1996, Authorization No. 90-0069.

Figure 77. *St. John the Baptist.* Musée du Louvre.

Figure 79. *Virgin on the Rocks.* Musée du Louvre.

Figure 80. *Plague at Ashod.* Musée du Louvre.

Figure 81. *The Arcadian Shepherds.* Musée du Louvre.

Figure 82. *Eliezer and Rebecca.* Musée du Louvre.

Figure 84. *Tancred and Erminia I.* The State Hermitage Museum, St. Petersburg.

Figure 85. *Tancred and Erminia II,* © 1635 by Nicholas Poussin. The Barber Institute of Fine Arts, University of Birmingham/Bridgeman Art Library.

Figure 87. *Death of Germanicus.* The Minneapolis Institute of Arts.

Figure 89. *Second Self-Portrait.* Musée du Louvre.

Figure 90. *Cassini map circa 1750 of Cardou with IGN topographical data overlain to show summit of Pech Cardou.* Cassini map, Archives de L'Institute Géographique National, IGN Map No. 2347OT © IGN Paris 1994, Authorization No. 90-0069.

Figure 93. *The hexagram in Paris.* IGN Map No. 2314OT © IGN Paris 1998, Authorization No. 90-0069.

Figure 95. *Templar Crosses over Paris.* ©CNES/SPOT Image Corp. 2000.

Figure 96. *The three roads forming a triangle with churches enclosed.* IGN Map No. 2314OT © IGN Paris 1998, Authorization No. 90-0069.

Figure 97. *The Two Templar Crosses on the Map of Paris with circles around them.* ©CNES/SPOT Image Corp. 2000.

Figure 98. *The Paris hexagram overlain on the hexagram at Pech Cardou.* IGN Map No. 2347OT © IGN Paris 1994, Authorization No. 90-0069.

"*Golgotha . . . reflects the legend that Adam was buried in or near the center of the earth. . . . The idea of the center of the earth at a sacred mountain, in a place where heaven and earth meet, is common to a number of religions.*"

Christian Mythology, George Every

To Lynne

TABLE OF CONTENTS

TABLE OF ILLUSTRATIONS

PREFACE

LIKE MANY OTHERS I have been curious about the Rennes-le-Château area for over ten years, ever since I read *Holy Blood, Holy Grail* by Baigent, Leigh and Lincoln. But it wasn't until I read *The Tomb of God* by Andrews and Schellenberger that I realized that there might be a connection between Freemasonry and a mountain on the northeastern slopes of the Pyrenees in the Roussillon region of southern France. My first thoughts were that perhaps the solution to the Rennes-le-Château mystery lay within the Masonic ritual and that likewise the "long lost secret," which all Freemasons are taught to seek, might be tied up with Rennes-le-Château. This particular puzzle has literally captured the imagination of millions. The manuscripts, though, which point to a solution were supposedly found in a "hollow column" and this adds a strange Masonic "dimension" to it.

My early discoveries quickly confirmed that the location of Pech Cardou is encoded within the Masonic ritual and my first reaction was that I had stumbled onto a Masonic secret from a higher rank than those that I hold. My inquiries in this area soon allayed my fears and my natural curiosity did the rest, driving me over the next two years to a solution of the puzzle. As I progressed with my research and more fellow-Masons became aware of where my findings were going, I was asked more than once, "Why are you doing this?" I am a "middle ranking" Freemason, and this question has caused me more than a little reflection; I have therefore devoted a few pages of this preface to explaining why I have decided to publish my findings.

At an early stage my research was providing evidence that beneath this Masonic ritual encoding of geographic landmarks identifying Pech Cardou, there appeared to be something else equally intriguing. It appears that particular lines of longitude may have been allocated to mark the resting-places of something of immense importance on its journey from the East to the West.

It is strange how this investigation expanded from the early discoveries of codes within the Masonic ritual to encompass much of France and particularly Paris. In the process, what had been a background curiosity became the focus of a large part of the last two years of my life. I am, however, convinced that this information is not so much a secret of Freemasonry, but more a secret of which Freemasonry is but a part.

My next comments are of necessity made from the perspective of an English Freemason; I am, after all, English and my Masonic activities come under the jurisdiction of the Grand Lodge of England. That a few people who already know of the secret which I have uncovered are Freemasons is beyond doubt, but I suspect that this probably accompanies their membership in Freemasonry, rather than being the result of it. Which brings me back to the question of whether I should publish my findings, which are unavoidably heavily laden with Masonic ritual and symbolism, and this has caused me some self-doubt. It has proved impossible for me to unfold this story without disclosing some Masonic ritual, in fairness, not as much as recent U.K. television programs. My problem is that I come from the "I prefer our ritual to be mysterious" side of the debate. An eminent Masonic colleague put it very well in saying that "our ritual is like a present—it should be nicely wrapped so that it comes as a pleasant surprise to any new candidate." There is, however, a considerable difference between disclosing our ritual, which might indeed take some of the "shine" off the initiation of candidates, and an open debate on our historical origins.

Freemasonry generally is passing through a difficult period. In the U.K. it is currently subject to discriminating laws on disclosure that do not apply to similar organizations. In the U.S.A. membership is also falling. Whether these matters are transient or signal the onset of a more profound change for Freemasonry, no one really knows. This investigation will show that the *raison d'être* of Freemasonry has been subject to continual watering down, and if you do that to any organization, the membership may eventually question why they joined.

The other problem for Freemasonry, the current public unease that Masonry is a secret society, probably owes much to the "hang-over" of the quite proper obsessive secrecy of the war years. In recent times, the senior ruling body of English Freemasonry, The United Grand Lodge of England, has gone to considerable lengths to make Freemasonry more open. Indeed, the second most senior person in English Freemasonry, Lord Farnham, the Pro Grand Master (and the "Pro" is not an abbreviation), recently stated that the only secrets in Freemasonry are the passwords and associated signs given to identify one's status as a Freemason. The problem here is that this openness removes one of the attractions for joining Free-masonry, the boost to one's self-esteem of being admitted to a secret that others don't know.

The concept of Masonic secrecy certainly does not bear the test of time. After the creation of The United Grand Lodge of England in 1717, indeed right up until the first quarter of the last century, public parades in full regalia were commonplace. These parades only stopped because the general population found the sight of hun-dreds of middle-aged men parading through the streets in aprons a matter for ridicule: *plus ça change plus c'est la même chose.*

In the early days of recorded Freemasonry it was also quite normal to publish one's views on its origins and history. Much of current Masonic knowledge owes a debt to those early Masons such as Dr. Anderson. The nineteenth century saw an explosion of pub-lications advancing this or that particular theory on the origins and meaning of Freemasonry. The very idea that the publication of research is a matter that should be restricted to "secret Masonic only" circulation has no historical basis. It is true that, from time to time, a Grand Lodge may offer an adverse comment on a publica-tion within its jurisdiction that it feels is inappropriate to the reputa-tion or perception of Freemasonry, but that is no different from the protective action that any organization would take.

One only has to read the Internet pages under Freemasonry to see that, particularly in America, very open and lively discussions on the topic of Freemasonry are in progress, and it is noteworthy that the many Grand Lodges have established their own Internet sites. The two leading research lodges within English Freemasonry have been kept abreast of my findings and have been aware of my interest in publishing this work for some time.

Indeed, no less an authority than John Hamill, the curator of the Grand Lodge of England library, addressed this very issue[46].

> *Whether we shall ever discover the true origins of Freemasonry is open to question.*

In conclusion, I can say that nothing that I have uncovered has altered my regard for the good work that Freemasonry does and the pleasure that it brings to so many. Speaking entirely for myself, I find it perfectly satisfactory, as the reader will discover, to find that our heritage is rooted in chivalry rather than construction.

As I have just explained, this book recounts an investigation that started off looking into a secret in the south of France. The fact that it quickly became apparent that the mystery embraced Freemasonry and then went on to uncover a conspiracy is particularly intriguing. It appears that certain people in France have been prepared to ensure that the symbolism of the Knights Templar is preserved in the arrangement of certain public buildings, particularly in Paris. There does not appear to be any malevolence behind these actions, simply a desire to say "we did that." An undertaking of this magnitude must have some eventual aim or goal towards which each action is aimed but that has not been so easy to uncover. These are people who appear to have no ambitions for power, simply back-room boys and "king-makers" who seem content to know that world events are moving in the direction they approve of.

ACKNOWLEDGMENTS

IT IS SIMPLY NOT POSSIBLE to write a book of this complexity without a lot of help. Foremost in line for thanks must be my wife, Lynne, who with more patience than I deserve put up with yet another of my obsessions. I must also make mention of David Ingram who helped out with local knowledge, photos, and climbers. The book would never have seen the light of day without Julie Nieves who turned my untutored writings into something that a publisher could work with. Michael Gauffman who provided a detailed critique and the many members of the Priory-of-Sion "egroup" list who provided me with so much support and informed debate. Finally, among my associates and friends I number several Freemasons who nudged and prodded me towards the solution. They know who they are and they know of my gratitude: I am forever in their debt.

On a more formal level, I would like to acknowledge the assistance given by the many libraries and other institutions that patiently helped me to locate the information I needed, often with little to go on from me. To those institutions who gave permission for their paintings and other works to be reproduced I also extend my thanks. The Barber Institute of Fine Arts, University of Birmingham and the Bridgeman Art Gallery, The Minneapolis Institute of Arts, The State Hermitage Museum, St. Petersburg, SPOT Image Corporation, Dr. Leen Ritmeyer, The Louvre Museum, Royal Library at The Hague.

CHAPTER 1 KEYSTONE

THIS HAS BEEN a very difficult investigation to untangle and an even more difficult one to describe on paper. To assist me in focusing my thoughts and allowing the same process to help you, the reader, I have adopted a technique recommended to me by a fellow researcher. This involves starting each chapter with a brief summary of where the chapter is going and why: this summary is called a "keystone," after the last piece of stone to be built into an arch, binding the structure together.

In 1982, a book appeared which entrapped many readers in a mystery. That book was *Holy Blood, Holy Grail* by Michael Baigent, Richard Leigh and Henry Lincoln. The mystery is based in the area surrounding a tiny village called Rennes-le-Château in the Languedoc/Roussillon region of southern France. The Rennes-le-Château mystery, as it has become known, concerns a legend suggesting that some treasure is or was buried there. The myth of buried treasure was heightened when a local priest, Abbé Saunière, made a discovery in 1885 that led to his becoming extremely wealthy. Although Saunière promised to make his secret available before his death, events dictated that this was not to be. The treasure referred to is presumed to be connected to the Knights Templar who had a very strong presence in the area.

For those readers who, like me, are Freemasons, there are a number of facets to the story which hold a special attraction. These are aspects of the story which have a strange Masonic "ring"

1

to them. For example, there was a set of supposedly ancient scrolls found in a hollow pillar and this bears some resemblance to the "constitutional rolls" of Freemasonry which, according to the ceremonial ritual, were lodged in the hollow pillars of King Solomon's temple in Jerusalem. So it was that I, just like thousands of others, became hooked on the Rennes-le-Château mystery and acquired each new book on the subject as soon as it hit the bookshelves.

The more I read about the mystery, the more I became convinced that the Knights Templar and Freemasonry were somehow inextricably linked. Seemingly unanswerable questions remained of "how and why?" But before the various threads that make up the mystery can properly be untangled and woven into sense, it is essential to gain an understanding of the main actors in this theater, for theater it certainly is and of the highest standard. We will start with the drama of the group that held the world stage and who are at the very center of this story—the Knights Templar—before leading on to their spiritual successors.

During most of their two hundred years of existence, the Knights Templar were based in the Holy Land and it was on that "stage" that they so vividly demonstrated their *raison d'être*. They had grown to eminence because of their pivotal role in maintaining the Holy Land and particularly Jerusalem under Christian control. The massive land and property holdings which the Templars acquired under countless deeds of gift were used for two main purposes. Firstly they generated funds to support the Templar operations in the Holy Land, and secondly they acted as recruiting and training centers for knights and sergeants who would, in time, transfer to the Holy Land. The intermittent counterattacks by the Muslims meant that there was a never-ending demand for new knights and sergeants to replace those killed or injured in battles and those who had simply grown too old to be of useful service.

The Templars were involved on other fronts of the Christian empire, most notably in Spain against the Moors, but the mainstay of their operations, the single activity which marked them out for greatness in the Christian West, was their defense of The Holy Land.

THE KNIGHTS TEMPLAR – I
THE OPENING

Sunday December 5th Bert said,
"You daft bugger, what you need is a good stint of hard work."

Sue Townsend, *The Growing Pains of Adrian Mole*

N O WESTERN MONASTIC ORDER has come even close to creating an aura of mystery such as that surrounding the Knights Templar. Their relatively short life of nearly two hundred years was a catalog of extremes: bravery to the point of foolhardiness, wealth beyond imagination, a permanent standing army greater than any nation, and finally total and abject capitulation without a murmur to a secular king.

This book will not make sense without some understanding of this order of fighting monks. Was Sir Walter Scott's portrayal of them as "treacherous" accurate, or were they something else? Historians seem to agree that, for the most part, the primary historical records of the activities of the Poor Fellow-Soldiers of Christ and the Temple of Solomon, or Knights Templar as we know them, treat the subject with veneration or scorn dependent on the paymaster of the chronicler. A number of letters, particularly from various Grand Masters to the Pope, still exist, and here one would hardly expect them to contain adverse comment on Templar activity. During their 189 years of existence—from 1118 until 1307—the Templars experienced the usual highs and lows, with many intervening years of boring routine. As in any modern organization, their performance was largely a reflection of the qualities of each individual "Master of the knights of the Temple" (*Magister Militum Templi*). The term Grand Master was not, in fact, used at the time although it will be adopted throughout this book because it has become common parlance. These qualities were severely tested by one Grand Master, Gerard de Ridfort, and the Templars were finally driven to destruction in 1307 under Jacques de Molay.

Each Templar castle, or preceptory as it was known, had its own Chapter, or governing body, made up of the most senior officers. The Order was divided into ten provinces, each of which had a Provincial Chapter made up of the Provincial Master and the masters of the individual preceptories in his region. Finally, at the top of the management tree was the Grand Chapter, which comprised the Provincial Masters together with the Grand Master and his Seneschal who was also his deputy. Once elected, the Grand Master enjoyed immense authority, but the Grand Chapter remained the ultimate authority able to change any area of business.

How then did someone who wished to become a Templar Knight do so? Having indicated his desire to be a Templar and being accepted by a majority of the Chapter, the candidate would be invited for his initiation. This ceremony was carried out in the utmost secrecy. No one has been able to provide a satisfactory explanation for the incredible degree of concealment involved or for the fact that the initiations took place at night. Any organization that hides its proceedings from the non-members lays itself open to the inference that they only do so because they have something to hide. Why an order of Christian monks should adopt such a policy, which was bound to raise the eyebrows of the uninitiated, remains a mystery. Electric lighting has resulted in the night holding few terrors for us today, but the Templars were around when the night was the devil's time and God-fearing men were in bed asleep. Perhaps the obvious explanation is the correct one, and they really did have something to hide. Anyway, the candidate for initiation was escorted through the Temple grounds and corridors, and as he passed through each door, it was closed and barred behind him. Eventually he stood before the assembled knights of the Chapter resplendent in their white mantles with a red cross on each shoulder and with their swords drawn. The swords would have glinted in the flickering light from the candles on the altar, the only light in the Chapter room.

The candidate was required to swear that he was of knightly caste, legitimate birth, unmarried, and in good health. He would also have to affirm that he embraced the Catholic faith and had not been excommunicated. He would also affirm that he had no allegiance to any other religious order. The questions would then begin. Each question was put three times and each time an affirmative answer was essential. Three times the candidate would be asked if he wished to join the Order, and three times he had to give a positive response. Three times he was made to beg humbly for bread and water and three times he would be warned of the consequences of joining the Order:

> *You must entirely renounce your own will, and entirely submit to that of another. You must fast when you are hungry, keep watch when you are weary, thirst when you would drink.*

If the candidate then affirmed that he would gladly suffer anything for God and wanted strongly to become a serf and slave of the Order, he was told to kneel and to repeat his request to join. The presiding knight would then say:

> *Dear brother, you ask a great thing, for you see only the outward trappings of the Order. You see only that we have good horses and rich equipment and eat and drink well and have fine clothing, and so you may imagine that life with us will be very pleasant. But you will find it very difficult to be unable to follow your own will in anything. When you wish to be in this country, you will be sent overseas, or if you wish to be in Jerusalem, you will be sent to Tripoli, or Antioch, or Armenia, Apulia, or Sicily, or Lombardy, or France, or Burgundy, or England. Do you swear to God and Our Lady that you will, all your days obey the Master of the Temple and all others placed in authority over you?*

To this, the candidate would reply, "Yes, sir, if God pleases." There followed more undertakings that the candidate would promise on his honor:

Never to lose his weapons or his horse.
Never to suffer a Christian to be unjustly treated.
Never to be the first to flee the field of battle.
Never to surrender property to the enemy.
To fight with all his strength against the infidel.
To embrace perpetual chastity.
To protect the members of all religious orders.

The presiding knight would then admit the candidate:

Then in the name of God and Our Lady Mary and St. Peter of Rome and our father the Pope and in the name of the brethren of the Temple, we accept you, your father, your mother and all your family whom you wish to participate therein, as sharing the good works which have been done by the Order since its foundation and such as shall be done to the end; and you accept us as sharing in all the good works which you have done or shall do. And we promise you bread and water, the poor mantle of the Order and much hardship and labor.

The new knight was then invested with his white cloak and cap while the priest intoned Psalm 133:

Behold how good and how pleasant it is for brethren to dwell together in unity. It is like precious oil poured on the head, running down on the beard, running down on Aaron's beard, down upon the collar of his robes. It is as if the dew of Hermon were falling on Mount Zion. For there the Lord bestows his blessing, even life forevermore.

The presiding knight would raise the knight to his feet and kiss him. The newly-made knight would be kissed by every other knight of the Chapter and he was taken by the hand and told:

Go and may God make you an honest man.

Having avoided every offer to withdraw, the Templar Knight had entered a new and very different world to the one that he left behind. There is, at this point, an observation that needs to be made about the ceremony and in the context of this investigation. The kiss by the presiding knight and the remaining members of the Chapter was the kiss of peace and was a perfectly normal and important rite in secular life; it was also normally given on the mouth.

What, then, of our new Templar Knight? Filled with apprehension and excitement, he would be taken to the Draper's office where he would be fitted out.

Shirts	2	Sword	1
Pants	2	Lance	1
Breeches - tight fitting	2	Mace	1
Tunic	1	Dagger	1
Jacket	1	Shield	1
Cape	1	Knife– bread	1
Mantle	1	Knife - all purpose	1
Surcoat - over chain mail	1	Pot - cooking	1
Haubeck - chain mail shirt	1	Basin - measuring barley	1
Chain mail for legs	1	Pestle & mortar	1
Shoes - iron	2	Cups - drinking	2
Shoulder pieces - iron	2	Flasks	2
Helmet - iron	1	Hatchet	1
Dipper	1	Saddle	1
Wallets	3	Tent - small	1

Staggering under the weight of his kit he would be told the standing orders, those items of "the rule" that he needed to know. The Templar "rule" was the written monastic code of discipline compiled under the guidance of St. Bernard at the Council of Troyes in 1128, when the Order received its papal authority. The original "rule" ran to seventy-two articles, all of which were explained to an initiate when he joined the Order. By the time the Order was disbanded, over six hundred articles had been added; they had become a secret and were dispersed strictly on a "need to know" basis. Typical of the restrictions contained in the original seventy-two articles were:

1. *No cutting of beards and hair to be kept short.*
2. *No bathing except with permission.*
3. *No medicine except with permission.*
4. *No bleeding oneself except with permission.*
5. *No walking abroad except with permission.*
6. *No decorations on stirrups or saddle.*

7. *No hunting except lions which were thought to be Satan.*
8. *No brawling.*
9. *No commerce with women.*
10. *No wounding of a Christian for revenge.*
11. *Where it is forbidden to walk, no horses shall be allowed.*
12. *Stirrups may only be shortened with permission and never cut.*

There were nine offenses for which expulsion was the penalty:

Simony, revealing information about the chapter, killing a Christian, theft, leaving the castle except by the gate, heresy, leaving the banner during battle, defecting to the Saracens and fleeing from the Saracens during battle.

Lesser offenses such as displaying anger, keeping undesirable company or disposing of the Order's goods would have been punishable by a penance usually of a year and a day.

But if he sleeps two nights outside without permission, and has returned in their entirety the things he should return, and has taken away nothing he should not, he may recover his habit when he has done penance for a year and a day. But if he takes away anything he should not, and sleeps two nights outside, and without permission, he is lost to the house forever.

A typical penance would have been to eat from the floor. This was in fact a particularly harsh punishment, negating the aspect of brotherhood that binds people together, the communal eating of bread, *cum panis*. This punishment was clearly meant to humiliate those knights subjected to it and to imply a penalty comparable to the Muslim punishment of having the eating hand, the right hand, cut off. The full significance of this punishment is apparent with the knowledge that the right hand is the only one that Muslims may put into the communal pot of food to eat with. Similarly, only the left hand is used for wiping after a visit to the toilet. Someone with his right hand removed is therefore condemned to eat alone forever, away from the communal table.

Each soldier-monk was provided with three horses and a squire. In return for all of this, a Templar Knight dedicated himself to a life of penance, battle, and chastity, accompanied at all times by the accumulation of "healthy" filth to humiliate his body and thus prevent him from becoming conceited. The provision of three horses should be seen as perfectly normal for any knight. The destrier or war horse was only ever ridden in battle; on route it would be led by the squire with his right hand; hence its name which is derived from the Latin word *dexter* meaning right. A well-trained destrier was the difference between life and death to a knight. In battle, the knight would have his lance in one hand and his shield in the other. It was essential that the destrier respond immediately to the knight's knee and body movements. Failure to do so meant that the knight might miss his target, or worse, he could get struck himself. For this reason, a good destrier was worth a similar amount to a new Rolls Royce motor car today. At other times, the knight would ride his palfrey, a well-bred but quieter horse, and finally there would be the packhorse to carry the knight's armor and other equipment. On horseback, a knight could travel around 35 miles (56 kilometers) in a day, but an army with wagons and foot soldiers would only manage around 8 miles (13 kilometers) per day.

And so, after the excitement of his initiation, our new-made Templar went to bed. He slept in a cell shared with one other brother and on a palliasse or a rug. There was one sheet, two blankets and a coverlet. The cell contained two small chests with no locks, plus a lamp that had to burn all night. As if the ever-present light was not enough to deter the knight from carnal thoughts, he was obliged to sleep in his shirt and breeches, the latter with girdles well fastened irrespective of the temperature. Sleep must have come easily because at midnight he was wakened for Matins and the repeating of thirteen Pater Nosters; he would then inspect the horses to ensure that they were well. Once back in bed, he was soon awake again, this time for the Office of Morning Prayers at four A.M., followed by an hour consecrated to the Holy Spirit. At mid-day came the Office of Sext followed by breakfast. Between the Offices of Prayer, there was the cleaning and greasing of arms and equipment. The horses needed regular attention and then there was the normal conversation relating to the business of the preceptory.

All conversation had to be polite and only for the purposes of Templar business. Meals were taken in silence and at three sittings, the most senior brethren attending the first sitting. During all meals the reading of the scriptures took place, but as these were in Latin it is unlikely that many of the knights understood a word of it.

The two main military orders, the Templar Knights and the Knights of the Hospital of St. John, or Hospitallers, treated their members with all the sophistication of modern bankers. They both operated internal labor markets, which meant that all promotions were from within and both declined to accept rejects from the other order. These are personnel policies that are only possible within organizations that are comfortable with the semi-monopolistic position they hold in the market place. The Knights Hospitaller had originally directed their efforts towards running a pilgrims' hospital in Jerusalem. The success of the Templars, however, led the Hospitallers to include a wing of military knights within their order. Whatever opinion one might hold of the existence of two military orders, it appears to have suited all of the major players, the Pope and the various European Kings. Two large mercenary armies ensured that neither ever became so powerful as to threaten a monarchy. It is also surprising that neither order ever became sufficiently large so as to be able to dominate the other. The appearance and occasional demise of other orders support the absolutely dominant position which the Templars and Hospitallers held in the Holy Land. The Teutonic Knights for example had a hospital for German pilgrims early in the twelfth century but did not copy the Hospitallers military arm until very late in that century. During the period of the Crusades they were perhaps the most successful third order, but they never came close to the size and power of either of the two main orders. The Teutonic Knights survive to this day, although they were obliged to drop their military function in the middle of the nineteenth century.

It has been suggested that, towards the end of their existence, when many were calling for the two orders to amalgamate, that Templar opposition was based solely on the personal aggrandizement of the Grand Master. This is certainly debatable because it clearly suited both of the military orders to maintain an equitable balance. This way they were not, nor could they reasonably be seen, as a threat. There are few other satisfactory explanations for two such organizations to maintain such parity over such a long period, other than by mutual consent. This argument also casts doubt on the suggestion of bitter rivalry between the Templars and the Hospitallers. Whenever such occurrences happened among the lower ranks, it is quite likely that senior Templars were content to let it occur to give the appearance of rivalry that would reassure the external powers.

As events turned out, at the dissolution of the Templars, not only were the properties of the Templars transferred to the Hospitallers but some Templar Knights also transferred. It is a theme of this book that these ex-Templars somehow came to dominate the internal management of the Hospitallers. Indeed, an example is quoted in Chapter 9 of how the Hospitallers left a "Higher Military Force" in Cyprus after they had moved their headquarters to Rhodes. This act was after the Templars had been disbanded and this "Higher Force" almost certainly included former Templars and may even have been made up entirely of them. It is certainly a matter of record that as the years went by the Italian order of Hospitallers became dominated numerically by Frenchmen. Returning to the personnel within a typical Templar preceptory, there would, as one might expect, have been a full range of staff able to perform every function within the quarters of a multinational security organization with an annual revenue of something like $400 million in today's money. In seeking to draw comparisons with similar sized organizations today, one should multiply the Templars' annual revenue many times to allow for the huge growth in money supply. As a proportion of the available wealth of the time, the Templars would have ranked alongside all but the most powerful of kings in terms of annual revenue.

The extraordinary sums of money available to the Templars have to be weighed against the huge costs of running the military support operation in the Holy Land. For example, the net cost of running Safed Castle was given as 40,000 French bezants per annum. Translating the value of money from times past is, as just evidenced above, always hazardous; however, one French bezant was then worth about half a dollar.

Using the price of dairy cows then and now to provide some feel for currency equivalents, we can estimate, albeit rather loosely, that a bezant would be worth close to $800 today. Applying the same logic, the annual net cost of running Safed Castle, after deducting internally generated revenue, can now be roughly estimated at something like $30 million. The Templars had up to ten castles in the Holy Land, which would put the total net cost of supporting their activities there at around $300 million per annum. It is certainly fair to say that the world-wide income of the Templars would have been very largely consumed simply by their commitments in the Holy Land.

At the top of the Templar hierarchical tree was the Grand Master, and under him in each country was a Provincial Master. Each temple, preceptory or commanderie had its own master and under him, his complement of knights. For each knight there would have been around ten support staff of either "sergeant" or "clerical" class. A typical establishment of fifty knights would therefore result in a household of some five hundred persons. These would be made up of chaplains, sergeants, bookkeepers, translators, masons, engineers, carpenters, artisans, armorers, smiths, tent makers, rope makers, vintners, shepherds, grooms, gardeners, millers, cooks, dairymen, field hands and laundry workers. There were two more groups which were "outside of the Templar family," namely the *turcopoles* or local mercenaries and slaves. All of the support workers would have been dressed in black or brown, these being the colors of the peasantry, with a red cross on the breast and shoulder. The Templar clergy were identifiable because they were clean—and wore green tunics with white gloves. It has been suggested that there were seldom more than 20,000 Western people in the Holy Land outside of the times of any particular Crusade. The Templars usually had around 500 knights in the Holy Land, which would indicate a total establishment of around 5,000 Templars. If the Hospitallers had a similar sized establishment to the Templars, then between them the two military orders were probably providing something like fifty percent of the total Western population of the Holy Land.

It was almost twenty years after the successful launch of the First Crusade, in 1118 AD, that nine knights from the Court of Champagne arrived in the Holy Land. Eighteen years earlier in 1100, Baldwin, Count of Edessa, was crowned Baldwin I, King of Jerusalem. It was also in 1118 that Baldwin I led his army on a quest to conquer Egypt, but he fell victim to one of the many local diseases of the Nile delta and died. Baldwin's cousin, who had meantime taken over as the new Count of Edessa, was brought to Jerusalem and crowned Baldwin II. That same year, the knights from Champagne approached Baldwin II and asked for permission to form the Poor Fellow-Soldiers of Christ and the Temple of Solomon, later to become known as the Knights Templar. This permission was duly granted, and it turned out to be a memorable occasion. The nine original knights are generally believed to have been:

Hugh de Payens
André de Montbard—the uncle of Bernard of Clairvaux
Geoffroi de St. Omer
Payen de Montdidier
Achambaud de St. Amand
Geoffroi Bisol
Godfroi
Gondemare
Rosal

The last two, Gondemare and Rosal, are believed to have been Cistercian monks who were simply changing orders. Bernard of Clairvaux was also a Cistercian monk, and the sheer depth of his involvement with the early years of the Templars seems to be more than coincidence.

Although as knights the nine new Templars were all of equal rank, they settled on Hugh de Payens as their leader. This may not be as surprising as might at first appear because Payens had made a pilgrimage to Jerusalem from 1104 to 1108, with Count Hugh of Champagne[22], and together they had returned to France. Count Hugh made another journey to Jerusalem in 1114 and returned finally in 1125 to become a Knight Templar. The role that the Templars proposed was simple. They promised to protect the pilgrims as they made their way through the Holy Land to Jerusalem, particularly from the coastal port of Jaffa. They also swore vows of poverty and chastity. The fact that the main source of revenue for the Kingdom of Jerusalem was from road tolls made this a task of considerable importance. It is not difficult to understand the high profile that this task would have generated. Pilgrims were travelling, sometimes with caravans and sometimes in large straggling groups that made them easy prey for the remnants of the armies of both sides of the earlier war. For soldiers, pillage was a way of life and the occasional absence of wars did little to assuage their natural inclinations. The formation of the Knights Templar was quickly seen as an asset to the area. Baldwin II of Jerusalem, the Bishop, and all of Jerusalem gave money to the new order and they were set up in the al Aqsa Mosque, which stood on Temple Mount near to the site of King Solomon's Temple.

The earlier visits to Jerusalem by Hugh de Payens and Count Hugh of Champagne may have been a perfectly innocent precursor to their return and the subsequent establishment of the Knights Templar. On the other hand, they may have uncovered information during their first visit—such as the existence and whereabouts of something of inestimable value and beyond their wildest dreams— that was in fact the real reason for their return. This suggestion is not as unlikely as at first it might appear because the Copper Scroll, one of the Dead Sea scrolls, has been deciphered and gives a list of burial sites for sacred items[67]. Some support for this suggestion can be found in the knowledge that the nine appear to have done very little in their early years apart from searching for something on the Temple Mount. The excavations carried out by the Templars were re-excavated by Lieutenant Warren and a team of Royal Engineers in 1867[4] and extended vertically for some 80 feet (24 meters) before fanning out under the site of King Solomon's temple.

During the ten-year period of the Templars' excavation work, they appear to have recruited few new members. Towards the end of the excavation work, Count Fulk of Anjou, who would later become king of Jerusalem, arrived, joined the Order, granted an annuity to them and returned home to his wife, a very unusual arrangement indeed. In 1124 the Count of Champagne also arrived, joined the Order and in so doing accepted Hugh de Payens—one of his vassals—as leader.

In 1128, Hugh de Payens departed the Holy Land to attend a Synod at Troyes, the capital city of Champagne and location of its court. During this first return by Payens, he carried letters from the

Patriarch of Jerusalem, King Baldwin II, and other dignitaries supporting his request for official recognition of the Knights Templar.
Before his death, Hugh de Payens again toured Europe, and wherever he passed through, local Templar preceptories sprang up. The
continuing approbation of Abbot Bernard, later Saint Bernard, ensured support and funding from those who wished to go to heaven
when they died, and that was almost everyone in the Western
world. Preceptories appeared in England in London, Essex, Buck-
inghamshire, Lincolnshire and Hertfordshire as well as in Scotland.
They sprang up in Provence and the Roussillon in France and also
in Spain and Germany. With the exponential growth in organization, systems and controls also fell into place. A senior group of
Templars in each preceptory formed a Chapter and these meetings
were held in secret; curtains were draped over doors and the
keyholes were filled. A knight was even stationed on the roof to
ensure that no one approached the Chapter room when a meeting
was in session.

This obsession with secrecy would in due time contribute to the
demise of the Templars, and even with hindsight it is hard to
understand what provoked it. The charges, which would later bring
down the Templars, included one of "secrecy" to which there was
no defense. Why then did they risk so much? It has been suggested
that they indulged in anti-Christian behavior, and much of the later
case against the Templars was based on this assumption. No one,
however, has ever satisfactorily explained why so many God-fearing men joined what they understood to be a Christian monastic
order and stayed if it was not. The suggestion that in the "safety" of
their secluded Chapter meetings some obscure rites were enacted
simply does not make any sort of sense at all. Subsequent study of
the records of the Templars' trial shows little more than the suggestion that during their initiation candidates were made to spit on the
cross but that was as bad as it got. Chapter 14, "The Grail Legend,"
includes an explanation for this act. In the Grail legend, the act of
spitting on the cross was supposed to be an act of contempt for the
object that had caused Jesus Christ such pain; it was not meant to be
an act of blasphemy. Whether there is anything in this explanation
does not alter the fact that it in any way explains the lengths that the
Templars went to in order to keep their meetings secret. They clearly

had something that was of extreme value to them, and about which no one else was to know. One explanation which makes sense is that they had knowledge of or possessed something that could only be discussed in conditions of extreme secrecy. There is of course one artifact that would fit this condition, and it is the Ark of the Covenant.

It can be argued that other religious trophies such as the Turin Shroud—although doubts persist as to whether it existed then—would fit the bill equally well, but none of the other known relics appears able to stand up to scrutiny. All of the other religious memorabilia, shrouds, pieces of the cross, bones of saints, etc., were all legitimate trophies held by churches around the Christian world.

There would have been no reason for the Templars to go to such lengths to maintain secrecy about any other known religious souvenir. The only artifact that appears to meet these conditions is the Ark, and there are good reasons for wanting to maintain secrecy. Firstly, historically it belonged to the Jews, and if the Templars did indeed have it, they could not allow that knowledge to be made public without incurring demands from the Jews for its return. Secondly and perhaps even more importantly, the Ark would have been an extremely attractive ornament to the Pope or to the Western kings, any one of whom could have threatened the very existence of the Knights Templar.

There are many tales of atrocious violence in the Holy Land perpetrated by both sides. The capture of Jerusalem by the First Crusade, when the streets "ran knee deep with blood," is but one. There are also many stories of incredible acts of kindness and honorable actions. One such story concerns a visit to Jerusalem by a minor Muslim prince, Usama of Shaizar, who gave the following account:

> *Adjoining the Mosque of al-Aqsa was a smaller mosque which the Franks had converted into a church. When I came to al-Aqsa, which was occupied by my friends the Templars, they assigned this little mosque to me for my devotions. One day I went in and glorified Allah. I was immersed in prayer, when a Frank pounced on me, seized hold of me, and roughly turned my face to the east, saying, "That's the way to pray!" A group of Templars hurled themselves upon him and threw him out.*

It is apparent that after only a few years the Templars, just like the Crusaders, were beginning to "go native." They obviously admired the honor and chivalry that the Muslims brought to battle and for their part they were recognized by the Muslims as honorable men. Whenever the Muslims made an agreement with the King of Jerusalem, it was always subject to the condition that the Grand Masters of the Templars and Hospitallers also signed. This was their guarantee that the agreement would be honored and helps to explain why the Templars and the Hospitallers saw themselves as one-third rulers of the Holy Land

In 1174 the King of Jerusalem, Amalric, died, and minds turned to the election of the next king. The crown of Jerusalem was kept in a vault in the Church of the Holy Sepulchre under triple lock. The Patriarch of Jerusalem held one key, another was held by the Grand Master of the Hospitallers and the last key was held by the Grand Master of the Templars. It was said at the time that the crown of Jerusalem rested on the three pillars of these three key-holders. Certainly, no one could be crowned King of Jerusalem without the consent of all three. It is perhaps now easy to see why the two Grand Masters might have thought of themselves as "king-makers." This system of tripartite leadership would later reappear in Masonic Royal Arch Chapters, and three pillars would appear on the Craft Freemasonry first-degree tracing board.

Although the Templars were answerable only to the Pope, there is an example of this having been ignored. It was the Spanish Templars who became involved with the Albigensian War, when King Pedro of Aragon found his lands on the French side of the Pyrenees threatened by Simon de Montfort's forces. He arranged for some Templars to defend his border to the south while he crossed to protect his French landholding. This action by the Templars indicates that in Spain they were prepared to divide their allegiance between the pope and the king. There appears to be no record of their being chastised for this action, which is probably an example of pragmatic politics by the pope. Another religious order sprang from the Albigensian Crusade, and it was an order that would cost the Templars very dear, some eighty-four years later. In 1215, the monastic order of the Dominicans was established with the aim of rooting out any vestiges of the Cathar heresy. By 1223 Pope Gregory IX had expanded their remit and established the Holy Roman and Universal Inquisition under Dominican direction.

In 1228 the Emperor Frederick II, under interdict from the Pope, had sailed to the Holy Land. Once there, and by nothing more than a show of force and solely by negotiation, he had been able to regain the city of Jerusalem and to conclude a ten-year peace treaty with the Sultan. The only exception to this deal was Temple Mount which would remain in Muslim hands but would be available to Christian pilgrims. The other temporal leaders of Islam contented themselves with heaping abuse on the Sultan. Pope Gregory IX, however, was apoplectic and ordered a Crusade against Frederick II for launching a Crusade when excommunicated.

The Templars and the Hospitallers were in disgrace because they had not taken Jerusalem by force when it was clearly a realistic option. The Templars were equally angry because Frederick had seen fit to bargain away their Temple site. The Grand Master wrote to the Sultan with a proposal to ambush and kill Frederick, but the Sultan, true to an earlier treaty, sent the letter to Frederick. Frederick was outraged; he surrounded the Templars' headquarters at Acre and threatened to march on their impregnable headquarters—Castle Pilgrim. This was not a threat that he could realistically carry out and news of a papal invasion of his Italian territories made it imperative for him to depart for Italy. On his arrival in Italy, he proceeded to seize all of the Italian Templar property. The Templars retaliated by throwing Frederick's Teutonic Knights out of Acre.

In Jerusalem, meanwhile, the Templars set about rebuilding the fortifications on Temple Mount. It is clear that they did not feel bound by a treaty about which they had not been consulted. Although the Sultan seemed unwilling to take any action over this breach, Frederick certainly was. He wrote to the Templars warning them that if they continued to break his treaty with the Sultan, he would confiscate all of their properties in Germany and Sicily. Any work on the defenses of Jerusalem would expose him to charges of perjury and he would stop at nothing to defend his honor. Work by the Templars halted forthwith and Jerusalem remained an open city. The Templars had taken a secular king too far and had been soundly put in their place.

By 1260, having survived the onslaught from the Mongols, the Holy Land came under sustained attack from the Egyptian Mamelukes. In 1264 the new Egyptian ruler Sultan Rukn ad-Din Baibars sacked Nazareth, followed by Caesarea. After days spent attacking the Templar fortress of Castle Pilgrim, Baibars gave up and moved on to the Hospitaller castle at Arsuf, capturing it and putting the residents in chains. The following year Baibars returned to settle with the Templars. His target was the castle of Safed where some two hundred Templars were stationed. After several assaults were repulsed, he adopted the successful tactic of tempting the castle's turcopoles, the local mercenaries, to abscond. Very soon the Templars did not have sufficient men to protect the castle, and at this point Baibars offered a truce. When the Templars allowed Baibars in, he offered them their lives only on the condition that they took the Muslim faith. The Templar commander declined and was flayed alive, a treatment accepted by several more Templars until, losing patience, Baibars had those remaining from the original two hundred beheaded because none were prepared to renounce the Christian faith.

This clear example of the martyrdom of the Templars, away from the heat of battle, is perhaps the clearest counter to the later allegations against them regarding anti-Christian behavior. The suggestion that the Templars were some sort of secret anti-Christian sect simply cannot stand against this example of its members choosing death by flaying rather than the alternative of renouncing their faith. As city after city fell to the Mamelukes, impassioned pleas were sent to Europe for more Crusaders and more knights for the military orders. King Louis responded and returned in 1270, only to die within days of landing in Egypt. The end of the Christian occupation of the Holy Land in 1291 encapsulated in microcosm its existence. The city of Acre was in fine spirits, the harvest had been excellent and the city was thronged with Muslim merchants. There were also some Italian soldiers from a recent expedition who were enjoying some rest and relaxation. Unfortunately, their pay was late and, as was the general situation with Crusaders, they lacked discipline. Before long a riot had started and the Italian soldiers vented their anger by massacring any civilian with a beard. The Mameluk Sultan Qalawun needed little excuse. He mobilized his army, but before he could move on Acre he died.

His son, al-Ashraf Khalil, was determined to fulfill his father's vow to leave not a single Christian alive in Acre. The resulting siege of Acre lasted forty-three days until the outer walls failed. The Muslims moved into the city to be met by Templar and Hospitaller knights charging on horseback. Every inch of the city was bitterly fought over; the Templar Grand Master was killed and the Hospitaller Grand Master evacuated only when he was seriously wounded. As the Muslims drove the Christians towards the sea, those who were able made off in small boats to the larger vessels moored in the bay. Eventually, the Templar preceptory was the only part of the city not in Muslim hands and so it remained for another four days. The Sultan offered free passage to those remaining in the preceptory. As a show of good faith, the Templar Marshall allowed a hundred Mamelukes to enter the preceptory and hoist their Crescent flag. The Mamelukes, flushed with victory, proceeded to violate the women and small boys. This was too much for the Templar Marshal who ordered the killing of the Muslim troops. When this was done, they barricaded the gate and pulled down the Crescent flag. That night the preceptory "treasure" and as many civilians as possible were taken out to the Templar ship.

This reference to the removal of the Templar treasure calls for examination. Could the historical records be drawing attention to the Templars placing money above human lives? These records report a Templar knight by the name of Tibald Gaudin carrying the "treasure" away. Because in those times, money was metal coin, usually heavy gold, this rather rules out some massive accumulation of cash that had to be saved. If, on the other hand, the Templars did indeed have something as valuable as the Ark of the Covenant, then it would indeed have been at the top of the list of items to be saved. Whatever this treasure was, it does seem improbable that it was simply money. There were civilians present, and if the Templars had really taken up a large amount of boat space that could have been used to save them, surely that would have been "newsworthy" and would have come out after the event. The allegation would surely have been that the Templars preferred to save their gold rather than the lives of fellow Christians. The records, such as they are, do not appear to suggest that the Templars ignored people in favor of gold, simply that the Templars saved their treasure. If support is needed for this suggestion, it comes in the knowledge that, on arrival at Sidon, the Templar who accompanied the "treasure," Tibald Gaudin, was elected the next Grand Master. There would have been reserves held at Sidon, just as there was at every other preceptory; it simply does not make sense to consider that the newly arrived Gaudin would have warranted such promotion simply because he brought some gold with him.

In August of 1291, the Templars were the last to leave Tortosa, followed by a withdrawal from Castle Pilgrim which never fell to the Muslims. There was simply no longer any reason to stay. They remained on the small island of Ruad some 2 miles (3 kilometers) off Tortosa for another thirteen years until, in 1303, the Muslims took this island as well, completing the clearance of Christian forces from their land. All that remained of the military orders who had been stationed in the Holy Land were now settled in Cyprus.

With the Holy Land gone for good, the Templars turned their attention to their remaining properties throughout Europe. Their lands and property comprised 9,000 manors, their taxes nil and expenses much reduced without the cost of keeping their military capability in the Holy Land. The last Grand Master, Jacques de Molay, was established in relative luxury on Cyprus and maintained good relations with the Pope. All seemed well, and the Templars continued to provide a banking service to travellers and monarchs alike. The involvement of the Templars in the banking industry started out of their concern for the welfare of pilgrims arriving in the Holy Land. The new arrivals were met with a bewildering array of peoples from different countries, speaking different languages and offering different currencies. To assist the pilgrims, the Templars set up money exchanges in the ports, and they quickly gained a reputation for fairness and honesty. As the number of their preceptories around the Western world grew, they moved into the area of travellers' checks—not quite the way we know them today, but equally effective at that time. For then, if a merchant wished to travel to a foreign land, he would, as a matter of course, need guards to ensure that he was not robbed during the journey, an expensive undertaking. The Templars devised a scheme whereby a merchant could deposit his money in a preceptory in one country, travel to another and withdraw his money from the preceptory there.

In these modern times, when we can speak to anyone, anywhere, with the aid of a small box of electronics, it is easy to overlook the complexity of such an operation. Today we can send pictures, fingerprints, personal details and history to the four quarters of the globe at the press of a button. And yet banks still operate the most sophisticated, state-of-the-art coding systems known to man to ensure that a tourist withdrawing money, in say Italy, has the available funds in the U.S. How much more difficult then, in Templar days, when the tourist or business traveller might arrive at his destination and require his funds before confirmation could have arrived there from the issuing preceptory. In those days, centuries before the wireless or telephone was even thought of, messages between countries could only travel by horseback or sailing ship, both alternatives being both slow and uncertain of arrival. Therefore, to have operated the financial facility outlined above, the Templars must have developed an elaborate coding system that enabled the destination commanderie to know how much money the traveller was entitled to, and equally important, that the traveller was the only person entitled to it—what we today would call a "travellers check."

The Templars had a reputation for financial astuteness and actually administered the national treasuries of France and England. In addition, the Templar commanderies were strongholds, and it soon became fashionable for rich merchants and indeed monarchs to deposit their wealth with the Templars for safe-keeping.

In France, King Philip IV had inherited a difficult financial situation with the wars against England and Flanders providing a continuing drain on his treasury. He could not help but notice that, by comparison, the Templars had a great number of assets, plus an excellent revenue stream. The economic burden of maintaining their presence in the Holy Land was now gone, and one inevitable consequence must have been that the Templars began to accumulate visible wealth. This can only have caused Philip to eye them with envy.

As the curtain rose on the Templars' final period, we will probably never know exactly what motivated Philip to act the way he did. Most commentators conclude that his motivation was greed, but there are certain flaws in this argument that will be brought out. One conclusion is nevertheless inescapable, and that is that he laid his plans carefully and thoughtfully. One of Philip's first acts on becoming king was to legislate against further growth by the Templars, preventing them from acquiring any additional property within his realm. The crown also took over inherited Templar property that had any dispute over ownership, no matter how small. At this point, Philip strangely turned back from this policy of confiscation. It may of course simply have been that he had run out of legitimate excuses. On the other hand, it might have been part of a softening up process. What happened next was that Philip proceeded to give all of the confiscated property back to the Templars. As if that were not enough, he issued patents giving the Templars absolute tenure of these lands and properties.

The Templars reciprocated the King's generosity by paying for his daughter's dowry on her wedding to the heir to the English throne. The King in his turn returned that favor by making Jacques de Molay godfather to his son. They had become one big family, or so it seemed. However, by befriending the Pope's military order, Philip was able to weaken the Pope's control. Philip IV was of course fully aware that the Templars enjoyed the protection of the Church. To gain control over the Templars he had to be prepared to gain control over the Church—a formidable undertaking and one that would need a formidable king to achieve it. His next move exploited the general air of religious defeatism and despair that had been simmering for many years and which finally matured when the Holy Land was lost. Could a Christian God really stand by and let the Muslims win? Even if they accepted that Islam and Christianity both worshipped the same God, onlookers felt that the conclusions were equally bad. Could it be that God was actually saying that He preferred Islam to Christianity? These were frightening questions for Christendom to face up to, but ones that were unavoidable. Against this background, Philip IV proposed that he, just like his grandfather—St. Louis—before him, would lead the next crusade. He could achieve lasting success with a few changes, for example:

1. The military orders would be united, and to avoid leadership squabbles the hereditary Grand Master would be the King of France, starting with Philip himself.
2. The incomes of all priests up to and including archbishops should be at a fixed level with surpluses going to the Crusade fund under the King's administration.
3. Monasteries should be allowed to keep a fixed income with the surplus also going to the Crusade fund. The monks would be directed to go out into the world to teach, as this would reduce the running costs of each monastery.
4. The hereditary grand Master of the combined military orders should have four votes at papal elections.

These proposals gained little favor among the military orders, the priesthood or, for that matter, the general population, and quietly they were allowed to fade into the background. It was in 1294 that a powerful cardinal ascended the papal throne of Rome, Boniface VIII. King Philip, clearly still in a combative mood, imposed another tax on the clergy, but this time the new pope responded with his bull *Clericis laicos,* which ordered that no taxes on the clergy were to be levied by any king without the consent of the Holy See. Battle had now been joined and Philip responded with a ban on exports of gold. Pope Boniface could not survive for long without the revenue from France and backed down, permitting the king to raise taxes on the clergy *"for the protection of France."* Although Philip had gained the ascendancy over Boniface in the areas of taxation, the pope had a very strong card in his hand. All clerical workers, and this included the king's own civil servants, had to gain their learning from the Church.

The Church had control over the distribution of knowledge, including the basics of reading and writing. Before someone could aspire to work for any noble in a clerical post, he needed to take minor Holy Orders. In those days very few men taking Holy Orders expected to work as a priest; most expected to use the skills that they had acquired in the service of a bishop or a lord. Philip turned his attention to this area of papal strength and proceeded to undermine it by appointing a Templar, Hugh de Peraud, as receiver of the king's taxes. At first sight, this might have been viewed as simply part of the continuing "love affair" between the king and the Templars. On the other hand, it is possible to discern an alternative intrigue. What Philip had started was a process which could not fail to irritate the French clergy. The more of his administrative functions that he gave to the Templars, the more the clergy would have felt that their particular area of expertise and control was weakened. Little by little Philip drove a wedge between the two parties that he wished to subjugate.

By the jubilee year of 1300, Boniface VIII had led the papacy to one of its pinnacles. He had also brought about peace between England and France. All of Italy boomed under the weight of pilgrim money from the hordes that flocked to Rome. He had also beaten off his rivals and the anti-papal forces. In the warm glow of his own success, he turned his attention back to the King of France. He demanded that Philip acknowledge that he owed his position to the grace of Boniface. Philip, true to form, reacted strongly and had the Pope's good friend, the Bishop of Pamiers, arrested and charged with treason, blasphemy, simony (selling church appointments), and fornication. Boniface responded with a bull *Salvator mundi* revoking all of Philip's privileges since the *Clericos laicos* bull. This was followed immediately by another bull *Ausculta fili* that condemned Philip and summoned all of the clergy to a General Council in Rome in November of 1302. It is a measure of the quality of legal advice available to Philip that, when the initiative passed back to him, he called an almost unheard of "Estates-General." This assembly of all three estates had last been used by Philip Augustus to harangue the English King John. It required prelates, barons and burgesses from the chartered towns to attend the King in April, 1302, to hear all the facts of the dispute. This appeal to the "voice of the nation," to the popular views, was a powerful weapon and one that could easily be manipulated with propaganda. The use of propaganda was a tool that Philip would hone to a sophisticated level. At the Estates-General, Philip railed against the injustice of Boniface. The papal bull was publicly burned and Philip called down a curse on any of his successors who admitted that they held France from anyone other than God. It was a powerful jingoistic appeal to nationalistic instincts and it prevailed. Nobles and commoners wrote to Rome calling into question the legitimacy of the Pope. Boniface then overreacted and issued his bull *Unam sanctam* that declared everyone, including kings, inferior to the Pope.

It is necessary to salvation that every human creature be subject to the Roman pontiff.

This action must have comforted Philip, but the Pope's next move brought about a truce. In the summer of 1303 Boniface announced that on September 8 he was going to excommunicate King Philip IV of France. The dispute had come to its inevitable head, for although kings had been excommunicated before and survived, it remained a serious matter and one that Philip did not relish. In the event, having drawn his ultimate weapon from its metaphorical scabbard, the Pope did not find it necessary to use it. A secret accommodation was reached between Philip and Boniface and the excommunication never took place.

This was hardly surprising because King Philip of France took his religious position extremely seriously. The Capetian line of kings began with Hugh Capet (938–996) who was crowned King of France in 987. The dynasty went to great lengths to ensure that their lineage became as revered as the Carolingian line which they replaced and the Merovingians who were the antecedents of the Carolingians. These preceding dynasties, to differing degrees, claimed to be of the same bloodline as Jesus Christ and therefore presented a latent threat to the Capetians. Philip's grandfather, Louis IX, later called Saint Louis, embarked on a mission to turn Paris into the New Jerusalem. Saint Chapelle, the palatine chapel of Louis IX, was built specifically to house religious relics and the stained glass windows attempted to juxtapose the Old Testament symbolism with the Capetian kingship. Philip's reign saw this theme continue strongly as power and culture passed from the old rural monastic centers to

Paris and particularly the royal court. From the mid-thirteenth century until as late as the sixteenth century "one king, one faith," "*un roi, une foi*," was the maxim.

Philip however had not given up the struggle. At the end of summer, 1303, Guillaume de Nogaret, the King's chief advisor, arrived in Italy with some large bankers' drafts that he drew on the Italian banks. Nogaret had been Professor of Jurisprudence at the School of Law in Montpellier as well as a legal counsellor to the King of Mallorca. In 1294 he became the senior judge in the Sénéchaussée of Beaucaire and a member of the Paris Parliament the following year. 1296 saw Nogaret a member of the Curia Regis and from then until his death in 1313 he was one of Philip's most trusted counsellors. Philip rewarded his service by ennobling him in 1299 and giving him a 400-square mile (1,000-square kilometer) estate near Nîmes. Guillaume was one of several legal specialists who helped Philip to firmly establish a royal absolutism. Such non-combatant knights were called the *chevaliers de l'hôtel*; perhaps "office knights" might be an appropriate modern translation: they were neither noble nor did they bear arms, but they ranked as knights. These "new" types of politician who owed their wealth and position entirely to the king shared a common opposition to the Church, whose place they hoped to fill in the administration of the state.

Unaware of Nogaret's plans, Boniface was reposing in the family villa in Anagni, a small town near Rome. Nogaret set to work with his money, seeking out all those with an axe to grind against Boniface. By September 7 Nogaret had joined up with Sciarra Colonna. Colonna was an Italian noble from a family from whom popes were regularly chosen and therefore an obvious rival to Boniface. Their dispute had been sufficiently bitter for Boniface to exile Colonna from Rome, and to rub salt into the wound, had excommunicated him. Together, Nogaret and Colonna assembled a force of some 300 anti-papist Italians, and under cover of darkness they marched on Anagni. The gates were opened silently by a bribed guard and very quickly the palaces of three cardinals were captured and the occupants forced to flee. The papal villa held out for a while until the adjacent church was torched, and this caused most of the Pope's retinue to run away. When the attackers entered the villa they found the eighty-six-year-old Pope lying in his bed, offering himself up to martyrdom. A dead Pope was not in the plans, and so the attackers contented themselves destroying anything of value, and there were of course many such artifacts. Despite much urging and threats against his life, the old man refused to abdicate and twenty-four hours later he was released. By now, the townspeople, fearful of the consequences of a Pope being murdered in their town, had organized themselves and set about the attackers. Nogaret escaped in disguise and most of the remainder were killed, but the damage to Boniface had been done. Four weeks after the coup, Boniface VIII died a broken old man.

The next pope, Benedict XI, granted absolution to Philip IV and nullified the damaging passages from Boniface's bulls. For Nogaret, the King's faithful servant, there was however to be no remission; he was going to be excommunicated and he was going to remain excommunicated. Benedict XI did not live long enough to bring the perpetrators of the attack on Boniface to trial and excommunication. After only eight months as pontiff, he died with symptoms which could very well suggest deliberate poisoning.

After the events of the previous year, it was hardly surprising that the next pope was not elected with any speed. It was almost a year later when the Archbishop of Bordeaux, Bertrand de Got, became Pope Clement V. King Philip must have felt that God was firmly on his side. He now had a French Pope, Clement V, and the continuing unrest in Rome meant that this French Pope based himself in France, initially at Lyons and later moving to Avignon. Clement was reluctant to move to Rome because he feared an Italian reaction to him as a French Pope in consequence of the French treatment of Boniface. Pope Clement V proceeded to issue a series of bulls undoing every bull that had previously been critical of Philip. Indeed, after a short while, Clement would send his draft bulls to Philip for agreement before they were formally issued. There was only one area that Clement would not back down on and that was the matter of Nogaret's excommunication. A cynical onlooker might conclude that it suited King Philip to have Nogaret at a disadvantage. Now that he had a compliant French Pope, Philip was able to resurrect the matter of a Crusade. During the next couple of years he spent a lot of time planning it with Clement. Unfortunately, Clement was not a healthy man, and often needed to take to his bed to recuperate. These periods of rest could last the best part of a year.

In the meantime, Philip's problems with money would not go away, and many adulterations of the French currency proved to be only short-lived solutions. Clipping of the coins reached such a level as to have halved their individual value, and this brought in its wake riots by the general population. In 1291 the King expropriated the funds of the Lombard bankers in France. Then in 1306 Philip, with the able assistance of Nogaret, decided on what would prove to be a full-scale dress rehearsal for his later actions. Throughout France all Jews were arrested and their property confiscated by the Crown. The surviving Jews were exiled and Philip declared all sums owed to Jews would be immediately repayable to the Crown. The whole operation went through without a hitch. The dénouement for the Templars was now at hand.

Ashlars—building blocks

Just as at the beginning of this chapter I explained why a feature called the "keystone" has been included, so, to assist readers in untangling this mystery, I have included a list of summary statements which are called "ashlars." Ashlars are the dressed or finished cut stones that are used in stone buildings or structures. Thus, in the same way that "ashlars" form the building blocks of a structure, so the following and later "ashlars" are here meant to be the metaphorical building blocks which will help in unraveling and understanding this mystery. Just as the Masonic ritual describes a "keystone" as fixing the arch that contained the Ark of the Covenant, so also in Masonic ritual a rough or unfinished block of stone represents a candidate for Freemasonry and an "ashlar" symbolizes the "new man" when he becomes a Mason.

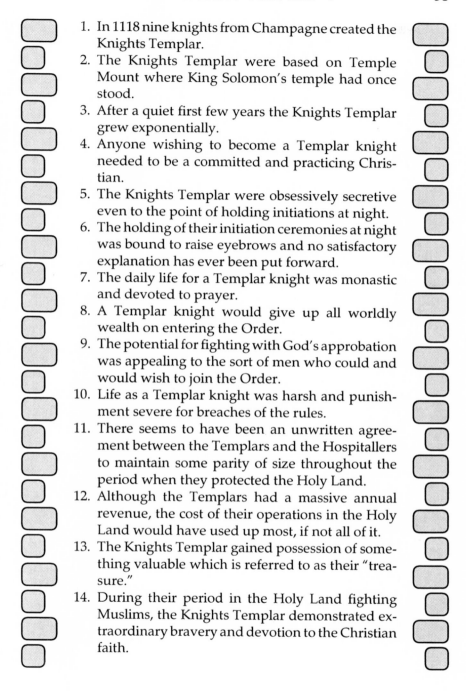

1. In 1118 nine knights from Champagne created the Knights Templar.
2. The Knights Templar were based on Temple Mount where King Solomon's temple had once stood.
3. After a quiet first few years the Knights Templar grew exponentially.
4. Anyone wishing to become a Templar knight needed to be a committed and practicing Christian.
5. The Knights Templar were obsessively secretive even to the point of holding initiations at night.
6. The holding of their initiation ceremonies at night was bound to raise eyebrows and no satisfactory explanation has ever been put forward.
7. The daily life for a Templar knight was monastic and devoted to prayer.
8. A Templar knight would give up all worldly wealth on entering the Order.
9. The potential for fighting with God's approbation was appealing to the sort of men who could and would wish to join the Order.
10. Life as a Templar knight was harsh and punishment severe for breaches of the rules.
11. There seems to have been an unwritten agreement between the Templars and the Hospitallers to maintain some parity of size throughout the period when they protected the Holy Land.
12. Although the Templars had a massive annual revenue, the cost of their operations in the Holy Land would have used up most, if not all of it.
13. The Knights Templar gained possession of something valuable which is referred to as their "treasure."
14. During their period in the Holy Land fighting Muslims, the Knights Templar demonstrated extraordinary bravery and devotion to the Christian faith.

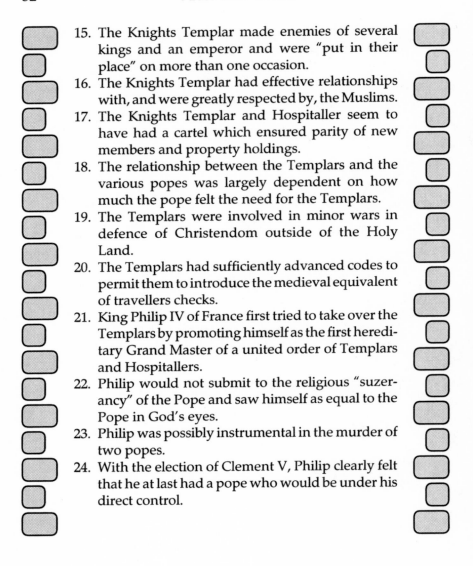

15. The Knights Templar made enemies of several kings and an emperor and were "put in their place" on more than one occasion.
16. The Knights Templar had effective relationships with, and were greatly respected by, the Muslims.
17. The Knights Templar and Hospitaller seem to have had a cartel which ensured parity of new members and property holdings.
18. The relationship between the Templars and the various popes was largely dependent on how much the pope felt the need for the Templars.
19. The Templars were involved in minor wars in defence of Christendom outside of the Holy Land.
20. The Templars had sufficiently advanced codes to permit them to introduce the medieval equivalent of travellers checks.
21. King Philip IV of France first tried to take over the Templars by promoting himself as the first hereditary Grand Master of a united order of Templars and Hospitallers.
22. Philip would not submit to the religious "suzerancy" of the Pope and saw himself as equal to the Pope in God's eyes.
23. Philip was possibly instrumental in the murder of two popes.
24. With the election of Clement V, Philip clearly felt that he at last had a pope who would be under his direct control.

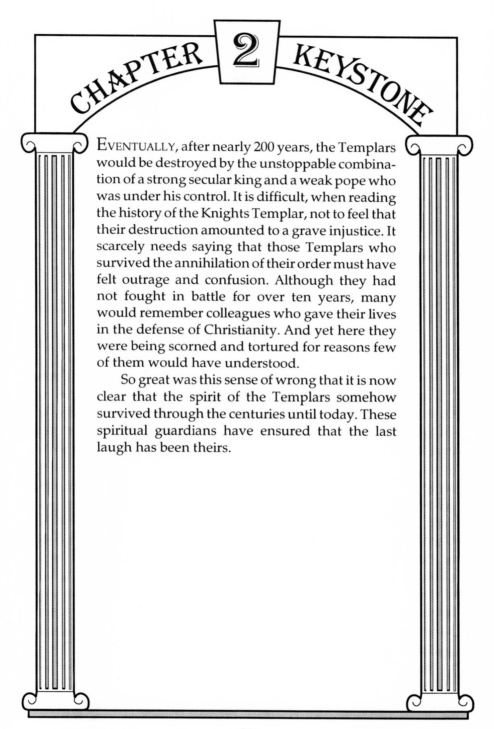

CHAPTER 2 KEYSTONE

EVENTUALLY, after nearly 200 years, the Templars would be destroyed by the unstoppable combination of a strong secular king and a weak pope who was under his control. It is difficult, when reading the history of the Knights Templar, not to feel that their destruction amounted to a grave injustice. It scarcely needs saying that those Templars who survived the annihilation of their order must have felt outrage and confusion. Although they had not fought in battle for over ten years, many would remember colleagues who gave their lives in the defense of Christianity. And yet here they were being scorned and tortured for reasons few of them would have understood.

So great was this sense of wrong that it is now clear that the spirit of the Templars somehow survived through the centuries until today. These spiritual guardians have ensured that the last laugh has been theirs.

THE KNIGHTS TEMPLAR - II
END GAME

I tried to close his eyes: to extinguish, if possible, that frightful, life-like gaze of exultation, before anyone else beheld it. They would not shut: they seemed to sneer at my attempts; and his parted lips and sharp white teeth sneered too!

Emily Brontë, *Wuthering Heights*

IN 1307 CLEMENT V summoned the Grand Masters of the Templars and Hospitallers to his base at Poitiers, to finalize plans for the next crusade. The Hospitaller Grand Master, Foulques de Villaret, excused himself on the grounds that his men were in the process of moving from Cyprus to Rhodes and he could not be spared. The Templar Grand Master, Jacques de Molay, eventually set off from Kolossi castle, accompanied by sixty knights, twelve packhorses of gold and the usual complement of support people. His first call was on the King in Paris where he had the honor of acting as pallbearer to Princess Constantine. After the funeral, he retired to the security of the Paris Temple. Jacques de Molay was in his mid-sixties and had been a Templar for some forty years. He was a Burgundian knight who eschewed learning and, since becoming Grand Master, had moved the Order back towards its military roots. There can be little doubt that he knew that something was afoot. It is equally clear that he was prepared to face it out—man to man.

It is probably fair to say that anything less from a member of the Order would have been unimaginable. Signs that the King had unpleasant plans were littered everywhere. The Templar "friend and treasurer" to the King, Hugh de Peraud, told a knight who requested to leave the Order that he was being wise and should act quickly. In an act of casual overconfidence, Philip had written to the other European rulers urging them to take similar action to that which he proposed to adopt. In the light of the Templars' known friendship with many European rulers, this act alone would probably have ensured that the Templars found out about Philip's plans. Finally, as if any more proof were needed, the King's bailiffs were going into the Templar preceptories and carrying out audits of goods and valuables stored there. In defense of the Templars, these inventories showed no evidence of the profligate lifestyle that had been a widespread criticism aimed at them.

This "writing on the wall" for the Templars began immediately after the fall of the Holy Land in 1291 when Fidenzio of Padua published a book, *Liber Recuperatione Terrae Sanctae*, that had been commissioned by Pope Nicholas. The remit of the book had been to examine strategies for re-taking the Holy Land. Fidenzio concluded that the Templars and the Hospitallers should be combined into one holy military order. Others followed and in 1294 Raimon Lull published *Petitio pro recuperatione Terrae Sanctae* and Galvano de Levanti, a doctor at the Court of Philip IV, published *Liber sancti Passagii Christicolarum contra Saracenos pro recuperatione Terrae Sanctae*, all continuing the argument for a Crusade led by a combined military order. Philip had decided that the time was ripe to renew his ambitions and his "hired hands" were preparing the way. In June of 1306 Pope Clement V initiated an inquiry into the feasibility of uniting the military orders and invited the Grand Masters of the Templars and the Hospitallers to respond in writing. Jacques de Molay's response is today held in the *Bibliothèque Nationale*.

The quality of advice available to de Molay would have been of the highest caliber, and against this background the memoir is remarkably thin in its argument against union. Fifteen anti-union reasons were put forward, ranging from the argument that it would not be honorable, taking into account their past service, to the suggestion that knights from each order would continue their mutual antagonism, and being armed it could create a dangerous situation. Only two supporting assertions were made: the first, that a combined order would be better able to defend itself against criticism and the second was the reduction in costs that would flow from amalgamation. There could be a number of explanations for the poor quality of de Molay's response. On one hand, his own lack of education coupled with a desire to put his personal stamp on the memoir could explain the mediocrity of his argument. Alternatively, it may be that the Templars and Hospitallers actually recognized the benefits that might come from combination of the two orders but felt that they had to put up a token resistance. At that time, de Molay was over sixty years of age, and it is hard to imagine that he opposed the suggestion for reasons of personal ambition.

Be that as it may, during Friday, October 13, 1307, acting on sealed orders, the King's seneschals arrested every Templar, sergeant and worker remaining in the preceptories throughout France. The Grand Master, Jacques de Molay, and the sixty knights that he had brought from Cyprus were no exception. In all, some 2,000 Templar personnel, out of a world-wide complement of around 15,000, were interned. Although most of those arrested were elderly, they did include some 200 knights, the remainder being support staff and priests. This action served to further reinforce Friday the thirteenth as an unlucky day. The question of why de Molay allowed this to happen has taxed the minds of every commentator on the history of the Templars. He had absolute control over the most powerful army in the world at that time, each knight being equivalent to a modern tank, measured against the military capability of the time.

Jacques de Molay had around fifteen hundred knights under his control world-wide. There is, however, a simple explanation. It would have been incomprehensible for a Templar Knight to turn against a King of the Blood Royal. Although rebellions by knights against their liege lord were not unknown, they were invariably prompted by ambitions to overthrow a ruler they considered inappropriate or incapable. The Templars could not claim that indulgence, and even if there was some hitherto unknown correspondence or discussion between de Molay and the Pope on the matter, it is inconceivable that a French Pope, of all people, would have sanctioned armed opposition to Philip. To make matters even more difficult, the Templars had their origins in French chivalry and their persecutor was the King of France. In these modern times, it is perhaps easy to overlook "the divine right of Kings." There was scarcely a more terrible act that a noble might commit than *lèse majesté*. This would not normally have been an issue for those below the rank of noble because it was extremely unlikely that they would get near enough to the King to effect any harm.

Once again, in an attempt to provide a "feel" for the essence of the time, a contemporary story from the 1340s is recalled, this time the rape of the Countess of Salisbury. The English King Edward III was very attracted to the Countess, but she rebuffed his advances. The King then arranged for the Countess' husband, the Earl of Salisbury, to travel to Brittany. When the Earl was away, Edward visited the Countess and on this occasion raped her. In fact, as King, this might have been viewed as his "divine right," in which case the Countess should perhaps have given herself willingly. This, however, was the age of chivalry and the King's behavior was a serious breach of the chivalric code. When the Earl returned to England, the Countess reported the King's actions to him. The Earl went straight to court—the Royal court, not the law—and divested himself of his lands and property in such a way as to provide his wife with a dowry for life. He then advised the King that he could no longer live in England and took himself off. The question of retribution against Edward for the terrible wrong he had done was never an option. Although today such behavior may seem strange, one has only to look back a few years to the affair between King Edward VIII and Mrs. Simpson to observe how Mr. Simpson declined to comment throughout the whole business. Ernest Simpson even agreed to provide evidence of his infidelity to allow his wife to divorce him in order that she could then marry Edward.

For Jacques de Molay, the Grand Master of the Knights Templar, immediate and total surrender was the only course of action open to him. Templar Knight he may have been, but his upbringing had been noble and the code of chivalry would have been instilled in him from the moment he could walk. The remaining Templar Knights were also of noble birth and could only have come to the same conclusion. The early warnings made it likely that de Molay would have given orders for no resistance to be offered and the remaining Templar staff would unquestioningly have followed his orders. They knew no other way. The chivalric code, which demanded disciplined comportment and loyalty to one's lord, made abject surrender inescapable. The inevitable consequence was that just like tethered goats they were led away to the awful events that awaited them all.

Philip and his loyal adviser Nogaret, who had just been promoted to Chancellor, had not forgotten the lessons of earlier years. On the day after the arrests, the "arrest order" against the Templars was read out to the nation in every square and market place. The word was also put out that all debts owing to the Templars were wiped out. The arrest order began:

A bitter thing, a lamentable thing, a thing horrible to think of and terrible to hear, a detestable crime, an execrable evil deed, an abominable work, a detestable disgrace, a thing wholly inhuman, foreign to all humanity, has, thanks to the reports of several persons worthy of faith, reached our ears.

With the Templars in France under arrest, the King wasted no time. The following day the inquisition began. The practice of inquisition took its name from the third of the forms of legal action available to the courts in those days: *accusatio, denunciatio* and *inquisitio.* It became a part of the proceedings for heretics in 1184 but entered formally as "The Inquisition" some fifty years later under Pope Gregory IX. An examination of practices from so long ago requires us to understand the precision with which those affairs were conducted. Overseeing the "torture" of the Templars was the Inquisitor General—a Dominican friar named Guillaume de Paris. The Inquisitor General was normally a university trained doctor of law. At the time when the Templars were exposed to this procedure, it was usual for the inquisitors to work in pairs so that neither could become too absorbed in the sadistic aspects of his work. The procedures were carefully regulated and governed by operating manuals written by such as the Dominican friar Bernard Gui. Such was the precision of Guillaume de Paris' work that later, when the Templars were able to employ legal representation, few grounds for complaint were found against the application of the inquisitorial procedures. These procedures were completely successful in achieving Philip's early goals. Within days, a list of confessions had been obtained and these formed the basis of subsequent charges at the trials of the Knights Templar. These charges were:

1. The Templars put themselves before moral and religious principle.
2. They were in secret correspondence with the Muslims.
3. Novices were required to spit on the cross and renounce Christ.
4. Anyone who tried to expose the Order was murdered.
5. They practiced absolution and idolatry, omitting the words of consecration in the canon of the Mass and despised the sacraments of the church.
6. They were immoral and practised sodomy.
7. They had betrayed the Holy Land.
8. They worshipped the devil, often in the form of a cat.

These charges were put up in the town squares, and very quickly everyone knew their nature. To every captive Templar, the questions were put under torture, with the justification that torture "could only extract the truth because God would protect an innocent person from the pain." Inquisitorial rules required that torture could only be applied once. This was, however, observed more in the breach by "continuing" the same torture the following day. A forced confession was considered then as now to be invalid; therefore a "voluntary" confession had to be signed three days after the first confession under torture.

The usual procedure was that with the confession came absolution from the Church for the specific crimes confessed, and the individual would be passed to the secular authorities for earthly punishment in the certain knowledge that his immortal soul was safe.

It was in these early days that the die was cast. Within twelve days Jacques de Molay had confessed that, some forty years earlier, he too had denied Christ, at his initiation by the Master of the London Temple—Humbert de Pairaud. De Molay admitted being ordered to spit on the cross but insisted that he had aimed at the floor. The following day he repeated this confession in front of an audience of theologians and lawyers from the University of Paris. Surprisingly, most Templars confessed only to some of the charges. Only three Templars confessed to sodomy and several of the younger knights refused to confess to anything. In Paris alone thirty Templars died in the first few days from "persuasion." When they were taken before their examiners for their voluntary confession, many had to be carried, having lost their feet or the use of their limbs. One of the "confessions" that resulted from the inquisition concerned the worshipping of a head, known as Baphomet, and there may have been a reasonable explanation for its origin:

> *After King Baldwin II's abortive attempt to capture Damascus, he did not venture out on another aggressive expedition. He was, however, obliged to send out his army again, because of the actions of one of his sons in law, Bohemond II. The Atabeg of Mosul, the Turk Zenghi had, by then, gained control over most of Moslem Syria. Bohemond, chose that time to attack his neighboring Armenian territory. His army was massacred and his embalmed head sent to the Caliph of Bagdad as a gift. Bohemond's wife Alice, who was King Baldwin II's second daughter, was so keen to retain her position that she offered Atabeg Zenghi homage if she could retain tenure. In order to head this off, King Baldwin II was obliged to rush his army to Antioch.*

It is possible that the embalmed head of Bohemond somehow found its way into Templar hands and perhaps by way of a salutary warning was displayed to novices. Whether this was the head in question or not, the Saracens regularly beheaded captives who had no ransom value, and this usually included captured Templars. It is therefore not unreasonable to presume that a head was displayed on the "if you're not careful this could be you" basis. There are, of course, any number of other benign explanations. One obvious example is that it was simply a tribute to Golgotha—meaning the place of the skull—the site of Jesus Christ's crucifixion. Alternatively the Templars may have acquired the severed head of John the Baptist, or at least what they thought was John's head, and accorded it some reverence.

Another theory may explain the fact that many Templars confessed to having worshipped a head. This theory derives from the word "Chapter" which is used to describe *inter alia,* a meeting of the Masonic Royal Arch. The French word for "chapter" is *"chapitre"* and it comes from the Latin *"capitulum"* which is the diminutive of *"capus,"* meaning a head. The word "chapter" also means a section of a book and has been used from early times. Thus, when cathedral church officers, monks of a monastery or knights of an order held formal meetings, the proceedings usually began with the reading of a chapter from their rule or from the scriptures. The gathering itself soon became known as the "chapter," and the room in which it was held was called the "chapter-house." When one recalls that the prayers during meal times for Templars were always in Latin and also that many if not most Templars were illiterate, might this be how the famous Baphomet mystery began? It is not difficult to visualize Templars sitting, perhaps eating and listening and hearing the word *"capitulum"* over and over again. It is equally easy to imagine that some were even moved to ask, "What does *capitulum* mean?" The answer of course was "head" and this provides a ready explanation as to why so many of them became convinced that they worshiped some sort of head. Couple this explanation with their probable knowledge of Bohemond's head encased in silver and a legend was born.

The symbolic skull and crossed bones have a place in Masonic ceremony as reminders of death, which awaits us all. It is therefore appropriate to pause and examine another explanation. On the walls of Limasol castle are two relief carvings, one of a skull and crossed bones (Fig. 1), and another of a knight in the same position as the dead Jesus Christ (Fig. 2). The similarity of the positioning of the head and crossed arms of the "Dead Christ" to those of the skull and crossed bones leads to speculation that the latter is an allegorical representation of the former. If this speculation were to be correct, then we can see immediately how the Masonic ritual compilers managed to get a representation of the Ark of the Covenant into a lodge room. The process of symbolical exchanges goes something like this:

Figure 1
Relief carving of skull and crossed bones at Limassol Castle.

Figure 2
Dead knight with crossed arms in "Dead Christ" posture
at Limassol Castle.

The skull and crossed bones	=	Jesus Christ
and	Jesus Christ =	God
and	God =	The Ark of the Covenant
therefore		
The skull and crossed bones	**=**	**The Ark of the Covenant**

This arrangement of allegorical exchanges at last provides an explanation of why the Templars chose as their naval battle flag the skull and crossed bones—a flag later borrowed to good effect by pirates. The powerful symbolism of the skull and crossed bones can at once be seen as an emblem to remind them of death and also their most precious possession—the Ark of the Covenant.

Returning to the story of the demise of the Order, it was on October 25, only two weeks after the arrests, that Jacques de Molay and other senior Templars were brought before an audience of theologians and lawyers from the University of Paris. Here they repeated their earlier confessions. The collapse, under torture, of their Grand Master cannot but have had a devastating effect on the remaining Templars. Where was the incentive to resist? Even if some younger men had felt able to withstand the torture, Jacques de Molay had in effect condemned the Order by his confession. De Molay's confession also made it impossible for the Templars' friends abroad to support them. Two days later help arrived, but it was already too late. On October 27, a vehement protest was sent to Paris from Pope Clement V. He demanded to know why he, as bishop and judge of the Order, had not been consulted. His attack on the king had two prongs:

1. The groups' wealth, essential to the next Crusade, had been appropriated by the King to cover up his own financial problems.
2. There had been an obvious attempt to injure the papacy, both its material possessions as well as its rights.

Clement continued with an attack on the Grand Inquisitor of France, Guillaume de Paris. For taking upon himself the interrogation of the Templars without seeking papal approval, Guillaume de Paris was removed from office for contempt of the Holy See. The Pope ordered the proceedings against the Templars to cease until they were conducted in a proper canonical manner. The King ignored this directive, and the proceedings continued. It was a month later, on November 22, that Pope Clement was able to wrest matters back under his own control. He issued the bull *Pastoralis preeminentiae* that ordered all Christian rulers to arrest the Templars in their kingdoms. The Pope cited Jacques de Molay's confession as grounds for this action. Although this action may appear to be conceding matters to King Philip, the reality was that it gave the Pope authority to act on the issue. Accordingly he dispatched Cardinals Bérengar Frédol and Etienne de Suisy to represent his interests in Paris. Faced with what he assumed were friendly inter-rogators, de Molay retracted his confession. Philip had been down this particular path before and was well versed in the next moves. He had Nogaret appeal to the Faculty of Theology of the University of Paris to rule on whether the civil powers were competent to act as they had. The answers that he received were somewhat less than he might have hoped for:

Question 1	May the King alone judge the Templars?
Answer	No.
Question 2	Are the Templars knights rather than clerks?
Answer	No.
Question 3	Are the confessions sufficient to condemn the Order, or at least to require a thorough inquiry?
Answer	Yes.
Question 4	Does apostasy render the Templars no longer Catholic?
Answer	Yes—but with reservations.
Question 5	Should the Templars not confessed retain status?
Answer	As for Questions 3 and 4.
Question 6	Should confiscated property go to King or Church?
Answer	Ambiguous, [it] wasn't given and Templars' property should be used and administered in [the] best way.

Alongside this maneuver came the usual propaganda generated by another of Philip's close advisers, the lawyer Guillaume de Plaisians. It stated that Pope Clement V was "greedy, selfish, petty, designing, tyrannical." Philip intimated that the Estates-General would need to be called again and left little doubt that it would be the Pope who would be under attack again. Was the guilt of the Templars not obvious for all to see? They had confessions in plenty; the guilt of the Templars was therefore beyond doubt. It necessarily followed that anyone who defended them must have something to hide. Clearly concerned for his own safety, Clement established himself in the well-defended town of Poitiers.

On May 1, 1308, events took a hand when the Holy Roman Emperor, Albert I, died. Philip wanted his brother Charles of Valois to be elected as the new emperor, and the pressure of these two important problems brought him to Poitiers as well. May 29, 1308, saw Clement grasp the nettle and hold a public "consistory" with both papal and royal courts present in Poitiers. Guillaume de Plaisians argued for the crown that Philip had been forced into the position of arresting and trying the Templars. The King had shown "great courage" in taking on this task that no one else was prepared to shoulder. Plaisians quoted the miraculous coincidence of the simultaneous arrival in France of the Grand Master of the Order and his retinue when the unmasking took place. The simultaneity of the Templars' confessions all over France was likewise quoted. He ended by pointing out that the church owed a far greater debt to Philip than to Clement. Was it not Philip who had instigated the studies of theology? Had not Philip's forebears and many French nobles spilled their blood in the cause of Christendom? The Pope responded by pointing out that the blood on which Christendom was founded was the blood of Jesus Christ.

The wheels of justice continued to grind slowly, and by November Count Henry of Luxembourg had been elected Emperor. The threat to the Papacy of being overwhelmed by the Capetian Royal family had thus receded. Henry was crowned Emperor on January 6, 1309, and immediately afterwards Guillaume de Plaisians renewed his attack. The verbal tussle went back and forth with de Plaisians at one point listing all the rumors that were going around

France about Clement himself. The Pope was on the defensive and it was finally agreed that the Templar assets would be reserved for the next Crusade. The liquid assets that had not already gone into Philip's treasury were being used to pay for the incarceration of the Templar prisoners so there was little point in arguing over them. The conclusion of Plaisians' attack was an open threat that if the Pope did not act, others would.

Two weeks later, seventy-two Templars were brought to Poitiers for trial in front of the pontiff. The confessions of these seventy-two Templars had the desired effect. In a series of three bulls, Clement forgave the King for his hasty action and restored the Grand Inquisitor to his post. Clement ordered episcopal inquiries into the Templar heresy with each commission comprising the appropriate bishop, two canons from the local cathedral, two Dominicans and two Franciscans. Finally, on August 12, 1308, he ordered an inquiry into the Order as a whole. The issue would finally be resolved at a general council of the Church to be held at Vienne on October 1, 1310. Philip appears to have been satisfied with this result because he withdrew his army and returned to Paris. In the meantime, the King of England, Edward II, wrote to Philip, the Pope, and numerous European rulers, asserting that the Templars had been maligned and urged the Pope to act for the Order. Edward's letter crossed with the papal bull, which had ordered the arrest of the Templars, and on receipt of this bull the sovereign dropped his opposition.

Eventually, in November 1309, the papal commission got under way, with the object of reporting its findings in 1310 as agreed between Philip and Clement at Poitiers. One of the first witnesses was Jacques de Molay, who began by challenging the jurisdiction of the commission over the Templars, intoning that "it is under the sole authority of the Pope." His fragile mental condition seems at one stage to have led him to challenge the commissioners to battle. They were evidently taken aback at the Grand Master's attitude but managed to persuade him to allow his original confession to stand. Two days later, de Molay returned to the commission and thanked them for preventing him from acting rashly and withdrew his hasty proposal to offer a defense. Instead he begged to be allowed to be taken before Pope Clement. With the benefit of hindsight, we should at least contemplate whether Jacques de Molay was, by this time, out of his mind. His failure over subsequent months to come forward and offer support and leadership to his beleaguered subordinates, even when they were desperately in need, is so out of character. Throughout the history of the Templars, if there was one characteristic that defined its Grand Masters, it was bravery, even if at times foolhardy.

The commissioners appear to have concentrated their inquiries in Paris, where some 537 Templar prisoners were held in various buildings. There were about 74 prisoners in the Paris temple and the remainder in hostels and church properties. The conditions, in the various holding areas, were evidently better than during the first few weeks of the inquisition although even those kept in lodgings were chained.

The lodging house owners would no doubt have considered the arrest as quite fortuitous. They were required to provide quarters for several years, and they were paid from the funds held at the Paris temple. Another consequence of this arrangement was the unexpected redistribution of wealth to the property owners of Paris. The apparent absence of any royal action to alter these arrangements seemed to detract from the popular story that Philip initiated the destruction of the Templars simply to get his hands on their wealth.

The introduction of the papal commission put new heart into the Templar prisoners. On February 3, 1310, fifteen Templars came forward and announced that they were prepared to defend the Order. By February 10, the numbers had increased to 81 and soon the trickle became a flood. Only a fortnight later 500 were ready to defend the Order; this number reached 561 within a further two weeks, amounting to practically every Templar held in Paris at the time.

As the trained lawyers from within the Templar ranks came to the fore, the detailed legal case began to evolve. Their first request was for the full list of charges to be provided in writing. The full list of 127 articles of accusation had been prepared at Poitiers and was repeated for the benefit of the defendants on March 14, although those lawyers who had already made themselves known were not present. It is possible that the Templars who had already exhibited legal knowledge were deliberately excluded. The 127 articles may be summarized into nine categories:

1. During their initiation, new brothers were required to deny Christ, God, the Virgin Mary and the Saints.
2. Initiates were required to commit various sacrilegious acts either on the cross or an image of Christ.
3. The installing brother received obscene kisses on the mouth, navel or buttocks.
4. The Templar priests did not consecrate the host and the brethren did not receive the sacraments.
5. The Order practiced idol worship of a cat or a head.
6. The Order encouraged and permitted sodomy.
7. The Grand Master and other officials absolved Templars of their sins.
8. The Order held initiations and Chapter meetings in secret and at night.
9. The Order abused the duties of charity and hospitality and used illegal means to acquire property and wealth.

Items 1 to 5 may be viewed as a rehash of the familiar heresies that had been previously trotted out for the inquisition of the Cathars. The remaining four items relate to the Templar "rule" that in turn had originally been designed by officers of the church and given Papal approval. In considering charge number 7, one should bear in mind that the Templars were a monastic order and the Master of each preceptory was in effect the Prior and quite entitled to give his members absolution. The reality of the charges, however, is that there was no evidence or proof. The whole of the prosecution was based on such phrases as "generally held" and "public talk, general opinion and repute." The melange of innuendo was enough, and the Templar prisoners were now required to rebut the charges.

The suggestion of a denial of Christ is certainly incompatible with the "rule," which insisted that all religious services had to be conducted in accordance with canon law. The reading of scriptures during meals, the complex rhythm of feast days and fasts, and the repetition of Pater Nosters clearly called into question the validity of the allegations: indeed, no less than twenty-five paragraphs of the "rule" were devoted solely to religious service. Up until the present time, there is still no evidence to suggest that the Knights Templar were ever anything other than the Order as created in 1118 with a code of conduct written in large part by St. Bernard. Turning to the allegations of sodomy, the constantly lighted candle in each brother's cell and the mode of dress at night is evidence of the care the Order took to discourage homosexual relationships. Sodomy was twice condemned, in rules 418 and 572. There is also a reference to two Templars from Castle Pilgrim who, caught caressing each other, were taken to Acre, stripped of their habits and clapped in heavy irons. Rule 418 provides a strong indication of how the matter was viewed:

> *If a brother is tainted with the filthy, stinking sin of sodomy, which is so filthy and so stinking and so repugnant that it should not be named.*

There were two charges on which the Templars stood condemned and for which there was no obvious defense—firstly, the charge of secrecy and secondly, the charge of meeting at night. The reader may notice a parallel with the first of these charges and modern Freemasonry. The second charge is not a contemporary problem because we no longer associate meetings at night with witchcraft. This particular issue has already been addressed at length and it remains extraordinary that the Templars felt the need for such secrecy combined with evening meetings.

Meanwhile, on March 27, the papal commission resumed its work only to find that some men, held outside of Paris, had now added their names to those wishing to defend the Order. The number had risen to 597. The large number of defendants created problems for the commissioners, which they resolved by holding the first day of the trial in the garden of the Bishop of Paris. It is immensely significant that the Grand Master was not present, and it is difficult not to admit the possibility that his absence was from personal choice. The weight of numbers of prisoners clearly intimidated the commissioners, who never allowed a repetition of such a large gathering. The commissioners asked for spokesmen to be appointed, and Renaud de Provins and Pierre de Bologna were selected. These two representatives were evidently discomforted by the absence of Jacques de Molay and stated that they could not present a proper defense without the opportunity to consult with their Grand Master. Their pleas fell on stony ground, and the commission gave them three days to prepare. There followed a period when a team of papal notaries visited the holding areas, taking statements at each. It was Pierre de Bologna who proved to be the best advocate, standing the original arrest order on its head and pointing it back at his accusers.

> *Just as the alleged crimes of the Templars were despicable, execrable, abominable and wholly inhuman, so were the articles of accusation shameful, wicked and detestable. There had never been the slightest trace of the heresies with which they were accused in the entire history of the Templars, and their order was to be considered pure and immaculate.*

Bologna was particularly articulate in his explanation of the confessions made under torture:

> *For all the Templars who say that these lies or some of them are true are liars themselves and speak falsely. Nevertheless they were not deceived, because they spoke them in the fear of death. Neither should they prejudice the Order or its members, because it is known that these things were said in the fear of death and the terrible tortures the confessors had suffered. And even if some of them were not tortured, they were in any case terrified by the fear of torture, seeing others who were tortured, and so they said what the torturers wanted them to say. So these [confessions] should not be taken into account, because the punishment of one is the fear of many.*

When it came to Renaud de Provins' turn, he added a new twist. He requested that all Templars who had spoken badly of the Order should be handed over to the church to decide whether they were telling the truth. He also asked for deathbed confessions of Templars who had confessed under torture to be taken into account. This was particularly astute because a deathbed has long been considered the most likely place where someone would tell the truth. It fell to another brother, Jean de Montréal, to provide the best demonstration of past Templar strengths. He challenged anyone who was prepared to accuse him of the crimes to mortal combat. It is doubtful whether such a challenge to a group of bishops was given much credence, and in the event no one took up the challenge.

Around this time, some complained about the cost of their board and lodgings. They were allotted twelve *derniers* per day to cover everything, but when they were required to travel to a hearing, they had to pay for a blacksmith to release them from their chains, and then put them back on when they returned. The prisoners were also required to pay any ferry costs should they need to cross the river to get to the hearing. The money to pay these costs was coming from the Paris temple, but it appears to have been inadequate to cover the increased costs when the trial got under way. More importantly, this remonstrance provides some evidence that the Templars were beginning to feel some measure of confidence and that affairs were moving in their direction.

On April 7, 1310, Archbishop Gilles Aicelin chaired the full commission. Pierre de Bologna and Renaud de Provins led the nine defenders. One might speculate that they decided on *nine* Templars to provide the defense in order to emulate the nine who started the Order. Bologna presented the defense with considerable skill. After complimenting the reverend fathers and commissioners, he stated that they could not defend the Order without the consent of the Grand Master who was still inexplicably absent from the proceedings. The prisoners were therefore, of necessity, defending themselves as individuals. On the question of torture, Bologna cleverly argued that it was not the poor knights who had confessed under torture who should be listened to. On the contrary, he suggested that it was those brave Templars who had withstood the torture and refused to confess to any crimes who should be believed. He proceeded to summarize the purpose of the Order.

Whoever enters the said Order makes four essential promises, namely obedience, chastity, poverty, and to devote his entire strength to the

service of the Holy Land, that is to conquer the Holy Land of Jerusalem
if God grants the grace to do so, and to maintain, guard and defend it
to the best of his ability.

He pointed out that this promise did indeed entail a kiss, but not
the obscene kiss alleged in the charges but the honest kiss of peace.
With regard to defiling the cross, the Templars wore the cross with
pride on their breasts. He conceded that, of course, occasionally a
brother acted in breach of the "rule," but that Templar knights were
subject to human fallibility just like everyone else.

He also pointed out that when any lapses from the "rule" came
to light, the individual was dealt with harshly. Pierre de Bologna
continued by suggesting that evil men had misled King Philip into
initiating the inquisition, and that the prisoners then had little
choice, under torture, but to confess. These false confessions had, in
turn, falsely misled the Lord Pope and the Lord King. The defense
team were aware that such an argument had little chance of success
so they proceeded to attack the procedural flaws. Bologna pointed
out that because no evidence existed before the arrests and because
there was no change in public opinion against the Order, the
commission could not technically proceed. Jean de Montréal followed Bologna and illustrated the falseness of the charges by drawing upon Templar history. Montréal listed the various rules and
punishments and concluded with the loss of the castle at Safed.
Eighty Templars had been taken before the Mameluk Sultan Baibars
who offered to spare their lives if they denied Christ. All refused and
were either flayed or decapitated; these, he argued, were hardly the
actions of people who could even contemplate the conduct contained in the charges against them.

From the perspective of this book, the next witness is probably
the most significant. Raoul de Presles was not a Knight Templar; he
had risen from humble origins to become a lawyer trained to advise
a local *bailli* or bailiff. Presles spent several years advising the bailli of
Laon in the region of Champagne. It has been suggested that the
Count of Champagne may even have sponsored him. Whether this
was the case or not, Champagne has entered the investigation once
more. Sometime around 1305, Presles moved to Paris where he

became an advocate at the *parlement*. It was during his time in Laon that as a Royal official he became "very friendly" with the Master of the local preceptory, one Gervais de Beauvais. Presles was to open a window onto the reasons behind the secrecy of the Chapters' secret meetings. He told how Beauvais had spoken to him about a certain "point."

> *So extraordinary and so well concealed that the same Gervais would rather have his head cut off than see the point revealed.*

The reader will notice the reference to the secret as a point. I will later explain how the "long lost secret of a Master Mason" is also referred to as a "point." Presles was not finished, and he proceeded to quote Beauvais as having told him that there was a second point.

> *That was secret to such an extent that if the same Master Raoul de Presles, or even the King of France, were by some misfortune to see this point, in spite of the punishment they would incur, those present at the chapter would do everything possible to kill them, bowing to the authority of no one in doing so.*

Once again, the reference is to a "point." Presles continued by informing the tribunal that Beauvais had informed him that the Templars had a book of secret statutes. Beauvais had acquainted Presles with his book containing the "rule," an astonishing act if true, and in clear breach of the statutes contained in it. He had also informed Presles that

> *He had another secret book which he would not be able to show him for all the world.*

It has been suggested that Raoul de Presles' testimony was fabricated, and this may well be so. However, the substance of the story is so supportive of the suggestion that the Knights Templar had possession of the Ark of the Covenant as to warrant further consideration. The reference to the secret as being a "point" must draw us to the Masonic ritual where the "long lost secret of a Master Mason" is called a "point." The reference to another "book" also bears a remarkable similarity to my interpretation of later Masonic ritual that the "word" is used as a metaphor for the Ark. The big, unanswerable question is—did Presles get this information from Beauvais or someone in the Court of Champagne? One thing is sure, however, and this is that Presles reported the matter to either the king or someone very close to the king.

When the trial was over, Raoul de Presles became very wealthy indeed. A number of royal rents were made over to him together with a house and revenues at Courdemaine and a manor near Filan. His wealth continued to multiply and within only a few years he was the largest landowner in the lower valley of Aisne, with mills and several villages. Before he died, he founded a school and a college. This evidence allows us to consider a totally different scenario for the whole sorry episode. Philip was clearly aware that the Templars had possession of something of immense value that was held in great secrecy. If this object was indeed the Ark, then Philip would probably have known and certainly lusted after it. Notwithstanding his access to gossip and other secret information in his capacity as king, Philip was married to the daughter of the Count of Champagne. So he may well have acquired knowledge of the Templars' "treasure" from "pillow talk."

The reason for Philip's persecution of the Order has generally been put down to his desire to get his hands on the "Templar treasure." There were times during the Templars' sojourn in the Holy Land and later when things were particularly dire when mention is invariably made that the "treasure" was saved. The final fall of Acre is one example, and the flight from the Paris temple by the haywain is another. If the "treasure" was indeed the Ark of the Covenant, then the contradictions, enfolded within the trial stages of this story, are explained. The near-obsession of King Philip with his divine right of rule and his enthusiasm to have his grandfather Louis IX canonized, all suggest that the Ark of the Covenant would have been an irresistible object for him to possess. There was, after all, the palatine chapel of Saint Chapelle in Paris waiting to receive it. It would also help to explain the strange behavior of Jacques de Molay. If, in reality, de Molay had been subjected to special torture in order to wrest the whereabouts of the Ark from him, that would help to explain his collapse under torture.

Assuming for a moment that this supposition is correct, we can speculate whether the Ark was still in Cyprus at that time or whether it had been removed from the Paris temple in the "haywain." In either eventuality, King Philip would have been unable to gain possession because, if it were still in France, then it is unlikely that any of those arrested would have known the location. If, on the other hand, the Ark were still in Cyprus, then the King would have been pushed to find a credible excuse to invade the island and Kolossi castle in particular. The real reason for any hypothetical invasion would have been far too sensitive to have been made public. This conjecture does provide us with an explanation for de Molay's apparent physical collapse. If, for the sake of discussion, he had confessed to this "assumed fact" under torture, then it is conceivable that this act alone brought about his mental collapse. As we shall later see, his extraordinary bravery at the end, after some six years of imprisonment, does support an alternative possibility: that he simply battened down his "mental hatches" in order to get through the experience in order not to betray the whereabouts of the Ark.

There is another facet of this story that warrants examination, and that is the inquisition process. As has already been mentioned, the inquisition was under the control of the Dominican order. It is hard to believe that two members of this order would indulge in the sort of activities that have been described above simply to gain possession of the Ark of the Covenant for the King of France. It is more plausible to believe, if this notion is correct, that de Molay was subject to other torture outside of that carried out by the members of the Inquisition. If this were to be the case, then there would have been no way that de Molay could have mentioned it without explaining the reason for it. From whichever angle one views this whole affair, it is strange. It is possible to extend this enquiry with the knowledge that no "primary source" evidence is available to support the contention that de Molay was ever tortured at all. If my conjecture is on the right lines, then it may be that he fabricated the "confession" at the outset in order to buy time for the "treasure" to be spirited away and made safe. Further support for the various propositions outlined above comes from the behavior of Philip. For someone who is purported to have been very short of funds, he was remarkably generous with his key helpers, Nogaret, Plaissans and now Presles, all of whom finished up incredibly wealthy. It is also apparent that for long periods he became almost bored with it all. Clearly, as king, there was never any prospect of his backing down and saying sorry, but after the initial round of torture, the Templars appear to have been treated no worse than any other prisoner of the time.

Meanwhile, back in Paris things were not going well for Philip. The city was alive with tales of the torture of the Templars, and stories of their bravery in resisting. With these tales came sympathy for the victims. Pope Clement had been very successful in giving the commodity they most needed, time—but Philip was to have no more of it. Almost three years after the arrest, Philip IV was able to achieve a breakthrough.

The Archbishop of Sens, Etienne Bécard, a renowned scholar of independent mind, died on March 29, 1309. This enabled Philip to arrange for the brother of his "counsellor and master of finances" to be appointed as the new Archbishop of Sens. Thus Bishop Guillaume de Baufet, the bishop of Paris, found himself the suffragan of a new superior, Philippe de Marigny, the new Archbishop of Sens. Marigny wasted no time in convening a Council of the Province of Sens to "pass judgment on the Templars in Paris." The prisoners were well aware of the consequences of this shift in power, and Pierre de Bologna made an impassioned plea to the commissioners to be allowed to address the new Archbishop. It was all to no avail. On May 12, 1310, the Council gave its ruling. The commission was interrupted in the middle of hearing evidence to be given the Council's verdict. The Templars would fall into three categories:

1. Those who were prepared to confirm their confessions would be allowed to dress in secular clothes and go free.
2. Those who had refused to confess were sentenced to life imprisonment, or until the day on which they were prepared to confess.
3. Those who had retracted their confessions were relapsed heretics, *perjurer relapsi,* and would be handed over to the secular authorities. That meant automatic burning at the stake.

This finding put every brother participating in the trial into the third category, and fifty-four were handed over to the Royal officers immediately. The commission members protested but to no avail. The royal officers drove the men to a meadow just outside the city walls and set fire to the wagons. As the flames engulfed them, the Templars, as one voice, loudly declared their innocence. When the fires had died down, the bones were broken into small pieces and re-burned until they were dust, and this dust was then disposed of, probably in the River Seine. At the same time, nine were burned at Senlis and two weeks later, on May 27, 1310, five more Templars were burned alive in the meadow outside of the Paris walls. A total of sixty-eight had "gone to the stake" and the Templar resistance was over. As a means of bringing matters to an end, the Council's decision was a success. Pierre de Bologna simply disappeared; he was either one of those burned or was murdered by the Royal guards. With no effective leadership, the Templars, firstly in groups and then singly, withdrew their defense until no one was left. The commission then adjourned. In October, 1311, the Ecumenical Council met at the small town of Vienne. Three hundred church dignitaries filled the town to overflowing. The first and second items on the agenda were swiftly dispatched; they were:

1. The next Crusade.
2. Sundry minor church reforms.

The third item *Factum Templarorium* concerned the fate of the wealth of the Templars, and Pope Clement delivered a major oration. He listed the overwhelming proof, by way of two thousand confessions and other evidence, and concluded the need to abolish the Order. The assembled church dignitaries would not hear of it without listening to the Templars' defense and voted at a ratio of six to one against the proposals. The Pope pointed out that defenders had been invited but none had seen fit to come. The council insisted that the invitation be put again. The response was breathtaking: seven Knights Templar in full uniform and on horseback rode into Vienne. They said that they represented fifteen hundred knights who had escaped to the hills around Lyons and who wished for them to attack the council and defend their order. Clement V was paralyzed; he ordered the arrest of the seven but the Council over-ruled him and they went free. The Pope adjourned the Council for six months.

In March, 1312, still in Vienne and in secret, Pope Clement, under the watchful eye of King Philip IV of France, issued his bull *Vox in excelso*, which proclaimed the dissolution of the Knights Templar to the whole world. In April, 1312, the public session of the postponed council opened. The King's army surrounded the town as the Pope read his bull. The evidence, he said, was insufficient to warrant canonical condemnation. However, events of the previous three years meant that the Templars were now discredited and could not take part in another crusade. There was clearly some concern that the suggestion might arise that the whole Templar episode had simply been a subterfuge to gain possession of their property. To avoid any such suspicion, the landholdings and other assets were to be transferred to the Order of the Hospital. The main exception was the land and property in what is now Portugal; here, the Templars changed their name to the "Order of Christ" and transferred their allegiance to King Dinis. The Knights Templar ceased to exist.

All that was left was the matter of the remaining prisoners. Most of those who had confessed and denounced their calling had al-ready been released. Some would even enjoy pensions paid from the Order's former estates. Jacques de Molay and the three Provin-cial Preceptors had repeated their confessions of guilt before three cardinals and had been sentenced to life imprisonment. The perse-cutors, however, could not resist one last act of public personal purification. On March 18, 1314, the four leading Templar Knights were taken by tumbrel to a wooden platform erected outside of Notre Dame Cathedral. One by one their confessions were read to the crowds, and one by one they were asked to affirm their guilt before God and the people. Hugh de Peraud and Geoffrey de Gonaville averred with heads held low. Jacques de Molay, by con-trast, raised his now seventy-year-old body to its full height and in an act that would reverberate down the centuries, made the follow-ing speech:

It is only right that at so solemn a moment and when my life has so little time to run, I should reveal the deception which has been practised and speak up for the truth. Hear me; before heaven and earth and all of you for my witnesses, I confess, I confess that I am indeed guilty of the greatest infamy. But the infamy is that I have lied. I have lied in admitting the disgusting charges laid against my Order. I declare, and I must declare that the Order is innocent. Its purity and saintliness have never been defiled. In truth, I had testified otherwise, but I did so from fear of terrible torture. Other knights who retracted their confessions have been led to the stake, I know. Yet the thought of dying is not so awful that I would now uphold my confession to foul crimes which were never committed. Life is offered me, but at the price of perfidy. At such a price life is not worth having. If life is to be bought only by piling lie upon lie, I do not grieve that I must lose it.

Geoffrey de Charnay spoke similarly, and Philip immediately ordered the provost of Paris to arrest the two "relapsed heretics." The following morning, on the tiny island of de Palais in the Seine, the two were burned at the stake, declaring their innocence to the end. It is said that with his dying breath the last Grand Master of the Poor Fellow-Soldiers of Christ and the Temple of Solomon, Jacques de Molay, called on King Philip IV of France and Pope Clement V to join him at their earliest convenience for judgment before God. Whether there is any truth in this suggestion cannot be proved, but one month later Pope Clement V joined Jacques and Geoffrey before his Maker. A mere seven months after the death of Clement, King Philip also shook off his mortal coil. Philip's three sons, in turn, succeeded him as Kings Louis X, Philip V and Charles IV respectively. Each of them reigned for less than six years, and none left a male heir. By 1328 King Philip IV's Capetian Royal House was no more. Nogaret, the "behind the scenes" schemer, also died before the year was out. Finally the King's prosecutor, Guillaume de Plaisians, also died in 1314.

Ashlars

1. King Philip had every Templar in France arrested without apparent reference to the Pope and without any opposition from the Templars.
2. The Templar Grand Master succumbed immediately and confessed to "spitting on the cross," after which further Templar defense became problematic.
3. The remaining imprisoned Templars put up a spirited defense but without de Molay it was to no avail.
4. It is possible that King Philip was after the Ark of the Covenant all along, and when it became clear that he would not get it, he washed his hands of the matter and let the Templars be destroyed.
5. The Capetian line of kings, to which Philip belonged, had prepared Paris as the New Jerusalem and the Ark would have made that preparation complete.
6. Those individuals who helped Philip to destroy the Templars were rewarded with large tracts of land and huge wealth.
7. Thousands of French Templars survived the arrest and were at large in France during the period of the trial.
8. The Order of the Knights Templar went to considerable lengths to ensure that homosexual behavior did not and could not take place.
9. On March 18, 1314, Jacques de Molay, the last Grand Master of the Knights Templar, made an impassioned speech on the steps of the Cathedral of Notre Dame declaring the innocence of the Order. This seminal event will be seen to have laid the foundation stones for events over the next seven hundred years.

Note:

These two Chapters have drawn very heavily on works by Edith Simon[9], Edward Burman[19], John Robinson[22] and Steven Howarth[29], and, for this reason, individual attributions have not been given.

CHAPTER 3 KEYSTONE

I BEGAN THIS STORY with the Knights Templar, but it has become clear that we must now move to the esoteric world of Freemasonry. The idea that Freemasonry and the Knights Templar are somehow linked is not new. Almost since Freemasonry stepped cautiously onto the public scene in 1717, members have put forward arguments in support of a Templar/Masonic link. The official line taken by the various Grand Lodges around the world is that "nothing has been proved." In order, however, to make sense of this investigation, the reader needs a basic understanding of Freemasonry.

When a man becomes a Freemason, he goes through three "craft" ceremonies:

Initiation—To the first degree when he becomes an **entered apprentice Freemason.**

Passing—To the second degree when he becomes a **fellowcraft Freemason.**

Raising—To the third degree when he becomes a **master mason.**

The term "craft" Masonry is used to distinguish it, within Freemasonry as a whole, from other Masonic orders. There are many other orders, or degrees, in Freemasonry, such as the Mark Master Masons, Royal and Select Masters and the Red Cross of Constantine. Craft Freemasonry, however, has only three degrees—as explained above—and it is these three degrees which will assume immense importance as this story unfolds. The reader will see that they might more appropriately be written as 3°.

Freemasons consider themselves to be "speculative" masons, as opposed to operative masons, the latter being workmen engaged in the building-trade of masonry. Craft Masonic ceremonies are centered on the loss of the genuine secrets of a master mason. These secrets were lost, according to Masonic ritual, when the architect in charge of the building of King Solomon's temple, Hiram Abif, was murdered.

Many "non-Mason" readers will have seen excerpts from Masonic ceremonies on television and will therefore be able to picture the following exchange, which takes place during the opening of a lodge in the third degree:

Junior Warden	*To seek for that which was lost, which, by your instruction and our own industry we hope to find.*
Master (of the lodge)	*What is that which was lost?*
Senior Warden	*The genuine secrets of a master mason.*

After he has been a master mason for four weeks, a Freemason becomes eligible to join another of the Masonic orders, a Holy Royal Arch Chapter.

If he applies and is accepted, he will undergo a single ceremony of being "exalted" to the rank of Companion of the Royal Arch. The very word "companion" comes from two Latin words *cum* and *panis* which, as was described earlier, mean to break bread together. The Royal Arch is a more subtle order with its message concealed under many layers of allegory.

Some 1800 years ago Clement of Alexandria stated that "all sacred truth is enfolded in enigmatic fables, legends and allegory," and speculative Masonry is particularly rich in such allegories. But the chief of all allegories of Masonry is "the search for the Word," not the Sacred and Mysterious Name, but the "Word" that has come down to us through the countless ages and always has the same meaning—The Will or Law of God.

From the explanation of the Royal Arch jewel

The Royal Arch is not, as is sometimes thought, a fourth degree; it is the completion of the Master Mason's degree. The United Grand Lodge of England, who see themselves as the "Mother Lodge to the World," recognizes only Craft Freemasonry and the Royal Arch. There are several other Masonic orders that are separate from craft Freemasonry. These other Masonic organizations are, however, warmly tolerated; indeed, most senior craft-Freemasons also hold positions of seniority in other orders, or side degrees as they are sometimes called. None of the side degrees, however, is accorded any superiority over craft Freemasonry. In the U.S. and elsewhere the side degrees are included within craft Freemasonry.

There are other references to hidden secrets that are identified, within the Masonic ritual, by symbols or cryptic words such as "center" or "point." The exchange during the opening of a lodge in the third degree, mentioned above, continues:

Master	*Where do you hope to find them?*
Senior Warden	*With the Center.*
Master	*What is a Center?*
Junior Warden	*A point within a Circle, from which every part of the circumference is equidistant.*
Master	*Why with a Center?*

*Senior Warden   That being a point from which a
master mason cannot err.*

During the course of this investigation, we
shall learn what is meant by *"that which was lost—
the Word,"* which Freemasons seek. It will also
become clear what is meant by *"center"* and *"point"*
and where they are.

Some readers will be unfamiliar with the
ritual used within the ceremonies of craft-Freemasonry and The Holy Royal Arch. The following
brief explanation is intended to be of help. The
ritual of craft-Freemasonry is constructed around
the story of the building of King Solomon's
temple. The Royal Arch ceremony is a continuation of this story and acquaints us with two more
temples. The first, the Tabernacle, is simply introduced, and it is the second temple, on Temple
Mount in Jerusalem, which plays a much larger
role within the Royal Arch ceremony. These three
temples are immensely important both to Freemasonry and to this investigation.

IN THE BEGINNING

*The time it took the sphere to swing from end to end was determined by
an arcane conspiracy between the most timeless of measures; the
singularity of the point of suspension, the duality of the plane's
dimensions, the triadic beginning of p, the secret quadratic nature of
the root and the unnumbered perfection of the circle itself.*

Umberto Eco, *Foucault's Pendulum*

THE PRECEDING TWO CHAPTERS have described an organization
which may or may not be related to the modern Freemasons
and which may have owned something as precious as the
Ark of the Covenant. In order to consider both of these possibilities,
we must start right at the beginning, at the earliest event which
binds both of these propositions together.

It was around 3450 years ago that Moses came down from
Mount Sinai and built the Tabernacle. Royal Arch Freemasons refer
to the Tabernacle as their First or Holy Lodge, and its purpose was
to house the Ark of the Covenant.

*The First or Holy Lodge was opened A.L. 2515, two years after the
exodus of the children of Israel from their Egyptian bondage, by Moses,
Aholiab and Bezeleel, on consecrated ground, at the foot of Mount
Horeb in the Wilderness of Sinai.*

From the Royal Arch Historic Lecture.

The reader will immediately have noticed that the first para-
graph refers to Moses descending from Mount Sinai, although the
excerpt from the Royal Arch historical lecture mentions Mount

Horeb. These are in fact two names for the same mountain, and this "red herring" is the first of many that are there to throw off the scent for anyone attempting to uncover the "long lost secrets."

Craft and the Royal Arch Freemasonry draw heavily upon the Bible for the ritual used in their ceremonies. The Bible records that God made the earth and created man around 4000 B.C. Freemasons recognize this date, and the Grand Lodge certificate that a brother receives on becoming a master mason is dated Anno Lucis (the year in which he was raised plus 4000). Thus 1999 becomes 5999.

In a Royal Arch Chapter room stand twelve ensigns, or banners, on staves. They represent the twelve tribes of Israel:

Judah	Issacha	Naphtali
Zebulun	Asher	Rueben
Dan	Simeon and Levi	Benjamin
Gad	Manesseh	Ephraim

These tribes take their names from the twelve sons of Jacob and Joseph who settled in different parts of Israel and established their dynasties. The Book of Exodus, in the Holy Bible 1:1 to 4 proceeds:

Now these are the names of the children of Israel, which came into Egypt; every man and his household came from Jacob. Rueben, Simeon, Levi, and Judah, Issacher, Zebulun, and Benjamin, Dan, and Naphtali, and Gad, and Asher.

Around 1880 B.C. many Israelites were taken into slavery in Egypt. Some 430 years later, or 1450 B.C., they left, and the Bible tells the story. In Masonic terms, this date was around A.L. 2510, or 2510 years after the "beginning of the world," and five years before the building of the First or Holy Lodge. The difference of three years between this calculation and the piece of ritual from the Royal Arch historical lecture above is irrelevant.

The Book of Exodus tells how a pharaoh became worried over the increasing numbers of "children of Israel" in Egypt. It is now thought that the pharaoh was either Ramases II or his son and successor Merneptah. However, as Ramases ruled for some sixty-seven years and Merneptah ruled from 1212 to 1204 B.C., this would cast doubt on the dates given above. The Israelite slaves by then outnumbered the Egyptians, and Pharaoh was concerned that in a war situation the Israelites might side with an enemy. His first solution to this problem was to set the Israelites to work building the cities of Pithom and Ramases. Unfortunately, these exertions seem to have improved the fecundity of the Israelites, and their numbers increased even more. Pharaoh decided on a more drastic solution and ordered the Israelite midwives to kill all new-born males. The midwives, however, ignored this instruction. Pharaoh then ordered all Egyptians to kill the new-born Israelite males. To avoid this fate for her child, a Levite woman sent her baby son down the river in a crib made from bulrushes. This baby was found by a daughter of the Pharaoh who arranged for him to be reared until she could take him as her own son. She called him Moses. On reaching adulthood, Moses remained loyal to his roots, and seeing an Egyptian beating an Israelite slave, he killed the Egyptian. Pharaoh came to hear of his deed and Moses had to flee for his life.

He settled in the Sinai desert near Mount Sinai or Mount Horeb as it is also called (Fig. 3). Here he befriended a local priest named Jethro and helped out by tending his sheep. Later, Moses married Zipporah, who was one of Jethro's seven daughters, and they had a son, Gershom.

It was when Moses was tending Jethro's sheep on Mount Sinai that God appeared to him from a burning bush. God ordered Moses to return to Egypt and to lead the Israelites to a land flowing with milk and honey. Moses was naturally reluctant; he could not believe that the Israelites would listen to him. Exodus 4:2 and 3 continues:

And the Lord said unto him, "What is in thy hand?"
And he said, "a rod." And he said, "Cast it on the ground."
And he cast it on the ground, and it became a serpent; and Moses
fled from before it.

This is the first mention of a snake within the context of this book, but it will not be the last. Following God's instructions, Moses returned to Egypt. He demonstrated God's power by turning his rod once again into a snake and then changing the waters in the rivers and lakes of Egypt into blood. Pharaoh was unmoved and so

Figure 3
Map of Egypt showing Mount Sinai or Horeb

Moses warned him that if his people were not allowed to leave, there would be a succession of plagues.

Pharaoh declined the offer until the first plague—of frogs—arrived and then agreed to Moses' demand conditionally on the plague going away. Moses entreated God to stay the plague of frogs, but as soon as they had gone, Pharaoh reneged on his promise. There followed eight more plagues on the Egyptians including lice, flies, locusts, and then darkness.

During each plague, Pharaoh agreed to Moses' demand, but once the plague was lifted, he reneged on his promises. God sent one more plague, the tenth, that caused all first-born Egyptian children and animals to die, including Pharaoh's son. Ramases II had around ninety children, many of whom did not outlive him, so this part of the legend is plausible. These deaths had the desired effect, and Pharaoh permitted the Israelites to leave, some 430 years after they had been taken into captivity. Shortly after the Israelites had left, Pharaoh changed his mind and ordered a muster of his troops and chariots to give chase. As the Israelites waited for the tide to go out on one of the deltas in the Sinai region, Pharaoh closed the gap between them.

Eventually the tide receded sufficiently to allow the Israelites to cross just as Pharaoh and his chariots came into view. The soft ground in the delta region slowed Pharaoh's pursuit, and many chariots became bogged down in the mud. As the Egyptians struggled to get their chariots across the delta, the tide began to advance. As is common in delta regions, the tide came in at a frighteningly fast rate. Many Egyptians were drowned, and Moses and his people were free. Moses took his people to the area that he had come to know well, the desert region near Mount Sinai. The lack of water was a problem until he struck a rock with his rod and water came forth. The journey to freedom had taken the Israelites three months.

After a few years, God again summoned Moses to Mount Sinai and this time gave him the Testament, carved on two tablets of stone. The Testament comprised the Ten Commandments and a list of crimes together with their attendant punishments. When Moses returned from the mountain after forty days, he found his people worshipping an idol in the form of a golden calf. He was so angry that he smashed the two stone tablets containing the Testament on the ground. After destroying the golden idol, Moses again climbed the mountain and returned with two more stone tablets. God also gave Moses instructions on how to build a container for the Testament; this was the Ark of the Covenant (Fig. 4).

The Ark or chest was made by Bezlel ben Uri and was made of shittim wood and lined inside and out with gold. Shittim wood is better known as acacia, and wood from the acacia tree was highly prized. The acacia tree, native to Egypt, only grows in dry riverbeds or wadis. It is a deep-rooted tree drawing moisture from the deep sub-soil, and because of this can survive for up to ten years without rain. Acacia holds a very important place within Masonic tradition.

At the point within the Masonic ritual when the murdered body of Hiram Abif, the legendary Architect in charge of the building of King Solomon's temple, was found buried, the masons who found the body marked the spot with a sprig of acacia. The ceremonial collar of a Grand Officer, the most senior group of officers to which a Freemason can be promoted and a member of Grand Lodge, has acacia leaves embroidered down one side.

Figure 4
The Ark of the Covenant

The lid of the Ark of the Covenant was made entirely of gold with two cherubim beaten out of that gold. When the lid was placed on the Ark it became a mercy seat where the Bible suggests that God would "sit" whenever He wished to speak to someone.

And there I will meet with thee, and I will commune with thee from above the mercy seat, from between the two cherubim which are upon the ark of the testimony, of all things which I give thee in commandments unto the children of Israel.

Exodus 25:22

And the Lord said unto Moses, speak unto Aaron thy brother, that he may not at all times into the holy place within the vail before the mercy seat, which is upon the ark; that he die not; for I will appear in the cloud upon the mercy seat.

Leviticus 16:2

Mircea Eliade[54] submits that the Tabernacle and subsequent temples served as the earthly residences for God. The cloud was there to replicate the clouds in heaven, in other words, to make God feel at home.

> *Then Solomon spoke: Yahveh has chosen to abide in dense cloud. I have accordingly built for You a royal house, a dais for Your eternal enthronement.*
>
> 1 Kings 8

Mircea Eliade continues, by saying that:

> *the Ark served as God's footstool, and his throne was formed by the arched, winged cherubs.*

The Tabernacle was not in any sense a place for worshippers and, as will be later explained, the Ark was considered a dangerous structure for humans to get close to. In addition to the tablets of stone, the Ark of the Covenant also held Aaron's rod, which had sprouted leaves, and a sample of manna, the food that had sustained the Israelites in the desert. The Ark of the Covenant was two and a half cubits long, by one and a half cubits high and wide. Depending on which cubits were used in this description (see Appendix II), this would make it around 4 feet (1.2 meters) long by 2 feet 3 inches (0.7 meter) wide and high. The amount of gold incorporated into the Ark would have made it extremely heavy. Jacobs[52] suggests that it could have weighed ten tons although this figure would have ruled out the possibility of it ever being carried on two poles. The Ark possessed deadly powers:

> *And Joshua the son of Nun called the priests, and said unto them, Take up the Ark of the Covenant, and let seven priests bear seven trumpets of ram's horns before the Ark of the Lord.*
>
> Joshua 6:6

> *and the people shouted with a great shout, that the wall [of Jericho] fell down flat*
>
> Joshua 6:20

And he smote the men of Bethshemesh, because they had looked into the Ark of the Lord, even he smote of the people fifty thousand and three score and ten men; and the people lamented, because the Lord had smitten many people with great slaughter.

1 Samuel 6:19

Then God instructed Moses to build a special enclosure with a tent to house the Ark of the Covenant and this he called the Tabernacle (Fig. 5). The Tabernacle was a portable construction covered in fabric made from goats' hair and was transported with the Israelites during the forty years they spent wandering in the Sinai desert. The Tabernacle would have stood out against the sprawling tents of the wandering Israelites because of the white curtain wall—7 feet 6 inches (2.3 meters) high—that surrounded it. The outer court was 150 feet (46 meters) long and 75 feet (23 meters) wide. Around fifty pillars, that were capped with silver and set in bronze sockets, supported the white linen curtain wall of the outer court.

In the outer court was the "laver" or water basin in which the priests would wash their hands and feet before entering the Taber-

Figure 5
The Tabernacle

nacle. In addition there was the Burnt Offering altar, also made of acacia wood but overlain with bronze, in which the ritual sacrifices to God were made. The Tabernacle was effectively the first Jewish temple, and it only served one purpose, which was to house the Ark of the Covenant. God chose to speak to His people from "between the cherubim on the Ark," and this is how the Ark became synonymous, in the Biblical writings, with God. When someone went before the Ark, they went before God.

Stanley James[67] provides an insight into the significance of this structure to Freemasonry as he describes the inside of the church in Rennes-le-Château.

> The blue roof with stars—in French stars are "étoiles." The Tabernacle was a curtained structure. The curtains were blue, scarlet and purple. They were made from fine linen and dyed. "Linen" is "toile" and "lined" would be "étoile" i.e. the same as "star." Thus the blue roof with stars could be the blue linen curtain covering over the Tabernacle.

With this explanation, James could just as well be describing the ceilings of many a Masonic lodge room.

With Moses back in their midst and the Testament mandate—as defined by the commandments—in place, the Israelites quickly grew tired of following God's will. They were soon heard complaining about the penalties for misbehavior, and the object of their resentment was God himself; so He sent a plague of snakes among the tents of the Israelites; many were bitten and died. Moses was distressed by the severity of God's punishment and prayed to Him for forgiveness for the tribes. God told him to make a bronze serpent and to put it on a pole. Those who looked at the bronze serpent, God said, would not die. Once again, the snake comes into the picture, but now it has become a symbol of God's power.

The winged rod with two snakes entwined is the caduceus of the Greek god Hermes and has been adopted as the emblem of the medical profession. From around 2000 B.C. the Sumerian kings were known to use a staff of office with two intertwined snakes.

Of arguably more interest is the knowledge that in the earliest days of the Royal Arch there was a part of the ceremony called "the passing of the veils." This particular piece of ritual is no longer

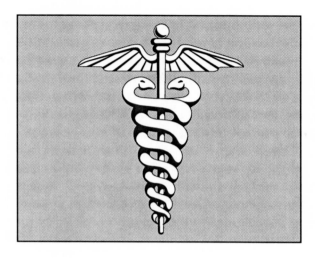

Figure 6
Moses' rod with the snake emblem—the caduceus

practiced in England, apart from the City of Bristol where it forms part of the "Bristol working." It is, however, commonplace in the U.S. The ceremony of "passing the veils" has variously three or four veils, which hang as curtains, and the candidate passes each one with a password. Where four veils are present in the ceremony, they are thought to represent the four elements of earth, water, air and fire. At the second veil it was usual to show the candidate a small replica of Moses' caduceus[59].

Gardner[1], drawing on more recent archaeological findings and ideas also put forward by Ahmed Osman, suggests an alternative history. He suggests that the earlier dates are wrong and argues that when the Pharaoh Tuthmosis died, it was his son the Pharaoh Amenhotep who created the problems for the Israelites. It was his son, by the daughter of the Chief Minister, that came under the edict to kill new-born male Israelites. The boy, also called Amenhotep, was born in 1400 B.C. and later changed his name to Akhenaten. When he became Pharaoh, Akhenaten suffered poor health and, blaming this on the current gods, closed the temples and built new ones to new gods. All of this made him unpopular with his people, and he was forced to abdicate in favor of his son Tutankhamen.

Akhenaten was banished from Egypt, taking his Jewish retainers with him, including families of the line of Jacob. Whether this or any of the other versions are ever proved to be correct will depend upon future archaeological discoveries. Although Gardner and other recent authors have suggested that Moses was not from Israelite stock, the fact remains that the Bible refers to Moses as the son of a Levite woman, and the brother of Aaron and as such clearly an Israelite. The debate is, however, still wide open, with Laidler[69] including Joseph's daughter in the Davidic family tree and mentioning that Judaic transmission is through the female side. In fact the female transmission is a relatively recent innovation and would not have applied to Joseph's daughter.

Another alternative is put forward by Zecharia Sitchin[2] who, drawing on other references, suggests that Moses dwelt in northern not southern Sinai. Sitchin suggests that the Lord spoke to Moses on Gebel Hall, a 2000-foot (600-meter) high limestone massif that stands in the middle of a vast alluvial plain. The Arabic term for Gebel Hall is "The Lawful." This particular explanation has an interesting Masonic connection. Masonic encyclopedias usually include the word *ghiblim, giblim or gibalim* as a significant word and also identify Giblites as the inhabitants of the city of Gebal. In either Hebrew or Arabic, the word *gibel* or *jebel* means "mountain."

As we will discover, a particular *mountain* will emerge as an extremely important feature in this story.

If we add Gebel Hall to Mount Sinai, Mount Horeb and the Deuteronomy reference to Mount Parah, it is apparent that more than a little doubt exists over exactly where the Lord spoke to Moses.

Ashlars

1. The Masonic ceremony of the Holy Royal Arch is linked to the Biblical story of Moses leading his people out of Egypt.
2. Snakes are introduced into the story, culminating in the building by Moses of the caduceus, which was once linked with Masonic ritual.

3. The wood acacia, which was used to build the Ark of the Covenant, also holds an important place in Masonic symbolism.
4. The Ark of the Covenant was covered in gold, and the lid or "mercy seat" where God sat was beaten out of solid gold.
5. The first or Holy Lodge in a Royal Arch Chapter was the Tabernacle used by Moses to house the Ark of the Covenant.
6. There is disagreement over much of the Biblical history of Moses.

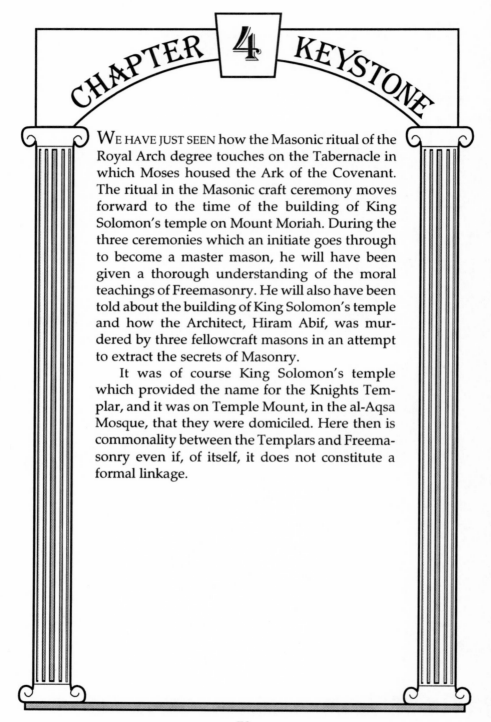

CHAPTER 4 KEYSTONE

WE HAVE JUST SEEN how the Masonic ritual of the Royal Arch degree touches on the Tabernacle in which Moses housed the Ark of the Covenant. The ritual in the Masonic craft ceremony moves forward to the time of the building of King Solomon's temple on Mount Moriah. During the three ceremonies which an initiate goes through to become a master mason, he will have been given a thorough understanding of the moral teachings of Freemasonry. He will also have been told about the building of King Solomon's temple and how the Architect, Hiram Abif, was murdered by three fellowcraft masons in an attempt to extract the secrets of Masonry.

It was of course King Solomon's temple which provided the name for the Knights Templar, and it was on Temple Mount, in the al-Aqsa Mosque, that they were domiciled. Here then is commonality between the Templars and Freemasonry even if, of itself, it does not constitute a formal linkage.

KING SOLOMON'S TEMPLE

My little hut upon the hill, no palace quite as fine;
Its every star bent to my will, its sun and moon incline.

Nikolai Tolstoy, *The Coming of the King*

FOR SOME FORTY YEARS the Israelites pursued a nomadic life in the Sinai desert. They then came within sight of Canaan, the land "flowing with milk and honey," in the general area of what we know today as Israel. It was here that Moses died, so close to the completion of the task that God had set him. Joshua succeeded him and led the people into Canaan where they settled. By around 1000 B.C. David had become King and united the two regions of Canaan, namely Israel and Judah, into one state. During David's reign, he brought the Ark of the Covenant into the capital city of Jerusalem and harbored an ambition to build a temple to house the Ark.

And God came that day to David and said unto him, "Go up, rear an altar unto the Lord in the threshingfloor of Araunah the Jebusite."

2 Samuel 24:18

Before David could realize his ambition, he received further word from God by Nathan:

Go and tell David my servant, Thus saith the Lord, "thou shalt not build me a house to dwell in."

1 Chronicles 17:4

79

Finally, David received word from God that it would be David's
son who would be charged with building the temple:

That I shall raise up thy seed after thee, which shall be of thy sons;
and I will establish his kingdom.
He will build me an house, and I will stablish his throne for ever.

1 Chronicles 17:11 and 12

The second quotation here, from 1 Chronicles 17:12, holds pride
of place on the ceiling of the Great Temple in Grand Lodge, Great
Queen Street, London.

Before continuing, it is important to recognize that a temple
(from the Latin *templum*, meaning holy ground) is not the same as a
church (from the Greek *ekklesia*, which was the open assembly
where policy decisions were made). This is a difficult concept to
grasp when viewed against such confusing signals as French Protes-
tants designating all of their churches as temples. This latter detail
owes more to the fact that some Christian denominations see their
faith as "the New Jerusalem" with the whole being representative of
a symbolical temple in which God dwells. Hinnells[55] makes the
point that:

Both church and synagogue are used in the Septuagint of the commu-
nity of Israel and both are used in the New Testament of a Christian
community, but from an early date "synagogue" has been reserved for
Jews and ekklesia for Christians.

De Breffney[51] points out that Josephus argues that the origins of
the synagogue, as a central feature within Judaism, can be traced
back to the time of Moses. He also explains that the more generally
held view is that the synagogue concept originated with those Jews
who went into captivity with the Babylonians around 586 B.C. He
states that the synagogue, in Hebrew—*bet ha-keneset*—literally
means "The House of Assembly." It is the place where Jewish people
gather to hear the Torah (the Jewish sacred texts) read and explained, and where they can pray to God. In time, the synagogue
became the center of the local community, a focus for social and
cultural life. Clearly, this description could apply equally to a Chris-

tian church building; the reality is that a synagogue and a Christian church fulfill similar functions.

The temple, in Hebrew—*bet ha-mikdash*—literally means "The House of Sanctuary" and is an entirely different concept. The temple was the Jewish spiritual center where they offered sacrifices to God. There was only one temple, which, when it was destroyed for any reason, was rebuilt as soon as was practicably possible. Douglas[53] argues that the temple at Jerusalem differed from any other religious structure because God chose to "dwell therein."

> *The temple is always the temple of God and not [as in the image of the body] of Christ. Where Christ is mentioned, he is thought of as part of the building.*

What Douglas is suggesting is that, excluding the Holy Spirit which resides in the main altar, there is no specific "place" for God within a church; God is all around and even in the stonework. In the case of the temple at Jerusalem, this was a place where God could "physically" visit and converse with man. In other words, the two types of structure accommodate two entirely different manifestations of God: the church for His being and the temple for His actuality—a difference between His essence and His substance.

The most important part of a temple is the chamber in which the image or statue of the god is lodged. In the first temple that Solomon built, the inner chamber was called the Holy of Holies or *sanctum sanctorum*. This room held the object that the Jewish people believe, and the Bible claims, "embodies" God—the Ark of the Covenant.

It is hopefully now clear that the places where Jews fulfill the obligations of their religion are synagogues. King Solomon's temple and subsequent temples in Jerusalem had only one purpose and that was to house the Ark of the Covenant and provide God with a place on earth for Him to visit and to give directions to man. The temple was unimportant in its own right: it was merely a structure to house the really important object which was the Ark. When the Ark was moved from the Tabernacle to Solomon's temple, the Tabernacle is no longer mentioned. Its time had passed and it was no longer of any importance.

After David's death in 970 B.C., Solomon succeeded and reigned as King of Judah and Israel until 930 B.C. He succeeded his father despite the superior claim of his elder half-brother, Adonijah. On becoming King, he set about the task of building a temple at Jerusalem to house the Ark of the Covenant. Around 950 B.C. Solomon completed the first temple on Mount Moriah at Jerusalem. He built it on the site of Araunah, the Jebusite King's threshing floor, and this is the al-Sakhra, the rocky mountaintop still visible today in the Dome of the Rock mosque. Royal Arch Freemasons refer to King Solomon's Temple as their "Second or Sacred Lodge" and, exactly like the Tabernacle, its purpose was also to house the Ark of the Covenant. Solomon's father David had purchased the site of the threshing floor from Araunah immediately after he had the vision of God telling him to raise an altar there. This site is thought to be the same one to which Abraham had years earlier taken his son Isaac in order to sacrifice him to God.

It seems possible that the site retained a sacred aura continually from Abraham's time. After King Solomon had completed the temple, the years passed and nature did her worst. The centuries of wind-blown sand and earthquakes took their toll. Invaders also sacked the city and knocked parts of the temple down as a gesture of the greater strength of their gods. In 922 B.C. the Egyptian Pharaoh Sheshouk sacked Jerusalem; then in 850 B.C. the Philistines and the Arabians followed their lead. In 786 B.C. it was the turn of Joash of Israel to conquer Jerusalem, to be followed in 604 B.C. by the Babylonians. Finally, in 586 B.C. Nebuchadnezzer sacked Jerusalem and completely demolished the temple, taking the Israelites into captivity in Babylon for seventy years.

One thing, however, is clear: the temple demolished by the Babylonians was not the same temple that was built by Solomon. This is apparent from the description in the First Book of Kings Chapters 6 and 7, that describe Solomon's temple and puts the height of the two great pillars at 18 cubits high. The description in the Second Book of Chronicles, Chapters 3 and 4, on the other hand, gives the height of the two great pillars as being 35 cubits high. Even if one description used Royal cubits and the other the smaller cubit, it would not account for this huge difference. There are other descriptive differences that support the proposition that two temples existed before the destruction by Nebuchadnezzer. The natural depredations of the structures, when added to damage sustained during the various conquests, makes the identification of archaeological evidence difficult. The Israel Ministry of Foreign Affairs has an Internet site, which states unequivocally that:

> *Until this very day, not a single archaeological remnant has been found of the Temple of Solomon.*

This statement should make us cautious of those who claim that Rosslyn Chapel in Scotland is a replica of King Solomon's temple. The reality is that it is the Bible that provides a description and measurements in the First Book of Kings Chapters 6 and 7. We are, however, able to draw inferences from the Bible together with archaeological evidence from other relevant sites. Such a site that dates from the time of Solomon's temple is at Tel Ta'inat in Syria, which is just north of Israel, where a long temple with three internal divisions has been unearthed. It is considered likely that King Solomon's temple closely resembled the Tel Ta'inat temple (Fig. 7).

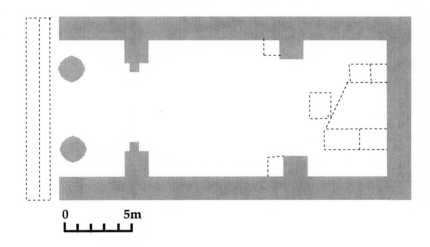

0   5m

Figure 7
The temple excavated at Tel Ta'inat in Israel

North of Jerusalem, but not as far as Syria, was the city of Tyre, and it is possible that Syrian architectural influences extended down to Tyre and even Jerusalem.

> *And King Solomon sent and fetched Hiram of Tyre. He was the son of a widow of the tribe of Naphtali, and his father was a man of Tyre, a worker in brass; and he was filled with the wisdom and understanding and skill to work in brass; and he came to King Solomon, and wrought all his work.*
>
> 1 Kings 7:13-14

The Israel Ministry of Foreign Affairs Internet site shows King Solomon's temple on Temple Mount, or Mount Moriah as it was earlier called, as part of the complex of the Royal Palace, all on Temple Mount. The Israelis attribute their conclusions to archaeological and written findings from neighboring countries.

Figure 8 shows Temple Mount existing in the time of Solomon's Temple, and this assumption is questioned by other archaeologists

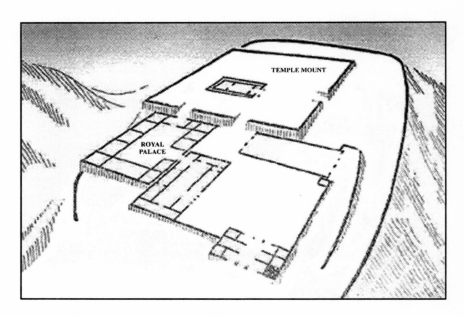

Figure 8
King Solomon's Temple and the palace
on the top of Mount Moriah in Jerusalem

Figure 9
Photograph of Jerusalem showing Mount Moriah and its surroundings

such as Leen Ritmeyer, of whom more later. The two different terms for the same mountain, Mount Moriah and Temple Mount, do in fact have a logical explanation. As you can see from the photograph (Fig. 9), Mount Moriah is not exactly a mountain as we would normally expect to see it. It does not rise that far or that steeply from its surroundings. Temple Mount, with the Dome of the Rock Mosque on it, runs across the middle of the photograph.

Dr. Leen Ritmeyer, who was introduced above, was the former Chief Architect on the Temple Mount excavations after the Six Days' War. His account[3] of the archaeological evidence is arguably therefore as good as any. Ritmeyer's conclusions go somewhat further than the official Israel Ministry of Foreign Affairs version. He suggests that when King Solomon built the first temple, it covered only the top of Mount Moriah (Fig. 10). The extension of Mount Moriah to form the platform, or pavement that we now call Temple Mount, must have been carried out at a later date, probably during the reign of Hezekiah (Fig. 11). The term "Temple Mount" does not appear until the reign of Hezekiah's son Manasseh, and it is considered unlikely that he would have carried out any building work on the temple complex.

The building materials for the walls that support Temple Mount and the rubble to fill the space between walls to form the pavement

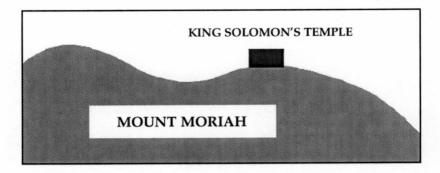

Figure 10
King Solomon's Temple on Mount Moriah

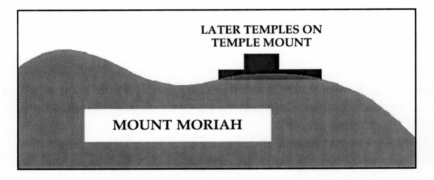

Figure 11
Temple Mount on top of Mount Moriah

probably came from the demolition of Solomon's palace. It is a small part of the remains of the original wall which supports the pavement that is now the "Wailing Wall." The flattening of the top of a mountain performed two important functions: first, it gave a much larger pavement for people to parade around, formally or otherwise. Second, it improved greatly the defenses of the buildings on the top of the Temple Mount. The original Temple Mount, probably built by Hezekiah, has been identified as having been 820 feet (250 meters) square. This is supported in the Mishnaic tractate Middot 2.1 which states *"Har habbayit* [Temple Mount] measured five hundred cubits by five hundred cubits[3]." The conversion used is the "Royal Cubit" of 16 inches (.5 meter). The Royal Cubit originated in

Egypt and is the same length as "the cubit and a handbreadth" quoted in Ezekiel 40.5, the cubit mentioned in Ezekiel being the "smaller cubit." Flavius Josephus, the first-century Jewish chronicler, provided a more accurate description of Temple Mount but understated the size by some 135 cubits.

When the Israelites returned from their exile in Babylon, they rebuilt the temple yet again. This third temple was finally completely rebuilt for a fourth time by King Herod the Great. The Roman Emperor Titus demolished this fourth or Herodian temple in A.D. 70. Finally, between A.D. 685 and 691, it was replaced with the Moslem mosque, "the Dome of the Rock" that still stands today. The third and fourth temples are dealt with in more detail in the next chapter.

During Ritmeyer's investigations into the temple complex on Mount Moriah, he made a significant discovery. He identified a depression in the al-Sakhra that fits the Ark dimensions precisely, and Ritmeyer believes that this is where the Ark of the Covenant stood and that this therefore also locates the position of Solomon's temple. Figure 12 shows where Ritmeyer contends that the temple was located in relation to the present Dome of the Rock Mosque.

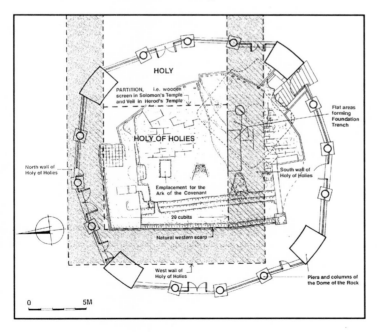

Figure 12 King Solomon's Temple and the Dome of the Rock Mosque

Reconstruction by Dr. Leen Ritmeyer

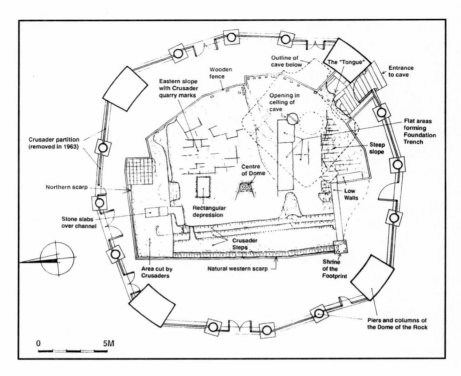

Figure 13
The al-Sakhra showing the cave and the damage caused by
the Templars and Crusaders
Reconstruction by Dr. Leen Ritmeyer

Figure 13, also Ritmeyer's, provides a closer look at the al-Sakhra
with the rectangular depression where the Ark of the Covenant
could have been sited, together with other details such as a natural
cave and various alterations made by the Templars and other
Crusaders at the turn of the first millennium. Finally, Figure 14
provides Ritmeyer's estimation of what a cross-sectional view
through King Solomon's temple might have looked like.

No discussion of Solomon's temple is possible without touching
on the Ark of the Covenant. The importance of both the temple and
the Ark to Freemasonry poses a question that cannot be avoided.
That question is when was the Ark in the various temples at
Jerusalem? We can accept that it was there when Solomon finished

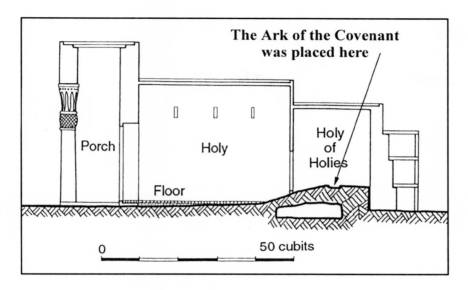

Figure 14
A cross-section through King Solomon's Temple
Reconstruction by Dr. Leen Ritmeyer

the first temple because the Bible says that it was, and there is little else to explain why he built it. It was also there during the reign of Hezikiah, who died around 687 B.C.:

And Hezikiah received the letters from the hand of the messengers, and read it: and Hezikiah went up unto the house of the Lord, and spread it out before the Lord.

And Hezikiah prayed unto the Lord, saying,

O Lord of Hosts, God of Israel, that dwelleth between the cherubim, Thou art the God, even Thou alone, of all the kingdoms of the earth; Thou hast made heaven and earth.

Isaiah 37: 14–16

We can be sure that these verses refer to the Ark of the Covenant because of the reference to "that dwelleth between the cherubim." As has already been argued, the Jewish people believe that God exists between the two cherubim on the lid of the Ark of the Covenant, and the Old Testament books of the Bible make many references confirming this point. The above verses are repeated almost word for word in the Second Book of Kings 19: 14–15. The last time that the Bible mentions the Ark is in 2 Chronicles 35:3 when King Josiah ordered it to be put back into the temple.

> *Put the Holy Ark in the house which Solomon the son of David king of Israel did build; it shall not be a burden upon your shoulders.*

This would have been around 623 B.C., and a number of conclusions can reasonably be drawn from this record.

1. The temple priests had moved the Ark to safe-keeping during the preceding turbulent times.
2. The Holy Ark was indeed returned to the temple because there is no reference to the fact that it was not, and that would have been an important event.
3. Those in authority, including King Josiah, were well aware that the Holy Ark had been safely hidden until the time that he ordered it to be returned to the temple.
4. The fairly off-hand manner in which this event is dealt with indicates that it was not unusual to hide the Holy Ark during periods of crisis.
5. Whatever and wherever the hiding place was, it had success-fully protected the Ark during the 327 turbulent years between 950 B.C. when Solomon built the first temple and 623 B.C. when King Josiah gave his direction to the temple priests.
6. The effectiveness of the hiding place is demonstrated by the knowledge that it remained a secret on at least four occasions when Jerusalem was over-run during those 327 years.

There are no further Biblical references to the Ark. However, it is highly unlikely that, if the Babylonians had taken or destroyed it, no mention would have been made. The various temples, through to the Herodian temple, offer compelling evidence that the Ark was available. If the Ark had been lost, why build these temples? The temples were, as has already been stated, structures to house the Ark—they had no other purpose.

There have been rumors that the Knights Templar recovered the Ark, although no record exists of their ever claiming to have had it. Before we can even consider such a contention, we must establish that the Ark could have survived from David's time, even until the beginning of the second millennium. For this to have been remotely possible, a secure hiding place for it must be identified. Even if we accept that the Ark was ever held in the Herodian temple, and Herod might have built his temple to provide him with credibility, there were later sackings as mentioned in the next chapter, until around 640 A.D. when the Muslims captured the city. Such a hiding place, however, can be identified.

Ritmeyer[3] is of the opinion that the Holy of Holies or the Inner Sanctum remained empty until the destruction of the temple by Titus in 79 A.D. Ritmeyer also reports "two stone slabs" conspicuously placed on the northern shelf. They cover an opening and channel previously investigated by Warren[4] and have been attributed to the Knights Templar who were "known to have dug tunnels on the Temple Mount in search of the Ark of the Covenant."

In the southeast corner is an entrance to a cave that is located under the al-Sakhra. Fourteen steps approximately 4 feet 6 inches (1.4 meters) wide descend to the cave which is about 23 feet (7 meters) long by 25 feet (7.5 meters) wide and irregularly shaped. The ceiling, which appears to be natural, is at a height varying from 5 feet (1.5 meters) to 8 feet (2.5 meters). There are no signs of rope marks, which rules the cave out as a cistern. This cave immediately brings to mind the Royal Arch ritual, which describes three master masons finding a vaulted arch under the site of the first temple—King Solomon's. The ritual refers to a vault, but what actually exists is a cave that might easily be represented ritualistically as a vaulted arch. It is furthermore likely that the Knights Templar, who occupied an adjacent site for many years, would have known of this cave.

On exploring the vault [I] found this scroll of vellum or parchment, but from the [lack of light] I was unable to read its contents. I therefore

signalled with my right hand, and my companions drew me up, bring-
ing the scroll with me. On arriving at the light of day, we found from
the first words therein recorded, that it was part of the long-lost Sacred
Law, promulgated by our Grand Master Moses at the foot of Mount
Horeb in the Wilderness of Sinai.

From the Principal Sojourner's story about the vault

One possibility, no matter how remote, is that the Royal Arch ritual refers to the discovery of the Ark of the Covenant by the Knights Templar. This would, in turn, link the Knights Templar directly to Freemasonry through its connection with the Royal Arch degree. There is other evidence of the possession of the Ark of the Covenant by the Knights Templar—for example, the castles at Kolossi and Limassol on Cyprus that were occupied by the Knights Templar when they left the Holy Land. A few years ago a friend told me that, during a visit to Cyprus, he had visited Limassol Castle and seen a stone container rather like a sarcophagus which the custodian had said was used to store the Ark of the Covenant. This information had sat at the back of my mind until now, and because it is so central to Masonic doctrine, I will return to it in more detail in Chapter 9.

Illustrations of the Ark of the Covenant can be found in several places in the Grand Lodge in Great Queen Street. There is a floor mosaic made from stones collected in Jerusalem by Brother Henry Mawdslay in 1877. The use of a mosaic is particularly piquant because the same word "Mosaic"—only the "M" is changed to a capital—means "pertaining to Moses." An Ark also features on the outside of the great doors to the Grand Temple. Finally, at the Memorial Window and Shrine commemorating Masons who gave their lives in the Great War, the chest containing the names of the fallen is called the Ark. In fact, the word "ark" simply means a chest, but the winged angels and the rings at the corners leave little doubt that this is a representation of the Ark of the Covenant.

Others have suggested that the Ark of the Covenant was found in King Solomon's stables (Fig. 15). These stables or subterranean halls where the Templars indeed stabled their horses were not built during the construction of the first or second temple. They were in fact built at the time that King Herod carried out extensive enlarging

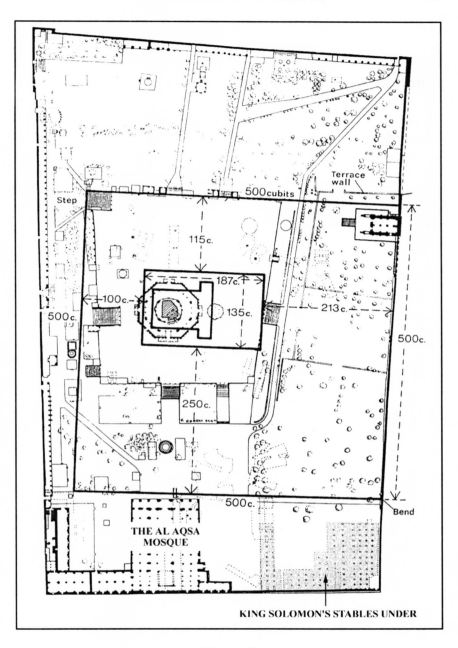

Figure 15
Overhead view of Temple Mount showing the location under the stables

Reconstruction by Dr. Leen Ritmeyer

and rebuilding. In the absence of conclusive proof, and nothing can be ruled in or out, the existence of the cave together with the Royal Arch ritual points away from the stables as being the hiding place of the Ark. More details of Solomon's stables are given in the next chapter.

Before we leave this chapter, one final point concerning the Knights Templar deserves mention. A number of the more recent popular publications on this subject include references to a declared ambition of the Templars: to build a temple on the model of the one described in the Bible book of Ezekiel. Subsequent chapters will show that these recent publications were quite right to record this Templar aspiration.

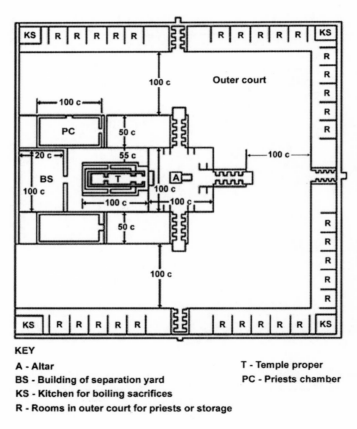

KEY

A - Altar

BS - Building of separation yard

KS - Kitchen for boiling sacrifices

R - Rooms in outer court for priests or storage

T - Temple proper

PC - Priests chamber

Figure 16
Layout of the temple complex as described in the Bible book of Ezekiel

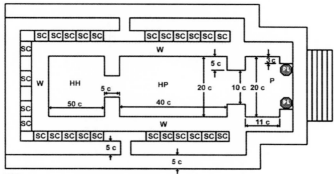

KEY
H - Holy Place (sanctury)
HH - Holy of Holies
P - Porchway
PL - Pillars
SC - Side Chambers of the Temple Sanctury
W - Wall of the Temple

Figure 17
Plan of the actual temple within
the complex shown in Figure 16

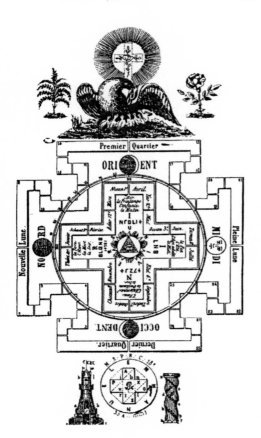

Figure 18
Stylized plan of Ezekiel's
Temple dating probably
from around the eighteenth
century

Ashlars

1. The Knights Templar and Freemasons share a common interest in King Solomon's temple.
2. The site on which King Solomon's temple was built had been a sacred site for hundreds of years before.
3. The Tabernacle, King Solomon's temple and later temples on Mount Moriah were not churches. They were buildings with a single purpose of housing the Ark of the Covenant.
4. There was probably another temple built on Mount Moriah after King Solomon's temple and before what we now know as the "second temple."
5. Nothing is known archaeologically about Solomon's temple, even as to what it looked like.
6. King Solomon's temple is known as the "second or Sacred Lodge" in a Royal Arch Chapter.
7. The temple priests were in the habit of hiding the Ark of the Covenant during times of crisis, and they were successful because the Ark survived several sackings of Jerusalem.
8. Under the *al-Sahkra* is a cave that dates back to early times and may have been the hiding place for temple valuables such as the Ark.
9. The Masonic ceremonial ritual of the Royal Arch points to someone finding the Ark under the ruins of King Solomon's temple.
10. There are rumors that the Templars found the Ark on the site of King Solomon's temple.
11. The Ark may have travelled to Cyprus.
12. The Grand Lodge of England, in London, contains Ark-related symbolism.

CHAPTER 5 KEYSTONE

AROUND 1730 a new ceremony or degree entered Freemasonry and it was called the Holy Royal Arch. Its appearance on the Masonic stage was not greeted with unanimous approbation. A few years earlier, in 1717, the first Grand Lodge was formed in London. From around 1730, when the Royal Arch appeared, and 1751, when a rival Grand Lodge "the Ancients" also appeared in London, Grand Lodge was implacably opposed to the idea that the Royal Arch should be integrated with Freemasonry as it then existed. Just before the union in 1813 when the "Moderns," as the first Grand Lodge became known in obvious counterpoise to the Ancients, voted on the continuing question of whether to admit the Royal Arch, they voted unanimously against the proposition. The curious aspect of this vote was that at the time all of the "Moderns," Grand Officers who voted against the incorporation of the Royal Arch, were themselves members of it. At the union of the Ancients and Moderns to create the United Grand Lodge of England that exists to this day, the compromise was that the Royal Arch should not be a separate degree but rather the completion of the master mason's degree. This arrangement has continued to this day.

In 1838 the Royal Arch ritual was greatly modified to provide the ceremony in much the same format as is practiced today. This ritual is built around the construction of the "second temple" at Jerusalem, the so-called Zerubbabel temple after the then governor of Judah.

REVELATION

I accept the risk of damnation. The Lord will absolve me, because He knows I acted for His glory. My duty was to protect the library.

Umberto Eco, *The Name of the Rose*

IN ADDITION TO THE FIRST OR HOLY LODGE described in Chapter 3, and the second or Sacred Lodge described in Chapter 4, Royal Arch Freemasons commemorate a Third or Grand and Royal Lodge, the purpose of which was also to house the Ark of the Covenant.

The third or Grand and Royal Lodge was holden at Jerusalem, and opened A.L. 3469, shortly after the return of the children of Israel from their Babylonish captivity.

From the Royal Arch Historical Lecture

The Masonic date of Anno Lucis 3469 puts this event at around 530 B.C., and it is a clear reference to the building of the second temple. In fact, as was explained in the previous chapter, the second temple, as commonly thought, is most likely the third temple to be built on Mount Moriah in Jerusalem. The total number of temples was arguably at least four not including the later Moslem Mosque. The Biblical book of Ezra tells the story of the return to Israel from Babylon of the children of Israel and their building of the temple.

In a ceremony to exalt a new candidate into the Holy Royal Arch, there is a character called Scribe Ezra who plays an important role. The Ezra who wrote the book in the Bible, however, probably lived at least 100 years later than the building of the temple, between 400 and 300 B.C. Among the thousands of people who are reported in the book of Ezra to have returned to Israel for the building of the temple were Jeshua and Zerubbabel, who was the Governor of Judah. Returning to the Holy Royal Arch ceremony of exaltation, the most senior member is Zerubbabel, and he is referred to as a prince. Jeshua is called Joshua and is referred to as:

the son of Josadech, the High Priest.

The third member of a trinity of leaders who act jointly in much the same capacity as the master of a craft lodge, is Haggai the Prophet. The Biblical book of Haggai 1: 1, 2, 7 and 8 dates the event precisely:

In the second year of Darius the King, in the sixth month, in the first day of the month, came the word of the Lord by Haggai the prophet unto Zerubbabel the son of Shealtiel, governor of Judah, and to Joshua the son of Josedech, the high priest, saying,

Thus speaketh the Lord of hosts, saying,

This people say, The time is not come, the time that the Lord's house should be built . . .

Thus saith the Lord of hosts; consider your ways.

Go up to the mountain, and bring wood, and build the house; and I will take pleasure in it, and I will be glorified, saith the Lord.

Darius became King in 550 B.C. and Haggai is reported as likewise being active in the late 6th century B.C. After the foundations to this temple were laid, there was a delay in completing the temple of some twenty years due to opposition from the population. Temples cost money to build, and, as with all public buildings, that means taxes. They also require a lot of labor for the construction work, and it appears that after their captivity in Babylon the Israelites wanted to relax and enjoy their freedom. They were not inclined to build a new temple.

It was not until around 440 B.C. that Nehemiah began to rebuild the walls around Temple Mount and this is described in the Biblical book of Nehemiah 3.1:

Then Eliashib the high priest rose up with his brethren the priests, and they builded the sheep gate; they sanctified it, and set up the doors of it; even unto the tower of Meah they sanctified it, unto the tower of Hananeel.

The Sheep Gate and the tower of Meah were situated at the western end of the North wall of Temple Mount and the tower of Hananeel supported the northwest corner. The Bible book of Nehemiah chapter 3 describes the rebuilding of the walls of Jerusalem and Temple Mount. The Temple Mount was further extended in 186 B.C. when Antiochus IV Epiphanes added a fortress to the South wall (Fig. 19). The new fortress was to house his Macedonian troops who were there to oversee, and control, the population of Jerusalem. The new fortress was known as the Akra.

In 141 B.C. some further modifications to Temple Mount took place when Simon the Maccabee demolished the Akra, and the Mount was extended over the area where the Akra stood. For the first time, the Mount was no longer square but oblong. It was circa 19 B.C. that King Herod set about rebuilding the whole temple complex (Fig. 20). The north, south and western walls were moved outwards to extend the pavement area to double its previous size.

Only the eastern wall remained visible after the extensions had taken place. The Herodian temple was of a much grander scale than anything that had preceded it and dwarfed even the present Dome of the Rock. The pavement area of Temple Mount was extended by some fifty percent, and this created considerable construction difficulties. Because they had been moved outwards from the center, the foundations of the outside walls were further down the hillside. This had the effect of making them very high, up to 155 feet (47 meters) in places. The construction methods available to Herod at that time would have made the width of wall necessary to retain the earth behind them impractical. Herod's engineers cleverly overcame the problem by filling behind the walls to a depth of 100 feet (30 meters) and then constructing vaulted underground halls on this filled ground that in turn supported the pavement above (Fig. 21). These subterranean halls are of considerable size, having a length of around 265 feet (80 meters) and a width of some 200 feet (60

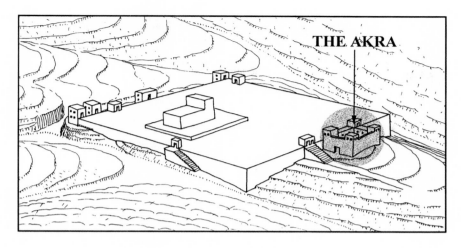

Figure 19
The third temple ("second temple") with the Akra fortress
Reconstruction by Dr. Leen Ritmeyer

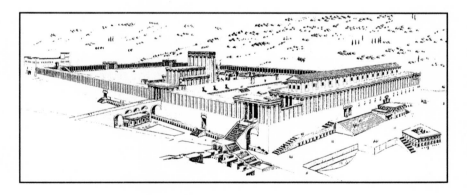

Figure 20
The Herodian Temple
Reconstruction by Dr. Leen Ritmeyer

Figure 21
"King Solomon's Stables" under Temple Mount

meters) with a ceiling height of 30 feet (9 meters). There are twelve rows of pillared avenues with arches spanning the rows of pillars. At the bases of the pillars are metal rings for tethering horses and it was known that the Knights Templar used the halls for this purpose during their stay in the al-Aqsa Mosque.

This summary of some of the historical and archaeological evidence relating to the various temples on Mount Moriah in Israel during the period from around 1000 B.C. to around 10 A.D. invites us to look again at the Masonic ritual and to remember that Freemasonry is allegorical:

> *Master:*   *What is Freemasonry?*
> *Candidate:* *A peculiar system of morality, veiled in allegory and illustrated by symbols.*
>
>   Questions to candidate during the second degree ceremony.

Someone with an inquisitive frame of mind, therefore, might be tempted to pose a couple of questions concerning the assumption that the Holy Royal Arch Third or Grand and Royal Lodge was ever held in the Middle East. The alarm bells begin gently to ring with the assertion that the Third or Grand and Royal Lodge was:

holden at Jerusalem.

If, as is commonly believed, this refers to the rebuilding of King Solomon's temple, then why not say so? Why should the ritual state that the second or Sacred Lodge was:

holden in the bosom of the Holy Mount Moriah.

Mount Moriah is also in Jerusalem. Either both lodges are in Jerusalem or both are on Mount Moriah. This use of two different versions to describe one location is odd and draws attention to this part of the ritual. There could be a subtle message hidden here, and it might be that there were indeed three lodges, but they were held at three different locations. The first or Holy Lodge is described in Masonic ritual as:

holden at the foot of Mount Horeb.

This clearly refers to the building of the Tabernacle by Moses. The second or Sacred Lodge is described again in the Royal Arch Masonic ritual as:

holden in the bosom of the Holy Mount Moriah.

This is unequivocally the building of the first temple at Jerusalem by King Solomon. One can use such a strong word as "unequivocal" because the three main Craft Masonic ceremonies draw, for their entirety, on the building of King Solomon's temple. The third or Grand and Royal lodge is described in the Royal Arch ritual as:

holden at Jerusalem.

This use of the term "Jerusalem" opens up the investigation and provides ample scope for speculation. The word "Jerusalem" has been used by various groups over the years to signify their wish to build new communities dedicated to Christian ideals. Indeed, that well known song that begins, *"And did those feet in ancient times walk upon England's mountains green"* is of course called "Jerusalem." In this instance Jerusalem is used in yet another context: here, Jerusalem refers to the legend that the young Jesus came to England and was involved with Glastonbury[1]. As far as the early devotees of Christianity were concerned, wherever Jesus Christ had walked was Jerusalem.

As the following chapters will show, this investigative story will take us to a region of southern France known as the Roussillon. In the early centuries after the death of Jesus Christ, rumors abounded that either Jesus Christ or his son[1] had lived in the Roussillon. In these circumstances, it would not be surprising to find the local people considering this area to be another Jerusalem.

The second part of the Holy Royal Arch ritual that casts doubt over the idea that the Third or Grand and Royal Lodge was the second or third temple at Jerusalem concerns the three rulers. The Holy Royal Arch ritual refers to the building of this Lodge as having been presided over by Zerubbabel, Haggai and Joshua. The assembly of these three people is certainly recorded in the Biblical book of Haggai, but one must be cautious in lifting sections from the Bible that appear to contain a coded message. It is unlikely that the compilers of Masonic ritual would not have been aware of this observation.

That these people lived is recorded in the Bible; it has been suggested, however, that Joshua was an allegorical figure "to prefigure the victorious militant Christ." The suggestion that they all lived at the same time is at least questionable. Another character in the Royal Arch ritual, Nehemiah, does not figure until 444 B.C., when he set about restoring the fortifications of the temple and Jerusalem in general. What is interesting, from an allegorical viewpoint, is that they represent King, Prophet and Priest—a commonly used euphemism in the Bible for Jesus Christ. In other words, this whole piece of Masonic ritual appears to be allegorical. But if the Third or Grand and Royal Lodge was not in Israel, where was it held?

Ashlars

1. The ritual of the Royal Arch ceremony is constructed around the building of the second, or perhaps third, temple on Mount Moriah.
2. The purpose of the "second" temple on Mount Moriah was the same as the Tabernacle and King Solomon's temple. It was to house the Ark of the Covenant.
3. This "second" temple is called in the Royal Arch the "third" or Grand and Royal Lodge.
4. The Royal Arch ritual points to the possibility of another Jerusalem somewhere.

CHAPTER 6 KEYSTONE

WE HAVE JUST SEEN that the Masonic ritual of the Royal Arch degree may be pointing to the possibility that the Third or Grand and Royal Lodge was not in Israel. If this could somehow be established, might this have something to do with the Templars and Rennes-le-Château? Could it also be part of the "long lost secret" which all Freemasons seek? To someone who is not a Freemason, such reference to secrets in this way must sound strange. Freemasonry is built around various secrets—passwords and other signs—that an individual Mason accumulates as he is promoted or joins other orders or degrees to distinguish him from others who are not at that level or in that degree. These extant Masonic secrets are quite categorically *not* the subject of this book. In solving the mystery of the Templar "treasure," this book will uncover the "long lost secret of a master mason" which is not described in any Masonic order.

This investigation started for no better reason than to try to untangle the mystery surrounding the little village called Rennes-le-Château in the Roussillon region of France. The "Masonic type" clues in the Rennes mystery have drawn us into the arcane ritual of Freemasonry, but quite where this is leading us is yet to become clear.

A SECRET PLACE

But Morse was a man who could never abide the incomplete, could never abide the not-knowing-immediately.

Colin Dexter, The Jewel That Was Ours

A S I HAVE DRAWN THIS ENQUIRY DEEPER into the realms of Freemasonry, I have several times talked about Masonic secrets such as the "long lost secrets of a master mason." The whole idea that Freemasons should spend much of their time searching for secrets is in part referring to one's individual pursuit of inner knowledge or the understanding of oneself. I am not concerned here with that aspect of Masonic teaching, but rather the search for a "hidden secret" that can be discovered. There exists within the Masonic ritual at least one place where this concept of a secret that a Freemason can uncover is clearly stated. That location is in the Holy Royal Arch description of "The Jewel of the Order." As Freemasonry has developed over the years, a number of different versions of the ritual for each of the different ceremonies have become established. There is no special reason why a lodge or Chapter might choose any particular variation of the ritual although a particular variation does seem to have become prevalent in one Province or another. An example of the sorts of variations that might take place between one set of ritual and another is apparent with the description of "The Jewel of the Order" just mentioned. The 1989 version of the Domatic Chapter of Installation ritual does not contain this particular piece of ritual but the Aldersgate version 1946 to 1978 does. Page 141 explains the reverse side of the Chapter Jewel:

Nil nisi clavis deest.

This translates as:

Nothing is wanting but the key.

The key however is not explained. In an old—1904—version of Royal Arch ritual, held in the Masonic Hall, London Road, Leicester Library, there is also a description of "The Jewel of the Order," but this version includes the following additional explanation:

 is *Templum Hierusolyma*   - the Temple of Jerusalem;
is *Clavis ad Thesaurum*   - the Key to the treasure;
is *Theca ubi pretiosa deponitur* - **a place where a precious thing is concealed**.

"A place where a precious thing is concealed." What an intriguing suggestion, that the triple tau has something to do with a location! The Masonic symbol is called the "triple tau." Tau is the Greek letter "T" and also the last letter of the Hebrew alphabet. The "triple tau" is described in detail in the Royal Arch ritual as:

That mark or sign spoken of by the angel, whom Ezekiel saw in the spirit, when it was said to the man with the writer's inkhorn, "Go through the midst of the city, through the midst of Jerusalem, and set a mark on the foreheads of the men that sigh and that cry for all the abominations that be done in the midst thereof."

Whatever else the "triple tau" might be, this it is not. This particular piece of Masonic ritual has been lifted directly from the Bible, book of Ezekiel 9:4, where it refers not to a triple tau but to a single tau,

ת

the last character of the Hebrew alphabet. The triple tau is actually three English "tees" rather than three Hebrew "taus." Notwithstanding this explanation, the questions however remain of where did it come from? What is it? It is possible to identify a triple tau within the medieval "T – O" map of the world, but it is upside down (Fig. 22).

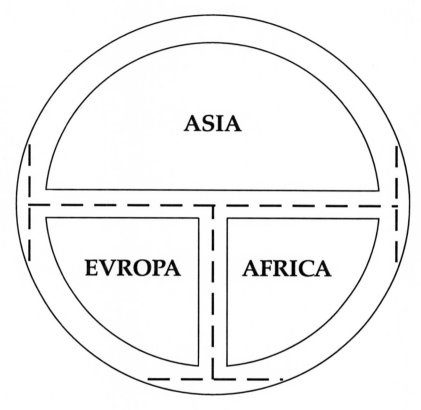

Figure 22
Circular "T" map of the world with triple tau discernible within it

On a medieval pictorial circular map of the world, the "T" shape was water, representing the seas that were thought then to separate the three continents of Asia, Europe and Africa. These seas were probably the Mediterranean Sea, the Red Sea and the Black Sea. There are also schematic circular maps of Jerusalem (Fig. 23), and the "triple tau" can similarly be made out within these in the same way as with the circular map of the world shown in Figure 23.

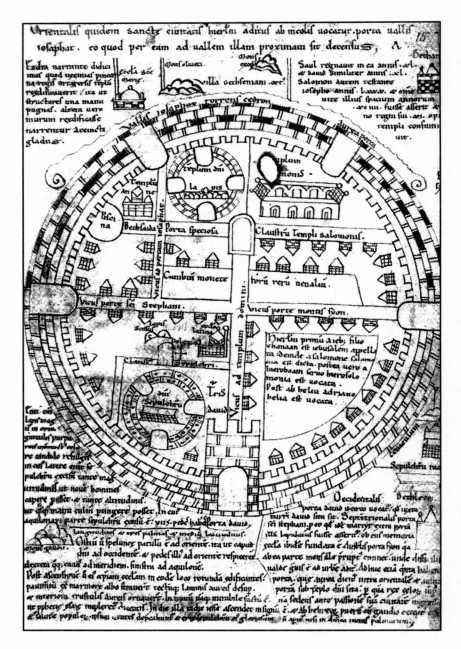

Figure 23
A typical circular map of Jerusalem

There is also a triple tau discernible within the mystical/sacred geometrical explanation of squaring a circle (Fig. 24).

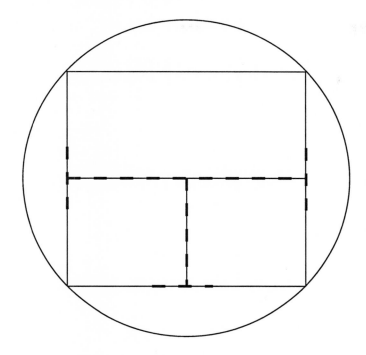

Figure 24
The sacred geometrical squaring of a circle

Once again it is upside down. Finally, the Holy Land of the Crusades had the regions of Antioch and Edessa at the North or top end that formed a letter "T," and, as this investigation unfolds, this might be seen as increasingly relevant.

Staying within the ritual of the Royal Arch, the next area examined was the "plate of gold." The Royal Arch ritual tells how this plate of gold was found by three master masons when they were excavating for the foundations of the new temple at Jerusalem. These three master masons referred to their leader as the Principle Sojourner. On the "plate of gold" were two geometrical shapes, a circle and a triangle, with certain letters also in gold, which spelt out words on those geometrical shapes. The whole assembly of shapes and letters rested on the square top of an altar that is a representation of a double cube of white marble. In 1988, under pressure from various religious groups and particularly the Methodists, this part of the ritual was radically altered, and different forms and wording are now used.

Because of the wide publicity given to the original wording at the time and because it has been radically altered, I consider it acceptable to publish part of an extinct Masonic secret. I have only shown the Hebrew characters and decoded those letters which have a Hebrew equivalent; the other letters are represented by either "X" or "Y." In reality, if anyone really wishes to know the identity of the other characters, or for that matter any of the other current Masonic secrets, he needs only visit his local reference library.

The Holy Royal Arch ritual describes how the three master masons found a plate of gold (Fig. 25):

with certain characters engraven thereon.

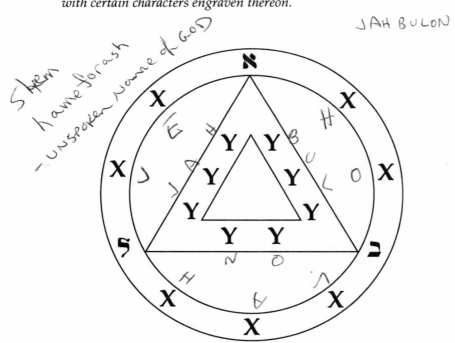

Figure 25
The plate of gold

א - Is the Hebrew character aleph

ב - Is the Hebrew character beth

ל - Is the Hebrew character lamedh

[handwritten margin notes]
A B - FATHer
BAL - LORD
AL - WORD
LAB - Heart or SPIRIT

The introduction of Hebrew characters onto the "plate of gold" provided the key to the solution of the code. The Hebrew alphabet comprises twenty-two letters, four fewer than the English alphabet and with no vowels. They do not correspond exactly to the English alphabet, but they do have the added benefit of having associated numbers.

A full list of the Hebrew alphabet with English equivalent and associated number is given in Appendix IV.

The code is therefore a substitution of a Hebrew character for each English letter and then the replacement of the Hebrew character by its associated number. The use of Hebrew numbers has drawn the investigation into the arena of Jewish mysticism. The branch of Jewish mysticism that encompasses the use of numbers is Cabalah, (Qabalah, Cabala, Cabbla, Cabbalah, Kabala or Kabbalah). Within Cabalah the technique of exchanging characters for numbers is called Gematria. Treating the actual Hebrew characters that were on the plate of gold separately, not necessarily in the order in which they appeared on the "plate of gold," and not disclosing those characters which have no Hebrew equivalence, the result for the circle is:

Letter	Hebrew character	Hebrew number
H	HE	5
H	HE	5

In addition to 2 Hs there were 5 other
English letters for which no Hebrew
equivalent character exists   0
Total for circle (excluding Hebrew characters) **10**

The Hebrew characters on the circle give us:

Letter	Hebrew character	Hebrew number
א	ALEPH	1
ב	BETH	2
ל	LAMEDH	30
Total for Hebrew characters		**33**

Applying the same logic to the triangle gives:

Letter	Hebrew character	Hebrew number
B	BETH	2
H	HE	5
L	LAMEDH	30
N	NUN	50 and 700
In addition to B, H, L and N there were 4 other English letters for which no Hebrew equivalent character exists		0
Total for triangle		**87**

Summary of results:

Total for circle (excluding Hebrew characters)	**10**
Total for Hebrew characters on the circle	**33**
Total for triangle	**87**

Hebrew scholars argue that one should not substitute letter for letter in this way. They say that taking a word like, for example, "Jehovah," this should first be transliterated into yôdh, hè, waw, hè ידה ‎ הוהי and only then should the numerical substitution using the technique of Gematria be attempted. The problem with this "correct" approach is that it leads nowhere. The resulting numbers are different from those given above and have no apparent significance. The formula used by the author, although unconventional, appears to be what the Masonic ritual compilers intended and it is after all a coded message. The problem of course is what on earth do these numbers mean?

It is at this point in the story that the paths of two other people, who were on a search for missing treasure, crossed that of the author. Andrews and Schellenberger[5] identified a mountain called Pech Cardou (Fig. 26) in their exploration of the mystery surrounding Rennes-le-Château.

Figure 26
Pech Cardou in the Roussillon region of France
Photograph by David Ingram

Around one third of all of the world-wide land and property holdings of the Knights Templar were in the Roussillon region of France. During nearly two hundred years of existence they accumulated vast wealth, much of which, it is suggested, was never recovered when the Order was dissolved by Papal decree. What makes Pech Cardou important to this story is the remarkable similarity between three pillars of rock quarried into one side of the mountain and the three pillars on the Masonic first degree tracing board (Fig. 27). Furthermore, the geological feature, whether natural or man-made, to the right of the rear pillar even resembles Jacob's ladder as shown on the tracing board.

Masonic tracing boards provide a connection with the time when operative masons would use them to draw up the plans of the building. Today, we would refer to such a piece of equipment as a

Figure 27
The First Degree Tracing Board
Photo by Anne Strachan

drawing board. In Freemasonry, the tracing board has a purely symbolic role and there are three tracing boards, one for each of the degree ceremonies. Each tracing board has a picture on it which symbolizes the ceremony of that degree, and part of each ceremony includes an explanation of the meaning behind the symbolism.

At a Masonic meeting when no candidate is available, a lecture on some aspect of Freemasonry is sometimes given by one of the members. One such lecture suggests that in the earliest days of Freemasonry, when meetings were held in public houses, it was the duty of the *Tyler*, the man guarding the door against strangers, to draw the appropriate tracing board on the floor with chalk. At the end of the meeting the man who had just been through the ceremony of joining Freemasonry would be given a bucket of water and a mop and told to clean it off. It is also said that, for this reason, in many lodges the members walk around the lodge and do not walk across the area where the chalked image of the tracing board would once have been drawn.

The beehive shape of the third or rear pillar on the site at Pech Cardou identifies the site with the Knights Templar, for whom the beehive—being St. Bernard's personal emblem—was an important symbol. Further support comes from the *capitelles*, a strange collection of many hundreds of beehive-shaped stone huts, which are to be found locally near Rennes-le-Château (Fig. 29). These strange structures, many in good repair and possibly rebuilt over the years, usually have a single doorway and a single narrow-window opening with one room inside. Some are square and some circular and a few are completely solid inside. It has been suggested that they resemble Neolithic beehive burial chambers. It is only fair to report that *capitelles* are also to be found elsewhere in France.

The identification of Pech Cardou permits us, at last, to find a use for the triple tau. If the triple tau is overlain onto the site at Pech Cardou, we can now see that it is the right way up (as viewed from the adjacent Roc Nègre) and that the ends of the upside down "T" fit over each of the three pillars.

The "fit" of the triple tau over the three pillars when taken in conjunction with the exchange of letters on the "plate of gold" enables us to look again at the tau from this new perspective.

Figure 28
Pech Cardou with the First Degree Tracing Board overlain

Figure 29
The Capitelles

Figure 30
Pech Cardou with triple tau overlain

Using a phonetic exchange, we could arrive at:

TAU = TOUR

In French, "tour" means tower, therefore:

TAU = TOUR = TOWER

Thus the triple tau becomes the **triple tower**, exactly as on Pech Cardou.

The identification of a possible link with the Knights Templar provides for yet another explanation of the "triple tau." As explained earlier, the Knights Templar originated in the French region of Champagne. At the heart of Champagne is the city of Rheims and it was there, in the cathedral, that the kings of France were crowned by the Archbishop. The Archbishops of Rheims lived adjacent to the cathedral in the *Palais du Tau*, so named because of its "T" shape. Thus, we have another exchange, but this time the substitution is synonymous using an algebraic paradigm.

The palace of the **Archbishop** = The palace of the **Tau.**

Deleting the identical features from both sides of the equation we get:

Archbishop = Tau.

The Archbishop was the king-maker, therefore:

The Tau is the king-maker.

Therefore:

The triple Tau becomes the three king-makers.

As has also already been illustrated, when the Knights Templar and Hospitaller were at the height of their power, the Grand Masters of both orders, together with the Patriarch of Jerusalem, held the three keys to the vault where the crown of Jerusalem was stored. They were *de facto* the three king-makers of Jerusalem. The exercise of overlaying the tracing board and the triple tau on the mountain identified by Andrews and Schellenberger—Pech Cardou in the Roussillon region of France—has indicated a link with Freemasonry.

The reader will recall that in attempting to decode the message on the "plate of gold" we ended up with three numbers.

Total for circle (excluding Hebrew characters)   **10**
Total for Hebrew characters on the circle   **33**
Total for triangle   **87**

The total substituted number for both the circle and the triangle but excluding the actual Hebrew characters is therefore:

$$10 + 87 = 97$$

An examination of the Institut Géographique Nationale (IGN) map, sheet 2347 OT, shows that the summit of Pech Cardou is at 795 meters above sea level. This figure is some 698 adrift from the total of the plate of gold. However, the Hebrew number for the last letter of the second word N (Hebrew NUN) is 50 **and** 700. The addition of the 700 brings the new total substituted number to:

$$10 + 87 + 700 = 797$$

This total, 797, is a tantalizingly 2 digits away from the map reference of 795. The connection between Pech Cardou and Freemasonry is getting stronger. It is worth noting that the Tarot card associated with the Hebrew Nun (N) is **death,** and the significance of this will shortly become clear. Andrews and Schellenberger[5] met a similar problem with one of their survey points at the Col de l'Espinas. Here the message, encoded on a parchment, purportedly found by Abbé Saunière, was 1 digit higher than the map reference, 681 against 680 on the map, and this prompted the following comment by the authors: "Could it be that someone was trying to make a point?" Knight and Lomas[6] display a copy of Henry Boudet's map that gives a height reference on Pech Cardou only 1 meter higher at 796 meters. Boudet was a close associate of Saunière, and this dates the map at around the turn of this century. The IGN map of the area dated 1944 also records the height of Pech Cardou as 796 meters, although interestingly it refers to the mountain as Pech Cardon.

Irrespective of the difficulties experienced by others with mountain heights, the reality is that modern surveying equipment has advanced by huge strides technologically. To find the levels within a couple of meters is a great credit to those French army surveyors who almost certainly carried out the original ordnance survey. In those days national armies had the monopoly on civil engineering skills. An ordnance survey was, in any event, carried out for use by the army in ranging their guns. In 1795 the French adopted the metric measure, a meter being one ten-millionth of the distance between the equator and the North Pole. In 1880 the standard meter was replaced by the composite platinum-iridium standard meter that exists to this day. The change to the "standard meter" must have generated some slight variation at that time. Furthermore, the change to a "standard meter" was effected after the Royal Arch ritual had been composed in much the same form as it appears today.

The Royal Arch as a separate degree can be dated from as early as the 1730s[59]. Very little, however, is known about the content of the ritual until the 1830s when, shortly after the union of the two competing craft Grand Lodges—the Ancients and Moderns—the ritual was extensively overhauled and revised. Bernard Jones[59] records that:

The earliest written copies of the ritual date from around 1850.

and

We cannot hide the fact that there is a considerable body of opinion in favour of the theory that Royal Arch masonry was a creation, a "fabrication," of French origin, brought to England round about 1730.

The necessary surveying expertise to measure the height of a mountain certainly existed during the eighteenth century. The Lambert conic projection currently used on French IGN maps was presented by Lambert in 1772. Gerardus Mercator, whose cylindrical projection is used in the international UTM system, lived between 1512 and 1594. In the early eighteenth century Jacques Cassini and his son César-François Cassini de Thury began the first triangulation survey of France, although this endeavor was not completed until 1818. Various interim maps were published during the survey period—including one of the Rennes-le-Château region in 1750. The Cassinis worked from the Paris zero meridian that is often attributed, wrongly, to Jacques' father Jean-Dominique Cassini[1].

It was, in fact, the Abbé Picard—Prior of Rillè in Anjou, who also held the chair of astronomy at the College de France—who recommended Cassini to Jean Colbert, the Chief Minister of Louis XIV. It was then only after some delay that Pope Clement IX consented to lend Cassini to France for what was expected to be only a year. This aspect of Cassini's move to France is the hardest to understand. On the one hand we are asked to accept that Cassini moved to take over the running of the Paris Observatory. And on the other hand he continued to be paid his salary from the University of Bologna in Italy, where he was the professor of astronomy, just as if he was on short-term loan to the French. Might not the answer lie in the fact that the French were in a pickle over the position of their meridian and called in the best astronomer in the world to help sort it all out. Cassini clearly didn't lay down the meridian because the building of the observatory started in 1667 and he didn't arrive in Paris until 1669. The observatory itself was finished in 1672. As events turned out, Cassini clearly enjoyed Paris, and he remained and took French citizenship.

The Paris Observatoire just happens to be sited in the middle of land that was and may still be owned by the Hôpital Militaire du Val de Grâce. Just to the north of the Observatoire and directly on the line of the meridian is the Palais du Luxembourg. Between the Observatoire and the Palais du Luxembourg, and in the grounds of the Palais, is the École Nationale des Mines. The most recent edition of IGN map 2347 OT states that the area covered was re-surveyed between 1982 and 1988, using photogrammetry or measurement from aerial photographs. This method is another potential source of slight differences. The juxtaposition of the Hôpital Militaire du Val de Grâce, the École Nationale des Mines and the Luxembourg Palace will, in due course, prove material to this investigation.

The next and fairly persuasive evidence of a linkage between Masonic Royal Arch ritual and the site on Pech Cardou comes with the remaining Hebrew characters that gave the total of 33. In 1804, the Ancient Scottish Rite, which some argue is the forerunner of Masonic ritual, was modified to introduce a new 33° rank. Furthermore, 33° is the most senior rank in the side degree of the Masonic Order of the Knights of Rose Croix of Heredom—more commonly known as Rose Croix. 33° is thus a very significant number in Freemasonry. If a line at 33° to the meridian is drawn through Pech Cardou (Fig. 31) at a distance of 5.8 kilometers south of Pech Cardou, there is a point called Pech de Rodès. The island of Rhodes was occupied in 1309 by the Order of Knights of St. John of Jerusalem, in short the Hospitallers, to whom the properties of the Knights Templar were ceded in 1312.

It may simply be coincidence that the Hospitallers occupied Rhodes only two years after the Templar fleet of ships fled from La Rochelle to avoid the persecution of the French King Philip IV. It may also be coincidence that the function of the Hospitallers on Rhodes was to keep the Eastern Mediterranean free of Muslims, a function that would have required a substantial number of ships. One further coincidence is the fact that the Hospitallers or "Knights of Rhodes" as they came to be called, were organized into units

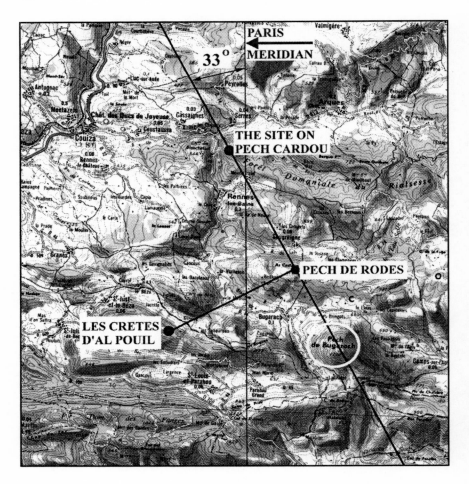

Figure 31
Map of Pech Cardou showing 33° line
IGN Map No. 72 © IGN Paris 1998, Authorization No. 90-0069

called *langues.* "Langue" in French means language or tongue, as in
Languedoc (langue d'oc) the language of Occitan. The Languedoc is
where the Templars had a strong base and Pech Cardou was situated; more recent boundary changes now place it in the Roussillon
region. It may be yet another coincidence that the Paris meridian,
that was probably intended to pass through Pech Cardou, finds its
origin in a Military Hospital site in Paris. The Hospitallers survive to
this day under their last name of Knights of Malta.

At an exact angle of 90° from the 33° line at Pech de Rodès, and also 5.8 kilometers to the west, is Les Crêtès d'al Pouil. It is on the north shore of Crete that the town of Iráklion (previously Candia) can be found. Indeed, Candia is the ancient Venetian name for the island of Crete. Furthermore, Candia is the fourth banner in the "United Religious, Military and Masonic Orders of the Temple and of St. John of Jerusalem, Palestine, Rhodes and Malta of England and Wales and its Provinces Overseas." Each banner has a meaning, and the meaning of the banner of Rhodes is also **death**, exactly the same as the Hebrew equivalent, NUN, of the last letter, N, on the plate of gold.

So, we have identified a number of locations in the general area of Pech Cardou that seem to have some positional interrelationship. How then might this additional information tie Pech Cardou to Freemasonry? Let us suppose that the Masonic ritual is a secret code that identifies the existence and location of something important. As has already been disclosed, the theme of a search "for the genuine secrets of a master mason" runs throughout Masonic ritual. The eminent Royal Arch Mason, Shepherd-Jones, OBE, could not have spelled it out more clearly in his explanation of the Jewel of the Order.

> *Some 1800 years ago, Clement of Alexandria stated that "All sacred truth is enfolded in enigmatical fables, legends and allegory," and speculative Masonry is particularly rich in such allegories. But the chief of all allegories of Masonry is "the search for the Word," not the Sacred and Mysterious Name but the "Word" that has come down to us through the countless ages and always carrying the same meaning—"The will or Law of God."*

This particular piece of ritual has been mentioned already, but it is sufficiently important to bear repetition. The allegorical nature of the clues pushed me towards the first question, which is where in the world is the "Word," which country? The predominance in Freemasonry of the hexagram, or "Seal of Solomon" as it is better known in Masonry, provides a clue. France used to be known as the hexagon because of its shape, and a hexagram fits perfectly into a hexagon. This knowledge would point to a probable location in France.

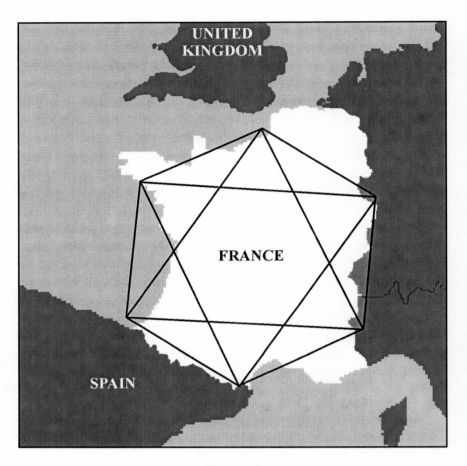

Figure 32
France with hexagon and hexagram overlain

If we assume for a moment that the landmarks are there to direct an inquisitive individual to a location, we are now able to center our inquiries on France. How then, might someone with knowledge of Masonic ritual be led to Pech Cardou? For the answer to this next question, we must return to the Masonic ritual of the second-degree ceremony, that of "passing."

Master: And when?

Candidate: *When the sun was at its meridian . . . the sun must*
always be at its meridian with respect to Freemasonry.

Questions to a new candidate for the second degree
by the Worshipful Master of the Lodge

Our attention has been drawn to the meridian, and running through Paris and approximately down to the middle of France is the Paris meridian. It is displaced from the internationally recognized Greenwich meridian by some 100 miles (160 kilometers) to the East. For navigational purposes, the Greenwich meridian is the international standard.

Running one's eye down the Paris meridian as far as Roussillon, Pech de Rodès comes into view, and this is the mountain identified above. The similarity to the word "R(h)odes" indicates a possible Masonic connection, as described above. The message from the plate of gold would call for a line to be drawn at an angle of 33° to the meridian. This line could be drawn from east to west or vice versa. A 33° line running from the southeast upwards towards the northwest would cut through the peak of "Pech de Bugarach," the largest mountain in the area, signifying that this is probably the correct elevation. In any event, Freemasons are encouraged to go to the west to find the secret:

Master: *What inducement have you to leave the East and go*
to the West?
Junior Warden: *To seek for that which was lost.*

From the third degree opening ceremony

For the next clue, it is necessary to refer back to the words of Shepherd-Jones, OBE:

What is sought, is the Word.

Within a Freemason's lodge, the place where the "Word" is kept is on the Worshipful Master's pedestal, and it is "The Volume of the Sacred Law" or the Bible (Fig. 33). The Bible is opened when the lodge is opened, and placed on the Bible are the square and compasses.

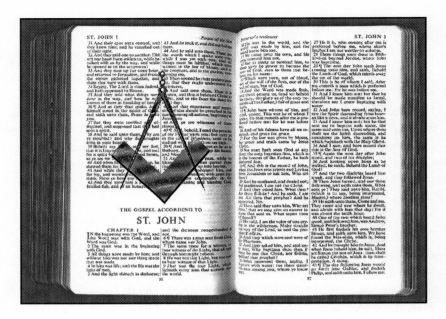

Figure 33
Bible with square and compasses on Worshipful Master's pedestal

These three items are referred to as the:

Three great, though emblematical, lights in Freemasonry.
> Master to candidate during initiation ceremony

In the third degree ceremony, when the Tyler or guard introduces the candidate, he is questioned:

Inner Guard: *How does he hope to obtain the privileges of the Third degree?*

Tyler: *By the help of God, the united aid of the Square and Compasses, and the benefit of a password.*

The Volume of the Sacred Law, or Bible, has drawn our attention to the square:

Master: *What is a square?*

Junior Warden: *An angle of 90 degrees, or the fourth part of a Circle.*

From the second degree opening ceremony.

The vertical edge of the square must now be placed against the 33° line, with the horizontal edge lying towards the West; and along this line is a place called Les Crêtès d'al Pouil. The decision to lay the square to the west would have been natural given the injunction just mentioned above:

To leave the East and go to the West.

The word "Crêtes" would have significance as also explained above. It is only now necessary to turn to the mariners' navigation tool, the compasses. Placing one point on Pech de Rodès and the other point on Les Crêtès d'al Pouil, then using the point on Rodès as the fulcrum and turning the Crêtès end of the compasses through an arc, it will after 90° meet the line drawn at 33° to the Paris meridian. The point of the compasses will now lie directly over the site on Pech Cardou (Fig. 34). With the "united aid of the square and compasses," we have once again arrived at Pech Cardou.

Of supporting interest to someone with Masonic knowledge is the adjacent site of Camp **Grand** (Fig. 35). We recall that in Chapter 5 we floated the idea that the Third or **Grand** and Royal Lodge might not be in Israel. Camp Grand is adjacent to the site of the Capitelles mentioned earlier and on a line from Pech Cardou through the Chateau de Blanchefort and extrapolated in a straight line. The ratio of the distances from Pech Cardou to the Chateau de Blanchefort is **1**, from the Chateau de Blanchefort to Camp Grand is **2** and from Pech Cardou to Camp Grand is **3**. Not surprisingly, these are the numbers of the three degrees in Craft Freemasonry. What is surprising, though, is that there should be such a clear relationship in terms of distances between Camp Grand and the site on Pech Cardou.

In addition to the excellent collection of Masonic books in the library of the Leicestershire and Rutland Provincial Grand Lodge building at London Road, Leicester, there is also a collection of ancient regalia and medals. Amongst the regalia is an old Masonic apron purporting to be French that has on it embroidery showing a

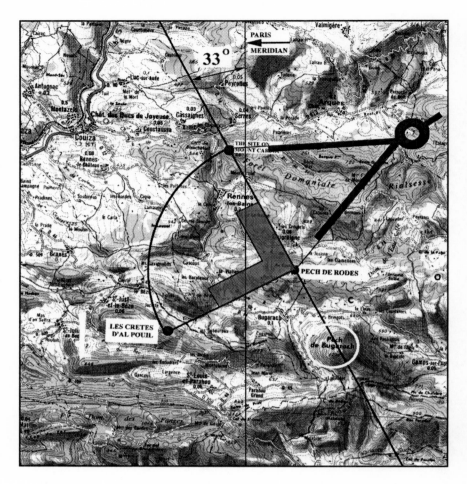

Figure 34
Map of Pech Cardou with 33° line, square and compasses overlain
IGN Map No. 72 © IGN Paris 1998, Authorization No. 90-0069

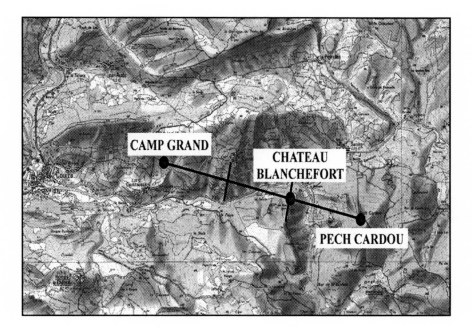

Figure 35
Map of Rennes-le-Château area showing the location of Camp Grand
IGN Map No. 72 © IGN Paris 1998, Authorization No. 90-0069

beehive on a mound between two pillars. If one were to stand on the Roc Nègre (black rock) and look across the valley towards the site on Pech Cardou, one might be forgiven for thinking that one was looking at the same ancient French apron. Built on the same ridge as Roc Nègre is the Château de Blanchefort, a Templar castle that would have allowed a permanent watch to be maintained over the site on Pech Cardou. Bertrand de Blanquefort was Grand Master of the Templars in the 1160s and the difference with the spelling of the name is probably a clerical error introduced at some time previously. Pope Clement V's mother belonged to the Blanchefort family, a further indication of the high esteem in which the name was held.

Further evidence in support of the suggestion that Pech Cardou in the Roussillon region of France is linked to Freemasonry can be identified within the ritual explanation of the first degree tracing board.

Our lodges are situated East and West

The rear pillar on the site on Pech Cardou and the front north-
erly pillar run directly east to west. Indeed, the positional locations
of the rock pillars and the Jacob's ladder feature on Pech Cardou are
on exactly the same compass bearings as their matching features on
the first degree tracing board.

Our lodges are supported by three great pillars. They are called
Wisdom, Strength and Beauty

These are the names that are engraved on the Royal Arch Jewel,
and it was the explanation of the Royal Arch Jewel that provided
many of the clues. There are also three pillars on the site on Pech
Cardou.

The Heavens He has stretched forth as a canopy; the earth He has
planted as a footstool; He crowns his temple with stars as a diadem

In many ways, this is one of the most significant pieces of
supporting evidence. As has already been explained in Chapters
Three, Four and Five, the Masonic ritual of a craft lodge encompasses the building of King Solomon's temple. Although there is no
archaeological evidence to support this argument, the Bible leaves
no doubt that this temple did indeed have a roof built from cedar
wood provided by King Hiram of Tyre. There is likewise little doubt
that the second, third and fourth temples on Mount Moriah all had
roofs. Finally, the Biblical description of the Tabernacle also states
that there was a roof, albeit of fabric.

Conversely, and in total support of the above section of Masonic
ritual describing the first degree tracing board, the site on Pech
Cardou has three pillars and is open to the stars. The use of landmarks within the Masonic ritual to identify Pech Cardou, located
under the watchful eye of the Chateau de Blanchefort, appears also
to bring the Knights Templar into this equation. The Masonic ritual
is clearly pointing to a site on a mountain which in turn appears to
have strong Templar connections. The adjacent site of Camp Grand
is hinting at this being the Third or Grand and Royal Lodge, as

discussed in Chapter Five, but it is too early to venture such a suggestion. There are still too many questions that require answers, and these must be addressed.

Ashlars

1. The triple tau symbol from the Royal Arch ritual is heavily laden with mystery and has been "marked out" as a clue to the solution to the Masonic secret.
2. The triple tau, "a place where a precious thing is concealed," fits neatly over the three pillars on Pech Cardou.
3. The characters on the old "plate of gold" add up to 33 and 797 when the Hebrew technique of Gematria is applied to them, and both of these numbers identify Pech Cardou.
4. From around 1730, the number 33, expressed as degrees, is very important within Freemasonry.
5. The quarried feature, on the side of Pech Cardou, resembles the Masonic first degree tracing board.
6. There is evidence that, when the Knights Templar were disbanded, a number of them joined the Knights Hospitaller who later also became known as the Knights of Rhodes.
7. Pech de Rodès and Les Crêtès d'al Pouil, two mountain peaks close to Pech Cardou, whose names are reminiscent of places where the Knights Hospitaller had bases, provide the location from which Pech Cardou can be located using 33°, a square and a pair of compasses.
8. France was at one time known as the hexagon.
9. The Paris meridian runs quite close to Pech Cardou and may well have been intended to run through its center.
10. There is something strange about the manner in which the Paris meridian was established and particularly the way in which Jean Dominique Cassini moved, apparently on temporary secondment, to Paris.

11. Camp Grand is close to Pech Cardou and has a positional relationship that can be expressed as 1:2:3.
12. The ruins of Château de Blanchefort, a one time Templar stronghold, sits overlooking Pech Cardou like a watchtower.
13. The pillars on the quarried feature, on the side of Pech Cardou, line up precisely with the pillars on the Masonic first degree tracing board.
14. The quarried feature on the side of Pech Cardou is "open to the stars" exactly as the Masonic ritual description of "our lodges" in connection with the first degree tracing board.
15. Before 1730 the Royal Arch degree did not exist; craft Freemasonry existed albeit in a more simplified version than is now practiced. Something must have happened around 1730 to create a need for an entirely new degree.

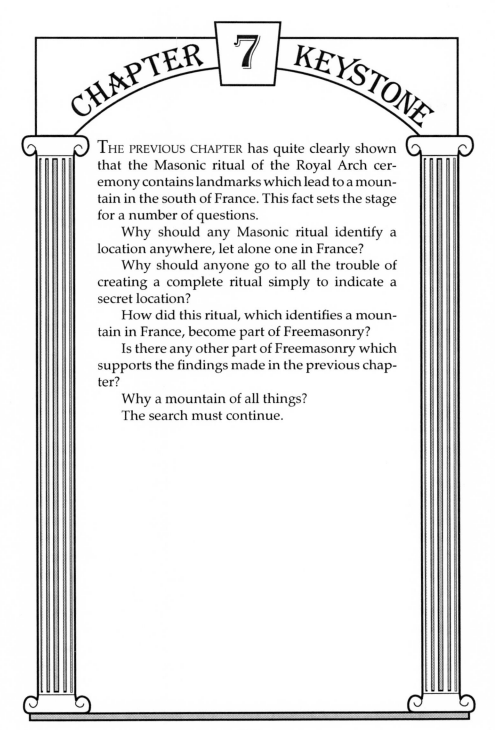

CHAPTER 7 KEYSTONE

The previous chapter has quite clearly shown that the Masonic ritual of the Royal Arch ceremony contains landmarks which lead to a mountain in the south of France. This fact sets the stage for a number of questions.

Why should any Masonic ritual identify a location anywhere, let alone one in France?

Why should anyone go to all the trouble of creating a complete ritual simply to indicate a secret location?

How did this ritual, which identifies a mountain in France, become part of Freemasonry?

Is there any other part of Freemasonry which supports the findings made in the previous chapter?

Why a mountain of all things?

The search must continue.

THE BOOK OF NUMBERS

That is, the errors which went into the calculations of "Blah blah blah 1940" are the same errors that went into the calculation of "Blah blah blah 1990." While both numbers might be wrong, there may still be value in contrasting them. It is true that, in the groves of academia, the orchards of the statisticians produce fake fruit. But I have tried to compare wax oranges only with wax oranges and plastic bananas with same.

P. J. O'Rourke, *All the Trouble in the World*

ALTHOUGH I HAVE UNCOVERED the remarkable existence within the Masonic ritual of clues pointing to a mountain in France, it is nonetheless premature for me to claim to have solved the secret embodied within the Masonic ritual. I decided to continue with the search by revisiting some of the other clues carefully left by those early ritual compilers. One such clue concerns the prominence of snakes in this story and in the Masonic ritual. The importance of a snake, to an English Freemason, could not be made more strongly than the observation that it is a snake-clasp that holds his apron on. A snake appears often throughout the Old Testament of the Bible as has earlier been mentioned. According to John Cohane[7] one of the words that run through most languages, apart from *oc*, is *asch*. Both of these words derive from the names of ancient gods; in the case of Asch, this god was a snake. David Wood[8] draws attention to a remarkable geological feature adjacent to the town of Peyrolles in the shape of a very large snake (Fig. 36). The remarkable thing about this feature is that an imaginary line of longitude drawn through the site on Pech Cardou would pass through the right side of the head of the snake. In the previous chapter, the location of the Paris Observatory was identified as being within the boundary of the grounds of the military hospital. It is now possible to identify the Paris meridian as more than just a positional link between Paris and the Rennes-le-Château area. For Peyrolles is phonetically the same as the surname of the designer of the Paris Observatory, Claud Perrault.

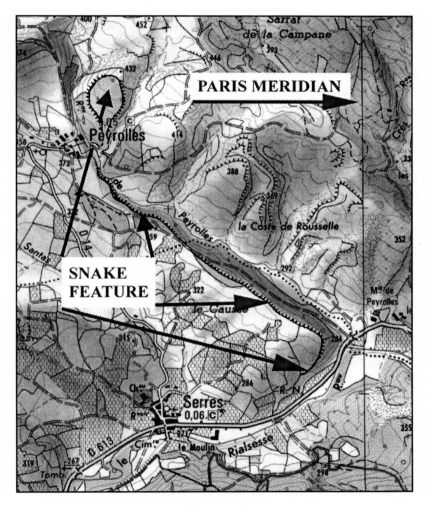

Figure 36
The snake feature at Peyrolles

At the southern tip of Greece and forming the shoreline of the
Gulf of Corinth is Achaea. This principality may hold a key to the
significance of the serpent because the French pronounce "ch" as
"sh," thus Achaea becomes Ashaea. After the sacking of Constantinople during the fourth Crusade, Achaea was appropriated by the
French Villehardouin princes. In the second half of the thirteenth
century, this principality was thought of as an extremely glamorous
settlement[42]. Under the Villehardouins, the court at Andravidha
was considered to be *the* finishing school for French knights. Achaea
retained its attraction, and in 1377 the Knights Hospitaller leased it
for five years. The coincidences do not end there because there is a
place where a sign very similar to the snake at Peyrolles can be seen,
and that is on the ceiling of the Great Temple in London's Grand
Lodge.

The similarity between yôdh, which is the Hebrew character for
"Y," and the snake at Peyrolles compels us to take a further look at
snakes in a Masonic context. We have earlier identified a number of
references, and another is in the Knights of Malta degree in an
extract from the Bible relating to St. Paul's visit to the Island of Malta:

*And when Paul had gathered a bundle of sticks, and laid them on the
fire, there came a viper out of the heat, and fastened on his hand.*

From the Bible, book of Acts 27 and 28

Figure 37
The sacred symbol yôdh from the ceiling of the Great Temple
in Grand Lodge

The snake is clearly an important symbol, but the precise reason why has not yet become clear. There was a Gnostic Ophite sect which revered Ophis, a snake, as a symbol of knowledge. They believed that the universe was made up of three parts: the superior world towards which man should strive, the inferior world of materialism and chaos, and the intermediate world of logos—reason or word—what we might now see as logic. Logos was depicted as a snake. A different, Iranian, form of Gnosticism was characterized by an absolute dualism between light and darkness. In this form Pneuma, the spirit, has been in perpetual conflict with chaotic and formless matter since eternity. Before leaving the subject of snakes, it is worth noting that in Kenneth McLeish's encyclopedia of mythology[47]—*Myth*—he identifies a link between snakes and circles. As has already been demonstrated in Chapter 6, circles also figure largely in this investigation. McLeish mentions that the image of a serpent biting its tail displays a circular shape. He also refers to an Egyptian legend that equates the serpent with the sea, the eternal ring, which encloses the world. Thus the circle, because it is without end, is seen as a sign of eternity.

The snake is similarly perceived as immortal because in biting its own tail it creates a circle. The snake has another claim to immortality, for when it sloughs its skin, it appears to be reborn. McLeish also maintains that coiled snakes represent the primordial ocean. McLeish[47] mentions other mythological references to snakes or serpents that may later be seen to have some relevance to this story. The second general line of myths relating to snakes derives from their propensity to live in dark cracks or holes. For this reason they have been regarded as guardians of the underworld, even messengers between the upper and lower worlds. There is a Hebrew fable which states that it was a snake that guarded the tree of knowledge, and this story finds expression in the tale of Adam and Eve in the Garden of Eden. The coupling of snakes with the underworld leads naturally to another Egyptian legend which identified Aapep—the god of chaos—as a serpent. Every morning and evening, Aapep would attack the sun as it rose or set in the sky; the sky would be drenched red with blood as the sun regularly defeated the serpent. It is generally thought that the ancient Egyptian "snake in the sky" was our own galaxy, the Milky Way. The reasons for this supposition are straightforward. First, the absence of background light in ancient Egypt would have made our galaxy much more clearly visible, and second, the way the Milky Way appears to be an extension of the River Nile when looking north provides an apparent link between heaven and earth.

There is, however, another candidate for the heavenly snake and that is the constellation of Draco which coils around the pole star, Polaris. Draco has been identified as a serpent or dragon for thousands of years. Indeed, although Polaris is the pole star, the effect of precession, or the way the earth wobbles on its axis rather like a child's spinning top, means that 4,000 years ago it was one of Draco's stars—Thuban or Alpha Draco—that was the pole star. It seems likely that the great pyramids at Gizeh were built with Thuban as a guide because at that time the star would have been visible day and night from the bottom of one of the pyramid airshafts. The mythology surrounding Draco can certainly be traced back to the writing of the Greek poet Publius Ovidius Naso in the first century B.C., when he identified it with the dragon slain by Europa's brother Cadmus. To reward this feat, the goddess Athena told Cadmus to plant some of the dragon's teeth, and armed men grew from the soil where the teeth had been planted. There was a dispute, and these men began to fight each other, and only five survived. Together with Cadmus these five men built the city of Thebes. Yet another version has the younger and older gods in a battle for supremacy during which monsters—"Titans," representing the forces of evil—were cast up from volcanoes. During one battle a Titan hurled a fierce dragon at Athena who caught it and hurled it high into the heavens. The dragon ended up in the northern sky as the constellation of Draco.

The constellation of Draco also finds its way into the Bible:

> By his spirit he hath garnished the heavens; his hand hath formed the crooked serpent.

> Job 26:13

Although it is not directly relevant to this investigation, an interesting coincidence with the number five is associated with the first version of this myth—the number of surviving armed men who helped to build Thebes. The earth's wobble or precession takes some 26,000 years to describe a full circle, and it therefore takes 72 years for the earth to describe one degree of arc—26,000 divided by 360 degrees. If we now consider the number 72 as an angle, we find that it is exactly one fifth of a circle and thus intimately associated with pentangles and the number five. Equally curious, while addressing astronomy and astrology, the number needed to take five to twelve—twelve being the number of astrological signs—is seven. I have included this minor detour because the numbers five, seven, and twelve hold a special position in the Bible, and five and seven recur regularly in Freemasonry. Perhaps the ancient use of these numbers simply indicates that the writer had knowledge of precession. He knew that the earth does indeed wobble on its axis.

Greek mythology provides us with the final strand of snake symbolism; Æsculapius had snake familiars which crawled over sick people while they slept and cured them. Snakes have also been representative of wisdom because they appear to ponder before striking their prey. These attributes explain why amulets, which coil around one's arm like a snake, are seen as lucky tokens. Finally, snakes, because of their shape, can symbolize the umbilical cord which binds the human race to "mother earth."

There is another Cabalistic symbol for God, and that is an eye within a triangle (Fig. 38), which is immediately recognizable as the symbol within the Grand Master's jewel. I will stay with Cabalism for a moment longer. For it now is evident that the Royal Arch double cube, the "altar of incense" on which the "plate of gold"

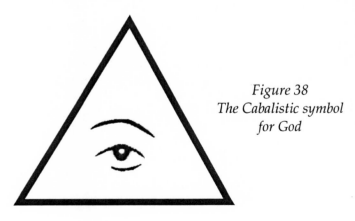

Figure 38
The Cabalistic symbol
for God

rested, has some significance. The cube in Cabalistic allegory refers to the earth and the first earth sign is three. A doubled three is thirty three—33.

Reverend F. de Castells published a paper[20], "Arithmetic of Freemasonry," in which he described Cabalists as intensely religious Jews who regarded the Deity as an "indivisible point, without limits and incomprehensible because of its purity and inexpressible brightness." The point, in "point, triangle," etc., is beginning to have meaning. Furthermore, the number three was very conspicuous, representing the voice, spirit, and word of the living God, and ether, air, and water being the three primordial elements. Interestingly, Castells refers to Samaël, the venomous beast or the angel of wickedness, and contends that one day Samaël will be restored to his original angelic nature and the first part of his name, Sam or *venom*, will be dropped. This would leave only the second part Ël and El is the common name [in Semitic languages] for all divine beings.

The candles in a Holy Royal Arch Chapter can now be seen to have significance. The six candles, on approximately 3-foot (1-meter) high candelabras, stand around the double cube altar. The three greater lights (larger candles), representing the Word, can metaphorically fold down to form a tetrahedron, the same as the first of the five platonic bodies that sit on the floor of the Chapter room just in front of the double cube altar. These five objects are the four-sided tetrahedron, the eight-sided octahedron, the six-sided cube, the twenty-sided icosahedron, and the twelve-sided dodecahedron. The inclusion of the cube permits us to call again to mind the Templars and their close relationship with the Muslims in the Holy Land. The most sacred Muslim shrine is the *Kaaba* at Mecca which is in the shape of a cube. The inclusion of a reference to "three lesser lights" seems to be directing us back to the craft Masonic ritual of "Initiation," when a new candidate is told that:

> The three lesser lights are meant to represent the sun [junior warden], the moon [senior warden], and the master of the lodge.

This potential arrangement of the candles seems to suggest that the three lesser lights refer to the master (of the lodge) and his two

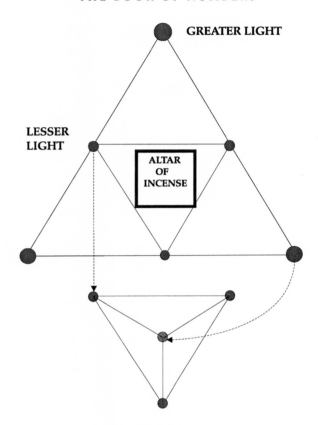

Figure 39
The layout of candles in a Royal Arch Chapter

wardens, sitting above the "Word" that is now buried centrally beneath them. Where else might this be, other than in Pech Cardou?

Apart from the tetrahedron explained above, none of the remaining platonic bodies appear to have any allegorical significance. It is, though, worth noting that the total number of the sides of these platonic bodies is equal to fifty and that the Kaaba is a cube with dimensions of 15 meters or a 50-foot cube.

There is mention of an event that has crept into recent Templar chronicles, and this is the "splitting of the elm." This story refers to an alleged schism between the Knights Templar and the Priory of

Sion, which is said to have taken place at Gisors. Andrews and Schellenberger[5] reproduce a copy of the coat of arms of King René d'Anjou from Professor Otto Pächt's *Studen ll* that clearly shows a split tree with a black rock on top and new leaves springing from the top of the dead tree. The new leaves look as if they could be acacia, and this, when taken with the black rock, indicates a possible link to Pech Cardou.

Gisors Castle was the venue of at least five conferences to settle the outcome of battles between King Henry II of England and King Philip II of France, with Henry's three sons—Richard, Henry and Geoffrey—adding to the confusion. Gisors was chosen because it sat on the border between the regions of Champagne and Normandy, or to put it in a clearer perspective, between the Kingdoms of England and France. Henry II and his son Richard I are referred to as Kings of England; however, this oversimplifies the confusion that surrounded France in those days. In fact both Henry and Richard were Frenchmen born and bred. Henry's kingdom included most of the U.K., although his hold over the more remote parts, such as Wales, was fairly tenuous. France, on the other hand, was split into two parts by a meandering line running from Dieppe to Toulouse: Henry ruled over the land to the West of this line and King Philip ruled much of the land to the East. When Henry II's sons reached maturity, he gave them the income from large tracts of his French lands but never sovereignty over them.

One consequence of this was that the sons regularly sided with King Philip of France whenever they felt that they might gain land from their father, Henry. Adding to this confusion was the behavior of those barons whose lands were close to the borders. They were minded to switch their allegiance to whichever side they felt might benefit them most. In particular this area of France and the Loire valley, the base of the English King, was in constant turmoil. It was immediately following the fourth conference at Gisors, in 1186, that King Philip cut down the elm tree which marked the border between the two kingdoms. It was a very public gesture and characterized his frustration over the lack of enforceability of such agreements. One thing is practically certain, and that is that the Knights Templar were not party to the squabbles between Kings Philip and

Henry. For if they had been, it would have been a most important departure from their role and the chroniclers of the time would have recorded the fact. That it has been introduced into "Templar history" can only mean that some unknown person or persons have left a deliberate clue for those who followed.

These mysterious individuals were undoubtedly involved with the compilation of the Masonic ritual, as this is the only explanation for the reason why the next piece of code is in the English language. If this were part of genuine Templar history, the code would be interchangeable with the French language, which it is not. The ritual compilers needed the word "elm," and Gisors is the place where an elm tree entered the history books.

The word under consideration then, is "elm." If we start by writing down the most simple transfer code, replacing a letter from the alphabet with the appropriate consecutive number, we get:

A	B	C	D	E	F	G	H	I	J	K	L	M
1	2	3	4	5	6	7	8	9	10	11	12	13

N	O	P	Q	R	S	T	U	V	W	X	Y	Z
14	15	16	17	18	19	20	21	22	23	24	25	26

The word "elm" can therefore be written as the numbers:

5 - 12 - 13

This, as any geometrician will recognize, is one of several right angle triangles with whole number sides.

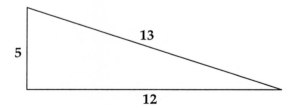

Could **"ELM"** be the password?—leading us to a simple exchange of alphabet letters for the appropriate consecutive number. Surely this is too easy or perhaps brilliantly clever: for who would metaphorically think of "looking in a children's book" for the key to one of the world's great remaining mysteries. There has already been a use of this type of code with the plate of gold, but on that occasion, there was an extra exchange of Hebrew characters for English and then into numbers. Let us look back at one of the pieces of ritual given in the previous chapter:

Inner Guard: How does he hope to obtain the privileges of the Third degree?
Tyler: By the help of God, the united aid of the Square and Compasses, and the benefit of a password.

Let us examine the four most relevant words, **"the square and compasses."** The use of the square, together with the compasses, has already been demonstrated in locating the site on Pech Cardou. Let us therefore try this simple substitution code on the word **"THE"** and we get:

$$T = 20$$
$$H = 8$$
$$E = 5$$

This adds up to **33!** We have indeed found the password and the exchange between the Inner Guard and the Tyler now sounds something like this:

Inner Guard: How does he hope to obtain the privileges of the Third degree?
Tyler: By the help of God, the united aid of 33, Square and Compasses.

"BY THE HELP OF GOD, THE UNITED AID OF 33°, SQUARE AND COMPASSES"

Exactly the proof used in Figure 34 in the previous chapter to locate Pech Cardou.

Pursuing the concept of exploring numbers, we can take the term "splitting the elm" at face value to get one of two alternatives. Firstly it is possible to split the "ELM" with the digit "1" by first representing "ELM" as numbers: 5 - 12 - 13 and then enlarging the digit 1 to form two barriers thus:

5 1₂ 1₃

Dropping the digits "1" leaves - **523**. The height reference given on the IGN map sheet 2347 on the top of the southern pillar on the site on Pech Cardou is **523**. Alternatively, we could split the number substituted word "ELM" into three separate numbers:

5 **12** 13

Splitting off the 5 and the 13 we are left with **12**, and 12 is the total of the numbers 3, 4 and 5. Once again we can recognize these numbers, 3, 4, and 5, as the three sides of a right angle triangle. Indeed it is a significant because it is the smallest right angle triangle with whole number sides.

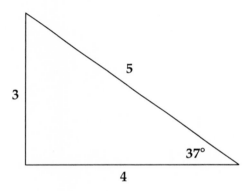

The fascination with numbers does not end there. During the ceremony of "passing" a new candidate to the second degree in Freemasonry, he is reminded of the seven liberal arts and sciences. The seven are grammar, rhetoric, logic, arithmetic, geometry, music and astronomy. However, in order to solve this puzzle, only four arts and sciences have been used, namely grammar, logic, arithmetic and geometry.

4 divided by 7 = 0.57

A right angle triangle with 57 degrees as one of the angles gives 33° as the third angle. The beauty of this solution knows no limits. No detail is too small to be included.

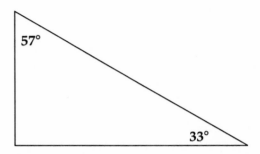

There is one piece of number-crunching that demonstrates the fun that the Masonic ritual compilers must have had. If the circular line, drawn on the map, between the site on Pech Cardou and Les Crêtès d'al Pouil is changed to a straight line, we get:

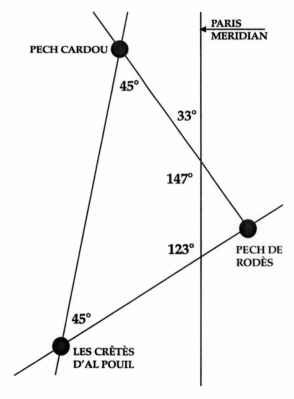

Figure 40
Angular arrangement at Pech Cardou

The sum of the angles contained within the quadrangle bounded by the meridian and the other three lines is:

$$45° + 147° + 123° + 45° = 360°$$

The angles contained within a quadrangle always add up to 360° and 360° is a circle!

Before leaving this chapter, I wish to draw attention to some numerical observations that I have made during the compilation of this book, starting, perhaps naturally, with the fascination that the Masonic ritual compilers had with the number three. Three threes are of course nine, the number of original Knights Templar. However, a series based on threes, but including the addition of the individual digits making up the product of the series, has an interesting result:

Number in series	Sum of digits	Multiplier	Result
3		1 x 3 = 3	1
6		2 x 3 = 6	2
9		3 x 3 = 9	3
12	1 + 2 = 3	1 x 3 = 3	1
15	1 + 5 = 6	2 x 3 = 6	2
18	1 + 8 = 9	3 x 3 = 9	3
21	2 + 1 = 3	1 x 3 = 3	1
24	2 + 4 = 6	2 x 3 = 6	2
27	2 + 7 = 9	3 x 3 = 9	3
etc.			
99	9 + 9 = 18	as 18 above	3
111	1 + 1 + 1 = 3	as 3 above	1
114	1 + 1 + 4 = 6	as 6 above	2

This particular series, or three times table, always appears to break down to a 1, 2, 3 series. It will perhaps come as no surprise to find that there is another series, the nine times table, that exhibits similar properties.

Number in series	Sum of digits	Result
9	0 + 9 = 9	9
18	1 + 8 = 9	9
27	2 + 7 = 9	9
36	3 + 6 = 9	9

Number in series	Sum of digits	Result
45	4 + 5 = 9	9
54	5 + 4 = 9	9
63	6 + 3 = 9	9
72	7 + 2 = 9	9
81	8 + 1 = 9	9
90	9 + 0 = 9	9

It is also obvious that this series between 9 and 90 is numerically "palindromic."

09 18 27 36 45 54 63 72 81 90

In fact, it is doubly "palindromic"; the numbers are still divisible by nine even when they are reversed.

Number	Reversed	Multiplier
09	90	9 x 10 = 90
18	81	9 x 9
27	72	9 x 8
36	63	9 x 7
45	54	9 x 6
54	45	9 x 5
63	36	9 x 4
72	27	9 x 3
81	18	9 x 2
90	09	9 x 1
99	99	9 x 11
108	801	9 x 89
117	711	9 x 79
126	621	9 x 69
135	531	9 x 59
144	441	9 x 49
153	351	9 x 39
162	261	9 x 29
171	171	9 x 19
180	81	9 x 9
189	981	9 x 109
198	891	9 x 99

This paradigm appears to work to infinity –1 and this would have made the number nine very special in the eyes of medieval mystics. When those medieval mystics recognized that nine had also the same totality as that of the most powerful gods of the Egyptian Ennead, the number nine itself must have become irresistible. This technique of taking the component integers of the product of two numbers and adding or subtracting them is also part of the Cabalah. The arithmetical procedure used earlier, Gematria, has a derivative section called Numerology that uses precisely these techniques.

It begins to look as if the selection of nine original Knights Templar was not an accidental choice, but rather the carefully thought out selection of a number with mystical power. The alternative is of course that through the years, those recording the history have substituted the number nine for the original number to provide the Templars with additional mystique. In today's world of computers and high levels of numeracy, these relationships may not be viewed as either important or relevant to anything. In the Middle Ages however, numbers were knowledge and special numerical relationships held magical power. I have not wasted too much time in this area, and others may be able to identify other similar relationships that put this observation into its proper perspective.

The next item of interest concerns the angle of 45°, subtended by the compasses in the Grand Master's jewel. This particular item of regalia comes into the picture during the next chapter. The choice of 45° is in itself symbolic because:

$$4 + 5 = 9$$

However, taking the 45° as part of a circle of 360°, it can be seen that the remainder of the circle is:

$$360 - 45 = 315 \quad \text{and} \quad 3 + 1 + 5 = 9$$

If we take the four quadrants of a circle, 90°, 180°, 270° and 360°, we get the same result:

$$90 - 45 = 45 \quad \text{and} \quad 4 + 5 = 9$$
$$180 - 45 = 135 \quad \text{and} \quad 1 + 3 + 5 = 9$$
$$270 - 45 = 225 \quad \text{and} \quad 2 + 2 + 5 = 9$$

The product is always the same—9—the same number as the original Knights Templar.

There is a drawing, shown in Chapter 11, that is open to a different interpretation using the paradigm just adopted for the 1, 2, 3 series of numbers. The drawing in question was a symbol used by Giordano Bruno, a well-known hermeticist from the sixteenth century, as the endplate to his book *DE TRIPLICI MINIMO ET MENSURA*.

As will become clear, the original solution to this puzzle would have involved a triangle within a circle with the top line of the triangle horizontal, not canted at 15° to the horizontal as it is in Bruno's sketch. Turning to the dotted line in the sketch, drawn at 45° to the horizontal, it can now be seen that this is at 135° to the vertical (45 + 90). And, as we have just seen:

$$1 + 3 + 5 = 9$$

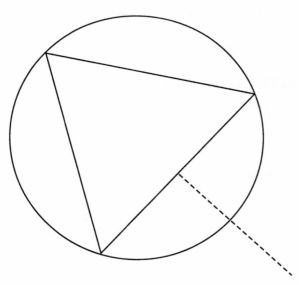

Figure 41
Bruno's Sketch from De Triplici

Giordano Bruno appears to have been inviting us to turn this drawing through 135° to arrive at the correct solution; the dotted line would then represent the Paris meridian.

And finally, the use of Gematria and the methods of interpretation discussed above throw up a possible solution for the name "Cardou." Using the replacement Hebrew characters and their numbers that were earlier used on the plate of gold, we get:

C	90
A	-
R	200
D	4
O	-
U	-
Total	294

$$\text{and } 29 + 4 = 33$$

Ashlars

1. Snakes feature large in Masonic symbolism and there is a large snake feature just north of Pech Cardou in the town of Peyrolles.
2. The layout of the candles in a Royal Arch Chapter appear to have very special significance.
3. With the use of a simple A=1, B=2 code, the completion of the landmarks for Pech Cardou is possible, and someone has drawn attention to this by bringing a bogus clue, the cutting of the elm, into Templar history.
4. There were nine original Knights Templar and the number nine can be seen to have properties when multiplied that must have seemed magical in medieval times.

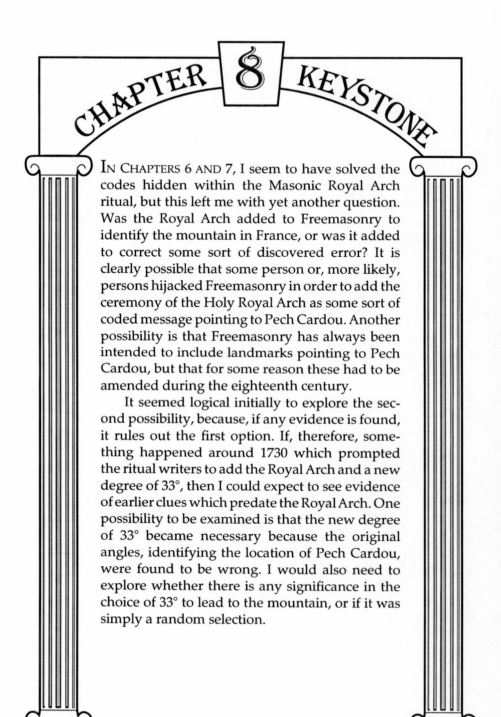

IN CHAPTERS 6 AND 7, I seem to have solved the codes hidden within the Masonic Royal Arch ritual, but this left me with yet another question. Was the Royal Arch added to Freemasonry to identify the mountain in France, or was it added to correct some sort of discovered error? It is clearly possible that some person or, more likely, persons hijacked Freemasonry in order to add the ceremony of the Holy Royal Arch as some sort of coded message pointing to Pech Cardou. Another possibility is that Freemasonry has always been intended to include landmarks pointing to Pech Cardou, but that for some reason these had to be amended during the eighteenth century.

It seemed logical initially to explore the second possibility, because, if any evidence is found, it rules out the first option. If, therefore, something happened around 1730 which prompted the ritual writers to add the Royal Arch and a new degree of 33°, then I could expect to see evidence of earlier clues which predate the Royal Arch. One possibility to be examined is that the new degree of 33° became necessary because the original angles, identifying the location of Pech Cardou, were found to be wrong. I would also need to explore whether there is any significance in the choice of 33° to lead to the mountain, or if it was simply a random selection.

JERUSALEM

Christopher Robin came slowly down his tree. "Silly old bear," he said, "what were you doing? First you went round the spinney twice by yourself, and then Piglet ran after you and you went round again together, and then you were just going round a fourth time."

A.A. Milne, *Winnie the Pooh*

ARLIER I SUGGESTED that an error had been made by whoever positioned the Paris meridian. The location of the Paris Observatory and the Luxembourg Palace hints that the meridian was meant to pass through Pech Cardou. If this were so, then the error was actually tiny, given the equipment and techniques available in the mid-seventeenth century. David Wood, in his second book on the Rennes-le-Château mystery[36], provides plausible support for this idea. He quotes Godfrey Higgins[45] as having identified a Latin word "cardo," derived from "cor" meaning "heart" or "wisdom." The "wisdom" would provide a clear link with the Masonic ritual references to the pillar named wisdom. It is, however, the other meaning, "heart," that fixes it closer to the meridian. Higgins maintains that the name "Cardo" was applied to a major line running north to south, in other words a meridian.

A "Cardo" would run through every capital or principal town.

and

Each having its own sacred Mount or Cardo . . . or stone circle.

155

Archaeological excavations in Jerusalem from 1978 have con-
firmed that the Knights Templar would have been well aware of a
Cardo running through the restored Jewish Quarter from the Zion
Gate—or thereabouts—to the Crusader section of the city. This
Cardo has been rebuilt using the original Roman and Byzantine
pavement, columns, and capitals.

What Wood does not pick up on is the variation in the name of
Pech Cardou between the 1955 IGN map and the 1977 IGN map. On
these different IGN maps, Cardou sometimes appears as Cardon. It
is only the final letter that has changed, from N to U; without either
of these letters, we are left with "Cardo." If the suggestion that Pech
Cardou had the meridian first is correct, then the error in transfer-
ring it to Paris is not difficult to understand. The distance between
Paris and Pech Cardou is around 415 miles (670 kilometers) so any
calculation of longitude required some form of celestial observation.
The first Harrison chronometer, with its accuracy of a few seconds in
24 hours, was not finished until 1730, and there is no evidence to
suggest that it ever went to France[30]. In any event, the Paris Observatory was built some sixty years earlier. Whoever located the Paris
meridian is not particularly relevant to this debate, although they
could have drawn on Jean-Dominique Cassini's updated set of
tables that relied on the position of the satellites of Jupiter to provide
longitudinal data.

Failing this method, they could have used the positions of
certain stars to determine the Paris Meridian. Cassini published his
revised tables of the positions of Jupiter's satellites in 1668 using data
first published in 1614 by Simon Marius and corrected in 1654 by
Battista Odierna. As things turned out, the Danish astronomer
Olaeus Rømer identified a systematic error of 10 minutes in
Cassini's tables. This last piece of information points away from the
use of Cassini's "Jupiter tables," because the error, on the ground at
Pech Cardou, is 0.8 mile (1.3 kilometers) easterly and yet a 10-minute
error would equate to some 8 miles (13 kilometers) in the same
location. Whichever of the available methods was used to lay down
the Paris meridian, it was slightly out, but nonetheless an extraordinary feat of astronomy and surveying at the time. In 1714, the British
Longitude Act offered a prize, worth several million dollars at

today's value, for an accuracy of ½° of a full circle. This measure of accuracy would have permitted an error of around 22 miles (35 kilometers) at Paris and 25 miles (40 kilometers) in the Roussillon.

When around 1750 Cassini's son, Jacques, published the map of the Rennes-le-Château area (Fig. 90), there must have been consternation because the existing Masonic landmarks did not work. Whatever the landmarks had been prior to the Cassini map, they clearly did not work now; the meridian was now 656 feet (200 meters) away from the summit of Pech Cardou. There was also another occurrence around this time which may have influenced the decision to ensure that a permanent record of the location of Pech Cardou existed. In 1792, the new French National Assembly confiscated all of the French property and goods of the Knights Hospitaller. This action was compounded in 1798 when Napoleon captured the main Hospitaller base on Malta. The Turks had previously ejected the Hospitallers from their home on Rhodes in 1523. It is probable that, with all of these attacks, the Hospitallers felt that they might go the same way as the Templars.

If these suppositions are correct, then there was indeed only one solution available: a new set of clues was required. But this, as has already been mentioned, raises the interesting question of what landmarks were there before? The obvious place to start was with the Masonic *Book of Constitutions,* and I still have a copy of the 1955 Edition which was given to me when I joined Freemasonry. The introduction to the charges includes the words:

Extracted from The Ancient Records of Lodges Beyond the Sea.

If there had been any doubts before of a link with Knights Templar, those words dispelled them. "Beyond the Sea" meant only one thing in days of old and that was *Outre-mer,* "the land beyond the sea," The Holy Land. The Holy Land was the base for the activities of the Knights Templar. The French word *outremer,* without the hyphen means ultramarine—deep blue—the color of a Grand Officer's apron and collar. After this, the clues came flooding in. In the Masonic Book of Constitutions, the collar of a past master is shown as having an angle at the base of 60°. In the center of the base and crossed by a line is a beehive, the symbol associated with the Knights Templar. The vertical line could be a reference to the Paris meridian, and the beehive to the site on Pech Cardou. The message in that case would be that 60° is the angle we seek.

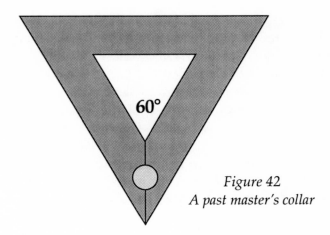

60°

Figure 42
A past master's collar

Likewise, in the Book of Constitutions, the jewels of Grand Lodge officers define similar angles. The compasses of the Deputy Grand Master, the Assistant Grand Master, and the Stewards are all set at **60°**. The swords in *saltire*, or crossed, of the Grand Sword bearer, his deputy and assistant are all at **60°**. The Grand Pursuivant's swords and those of his assistant are also at **60°**, but turned

Figure 43
Two Grand Officers' jewels

through 90°. Finally, the standards of the Grand Standard bearers are also at **60°**.

In fact there are only two jewels that have different angles subtended within them. The Grand Master's jewel has the compasses set at 45° and the Grand Director of Ceremonies' batons are set at 48°. The difference between the angles of these two jewels is **3°**.

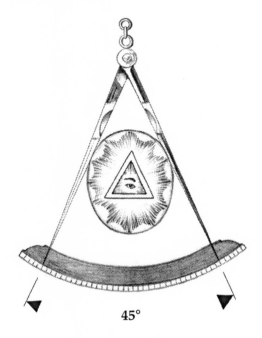

45°

Figure 44
The Grand Master's jewel

This difference, of 3° gives the clue to the earlier angle of 33°:
30° + 3° = 33°

30° is half of 60° and is the other angle in a 30°, 60°, 90° right angle triangle.

This investigation has thus far considered that there was an error in the original landmarks which were incorporated into Masonic Craft ritual for locating Pech Cardou. An angle of 3° has been identified as the probable error, and this degree of error can be seen close to the very heart of this mystery. The magnificent gardens of the Luxembourg Palace, which are about half a mile (.75 kilometer) long, have leading off them a similar length walkway that leads straight to the Paris Observatory. Everything in the gardens, including the centrally placed obelisk, are placed in a straight line between the center of the Palace and the center of the Observatory. And yet, all of this symmetry is nearly 3° to the east of north. The Luxembourg Palace, the Paris Observatory, and the location of Pech Cardou all appear to have a similar surveying error, an error of 3°. Thus far I have identified three angles which appear to provide part of the key to the solution to this part of the puzzle, although the angles of 30° and 60° look as if they may be interchangeable. Therefore, to uncover the earlier Masonic landmarks, I needed to find a way of using 30° or 60° and somehow or other a 3° offset. An angle of 60° brought to my mind a clue that no one has previously found a use for—the Dalle de Coume Sourde.

The only record of this stone slab, which is said to have come from Coume Sourde, a village near Rennes-le-Château, is a drawing. The illustration bears a resemblance to one leg, or the fourth part, of a Templar cross, particularly if the top horizontal line is deleted. It was Gérard de Sède[25] who reproduced the drawing of the stone. It is possible that he may not have realized the significance of the angles or alternatively deliberately modified them to put others off the scent.

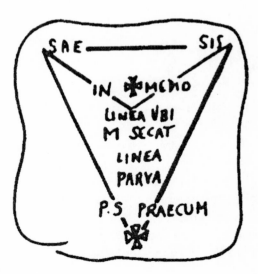

Figure 45
The Dalle De
Coume Sourde

In order to progress the investigation, I assumed that the angles included within the Dalle de Coume Sourde are 60° and 30°. Using the two pieces of directional information thus far identified, angles of 3°, 30° or 60°, I returned to the IGN map. At first I drew a line through Pech Cardou at 3° to the east of north, but there was nothing of significance anywhere to be seen. Perhaps the apparent error at the Luxembourg Palace was simply to mirror and thus to draw attention to the error at Pech Cardou, in which case the perpetrators were signalling the necessary correction at the Palace. To test this theory, I drew a new line through the site on Pech Cardou at 3° to the west of longitude. This new line cut the head of the snake at Peyrolles exactly in two; clearly this was the right track. At last, the significance of the Peyrolles snake, snakes throughout the Masonic ritual, and the Grand Lodge sacred symbol of yôdh, was becoming clear. Next I drew a line at 90° to the 3° line and just touching the top of the snake's head, which, with the 3° line formed a letter "T" leaning the same 3° to the left.

At this point I had to make an assumption. If the angles within the Dalle were 60° and 30°, then the distance from the top of the snake to Pech Cardou had to be half of the distance from Pech Cardou to the base of the triangle. This calculation is effected with the knowledge that the tangent (or the ratio of the opposite side over the adjacent side) of a 30° triangle is 0.577, and the tangent of a 60° triangle is 1.732, or 3 times the tangent of a 30° triangle. I drew in this line, and to my surprise it exactly reached the line between *les Crêtes d'al Pouil* and *Peche de Rodès*, the same line that I had used earlier for the 33° solution. As I was now in possession of the inclination of the top line, the 60° internal angles and the point of the inverted apex of the equilateral triangle, its completion, in conformity with the "Dalle" shape, was straightforward (Fig. 46). The top left-hand corner of the triangle is at a point on the map called *La Borde* and the top right hand corner is at a place called *La Borde de Roudeil*. Monsieur Planques, the *Chef du Service de la Documentation Géographique* at the *Institute Géographique National* (IGN), advised me that *borde* means a small farm or small holding. The closeness of *Borde* to the word border as "between countries" invites a closer look. The French-English dictionary, Larousse 1994, gives no French word

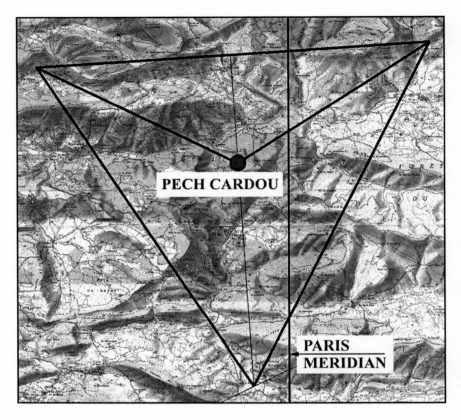

Figure 46
Pech Cardou with the 3° offset and
Dalle De Coume Sourde layout superimposed
IGN Map No. 2347OT © IGN Paris 1994, Authorization No. 90-0069

borde; it does however give *bord* without the "e." *Bord* is described as *côté d'un domaine* which translates as "the edge of an estate." Larousse also provides *bordé* meaning "trimming" and *border* meaning "to edge or to trim." It does look as if this could be yet another example of phonetic word exchange or pun that has already been demonstrated by the ritual compilers.

The next step was relatively straightforward. Andrews and Schellenberger [5] had been convinced in their solution of the need to introduce a canted square. This seemed appropriate because Royal Arch Chapter "fire" is done to the words:

Point, triangle, circle

From the Royal Arch Chapter fire

This is a variation of Craft Masonic "fire" which proceeds, "Point left right, point left right, etc.," with the index finger describing the shape of an upturned triangle, and completes a formal—such as the "Loyal"—Masonic toast. The Royal Arch variation "point, triangle, circle" also refers to the shapes drawn in the air with the index finger of the right hand. The craft fire is said to date back to Admiral Nelson who, it is said, gave his seamen a test on entering or leaving port that involved pointing the guns left, then right, and firing blanks after each movement. It is also said that the seamen on the deck who completed first got an extra ration of rum. The true origin, however, of masonic "fire" probably owes more to the fact that an upturned triangle is the alchemical symbol for fire.

I already had the "point"; I also had the "triangle," but a circle around the triangle produced nothing of interest. Canted squares, triangles, etc., feature in a number of old drawings of which probably the most famous are the sketches by Leonardo da Vinci owned by Her Majesty the Queen and held at Windsor castle.

The problem now was to decide where the canted square might go, based on which corner and at what offset angle to the triangle. The alternatives are unlimited. The answer was to be found, as earlier, amongst the jewels of the Grand Officers, but this time it was the Royal Arch Chapter jewels which provided the solution. Indeed, it was the jewels of the three Grand Principals that provided it. Figure 48 shows the jewel of the First Grand Principal, the most senior Royal Arch Mason, a post normally held by the Grand Master of Craft Freemasonry, and the interlocking triangles at the base of this jewel clearly identify a 15° canted angle.

It was shown in Chapter 6 that the Craft jewels provided certain clues and the Royal Arch jewels are no different. The Sojourner's jewel has a right angle square within an equilateral triangle subtending two angles each of 15° between the triangle and the square. Generally the staffs of office are crossed at 60° to match the three angles within the equilateral triangles in which they sit. However, the Grand Sword Bearer's swords are set at 70° within a similar equilateral triangle of three 60° angles, subtending two angles be-

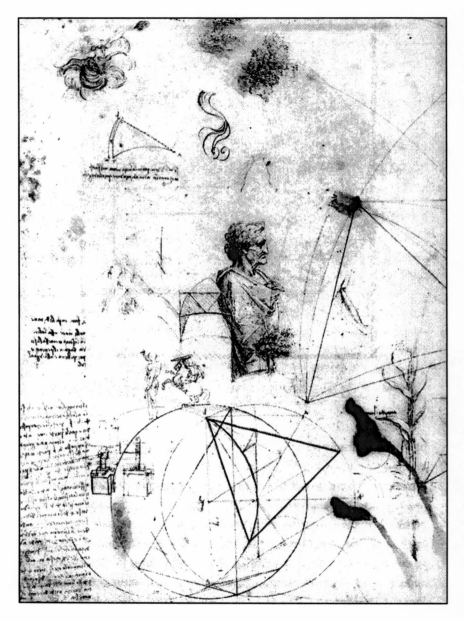

Figure 47
Sketches by Leonardo Da Vinci from The Royal Collection
at Windsor Castle

tween the swords and the triangle each of 5°—not exactly the 3° I was looking for, but a curious phenomenon in any event, and one which could simply be drawing attention to the two mirrored 3° angles at Pech Cardou and the Luxembourg Palace.

It is clear from Figure 48 that the canted square fits over the top left hand corner of the triangle and is offset equally on both sides by 15°. A canted square was duly drawn over the triangle (Fig. 49). The top left-hand corner was at the same site as the top left-hand corner of the triangle, *La Borde*. The top right-hand corner was at *Borde des Aouzis*. Not far from the bottom left-hand corner is *Borde d'en Mathurin*. Finally, the bottom right-hand corner is at *Roc de l'Aigle*, rock of the eagle. The eagle is one of the banners in a Royal Arch Chapter. Finally, I drew a circle around the square (Fig. 49). Point, triangle, circle, square, the complete Royal Arch Chapter fire. This turned out to be much easier that one might have thought. Whoever carried out the IGN survey placed 33 ordnance survey points exactly on the line of the circle (there is that ubiquitous number 33 yet

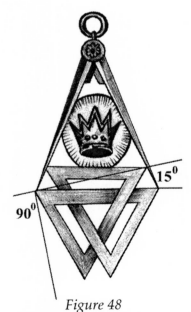

Figure 48
The First Grand Principal's jewel with 15° canted angle

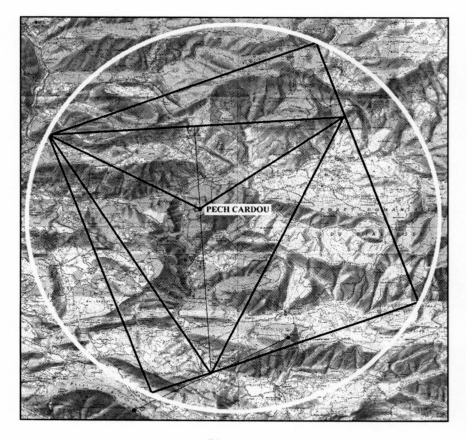

Figure 49
Pech Cardou with the canted square and circle overlain
IGN Map No. 2347OT © IGN Paris 1994, Authorization No. 90-0069

again). If I had known where to look, it was simply a matter of joining up the dots as in a child's drawing. The circle has an axis at:

    Longitude 445.8 UTM

    Latitude   4753.4 UTM

It is exactly 9 miles (14.5 kilometers) in diameter—the same number as the number of knights who originally established the Knights Templar. The axis of the circle is a mere 660 feet (200 meters) to the west of the Paris meridian, and this is such an infinitesimal distance in geodesic terms that it can be ignored. The spherical shape of the earth means that any attempt to transcribe it onto a flat sheet of paper leads to compromise "errors." The alternative "projections," such as Lambert and Mercator that were mentioned in Chapter 6, are different geometrical solutions to this problem. The complex use of the original 3° error, a triangle and then a canted square, as a means of creating an off-set, brings about a compelling message. The Paris meridian should have passed through the site on Pech Cardou. When the Cassini triangulation of France was complete, it was abundantly clear that the meridian did **not** pass through Pech Cardou.

For a secret society with an apparent claim to "control the longitudes," this must have been extraordinarily frustrating. The lines of Masonic ritual that allude to "the sun always being at its meridian with respect to Freemasonry" were now inaccurate. Something had to be done to wrest back control of this area of human knowledge, and the results are now clear. One additional, although tiny, benefit to flow from this inquiry is that we can now date when these words of the Masonic ritual were written:

The sun is always at its meridian with respect to Freemasonry.

The lines of Masonic ritual must have been included after the meridian was laid down around 1680—because otherwise they are meaningless—but before the error was uncovered in 1750—because at that point they would have realized that the ritual was incorrect. One important question, however, is what is so important about Pech Cardou as to warrant its inclusion in Masonic ritual and on the National Cartographers' maps? The evidence appears to be mutually supportive and suggests that either it was in Pech Cardou that a group of people, possibly the Knights Templar, created something special, or that someone with access to the preparation of the IGN maps appears to want to give that impression.

The nine-mile diameter circle, identified on the IGN map 2347 Quillan, is also special for another reason—that is, its remarkable similarity to the circular map of Jerusalem kept at the Royal Library at The Hague and usually referred to as the Templar map of Jerusalem. The first point that needs to be made about this particular map of Jerusalem is that it is not quite the same as other circular maps of Jerusalem, as comparison with Figure 23 will demonstrate. In par-

Figure 50
Part of IGN Map showing six survey points on the line of the circle
IGN Map No. 2347OT © IGN Paris 1994, Authorization No. 90-0069

ticular, no roads outside of the circle are shown, and the roads inside of the circle have houses alongside them, indicating that the place is a town or city. Several other features such as *lapis scissus, turris david* and *eccta Launa* are missing from other circular maps of Jerusalem.

On the Templar map, as with other circular maps of Jerusalem and the world, north is to the left. It is possible to match every feature on the Templar map with a similar one in and around the nine-mile diameter circle in the Roussillon.

Roads

The two "banners" streaming from the bottom of the Templar circular map of Jerusalem have the name *Vicus* meaning "street" in Latin. They correlate very closely to the D118 that leaves *Couiza* to the north and south at the junction with the D613. The D613 runs west to east through the middle of the nine-mile diameter circle and matches the road shown running vertically down the center of the Templar map circle. The similar road on the Templar map running from 11 o'clock just above the line of the circle round to 3 o'clock can be identified with various roads. Starting at the 11 o'clock position, the D129 travels from *Bouisse* around to *Albières*. At *Albières*, the road doglegs a short distance westward along the D613 before turning south onto the D212 and running down to *Soulatgé*. At *Soulatgé*, the D212 joins the D14 that runs due west until it reaches *Cubières* where it divides exactly as shown on the Templar map with the D10 travelling south and the D14 continuing northwest to *Bugarach*. At 3 o'clock, inside the circle is a feature similar to a road running horizontally across the circle: on the IGN map is a footpath running through *Sougraigne* down to *Bugarach* roughly in the same position. The point of particular interest about this feature is that it is referred to on the Templar map as *Claustrum calomons*, and *claustrum* in Latin can mean the **"key to a position."** The footpath shown on the IGN map goes across **Pech de Rodès**.

Mountains

At the top right-hand corner of the Templar map, or 10.30 o'clock, is *Beo Phage,* which could be Latin for "blessed fish." This may be in turn an allusion to the local Occitan name for mountain peaks as *Pech* because the French for "fish" is *pêche*. There is a mountain on the IGN map in this location called *Bouno Mort*. At 11 o'clock, and still outside of the circle, on the Templar map is another mountain, *Ascensio dus*, and this is matched on the IGN map by *Col de l'homme Mort* (Mount of the dead man). Further round, at 5 o'clock on the Templar map, is *Mons Syon* (Mount Sion) and *Mont Raymond Guiraud* matches this on the IGN map. The choice of the name Raymond Guiraud is interesting and despite a thorough search I have been unable to identify a character from history who might warrant having a mountain named after them. However, mindful of the region, it may be pertinent that the first Grand Master of the Hospitallers was called Gerald, Gerard or even **Guiraud** (these names from history are largely recorded phonetically) and the second Grand Master was **Raymond** of Provence. At 7.30 o'clock on the Templar map, at the left end of the D118 from *Couiza*, is *Mons Gaudy*. *Mons Gaudy* translates to Mountjoy and this was the name given by pilgrims travelling from the west to the mountain from which they caught their first glimpse of Jerusalem. *Mons Gaudy* corresponds on the IGN map with *Pic de Brau*. As if to further emphasize this point, a mile or so down the road, in Couiza itself is the château of the Ducs du Joyeuse.

Inside the circle on the Templar map, at 8.30 o'clock, is a mountain or feature *lapis scissus* which in Latin could mean cutting or sharpening stone; there are a number of rock features around *Véraza* that might be said to match this feature. In particular, to the southeast of *Véraza* is a deep valley, with straight sides set at around 45° to each other: it would be the easiest thing to imagine that the nickname for this valley was "the scissors sharpener."

Buildings (outside of the circle)

Commencing at 12 o'clock on the Templar map there is *Villa Gethsemal*, which is matched by *Albières* on the IGN map - Quillan 2347 OT. At 1 o'clock is *Jhevisco* matching *Fourtou* on the IGN map. At 2 o'clock can be seen *Bethania*, which on the IGN map is *Camps-sur-Agly*. Further round, at 3.30 o'clock, is *Cenaculu* representing *St.-Louis-et-Parahou*. At 4 o'clock is *Sepulchrum*, which is coincident with *St.-Just-et-le Bézu*. Also at 4 o'clock but further from the center is *Bethleem* matched by *St.-Julia-de-Bec* on the IGN map. At 7 o'clock there is *eccta beau Crepha* on the Templar map and on the IGN map is *Antugna*. Finally, outside the circle at 11 o'clock is *eccta ste marie* represented by *Missègre* on the IGN map.

Buildings (inside of the circle)

Starting at 1 o'clock on the Templar map, there is *Templu Calomonis* represented on the IGN map by *Sougraigne*. At 4 o'clock there is *Eccta Launa* coinciding with *Rennes-les-Bains*. Also at 4 o'clock but further from the center is an unnamed tower that is shown on the IGN map as *Bézu*. At 5 o'clock can be seen *turris david* (tower of David) and this is represented by *Rennes-le-Château*. Moving round to 8 o'clock there is *Golgotha* (the place of the skull) and this coincides with Pech Cardou. At 10 o'clock can be found *teplu sté osaris* in the same location as *Peyrolles*. Finally, inside the circle at 11.30 o'clock is *teplum oses* (*templum* is holy ground and *os* is bone in Latin) and this is represented on the IGN map by *Arques*. It seems as if both *Peyrolles* and *Arques* hold or represent "holy bones" of some sort or another.

Practically every single feature on the Templar map held in the Royal Library at The Hague can be seen to represent a similar feature on the IGN map in the vicinity of the nine-mile circle. This alone is quite remarkable because the "Hague" Templar map is purely schematic and yet the area around Pech Cardou matches the schematic "on the ground."

Most families accumulate possessions over the years as older family members go on ahead. My own family numbers among these an old leather-bound Bible, some 12 inches (30 centimeters) x 10 inches (26 centimeters) x 3 inches (8 centimeters) thick, with brass hasps and staples. This magnificent tome is of indeterminate old age and the publisher is unknown, the front three pages long since having been damaged beyond repair. In addition to the very detailed footnotes which take up around a quarter of each page, and which have been so helpful to me in the preparation of this book, there is an old Ordnance Survey map of Jerusalem, Figure 51. Careful examination of this old map shows that the many of the roads and footpaths on it have been replicated in the area around Pech Cardou.

The Roussillon roads do not just mimic the Templar schematic circular map; they are a close duplicate of the roads as they were when the Ordnance Survey map was produced and that was probably at some time in the nineteenth century. The strange degree of conformity can be explained only as yet another remarkable coincidence or a deliberate act to reproduce one area of the world, Jerusalem in Israel, in another area of the world, the Roussillon in France.

It is fast becoming more difficult to argue that the Templar map does *not* represent an area in the Roussillon region of France than to accept the alternative conclusion that it does. This same area has a circle clearly marked on the IGN map, so at the very least someone has to provide a logical alternative explanation. On the basis of the evidence, a message is becoming clear. The Hague "Templar" map, the Ordnance Survey map above and the circle of nine miles diameter identified on the IGN map, all seem to suggest that this circle

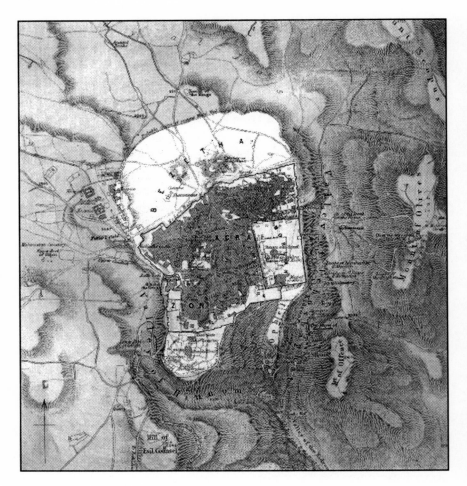

Figure 51
Nineteenth-century ordnance survey map of Jerusalem

defines the New Jerusalem of the Knights Templar. Once again the same caveat has to be applied; either this **was** the Templars' Jerusalem, established when they left the Holy Land for good in 1291, or maybe someone at the IGN wants us to think that it was.

It is of course possible that a member of the IGN staff, having completed the same exercise as I, decided to leave a permanent record of his work. If this interpretation were to be correct, it is unlikely that it was solved simply from the Templar map at The

Hague; the precise coincidence of the Masonic clues and the points on the IGN map point to another explanation. There are two fundamental weaknesses in the notion of an unauthorized act by a member of the IGN staff. Firstly, a remarkable extent of freedom would have been needed within the IGN for such an audacious act to succeed. Secondly and possibly more importantly, why, with this level of freedom, include the 660 feet (200 meters) off-set of the axis of the circle from the Paris meridian? Why not set it precisely on the meridian?

Setting aside the remote likelihood of a member of staff at the IGN marking up the map with the 33 survey points describing a circle without approval from the management, the question remains of how genuine is the circle? There is indeed an almost complete ring of mountains, ridges and other natural boundaries such as the river roughly on the line of the nine-mile circle. These natural boundaries work perhaps a little better than the one above—marked out with 33 ordnance survey points—if a circle around the original triangle centered on Pech Cardou and the snake feature at Peyrolles is used. This is perhaps understandable because the larger circle to accommodate the error in the meridian is obviously a later addition. The occurrence of roads and footpaths, also close to the line of and covering around half of the line of the circle, in addition to the natural barriers, does support the idea that this was indeed something real, something that did exist. There can, of course, be no question of the Knights Templar being involved in setting out this circle in so precise a manner because the necessary surveying equipment was not available. So who on earth put these data onto the map?

There was only one way to find out, and so I entered into a protracted cycle of correspondence with Monsieur Pierre Planques at the IGN in Paris. The result of this part of the investigation was inconclusive with M. Planques agreeing on a circle of 33 points but maintaining that it was random chance. It is perhaps fitting that M. Planques' name can translate as "rock hideaways." In fact, in order to calculate approximately the odds against such an occurrence, one must visualize a circle of 46 square kilometers strung together in a circle like a necklace. It requires 46 square kilometers to produce a

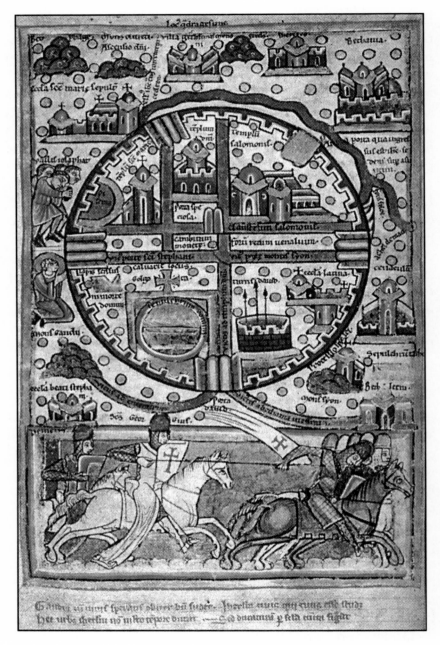

Figure 52
The circular map of Jerusalem
The Hague, Koninklijke Bibliotheek, 76 F 5, fol. 1r.

circle of 9 miles or 14.5 kilometers diameter. M. Planques volun-
teered the information that there are 4 survey points per square
kilometer on a 1:25,000 map, implying some two million survey
points for the whole of France.

Before proceeding further, I must show, by calculation, the odds
of 33 ordnance survey points appearing on the IGN map in a 14.5 km
(9-mile) diameter circle by chance. To do this it is necessary to
imagine these 46 square kilometers strung around the line of the
circle like a necklace, each square having 2 sides parallel to the line
of the circle.

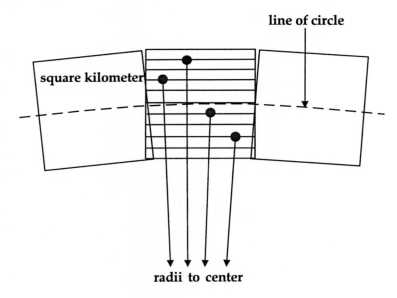

Figure 53
Four ordnance survey points in a kilometer square
on the line of the 14.5 km diameter circle

You must now divide each square into 10 strips each 100 meters
wide and also tangential to the line of the circle as Figure 53.
Running through one of the middle two strips will be the line of the
circle. There are 4 ordnance survey (OS) points per square kilometer
so the probability "p" of an OS point in a square kilometer being on
the line of the circle, to ± 50 meters, is:

$$p = 4/10 = 0.4$$

There are 46 square kilometers around the line of the circle therefore there should be:

$$46 \times 0.4 = 18.4$$

Say 19 OS points on the line of the circle to within ± 50 meters.

There are in fact 33 points so we have 14 more than random chance would suggest. The probability of each additional OS point being on the line of the circle—as just explained above—is:

$$p = 0.4$$

Therefore, to have 14 extra points the probability is 0.4 multiplied by itself 14 times or 0.4^{14} and this is:

$$0.0000066$$

Probability is measured on a scale of zero to one, where 0 is an impossibility and 1 is a certainty; an even chance comes out at 0.5. It is clear that 0.0000066 is a long way towards zero, making the occurrence of 33 OS points being located near to the line of the circle very unlikely to have been random chance. The reciprocal of 0.0000066 is 151,515; therefore the odds of the 33 OS points on the IGN map being there by chance are 151,515 to 1 against.

The calculation to determine the statistical odds against any number of OS points being in a particular arrangement in greater numbers than chance would suggest depends on the accuracy of their locations. In the case of the OS points on the 14.5 km diameter circle, this is a function of the radius measurements. These radii figures show that although there are 33 OS points within ± 50 meters there are also 24 OS points within the range ± 25 meters. It is as well to bear in mind that on a 1:25,000 map 25 meters is only 1 millimeter or not much more than the thickness of a pencil line. The methodology for calculating the odds against this is exactly the same as just described for the 33 OS points except that each kilometer square is divided into 20 strips.

The probability of an OS point, in a square kilometer, being on the line of the circle to ± 25 meters is therefore:

$$p = 4/20 = 0.2$$

There are the same 46 square kilometers around the line of the circle; therefore, there should be:

$$46 \times 0.2 = 9.2$$

Say 10 OS points on the line of the circle to within ± 25 meters.

There are in fact 24 points so we have 14 more than random chance would suggest, oddly the same number as with the previous calculation. The probability of each additional OS point being on the line of the circle is now:

$$p = 0.2$$

Therefore, to have 14 extra points the probability is 0.2^{14} and this is 0.2 multiplied by itself 14 times and is:

$$0.00000000016$$

The reciprocal of 0.00000000016 is 6,250,000,000; therefore, the odds of the more accurate 24 OS points on the IGN map being there by chance are 6,250,000,000 to 1 against.

The IGN have suggested that the OS points on the line of the circle are simply coincidence but the above statistical calculations confirm that it is extremely unlikely that this is the case. I have suggested above that a realistic explanation for the circle of 33 points is essential and "random chance" falls some way short of that criterion.

The next step was for me to visit the IGN in Paris to determine when the circle of numbers first appeared on the IGN map. The visit to the IGN *Cartotheque* was less than satisfactory. The staff there informed me that they had nothing earlier than 1944, which seems at odds with the publication of Cassini's 1780 map by Andrews and Schellenberger[5]. Three 1944 1:25,000 maps covering three-quarters of the area included by the 2347 Quillan map and one 1970 1:25,000 map were produced because "there is no copy of the 1944 map." The maps produced were:

Quillan 1 & 2	1944
Quillan 3 & 4	1944
Quillan 5 & 6	1970
Quillan 7 & 8	1944

Pech Cardou was shown on Quillan 1 & 2 but interestingly it was spelled differently as CARDO<u>N</u>. This particular spelling is also used on the IGN 1:100,000 map number 72 (Béziers and Perpignan). On Quillan 7 & 8 there was no mention of Pech de Rodès and on none of the 1944 maps was there any survey points on the line of the circle. Maps from 1956, the next survey date of the areas covered by the 1944 maps, were inspected but again there were no survey points on the line of the circle. The circle of 33 survey points first appears in the 1970 edition of the maps and this was also the first time that photogrammetry, or stereo-photography, was used to determine levels. Pech de Rodès and Les Crêtés d'al Pouil also appear for the first time on the 1970 maps.

This information sparked off another round of correspondence with Monsieur Pierre Planques at the IGN. The two site names, Pech de Rodès and Les Crêtés d'al Pouil, he maintained, have been added by the region's Local Authorities and the name "Cardon" seems to be the original. M. Planques had been able to access an 1880 map that was not made available to me during my visit to Paris. It is an undeniable fact that the two solutions to this mystery both rely on data published on IGN maps. The IGN do not appear ready to offer a realistic explanation to me but perhaps someone with better French language skills will pursue this enigma.

The knowledge that Cardon is the earlier name opens up an interesting new line of enquiry, for although Cardou has no apparent meaning, "Cardon" is a thistle, from the Latin *carduus*. Woodward's Treatise on Heraldry[48] informs us that the earliest appearance of the thistle was on the coinage of James III of Scotland in 1474. By 1540, the thistle had become recognized as the Scottish national emblem. Woodward reports:

> *A curious use of the thistle occurs in the arms of the National Bank of Scotland [granted 1826].*

When one recalls the banking role of the Knights Templar, this is indeed an odd coincidence. Fox-Davies' *A Complete Guide to Heraldry*[49] expands on this topic.

> *The Order of the Thistle was instituted by James V, in 1540.*

This order is now called The Most Ancient and Most Noble Order of the Thistle and was revived in 1687. It is headed by the Sovereign, Her Majesty The Queen, and has two royal knights, HRH The Prince Philip, Duke of Edinburgh and HRH The Prince of Wales, Duke of Rothesay. The remaining knights, who can total sixteen, are drawn from among the good and the great of Scotland. The Secretary and Lord Lyon King of Arms is Sir Malcolm Innes of Edingight, KCVO. *Who's Who* informs us that Sir Malcolm is also a member of the Order of St. John of Jerusalem. Another coincidence is the use of the terms "Most Ancient" and "Most Noble" in the title of this order because they are reminiscent of the piece of Masonic ritual which is recounted to a new brother when he receives his apron for the first time: it includes the words:

> *It is more **ancient** than the Golden Fleece or Roman Eagle, more **honorable** than the Garter or any other Order in existence, being the badge of innocence and the bond of friendship.*

"Noble" is of course one of several synonyms for "honorable" so it can be seen that both orders are claiming similar seniority and distinction. In claiming to be the oldest order, each is implicitly aligning itself with the Knights Templar who arguably can claim to have established the first knightly order in 1118. Fox-Davies' analysis of the origin of the thistle discounts the legend which attributes it to a "mythical" King **Ach**aius in 809. The use of this particular name is rather close to one of the themes that runs through this book, namely the serpent or snake. Fox-Davies continues:

> *The reason for the assumption of the thistle . . . has been raised, over and over again, but we never get one step nearer than the well-worn story that at the battle of Largs one of the Danish invaders trod with his bare foot on the prickly flower, and his cry of pain caused the failure of the attempted surprise.*

The stylization of this legend would permit it to sit comfortably within practically any piece of Masonic ritual. Of the European families who incorporate a thistle, or more commonly three thistles, into their coats of arms are the Cardonas of Spain, the Cardon and Debbits of Flanders and Chardon du Havet of France (*chardon* is the modern spelling of *cardon*). Finally, before leaving this interesting detour, there is one final coincidence, and this is that knights of the Order of the Thistle may use the abbreviation K.T. after their names and these just happen to be the same initials as the Knights Templar.

The use of Pech Cardou and Pech Cardon allows for an even more esoteric explanation. The two interchangeable letters are "u" and "n" and if the "u" is placed over the "n" we get an "X" and if the "n" is placed over the "u" we get an "O." These two letters make "ox," and the ox was one of the animals that was sacrificed in King Solomon's temple and also makes up one of the banners in a Royal Arch Chapter.

This manipulation of the last letters of Cardou and Cardon leads to even stranger interpretations. Firstly, the letter "X" made as described above does in fact resemble a hieroglyphic scarab which may in turn represent an insect. The introduction of an insect must lead us to the mysterious "shamir." The Bible states that when God directed Solomon to build his temple He laid down the condition that no metal tools were to be used to cut the stone. This may explain why all new candidates for Freemasonry are divested of metal before entering the lodge room. It is said that Solomon used "shamirs" which are variously recorded as worms or insects which had the power to split lumps of rock into perfectly formed ashlars. It has even been suggested that perhaps this was the "mason's secret" for which Hiram Abif, the architect in charge of the building of King Solomon's temple—according to Masonic ritual—was killed. A more likely explanation is that "shamir" is a corruption of the Greek word "smiris" meaning emery which was available at that time on the Aegean island of Naxos[62]. And secondly it cannot be ignored that "n" is simply a "u" turned through 180°. If on Mount Moriah the temple was on the top, this turning of the last letter is suggesting that the temple is now beneath the ground. If we ignore whether any of these three esoteric explanations is correct, we are still left with the important issue which is that they are all linking Pech Cardou with Mount Moriah.

It was during my visit to the IGN that I became aware of a most interesting aspect, stemming from its location. The main offices of the IGN are on the outskirts of Paris on the edge of the Bois de Vincennes and share a plot of ground with the Hôpital Militaire

Bégin. A little way up the Avenue de Paris is a castle—Château de Vincennes—and next to the château is *Fort Neuf*—Fort "New" or Fort "Nine." Here was an immediate problem because *neuf* in French can mean either "new" or "nine." We are back into the realm of word exchanges yet again. This particular variation permits the user to pay discreet homage to something connected with the number nine. If anyone asks, the meaning is of course "new," but for those in "the know," it really means "nine" to commemorate the nine original Knights Templar. With this possible interpretation in mind, other celebrations of *neuf* are apparent in Paris. Pont Neuf, the oldest bridge over the River Seine, seems an unlikely candidate for the title "new," but "nine" would clearly mark it out as special. There is after all, no Pont eight, seven, six or anything else, only nine, the number of the original Knights Templar. The use of *neuf* is unusual in another sense, and that becomes clear when the Cabalah technique of Gematria is applied. Using the code A=1, B=2 etc., as used in Chapter 7, both words "new" and "nine" add up to 42 and 42 minus 9 is **33**.

The picture continues to clear. The Paris Observatory is in the grounds of a military hospital and the offices of the IGN are likewise in the grounds of a military hospital. The IGN do have another office, in between the Hôtel des Invalides and the Ministère de la Défense, a military and hospital connection yet again. It is apparent that in France matters relating to astronomy and geodesic surveying appear to be, or have been, under the eye of the military hospital authorities. It does not take a blinding leap of intuition to make the obvious connection that it was to the Knights Hospitaller that the property and many of the Knights Templar themselves went when the Templars were disbanded. The control which the "military" hospital authorities appear to have exerted over matters astronomical and cartographical helps to explain another Masonic anomaly. Within the Masonic ritual, the two pillars at the entrance of King Solomon's temple are described, in part, thus:

> *Those pillars were further adorned with two spherical balls on which were delineated maps of the celestial and terrestrial globes, pointing out Masonry universal.*
>
> From the explanation of the second degree tracing board

These pillars are described in detail in the Holy Bible but without any mention of spheres. A sphere is however included atop the pillar in Poussin's painting of Eliezer and Rebecca in Chapter 13, suggesting that he at least is trying to catch our attention. Once again it is at the point where the Masonic ritual strays from the original Biblical text that points to a message, and the Masonic message in this instance appears to be "we control these two areas of human knowledge."

It is equally easy to conclude that from within the ranks of the Hospitallers the spirit of the Templars has been kept alive through-out the centuries. It appears that these same people have jealously guarded the knowledge of the hidden purpose of Pech Cardou and whatever secret it contains. It seems to follow, from my discoveries, that these same people are ready, or nearly ready, to make some public pronouncement and have begun to prepare the way by entering data onto the IGN maps. Once the possibility that some momentous announcement is imminent is accepted, the new mil-lennium must be a favored choice. If we discount, for the sake of discussion, the possibility that the points marking the circle were an odd coincidence, then we are left with several questions. Why, for example, the IGN should choose 1970 to mark the maps of the Roussillon area to show where the Knights Templar had their Jerusalem. Is this something that we are going to be told? If the alternative possibility is true, that the 33 survey points are not known to some senior staff at the IGN, then this implies a level of slipshod behavior that somehow does not fit with a national cartog-rapher. It must follow from this line of argument that the 33 survey points are acceptable to some senior staff at the IGN. Why did they not take the opportunity to remove them during the 1982–1988 re-survey?

Whoever is behind this mystery is clearly not yet ready to make a pronouncement; otherwise they would presumably have con-firmed my findings. One thing, however, is now certain and that is that this site in the Roussillon, this possible New Jerusalem, perhaps set out originally by the Knights Templar, is known to IGN staff of sufficient seniority to enable the 9-mile circle to find its way onto their maps. This circle clearly had a purpose and that purpose may well still exist, for sitting almost at the center of the circle is Pech Cardou.

The error, between the old and new landmarks identifying Pech Cardou within the Masonic Craft and Chapter rituals, has been identified as 3°. Such a serious error rules out any connection with those who laid down the Paris meridian. The probability is that the site at Pech Cardou and the snake feature at Peyrolles were created much earlier. It is at least conceivable that the original landmarks included in the first Craft ritual used magnetic north. Magnetic north was in use from the first century BC; however, it was not until around 1450 AD that the makers of sundials became aware that there was a variation between magnetic and true north. From data kindly provided by the British Geological Survey for nearby Quillan:

Year	Variation of magnetic north from true north
1500	Variation 5° east of true north
1550	Variation 9° east of true north
1600	Variation 10° east of true north
1650	Variation 2° west of true north
1700	Variation 7½° west of true north

It is possible to extrapolate approximately, back to a date of 1400 ± 50 years, when the variation at Pech Cardou would have been 3° west of true north. The next occasion when this variation occurred was around 1675, but by then the level of surveying knowledge effectively rules out an error of this magnitude. The significant fact is that the 1400 date fits the thesis of this book.

At the beginning of this chapter I touched on the fact that the 3° line through the site of the pillars on Pech Cardou passes through the center of the head of the snake at Peyrolles. This massive mound of red marble, obviously cut by many hands, is without doubt the *serpent rouge* brought up in the locally published pamphlet of the same name and was also discussed by Gérard de Sède.

It is appropriate here to consider what might have been in the minds of those ancient Templars who, having been forced out of the Holy Land, contemplated their future. What we must consider is the possibility that they started to quarry Pech Cardou *before* the Templars were dissolved. In this scenario, they would have had a

Figure 54
The head of the serpent rouge at Peyrolles
Photograph by David Ingram

different agenda compared to the people who came along afterwards and created Pech Cardou landmarks to parallel the Masonic
ritual. Based on this alternative proposition, the *Cardo* can be drawn
through the Peyrolles snake's head and the pillars on Pech Cardou.
A circle, centered on the site on Pech Cardou, can now be drawn
touching the snake's head and—curiously—the five-pointed "Place
of Interest" marker on the IGN map for the Source de la Madeleine.
The Source de la Madeleine is a spring feeding into the river Sals at
Rennes-les-Bains. This immediately draws our attention to another
"Place of Interest" marker on the IGN map, that for the Pierre Dresée
(Fig. 55).

Pierre Dresée literally translates to "standing stone" or "erected
stone" although the more usual French word for such an object is
menhir. A line drawn at right angles to the Cardo and through the
Pierre Dresée marker permits an equilateral triangle to be constructed with the inverted apex at the Source de la Madeleine
creating a shape remarkably similar to the caduceus (Fig. 6) shown
in Chapter 3.

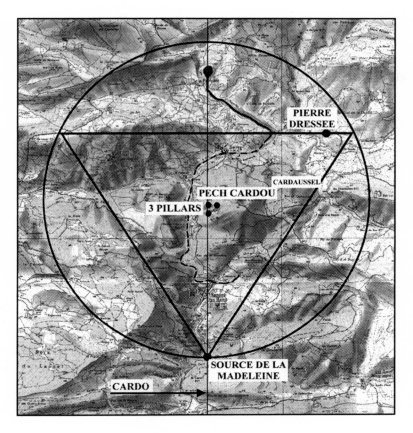

Figure 55
Speculative caduceus at Pech Cardou

Perhaps those ancient Templars wished to create a permanent memorial to Moses, who had been so instrumental in the creation of the Ark, which they believed now rested within their temple in Pech Cardou. Perhaps their successors, after the Order was banned, ceased work on the snake when the 3° error became apparent. Certainly it is possible to continue on the line of the natural geological features, as identified by the D613 and D14 roads and as indicated by the dotted line on Figure 55, to complete the snake coiled around an imaginary staff represented by the Cardo. Maybe the completion of the snake feature does exist under the surface of the

D613 and D14 roads. If this alternative explanation is nearer to the truth, then, when the meridian was also found to have missed the position of the staff, those involved must surely have questioned whether they really did have God's approbation.

The introduction into the debate of a speculative caduceus "coiled" around a Cardo takes us sharply back to Chapter 7 which is where I first mentioned the constellation of Draco. I am indebted to Tim Carmain, a contributor to the Priory-of-Sion Internet group at http://members.xoom.com/priory_sion, for drawing my attention to the apparent links between this investigation and the mythology surrounding Draco. One of the stars in Draco—Thurban—was the pole star at the time the pyramids were built in Egypt, and Thurban was the leader of the "Imperishable Ones," the stars that never set. What better link could there be for a group of people, the Knights Templar, who set out to show that they are indeed "imperishable." There is another aspect of Draco which may help to explain another legend, that of King Arthur and the Knights of the round table. The constellation of Draco coils around another constellation, Ursa Minor or the "little bear" from which we can derive Ursa ≅ Uther (Pendragon) and bear = Artorius ≅ Arthur.

It is, however, the fact that Draco winds around the pole star Polaris that affords the best link between Cardo, Pech Cardou, Draco and the astronomers who, in the eighteenth century, began to lay down the landmarks that have led me to the solution of this puzzle.

There in the sky is the explanation for Moses' caduceus and the reason why it became the symbol of God and able to save men from death by snake venom. Draco winds around the pole star that sits at the very top of the imaginary staff or pole around which the world rotates. When Moses took the caduceus in his hand he metaphorically mimicked God who has the whole world in his grasp. The wings at the top of the caduceus simply provide a clue as to where the answer lies—in the northern sky.

If we now turn our eyes away from the heavens and back to the speculative caduceus on the ground at Pech Cardou, as shown in Figure 55, we can see that this particular arrangement of lines brings those enigmatic mapmakers at the IGN once more into focus. For

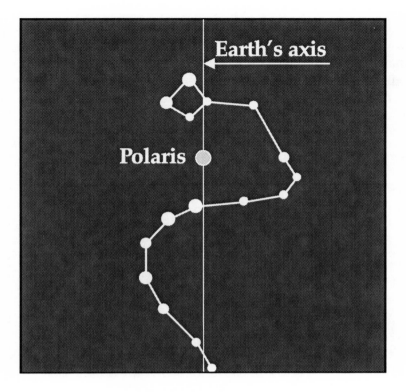

Figure 56
The constellation of Draco

there, on cue and coincidentally in exactly the right place, is a "Place of Interest" marker for the Lac de Barrenc. A line drawn at a right angle to the Cardo and through this star permits the completion of the Seal of Solomon or hexagram.

This second triangle has another interesting characteristic, for, if this triangle is set inside the triangle identified in Figure 46 (Chapter 8), it creates the layout of the candles in a Royal Arch Chapter room (Fig. 39, Chapter 7).

It is fair to point out that the orientation of these points at Pech Cardou differs from the layout of the Royal Arch candles by 57° anti-clockwise. The angle of 57° is 60° minus the 3° error discussed in Chapter 8, and 60° was the angle which dominated Poussin's paintings. If we now add the circle and hexagram from Figure 57 to the

large triangle in Figure 58 and then turn the picture through 57°
anticlockwise, we get a near perfect reproduction of the Royal Arch
Grand Superintendent's jewel, even down to the three small stars
which are exactly the same shape as a "Place of Interest" marker on
an IGN map.

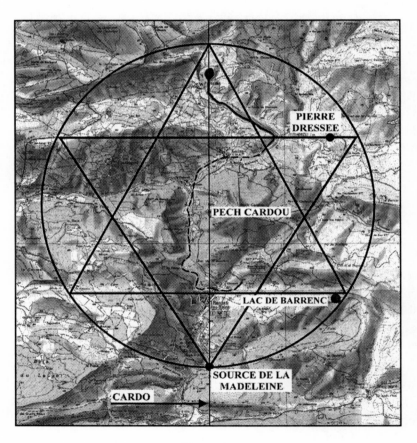

Figure 57
Hexagram markers at Pech Cardou

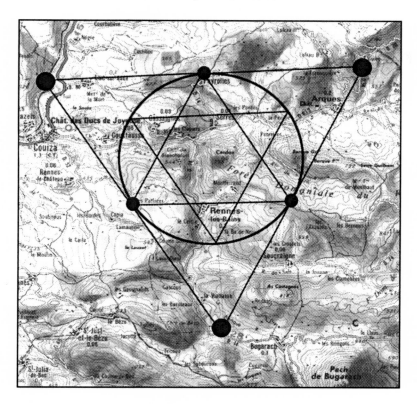

Figure 58
Chapter candles layout at Pech Cardou with the
hexagram from Figure 57 superimposed
IGN Map No. 72 © IGN Paris 1996,
Authorization No. 90-0069

Figure 59
Jewel of the
Grand Superintendent

Ashlars

1. There is strong support for the idea that the Paris meridian should have passed through Pech Cardou.
2. In 1750 whoever was behind this mystery realized that the meridian was in the wrong place and that another Masonic degree was required.
3. The Palais du Luxembourg seems to be implicated in this mystery by having an equal and opposite 3° tilt from true north in its half-mile (.75 kilometer) long gardens.
4. The Craft Masonic regalia contains hidden clues that point to the same mountain in France, Pech Cardou, but using different angles of 3° and 60°. Combining Craft and Royal Arch ritual symbolism, a circle of nine miles diameter can be identified on the IGN map, with Pech Cardou almost at its center.
5. There is a 2-mile (3.2-kilometer) long snake feature at Peyrolles which is necessary to identify and locate the 9-mile diameter circle around Pech Cardou. The huge head of this snake has been deliberately left uncut in a red-marble quarry; this identifies it as the *serpent rouge* from a small booklet of the same name which can be found on bookshelves in the area.
6. The Paris meridian would have gone through the site on Pech Cardou and it would also have split the snake had it not been for the 3° error.
7. The triangular clues which locate the 9-mile diameter circle around Pech Cardou, when added to the Grand master's jewel, create the Seal of Solomon.
8. A magnetic variation of 3° west of true north existed at the end of the fourteenth century.
9. There is an equal and opposite 3° "error" in the layout of the gardens at the Luxembourg Palace.
10. The nine-mile diameter circle is clearly marked on the IGN map 2347 Quillan scale 1:25,000 by 33

ordnance survey points exactly on the line of the circle.

11. The nine-mile diameter circle also matches the circular map of Jerusalem held at the Royal Library at the Hague and which is known as the "Templar map of Jerusalem."

12. The Masonic ritual includes a reference to two spheres with maps of the heavens and earth, as an amendment to the Biblical story. These suggest that a group of people are making the statement that "we control these two areas of human knowledge—heaven and earth."

13. Various "Points of Interest" markers on the IGN map, combined with the Serpent Rouge and Pech Cardou, facilitate the drawing of Masonic symbols including a caduceus.

14. The nine-mile diameter of the circle shown on the IGN map by 33 ordnance survey points suggests the nine original Knights Templar.

15. The IGN organization in Paris appear to have old ties with the Knights Hospitaller. It was to the Knights Hospitaller that many of the Knights Templar transferred when the Templars were disbanded. The "military" hospital authorities in France appear to have some control over matters of celestial and terrestrial surveying.

16. Pech Cardou was also sometimes called Pech Cardon. Cardon is a thistle and there is an old Scottish order called the Thistle.

17. The last letters of Cardou and Cardon, "n" and "u," can be manipulated to give apparent links between Cardou and Mount Moriah.

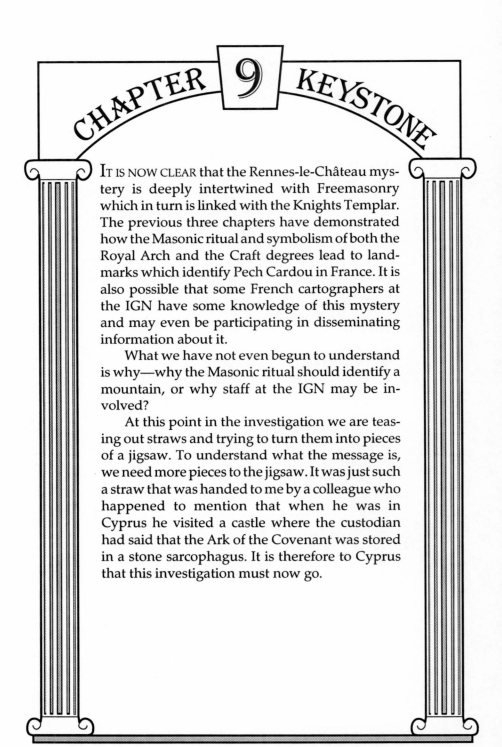

CHAPTER 9 KEYSTONE

IT IS NOW CLEAR that the Rennes-le-Château mystery is deeply intertwined with Freemasonry which in turn is linked with the Knights Templar. The previous three chapters have demonstrated how the Masonic ritual and symbolism of both the Royal Arch and the Craft degrees lead to landmarks which identify Pech Cardou in France. It is also possible that some French cartographers at the IGN have some knowledge of this mystery and may even be participating in disseminating information about it.

What we have not even begun to understand is why—why the Masonic ritual should identify a mountain, or why staff at the IGN may be involved?

At this point in the investigation we are teasing out straws and trying to turn them into pieces of a jigsaw. To understand what the message is, we need more pieces to the jigsaw. It was just such a straw that was handed to me by a colleague who happened to mention that when he was in Cyprus he visited a castle where the custodian had said that the Ark of the Covenant was stored in a stone sarcophagus. It is therefore to Cyprus that this investigation must now go.

CYPRUS

On Earth most fair, Pierian hill-sides, And melody there,
The voice of the Nine, Is borne on the air,
Over the hill-sides, And I would be there, Olympian hill-sides,
For Heaven is there, With spirits divine.

Part of Euripides "Bacchæ II" translated by J.F. Roxburgh
the first Headmaster of Stowe.

AMONG MANY OTHER STRANDS for investigation, the earlier chapters have identified the importance of an angle of 33°, and this turned my attention back to something I had heard earlier. In Chapter 4, I made reference to the possibility that the Ark of the Covenant was stored in the Templar commanderie at Limassol on the island of Cyprus. This begs the question of whether the Ark of the Covenant has anything to do with Freemasonry and here the answer is emphatically yes.

As described earlier in the Royal Arch ceremony of Exaltation the Principle Sojourner found:

a scroll of vellum or parchment.

When he reached daylight, he and his fellow companions found that it was:

from the first words therein recorded, part of the long-lost Sacred Law,
promulgated by our Grand Master Moses at the foot of Mount Horeb
in the Wilderness of Sinai.

The Sacred Law, referred to in the above ritual, was the Ten Commandments, and these were stored in the Ark of the Covenant. The Royal Arch ritual appears to be suggesting that it was the Ark of the Covenant that was found.

The earlier reference to the "plate of gold" might also be seen as an allusion to the gold covering of the Ark. If this deduction were to be correct, then it becomes conceivable, from the Masonic/Templar links identified in the previous chapters, that it could have been the Templar Knights who did the finding. This is worthy of further investigation because, if this hypothesis were to be found to be right, then it must follow that the original compilers of the Masonic ritual were aware of this information.

It was near to the end of this investigation that another "literary angel" appeared—another of those strange coincidences that move matters forward. This time it came in the form of a Masonic colleague who inherited an early book of Masonic ritual on the death of a close relative. My friend was aware of my interest in early Masonry and so he loaned the book to me: it is called *Ritual of Freemasonry—With Illustrations* and was published by William Reeves. This somewhat battered old book, with its spine hanging off, was undated, but from advertisements in the back it was possible to date it to around 1912. With this veritable "treasure" clutched tightly to my breast, I sped off home where I quickly scanned through until I came to the ceremony of the Royal Arch. The ceremony of the veils was all there, followed by an explanation of what, until then, I had only known of as "riding the goat." It has nothing to do with goats, other than providing a connection to the composition of the linen covering the Tabernacle, but a better and more vivid description of that part of the ceremony would be hard to find. It was the next section which made me draw in my breath sharply.

> *In pursuance of your orders, we repaired to the secret vault, and let down one of the companions as before. The sun at this time was at its meridian height, the rays of which enabled him to discover a small box, or chest, standing on a pedestal, curiously wrought, and overlaid with gold: he gave the signal of ascending, and was immediately drawn out. We have brought the ark up, for the examination of the grand council.*

So there it was; my assumptions appeared correct, for at the beginning of this century what was found was not the "word" but the Ark of the Covenant. I read on to find that the Grand Council inspected what was inside of the Ark, and then the High Priest says:

You now see that the world is indebted to Masonry for the preservation of this sacred volume [he is referring to the book of law found inside the Ark]. Had it not been for the wisdom and precaution of our ancient brethren, this, the only remaining copy of the law, would have been destroyed, at the destruction of Jerusalem.

This amazing discovery had at once confirmed my theory and immediately raised two more questions. Was this book genuine? And if so, why had the ritual been so extensively modified around the time of the First World War?

The first question proved easier to resolve than I had imagined. A search through the antiquarian inventories turned up *A Ritual of Freemasonry Illustrated by Numerous Engravings* written by Avery Allyn and published in Philadelphia by John Clarke in 1831. As before, it was the section on the Royal Arch to which I turned. Remarkably the ritual was substantially the same as the book, eighty years later, quoted above. It was certainly reassuring to find that a book of Masonic ritual, which was published around the time that Masonic historians say that the written ritual can be dated, had further confirmed my assumptions. I was, however, left wondering why the ritual had been so changed at the beginning of this century.

We now have several strands of this investigation that appear as if they will fit neatly together:

1. There is a clear and defined relationship between Freemasonry and a mountain in France—Pech Cardou.
2. There is a clear and defined relationship between Freemasonry and the Ark of the Covenant.
3. It has been postulated that, on the basis of local landmarks, Pech Cardou might be the Masonic Third or Grand and Royal Lodge.

Now, if Pech Cardou is indeed the Masonic Third or Grand and Royal Lodge, then its purpose is clear: it held the Ark of the Covenant, discovered—so they claimed—by the Freemasons. The circle is apparently complete, but questions remain. At the very least, it now seems possible that the Ark was stored in Pech Cardou starting perhaps as early as the fourteenth century. If this speculation is correct, then what happened in the early part of the twentieth century to cause the rulers of Freemasonry to so dramatically alter the ritual and remove any mention of the Ark of the Covenant?

Perhaps it was the approach of the German army on France that caused the guardians of the Ark to take fright and move it further west out of the reach of the German forces. And just maybe the rulers of Freemasonry discovered for the first time that the box they so casually discovered in their ritual was in fact real. That might certainly have caused them to modify the ceremony of the Royal Arch and to replace the Ark with "the word."

Alternatively, they may have known all along that the Ark existed, but that the emergence of a Jewish nation held out the possibility of the Jews demanding the return of their Ark. It was in 1917 that the U.K. pledged its support for the Balfour Declaration that led in 1920 to the assignment of Palestine to the British as a Protectorate under the League of Nations. The British Mandate expired in 1948 when the Jews declared Israel as a Jewish state, and the controversy has continued until the present time. Some support for this alternative suggestion can be found in the fact that when the two competing English Grand Lodges—the "Ancients" and the "Moderns"—reached agreement on union, the then Grand Superintendent, John Sloane, in 1813 built an "Ark of the Masonic Covenant" to hold the original "Act of Union." This ark was destroyed by fire in 1883, although the manuscript containing the Article of Union was saved. It is almost as if at the point of the union the Grand Lodge members were forced to face up to the knowledge of the whereabouts of the real Ark of the Covenant and created a suitable cover story. Both time scales are consistent with the alterations to the ritual, so both explanations are plausible, and of course there may have been a totally different explanation. It is equally possible that the activities of Abbé Saunière convinced the "guardians" that, guided by the new clues, someone else might now uncover the secret.

This investigation is beginning to fragment, so the strands must be pulled together. We certainly have a mountain in the Roussillon identified from landmarks within the Masonic ritual. We now also have the Ark of the Covenant and the Knights Templar, and the question that has been posed is—do they fit together?

At this stage in the investigation, it is probably only possible to link the Ark of the Covenant to the mountain—Pech Cardou—if it can be shown that the mountain is the Masonic Third or Grand and Royal Lodge. If this argument could be sustained, then it would have had only one purpose, and that was to store the Ark of the Covenant, just like the previous two discussed in Chapter 3. The "first" or Holy Lodge, you will recall, was the Tabernacle in was stored the Ark. The "second" or Sacred Lodge was King Solomon's temple in which also was stored the Ark. I have already intimated that the third or Grand and Royal Lodge may not—as the Masonic ritual states—be Zerubabbel's temple in Jerusalem—in which was stored the Ark—but another temple somewhere else. I decided to persist with this line a little longer and adopted, purely for convenience, the presumption that the Ark of the Covenant was stored or lodged in Pech Cardou. This presumption enabled me to drop certain pieces of the jigsaw into place.

It now becomes possible to visualize the Ark as buried at some point within a triangle—the triangle in question being drawn between the three pillars prominent on the site at Pech Cardou. For the ritual compilers to have included a reference to "a point within a triangle," may well have been considered by them to have been too obvious. They would probably have searched for a substitution or cipher word, and one was at hand; it is "circle." Circles are synonymous, in Masonic ritual and symbolism, with triangles, particularly equilateral triangles. Evidence abounds for this proposition, and almost all of the Masonic jewels that Freemasons wear to denote their Masonic rank display *inter alia* a triangle set within a circle. This is nowhere more apparent than with the seal of Solomon in the Royal Arch Jewel.

Indeed, if an equilateral triangle were to rotate on its axis, it would describe a circle. The ritual compilers left clues:

Candidate: *The earth constantly revolving on its axis.*

                    From the questions to a candidate for the second degree

How then, did the substitution of "circle" for "triangle" manifest itself in the ritual?

Master: *Where do you hope to find them?*
Senior Warden: *With the Center.*
Master: *What is a Center?*
Junior Warden: *A point within a Circle, from which every part of the circumference is equidistant.*
Master: *Why with a Center?*
Senior Warden: *That being a point from which a master mason cannot err.*

                    From the third degree opening of a Craft lodge

This particular piece of ritual makes no sense unless the point within the circle contains something with guardian-like qualities. The Ten Commandments certainly possess such properties and no one, certainly not a master mason, would err if he followed those commandments. The Ten Commandments were/are kept in the Ark of the Covenant, and it has already been argued that the Masonic Royal Arch ritual is pointing to the fact that the Knights Templar recovered the Ark of the Covenant from Temple Mount. If the Knights Templar took the Ark to the site on Pech Cardou and stored it there for safe-keeping, then they would certainly have wanted a record of what was buried and where.

It is beginning to look as if the landmarks identified earlier are not so much there to direct someone to the location, but rather to be able to say at some future point that "we did this, and here are the directions to prove that we did." These directions exist in a cleverly coded form, hidden within the ritual of Craft and Royal Arch Freemasonry. The Coat of Arms of Grand Lodge (Fig. 60) supports this proposition; above the Arms, where the crest might normally sit, is the Ark of the Covenant. Furthermore, the two "creatures," one on each side of the arms, are cherubim, who traditionally guarded the Ark. This does, of course, beg the question of why anyone should wish to set up something as elaborate as this. One explana-

Figure 60
The Coat of Arms of The United Grand Lodge of England

tion might be if the organization had been destroyed and wished to make a statement to the effect that "we have returned."

We have already examined the importance of an angle of 33°, and this turns our attention back to the earlier reference of the possibility that the Ark of the Covenant was stored in the Templar commanderie at Limassol on the island of Cyprus. The reason for this is that the castle at Limassol sits almost exactly (within 2 to 3 miles or 3 to 4 kilometers) on the line of longitude 33° east. It might just be possible to ignore this as a coincidence if it were not for the involvement of astronomers and surveyors throughout this story. Mention has already been made of Jean-Dominique Cassini and the Paris Meridian. The Paris Meridian was obviously intended to pass through Pech Cardou, and this ties the early French astronomic establishment into this investigation. Cassini also had connections with the Greenwich Observatory through the medium of Christiaan Huygens. Huygens was "head hunted," just like Cassini, to become a charter member of the French Académie Royale des Sciences which was founded in 1666. Huygens, who was Dutch, travelled to

England on a number of occasions to discuss matters of longitude with his English equivalents[30]. Four years earlier, in 1662, the British Royal Society had received its Royal Charter from King Charles II.

The Royal Society had started in 1645 in London but met in 1648 and 1649 at Oxford, returning permanently to London from 1658. It has been shown that at least a quarter of the early members of the Royal Society were Freemasons, and they included Christopher Wren and Samuel Pepys as well as Robert Boyle and Isaac Newton, who were purportedly also masters of the Priory of Sion. It was not until 1675 that Christopher Wren built Greenwich Observatory, and this would in time become the internationally recognized zero Meridian. Interestingly, it was Robinson[16] who identified the fact that Wren was not an architect by training but that he had been a professor of astronomy at Oxford. The linkage between the French astronomical establishment and the parallel English elite is thus made. It was only right and proper that such eminent scientists should have sought to exchange views and knowledge. However, before suggesting that particular lines of longitude could have been associated with any historical event, it is necessary to identify that such collusion was at least possible and this can now be done. Support for the supposition comes with the knowledge that the Italian astronomer and geographer Benedetto Bordone travelled to Cyprus nearly 150 years earlier, in 1528[41]. Both the means and the opportunity have thus been established, and a precedent has also been identified with the relationship between the Paris Meridian and Jerusalem.

Although I have used the term "almost exactly" above to describe the location of Limassol Castle, in doing so I have taken into account the relatively recent advances in terrestrial measurement capability. The prize offered in 1714[30] by the British Government to anyone who could determine longitude to within ½° would have permitted an error of 28 miles (45 kilometers) on Cyprus. A variation of a degree, or any other angle, results in different distances depending on how near or far one is from the equator. The nearer to the north or south Poles one is, then the smaller is the distance.

In Limassol Castle then is a building that has known associations with the Hospitallers and Templars. These two military orders, with the Patriarch of Jerusalem, each had a one-third control of the Holy Land during the period when it was in Christian hands. The crown of Jerusalem was kept in a vault, and the Patriarch and the Grand-Masters of the two orders each had a key. No one could be crowned king of Jerusalem without the agreement of all three. This castle therefore commemorates the number one-third, and it sits on a line of longitude that in percentage terms, 33%, is equal to one-third. Furthermore, the number 33 had already been used in this context. Jesus Christ was crucified at the age of 33 years; some theologians however attribute the use of 33 years of age as a symbolic reference to Christ's one-third role in the trinity. It therefore requires a suspension of disbelief to conceive that this is yet another coincidence.

Without doubt, the commanderie was there first, and the decision to allocate the 33rd line of eastern longitude was made much later, probably at the beginning of the sixteenth century. If this is true, then there is only one consequential conclusion that must follow, and that is that the observatory at Greenwich was deliberately sited to accommodate the 33° line of longitude that passes through Limassol. It follows, therefore, that Limassol must have held something quite remarkable to warrant such an honored position in the world of astronomy and navigation. The available evidence is suggesting that Limassol Castle did, at one time, hold something quite remarkable and that it was the Ark of the Covenant.

One would be forgiven for taking the view that this suggestion is outrageous. The very idea that the Ark of the Covenant might even exist, and that the Greenwich Meridian was only there to coincide with some castle in Cyprus, is indeed breathtaking—until one recalls that the Paris Meridian is positioned 33° west of Jerusalem. Based on the Paris Meridian, Jerusalem sits on a line of longitude 33° east, just as Limassol Castle does from the Greenwich Meridian. In reality, Jerusalem doesn't sit exactly on the line 33° east; it is some 6 miles (10 kilometers) to the west. This is an error of around 6 minutes of arc representing a quite incredible degree of accuracy for the early 17th century when it must have been established. The 33°, or one-third, relationship between the Paris Meridian and Jerusalem cannot be written off as coincidence because the French used this fact in their argument to the International Commis-

Figure 61
Limassol Castle

sion for the Paris Meridian to be the International zero Meridian. I have now established precedent, means, and opportunity.

The question still remains, why? What connects Jerusalem with Limassol Castle?, and the answer is the Knights Templar.

Limassol Castle certainly holds out the possibility of having once been a repository of the Ark of the Covenant. It was rebuilt around 1450 with many remarkable features. It has ceilings the height of which are one-third of the width of the room. It also has a fireplace positioned one-third of the way along the wall that demonstrates the paradigm used to identify Pech Cardou: i.e., the square and compasses (Fig. 34). Which use of this paradigm came first, Limassol or Pech Cardou, it is impossible to say. The fireplace, however, is probably an allegory for the Ark of the Covenant.

> *And Nadab and Abihu, the sons of Aaron, took either of them his censer, and put fire therein, and put incense thereon, and offered **strange fire** before the **Lord**, which he commanded them not.*

*And there went out fire from the **Lord**, and devoured them, and they died before the **Lord**.*

Leviticus 10:1-2

In these two verses from Leviticus, strange fire means an unlawful offering. The word "Lord" refers to the Ark, because God spoke from between the cherubim. Subsequent injunctions not to take strong drink, in verses 9-11, lead some to conclude that God struck down Nadab and Abihu because they had entered the tabernacle when they were under the influence of alcohol. This is only one of many Biblical references to the Ark spewing forth fire and suggests the use of the fireplace as an allegory.

Limassol Castle has other features that point to it having held the Ark of the Covenant. The first of these is a stone sarcophagus (Fig. 63) which, a friend of the author's was told by a guide during a visit, served as a storage vessel for the Ark; the internal dimensions of the sarcophagus are of the right order to have allowed it to have done so.

Figure 62
Fireplace at Limassol Castle

Figure 63
Stone sarcophagus at Limassol Castle

Figure 64
Recess in the floor of Limassol Castle

Another feature at Limassol Castle is the strange recess in the floor that would have comfortably held the sarcophagus shown in Figure 63. The rebates at the top of the recess are obviously there to receive timbers that in turn could have supported stone slabs. When the timbers and slabs were in position and the joints filled with mortar, the hiding place would have been totally secure and reminiscent of the covering to the cave under the al-Sahkra.

Limassol Castle also has some 15 miles (25 kilometers) of tunnels leading out from the cellar. Tunnelling was a common Templar activity, providing as it did the means of undermining walls and a means of escape from their own castles.

Although I have dealt at length with Limassol Castle, there is another castle close by which offers similar potential as a refuge for the Ark, and this is Kolossi Castle. The first castle or commanderie at Kolossi was built on the site of the camp of one of Cyprus' rulers, Isaac Comnenus, who was defeated and captured by King Richard I in 1191. Richard originally sold Cyprus to the Knights Templar in order to raise funds for his Crusade in the Holy Land.

Figure 65
Kolossi Castle

The Knights Templar were, however, less than successful in governing the island and were happy to sell it back, through Richard, to Guy de Lusignan, who had lost out in the election for the crown of Jerusalem to Henry of Champagne. Guy declared himself King of Cyprus, and his family ruled as sovereigns until the fifteenth century. The Lusignans granted the site of Kolossi Castle, together with surrounding farms, to the Knights Hospitaller in 1210, and it looks as if they built the first castle on the site.

When they finally left the Holy Land in 1291, the Hospitallers set up their headquarters at Kolossi, although there was a brief period from around 1303 when the Knights Templar occupied Kolossi. This can only have been by mutual agreement with the Hospitallers, and points to an extraordinarily important role for the castle and a role that only the Templars could perform. If this had been to store the Ark of the Covenant, then this might explain why the Hospitallers ceded occupation to the Templars. Kolossi reverted to the Hospitallers in 1308 when the Templars became a proscribed organization by order of the Pope. In 1310, the Hospitallers moved their headquarters to the island of Rhodes, probably leaving the previous Templars in charge and now operating under the name of the organization to which they had transferred *en bloc*—the Knights Hospitaller. Cyprus, including Kolossi, was ravaged by the Genoese in 1373 and again in 1402, and finally the Egyptian Mamelukes razed the commanderie in 1425-6.

The commanderie keep that stands on the site to this day was rebuilt in 1454 by the Hospitallers under the guidance of their Grand Master Louis de Magnac, whose coat of arms still adorns the castle wall. It was then allowed to fall into disrepair but restored to its present condition by the British Colonial Service in 1933; the reader will notice the recurrence of "33" yet again. Kolossi Castle is notable for several reasons. The keep, ignoring the basement, is approximately a fifty-foot cube, the same size as the Kaaba or Holy Shrine in the courtyard of the Muslim Mosque at Mecca. The basement, which has access through a trap door and down twenty-four steps, is divided from east to west into three rooms with pointed vaulted ceilings. The rooms are 40 feet (12 meters) long by 12 feet (3.6 meters) wide and have connecting arched doorways. In the basement are two water cisterns that were probably used for wine making and storage. The first-floor level is divided into two rooms, this time from north to south. The room to the west appears to have been the kitchen by virtue of having a fireplace, and the eastern one was the entrance hall with access via a drawbridge that has long since been removed.

The second floor, accessed by a winding staircase with 33 steps (there's that **33** again), also has two vaulted rooms also divided north to south as the floor below. Both of these second-floor rooms have fireplaces. There is also provision in these rooms for timber joists to be set into the walls halfway up, to make another floor presumably for sleeping quarters. The spiral staircase continues on up to the battlements. The external walls are 2.7 meters or 9 feet thick, and the castle itself is nine miles from the center of Limassol; the use of the number nine is, perhaps, another salutation to the

Figure 66
Winding staircase at
Kolossi Castle

nine knights from the Court of Champagne who formed the Order of the Knights Templar.

Beside Kolossi Castle stands a tropical acacia tree, the clearest possible symbol of a link with Freemasonry and the Ark of the Covenant. The ownership of the castle passed to the Cornaro family in the sixteenth century and they held it until 1799. In 1913, H.R.H., the Duke of Connaught, who was also the Grand Prior of the Order of St. John (in the U.K.), attempted to purchase Kolossi Castle[32] and return it to "the family." In the event, the owner, a Mr. Bishara, reneged on the day of transfer because his wife had had a vision suggesting misfortune for the family if they sold. The Order of St. John was able to purchase a small part of one of the second floor rooms (from a total of 132 sub-owners) to give them some ownership of the castle.

Perhaps in time a tunnel linking Limassol with Kolossi will be identified and then any doubts removed. I put these points to the Cypriot Ministry of Communications and Works, but as so often happens with this area of interest, one's enquiries are brushed peremptorily aside. One small gem of information from the Cypriot Ministry, however, is their confirmation that it was from Kolossi Castle that Jaques de Molay, the last Grand Master of the Templars, left for his final and fatal trip to Paris. In terms of this investigation, I cannot help but feel that Kolossi, almost against the evidence, was the last home for the Ark when it was in Cyprus. In reality it doesn't matter whether it was Kolossi, Limassol, both of them, or some other nearby castle. The argument is not affected.

The line of longitude 33° east passes almost equidistant between Kolossi and Limassol, so both qualify as candidates for the honor of this line of longitude. Whether any records exist to permit the true candidate to be identified, only time will tell.

It is only right, now, to consider other relics or artifacts that might also be seen as worthy of the honor of having lines of longitude used to record their progress. One that springs to mind is the "Turin Shroud." There are two reasons why this particular religious relic may be discounted.

1. It has been carbon-dated to around the turn of the millennium, and therefore the Templars were probably aware that it was not genuine.

2. Given that it is in the "public domain," there is no logical explanation as to why anyone should continue to act with secrecy or to add points in a circle on an IGN map.

These two arguments apply equally to every other known religious relic, and it is hard to imagine that there is another artifact that has never been mentioned. If there is, what on earth could make it the subject of such secrecy? Unlike the Ark of the Covenant, there can be no other competing claims of ownership for something that no one knows about. One conclusion, that can reasonably be drawn from the findings to date, is that the creators of whatever Pech Cardou holds must have selected a few people to act as guardians of its secret, and these chosen people have passed the secret down through the ages. Some from among their number allocated the number thirty-three to the line of longitude that passes between Limassol and Kolossi Castles on the island of Cyprus. The decision to allocate this number must have been made before 1675 because it was then that Sir Christopher Wren built the observatory at Greenwich for King Charles II. The intention was clearly to allocate the zero Meridian to Greenwich and thus to set in perpetuity the 33° line of longitude through Cyprus.

It was Eratosthenes (275–195 B.C.), a Greek and a friend of Archimedes, who first conceived of the idea of meridians. Although it actually means mid-day (A.M. and P.M. are ante and post Meridian), the word "Meridian" has over the years come to mean the zero line of longitude, and the internationally agreed zero is through Greenwich. This agreement was not in fact made until 1884, which says much for the manner in which the great secret has been passed down through the ages through the hands of prominent intellectuals. The generally accepted reason for the selection of Greenwich is that the first director appointed by King Charles II, one John Flamstead, spent forty-three years plotting the times, when three thousand different stars were over his observatory. These data were a major breakthrough in assisting navigators because of their reliability and comprehensiveness. The reality, however, is that there was a delay of one hundred and sixty-five years after Flamstead finished his recordings before Greenwich was adopted as the International zero Meridian. During the negotiations to agree on a zero Meridian, France argued strongly that theirs was preferable because it was based on Jerusalem. It is now clear that the learned men responsible for establishing the positions of the lines of longitude and latitude worked in collusion. The two locations that appear to be at the center of things are Jerusalem, from which the Paris Meridian is worked, and between Limassol and Kolossi Castles in Cyprus, the basis for the Greenwich Meridian.

One can identify many historic events that make Jerusalem in Israel a favored base point, but few of them also link with either Limassol or Kolossi Castles. The Knights Hospitaller were common to both and appear to exercise some control over matters relating to longitudes, but, apart from the excellent work they do and have done throughout the years, it is hard to understand why they should be so honored and, more importantly, why so secretively? The Hospitallers were originally an Italian organization, and this makes a French or British honor hard to understand. The Templars were also common to both Jerusalem, Limassol Castle and Kolossi Castle, but they were French, and that makes a British honor hard to comprehend and a secretive honor even more difficult to grasp.

Few artifacts—other than weapons of war—are of such immense importance that either their existence or whereabouts must be kept secret. One religious relic that does come into this category, though, is the Ark of the Covenant. It now appears that the foundations of the two major systems of longitude at the time, the Paris and Greenwich Meridians, both paid tribute to this same artifact—the Ark of the Covenant.

Ashlars

1. The current Royal Arch ritual describes a group of masons finding what could have been the Ark of the Covenant.
2. Early written Masonic ritual leaves no doubt that early masons found the Ark of the Covenant.
3. The Knights Templar were rumored to have found the Ark of the Covenant.
4. If Pech Cardou was used to store the Ark of the Covenant, it would explain why the mountain

was sufficiently important to warrant being identified within the Masonic ritual.

5. 33° east of the Paris Meridian is Jerusalem, and 33 percent is one-third. The Knights Templar and the Knights Hospitaller each considered themselves to be one of three pillars on which the Holy Land stood.

6. 33° east of the Greenwich Meridian stands Limassol and Kolossi Castles in Cyprus.

7. It was to Limassol and Kolossi Castles that the Templars went in 1303 when they left the island of Ruad off the coast from Tortosa, in what had been the Holy Land.

8. There was a co-association of membership between the astronomic world and Freemasonry in the early days of both disciplines.

9. There is physical evidence in Limassol Castle of a "hiding place" where the Ark of the Covenant might have been stored.

10. There are physical features built into both Limassol and Kolossi Castles which are reminiscent of features from Rennes-le-Château and from Masonic symbolism.

11. Although religious relics of one sort or another have always been "collectors' items" for monasteries and churches, it is hard to find another relic of the value of the Ark of the Covenant which would warrant secrecy over its ownership.

CHAPTER 10 KEYSTONE

As we unravel more pieces of this jigsaw, so the picture is beginning to clear. The ritual used in Masonic Lodges and Royal Arch Chapters identifies Pech Cardou, a mountain in the Roussillon region of France. This is a bold assertion, but one about which there can be little doubt. It has also been suggested that Freemasonry is somehow linked with the Knights Templar and because of that link the Ark of the Covenant may have been stored in Pech Cardou. The assertions concerning the link between the Knights Templar and the involvement of the Ark of the Covenant are necessarily circumspect, based as they are on assumption and ancient ritual. The link with Pech Cardou has been demonstrated by physical measurement; support for the other two theories can only be speculative and built up iteratively, one argument at a time.

If a formal relationship between the Knights Templar and Freemasonry were to exist, then one should expect to find further links in the Masonic ritual or constitutions. The two organizations do share at least one attribute. The Knights Templar went from being an organization with nine founding members to the largest such organization in the world at that time in only one hundred and eighty-seven years. In a similar length of time, Freemasonry has also become the largest such organization in the world.

CHIVALRY AND OTHER BONDS

Roi ne suis,
Ne prince ne duc ne compte aussi;
Je suis le sire de Coucy.

Motto of Baron Coucy of Picardy

T HERE IS CLEARLY SOMETHING within Freemasonry and there was something within the Knights Templar that is, or was, very attractive to men, women being excluded from both organizations. Might this attraction be chivalry? Grant Uden[13] refers to Léon Gautier, a French scholar who devoted his life to the study of the literature of chivalry. Gautier developed ten commandments, or what he called the decalogue, covering the conduct of a knight. These are listed below with the appropriate Masonic ritual copied with each rule. That there is indeed a common thread is confirmed. The examples of Masonic ritual are, for the most part, taken from the first-degree Charge. This piece of ritual, repeated from memory to every new candidate for Freemasonry, bears a strong resemblance to the sermon that was preached to candidate knights when the Church took over their investiture. This topic will be developed later in this chapter. The themes of chivalry, honorable behavior, honesty, and fairness permeate Masonic ritual, and the precepts are embedded in Masonic teachings. In the interest of brevity and to avoid repeating large portions of Masonic ritual, generally the most appropriate comparison only has been used to demonstrate this point.

GAUTIER'S DECALOGUE
1. Unswerving belief in the Church and obedience to its teachings.

MASONIC RITUAL
Charging you to consider it [the Bible] as the unerring standard of truth and justice and to regulate your actions by the divine precepts it contains.

Part of the first-degree charge

GAUTIER'S DECALOGUE
2. Willingness to defend the Church.

MASONIC RITUAL
To commemorate the valour of those men who assisted at the building of the Second Temple, who, with trowel in hand and sword by their side were ever ready to defend the city and Holy Sanctuary against the unprovoked attacks of their enemies.

Part of the Royal Arch Symbolical lecture

GAUTIER'S DECALOGUE
3. Respect and pity for all weakness and steadfastness in defending them.

MASONIC RITUAL
To your neighbour . . . by rendering him every kind office which justice and mercy may require, by relieving his necessities and soothing his afflictions.

Part of the first-degree charge

GAUTIER'S DECALOGUE
4. Love of Country.

MASONIC RITUAL
Ever remembering that nature has implanted in your breast a sacred and indissoluble attachment towards that country whence you derived your birth and infant nurture.

Part of the first-degree charge

GAUTIER'S DECALOGUE
5. Refusal to retreat before the enemy.

MASONIC RITUAL
This item is not relevant in modern society.

GAUTIER'S DECALOGUE

6. Unceasing and merciless war against the infidel.

MASONIC RITUAL

Neither is this one.

GAUTIER'S DECALOGUE

7. Strict obedience to the feudal overlord, so long as those duties did not conflict with duty to God.

MASONIC RITUAL

By never losing sight of the allegiance due to the Sovereign of your native land.

Part of the first-degree charge

GAUTIER'S DECALOGUE

8. Loyalty to truth and the pledged word.

MASONIC RITUAL

Let prudence direct you, temperance chasten you, fortitude support you, and justice be the guide of all your actions.

Part of the first-degree charge

GAUTIER'S DECALOGUE

9. Generosity in giving.

MASONIC RITUAL

Be especially careful to maintain in their fullest splendour those truly Masonic ornaments . . . benevolence and charity.

Part of the first-degree charge

GAUTIER'S DECALOGUE

10. Championship of the right and the good, in every place and at all times, against the forces of evil.

MASONIC RITUAL

And to yourself, by such a prudent and well-regulated course of discipline . . . thereby enabling you to exert those talents wherewith God has blessed you, as well as to His Glory as the welfare of your fellow creatures.

Part of the first-degree charge

There can be no argument that Freemasonry incorporates a chivalric pattern of behavior as the model to be followed by its members. Although there are many sections of Masonic ritual which could be used to support individual items of Gautier's decalogue, only that piece of ritual which best demonstrates the argument has been quoted. The proposition that Freemasonry is based on chivalric principles should be evident elsewhere. As we look back from these more egalitarian times to those days when battles were to a large extent fought hand-to-hand, one can get a feel for the age with the knowledge that English long-bows were considered, by the French knights, to be unfair. In those days a knighthood was the birthright of any male born into nobility. It was the role of the second estate, the nobility, to fight for and defend the realm. Before the eleventh century, therefore, the bestowing of a knighthood was very much a family affair. Joan Evans[14] tells how a father bestowed knighthood on his son.

> *He raised his palm, and brought it down upon his neck.*
> *"Be a knight," said the father, "fair son, and show courage in the face*
> *of thine enemies."*

By the end of the eleventh century, the Church had taken over the role of conferring knight-hoods. As one might expect, the ceremony became more ornate and more symbolic. The initiate received a ritual bath, made a confession, and received Communion. He was then required to pay attention as the priest intoned a sermon on the duties of a knight:

> *To be pure, honest and faithful,*
> *To protect the Church,*
> *To protect widows and orphans,*
> *To protect all that are desolate and oppressed.*

The first line of this sermon echoes throughout Masonic ritual, particularly that of Craft Freemasonry. With regard to the second line, it is now a condition of entry into Freemasonry that a candidate must state his belief in a single God rather than a specific church. In the early years, Freemasonry was exclusively a Christian order.

When a non-Christian candidate swears his obligation, the Bible is moved to one side and the candidate's appropriate Holy Book, such as the Koran, replaces the Volume of the Sacred Law. There is a piece of Royal Arch ritual that captures the gist of line two of the sermon:

And grant that during our sojourn in this world of sin, we may overcome the powers of darkness, and ever live according to Thy Holy Will and Commandments.

Part of address during the Royal Arch installation
of the Second Principal

The third line from the above sermon could have been written for Freemasons. They consider themselves to be "sons of the widow" because Hiram Abif, the architect in charge of the building of King Solomon's temple, was "a widow's son."

And King Solomon sent and fetched Hiram of Tyre. He was the son of a widow of the tribe of Naphtali.

1 Kings 7:13-14

In the past, English Freemasons owned their own Girls and Boys Schools for children of Freemasons who had died. In more recent times, the Boys' school has been sold and an endowment charity established to pay for their private education. The Girls' school is now called Rickmansworth Masonic School and is considering becoming a co-educational establishment. The decision to move partly to an endowment charity came about from the need to have these benefits shared throughout the U.K., thus enabling children to be nearer to their remaining relatives. It moved the position away from one in which all of the Masonic support establishments were in London.

The final line of the sermon might also have been written for Freemasons, but it does create a problem for them. Charity for a Freemason is a personal matter. Non-masons may be aware of the Masonic Charities and conclude that all Masonic giving is directed inwardly, but this is not the case. Every year Freemasons give well in excess of $1.5 million to non-Masonic charities in England alone. In England, most if not all of the well-known charities devoted to the care of the young, the old, and the disabled, as well as churches, cathedrals, and disaster funds will receive donations. A little known fact is that over the years Freemasons have bought ten of the lifeboats that operate around English shores. This level of charitable work is replicated around the world including the U.S., where the amount donated to charity by Masonic institutions exceeds $1 million each day.

For the Freemason, charitable giving is not a matter for public display; it is a private affair for those who follow the teachings of the Craft and see charity as the singlemost important objective. Such are the feelings for privacy that it is not unknown for the recipient of a Masonic Charitable donation to be unaware of the source of a banker's draft.

Other reminders of Masonic ritual appear throughout the texts on chivalry. Joan Evans[14] refers to the Pontification of Guillaume Durand, and includes the following words (p. 20).

And may thy servant, armed with Thy love, tread all his enemies underfoot.

This bears a similarity to part of the third degree charge that reads:

Will enable us to trample the king of terrors beneath our feet.

The evidence is compelling. It is quite apparent that in framing the Masonic ritual the compilers have built in medieval chivalrous qualities. Freemasonry makes no overt claims to be a chivalrous organization, but this is undeniably implicit within its ritual. In the case of the Knights Templar, chivalrous requirements were explicitly built into the Order. The question that must now be addressed is, quite where does this take this investigation? Certainly, one point can be made with some degree of confidence: the Masonic ritual is pointing away from it being rooted in the activities of operative masons. If one runs with the assumption of Freemasonry going back to the earliest masons, who developed their ritual as a means of identification for itinerant craftsmen, there is a class divide built into the existing ritual. Building workmen, belonging to "no matter what" particular craft, were by definition from the third estate, the peasantry. Chivalry was a preserve of the nobility. It is simply inconceivable that working-class operatives would have access to, never mind a desire to replicate, the chivalrous mores of the upper classes.

Having punctured the argument that Masonry developed out of craft mason guilds, I have rather limited the creation of Freemasonry to some other group who must have had a good reason to go to all the trouble. The Masonic ritual of the nineteenth century speaks of "masons" engaged in the building of the "second temple" discovering the Ark which had been hidden earlier by fellow "masons." This momentous discovery is not recorded in the Bible or any other contemporaneous historical document. It is therefore fictitious, a secret, an allegory or a combination of some of these. What is known is that the twelfth century Templars excavated vertically into Temple Mount to a depth of 82 feet (25 meters) and then fanned out horizontally under the site of King Solomon's temple. This knowledge comes from the fact that in 1867, Lieutenant Warren[4] and a team of Royal Engineers retraced the steps of the Templars and found remnants of their labors such as a spur, a Templar cross and part of a lance. Therefore, we can reasonably surmise that it was the Templars who found the Ark and kept the find a secret. If this supposition is correct, then the Templars, or rather those who carried the torch after the destruction of the Templars, certainly had a good reason to create the Freemasons. Indeed they had at least two good reasons. They needed to create a vehicle to carry the Templar ethos forward, and they needed to create a record of where their "treasure" was stored, and Freemasonry can now be seen to have been designed for both of these roles. But if we are now arguing that Freemasonry developed out of the wreckage of the Templars, then there must be more evidence within the Masonic ritual and symbolism.

The clues which point towards the answers were to be found, as before, in the building known as Grand Lodge in Great Queen Street, London. The first Grand Lodge of England met in 1717 in a pub, the Goose and Gridiron Tavern not far from St. Paul's Cathedral. In 1773 Grand Lodge bought 61 Great Queen Street and in 1776 the first hall was built in its garden. In 1860, a new hall was added that is now the main hall of the Connaught Rooms. The Connaught

Rooms are named after H.R.H. the Duke of Connaught, who was the Grand Master from 1901 until 1938. The Duke was very instrumental in the building of Grand Lodge and, as discussed in the previous chapter, also attempted to purchase Kolossi Castle in Cyprus. Work began in 1927 on the present Grand Lodge and was completed in 1933; note the significant final two digits of the year of completion. Many of the nineteen lodge rooms in Great Queen Street have an eight-pointed star on the ceiling. These and other stars provide the links which, once realized, are so obvious that it is a wonder that no one has published the fact previously.

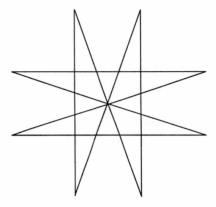

By dropping the vertical and horizontal lines, and adding small vees at the ends, we get the Templar cross.

The link is made, but more must be done to squeeze everything from this particular clue. First, we need to recall the shape engraved on the Dalle de Coume Sourde:

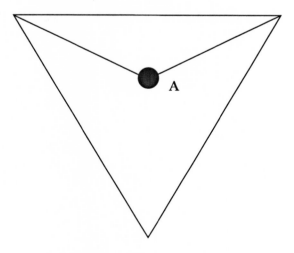

The point on the Dalle de Coume Sourde marked "A" would, if the triangle was drawn within a circle, coincide with the center of the circle.

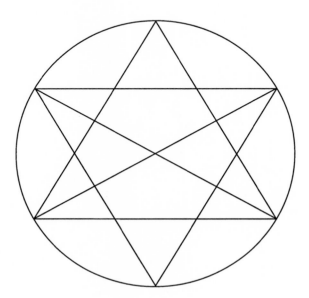

If the Dalle figure is inverted to form a Star of David, there across the center can be seen one leg of the eight-pointed star from the ceiling of the Great Queen Street Lodge rooms. Within this leg of the star are two arms of the Templar cross. More remarkably, if the leg of the eight-pointed star is removed, we are left with:

And this shape is immediately recognizable as a symbolized square and compasses.

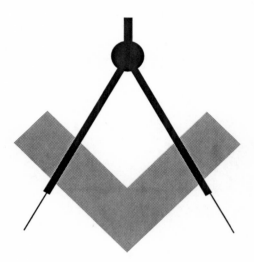

This particular maneuver with Masonic signs and symbols clears the way for what may be the convincing proof. The one manipulation of lines and signs is so obvious that even the most profound sceptic might find difficulty in refuting its significance. We must start by visualizing what the landmarks would have looked like if the 3° and misplaced Meridian errors had not crept in. The snake feature was there at Peyrolles; the circle was there, and the triangle clearly had a large part to play as evidenced by the Masonic jewels.

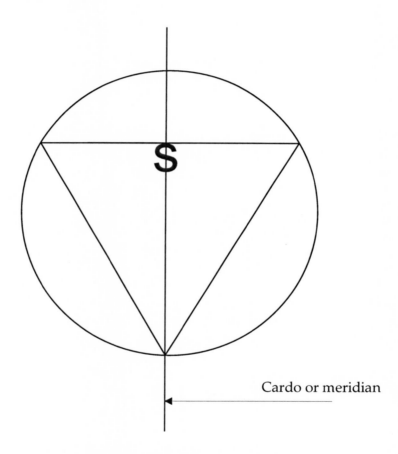

Cardo or meridian

All that needs to be added is the triangle and eye from the Grand Master's jewel.

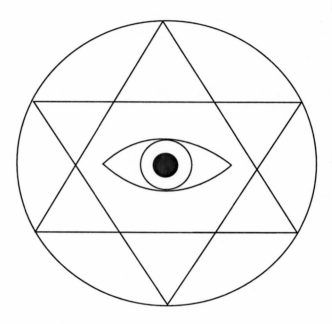

There it is then; all the signs, all of the symbols, all of the triangles, circles and squares now make sense. When you put them together, you get what those ancient ritual compilers wanted us to see—the Masonic Seal of Solomon with the Cabalistic sign of God, representing the Ark of the Covenant in Pech Cardou, at the center. It is now easy to imagine why the 3° and Meridian errors highlighted for all to see around 1780 had such a profound effect. The beautiful landmarks linked so carefully to the imagery of the jewels and signs simply did not work any more. It was back to the drawing board, and the results have all been explained.

This display of the original landmarks brings an earlier discovery into focus. In Chapter 6, a solution was given that showed Cardou to have a Gematria numerology value of 33 as in 33°. Earlier in this chapter, it was noted that the name of Pech Cardou on the 1944 IGN maps was Pech Cardon. This slight variation makes no sense until the technique of Gematria, using Hebrew equivalent numbers, is applied.

C	=	90
A	=	0
R	=	200
D	=	4
O	=	0
N	=	50
New total	=	344

which, using gematria and numerology as previously described, can be broken down to:

34 - 4 = 30

You will recall that 30° was an angle required for the first set of landmarks.

As we are on the subject of stars I should mention that there is a different star in the Great Temple at Great Queen Street. It is a magnificent light made in the form of a sixteen-pointed star. In order to create a Templar cross we need to ignore four of the shortest points of the star. The remaining twelve points can be joined to create a distinctive cross that will become more obvious as the book proceeds. Almost as if there were no other way to create the Templar cross, only angles of 45° and 60° are used. The sixteen-pointed star is nothing less that a symbolic representation of the Knights Templar cross, and it holds pride of position in the Great Temple at Great Queen Street.

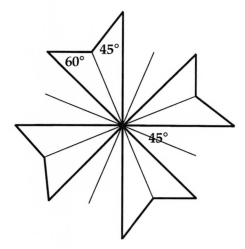

Pope Eugenius III awarded the conventual cross, the sign of the Knights Templar, to them in 1146. Before that they carried a representation of the cross of Lorraine which had been awarded to them by the Patriarch of Jerusalem at their inception. The cross of Lorraine was said to have been made from pieces of the original cross on which Jesus Christ was crucified; and the two cross-bars are each said to be on the "Golden Mean."

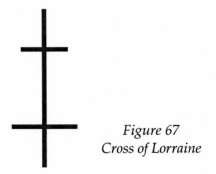

Figure 67
Cross of Lorraine

The Royal Arch Chapter fire can now be seen to point to the Templars' New Jerusalem, and the various stars in the Great Queen Street lodge rooms are symbolic illustrations of the Templar cross. The ties between the two groups, Freemasons and Templars, are becoming stronger. Even the 45° angle in the Grand Master's Jewel can be seen to represent the angle in the Templar Cross. An explanation is still required to explain the relevance of the "point, triangle, circle" in the Chapter fire. Just such an explanation is easy to construct.

If there was a circle, let us say from the early fourteenth century, then it was there to define a new Jerusalem with Pech Cardou at its center. The triangle similarly was part of the original landmarks which were built into the early Masonic ritual. The canted square was included later to correct the surveying error made by Cassini, or whoever laid down the Paris Meridian. A geometrical technique was needed to move the size of the circle eastwards to permit the Meridian to pass through its center. It is a tribute to the skills of these surveyors and mathematicians that the solution included a circle of fourteen and a half kilometers or nine miles diameter. It had clearly been intended to cement the importance of Pech Cardou by having the Paris Meridian run through it: the link between Jerusalem and Pech Cardou would thus have been cast in perpetuity. However, just like their predecessors who had positioned the snake at Peyrolles, they did not have the necessary surveying equipment to do so. The lesson to be learned thus far is that nothing was done without some deeper meaning, and we now need to return to the layout used at Pech Cardou: to move the center from the summit of the mountain onto the line of the Meridian. We already understand why this technique was used, but how does it link us to the Knights Templar?

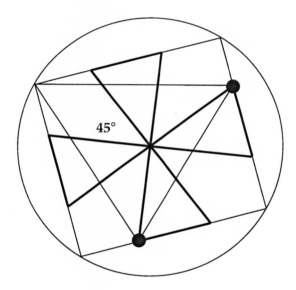

Yet again the sheer brilliance of these designers is breathtaking. The points where the triangle touches the square provide the launching points for a Templar cross where the angles between the arms of the cross are 45°, just as is shown within the compasses on the Grand Master's jewel.

In order to complete this examination of Masonic symbolism we need to revisit the six-pointed star, the hexagram or Seal of Solomon. It has already been demonstrated how this represents France, where the site is located, but there is more to tie us back to the Templars.

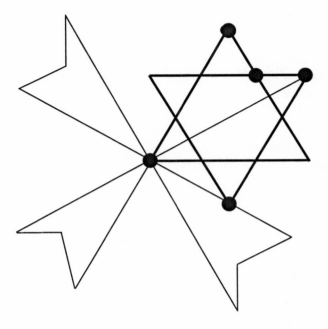

Once again, the sheer beauty of the solution is breathtaking. One can only wonder in awe at the time that must have been expended to produce two such elegant symbolized solutions. It is now clear that, within Freemasonry, nearly all stars lead back to the Templars. The pentagram identifies a fourth part of a Templar cross; the six-pointed star enables a Templar cross to be "grown" from the side, and the eight-, twelve- and sixteen-pointed stars provide the complete Templar cross.

It is at this point, before closing the chapter, appropriate to examine two more relevant geometrical shapes. The first, the purpose of Euclid's 47th proposition in the Past Master's jewel, can be disclosed. There, at the heart of the Past Master's jewel, is the fourth part of a Knights Templar cross. If one were to put four triangles together to make the square indicated by the dotted lines, one would finish up with the complete Templar cross. In terms of the way the solution has been arrived at, it is equally true to say that the fourth part of the Templar cross is in the fourth part of a circle. And what is the fourth part of a circle, no less than an angle of 90° or a square. The ritual really has taken us full circle.

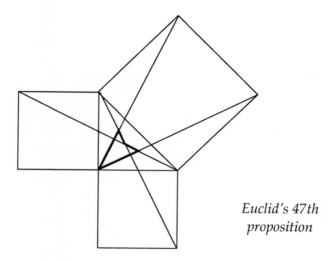

*Euclid's 47th
proposition*

It is worth exploring, before leaving this examination of Templar symbolism, where the source of these symbols might lie. We have already been drawn gently into Jewish mysticism through one of its arms, Cabalah, and there is a part of this mystical branch of Judaism that includes the very shapes that permeate the Masonic rituals— the ten *sefirot*.

1. Keter   The Supreme Crown, the unknown deity.
2. Hokhma   Wisdom, the location of the primordial idea of God.
3. Bina   Intelligence, the organizing principle of the universe.
4. Hesed   Love, the attribution of goodness.
5. Gevura   Might, the attribute of severity.
6. Tif'eret   Beauty, the mediating principle between the preceding two.
7. Netzah   Eternity.
8. Hod   Majesty.
9. Yesod   Foundation of all power active in God.
10. Makhut   Kingship, identified with *shekhina* or prescience.

It is immediately possible to identify the three pillars from Craft and Royal Arch ritual: Wisdom *(hokhma)*, Strength *(gevura)* and Beauty *(tif'eret)*. From this we can deduce that Beauty refers to the Patriarch of Jerusalem, Strength to the Grand Master of the Knights

Templar, and Wisdom to the Grand Master of the Knights Hospi-taller. The logic behind the allocation of "Wisdom" to the Hospi-tallers is simply that they were wise enough to move their order to the island of Rhodes and thus avoid the fate of the Templars. The ten *sefirot* become even more significant when they are seen transposed onto the human body. The triangular shape of the three pillars at Pech Cardou can be seen to connect Wisdom, Strength and Beauty. The fourth part of a Templar cross is evident when Love is joined to the other three.

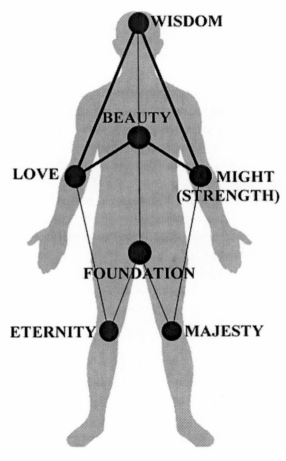

Figure 68
Seven of the ten Sefirot

The ten *sefirot* are more usually found, within Cabalah, on the "Tree of Life."

NOTE D = DAATH

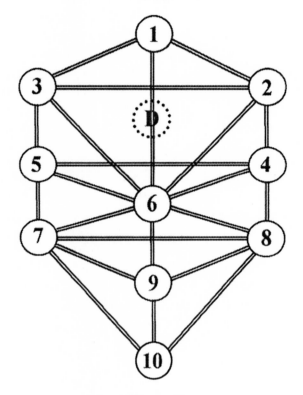

Figure 69
The Tree of Life

Rheeders[39] explains the ten *sefirot* on the "Tree of Life" as representing personality traits (spheres 7–10), soul (spheres 4–6) and spirit (spheres 1–3). The twenty-two interconnecting paths, one for each letter of the Hebrew alphabet, define the relationship or feelings generated by the two spheres. As shown in Figure 68, each sphere and path is also identified with a part or organ of the body. Put rather over-simply, Cabalah is the understanding of this complex of interrelationships between spheres and branches.

There is an additional "sphere" shown on Figure 69 as "D" or Daath; and this is a gateway to the dark side of each of the spheres. The whole "tree" is thus three-dimensional with each facet having two sides, light and dark, good and evil. The closeness of this word to "death," the name given to the Hebrew character Nun, which featured on the "Plate of Gold" and also to the Masonic Knight Templar banner of Candia, which you will recall was also given the word "death," poses the question of whether the choice of "death" is deliberately pointing us towards the Cabalah. It is within Cabalah that the Archangel Michael is described as "at war with the serpent," and the serpent is identified with Samaël. This is the same Samaël about whom Reverend F. de Castells' comments[20] were discussed earlier in Chapter 7. Colin Law[37] states that within the Cabalah, Samaël is identified with the serpent from the Garden of Eden; he is the source of "all of the nastiness in the world." Law also asserts that Samaël appears in different guises as the "Dark Angel" and more particularly, the Angel of Death. Cabalists are apparently divided over whether Samaël should be placed at the head of the demonic hierarchy or treated as the less attractive side of human nature. There is a saying that, before leaving this brief foray into the world of the Cabalah, somehow catches the essence of the Cabalistic concept:

> When someone stands in the light but does not give it out, then a shadow is created.

The idea is that it was God who **gave** us life, and to understand God we must act like Him and **give** to others, and that is a fairly clear statement of what Freemasonry has to teach.

I would like, before leaving this particular chapter which has taken us through the rich symbolism of the stars, to tuck in one more legend that seems to have a role in this story. Freemasonry is at least three hundred years old, and many would argue that it is a lot older. Over the years many legends, theories, and assorted books and papers have been published offering various ideas on how the Order started. Surely amongst all of these, there is something that supports the author's thesis, and there is. There have over the years been a number of publications suggesting that Freemasonry originated from the Knights Templar[16]. The official line has always been gently to distance Freemasonry from this idea.

> *Many well-meaning but misguided historians, both Masons and non-Masons, have tried to prove that Freemasonry was a lineal descendant or a modern version of the mysteries of classical Greece and Rome or derived from the religion of the Egyptian pyramid builders. Other theories reckon that Freemasonry sprang from bands of travelling stonemasons acting by Papal authority. Others still are convinced that Freemasonry evolved from a band of Knights Templar who escaped to Scotland after the Order was persecuted in Europe. Some historians have even claimed that Freemasonry derives in some way from the shadowy and mysterious Rosicrucian Brotherhood which may or may not have existed in Europe in the early 1600s. All of these theories have been looked at time and again but no hard evidence has yet been found to give any of them credibility. The honest answers to the questions when, where and why Freemasonry originated are that we simply do not know. Early evidence for Freemasonry is very meagre and not enough has yet been discovered—if indeed it even exists—to prove any theory. The general agreement amongst serious Masonic historians and researchers is that Freemasonry has arisen, either directly or indirectly, from the medieval stonemasons (or operative masons) who built great cathedrals and castles.*
>
> The Grand Lodge of England Internet site

In the mid-eighteenth century, an eminent French-domiciled Scottish Freemason, Chevalier Michael Ramsay, asserted that all Freemasons were crusaders[31]. It is however in the legend of Enoch[31] that perhaps the clearest clue as to what is in Pech Cardou exists.

The legend of Enoch, the seventh of the Patriarchs, says that he was inspired by God to build into Mount Moriah nine brick vaults (the reference to the number nine hints at Templar involvement). These brick vaults were said to have been built perpendicularly one above the other. In the lowest vault, he placed a gold triangle with 18-inch (.5-meter) long sides on top of a marble cube. Engraved on the golden triangle was the word "Jehovah." The reader will notice the similarity here to the section of Holy Royal Arch ritual discussed in Chapter 6. In order that his secret would not be lost, Enoch constructed two pillars above ground to mark the spot. One pillar was made of marble, and one of brass. If one were to speculate on what is inside of Pech Cardou, then nine brick vaults, one above the other, has to be among the favorite suggestions. Albert Mackay[31] also reports on Talmudist tradition, which suggests that when King Solomon built his temple at Jerusalem, he constructed an underground vault to store the Ark of the Covenant during times of trouble and unrest. Just as in the legend of Enoch, there was in this vault a cube of stone on which the Ark stood. Within the ritual of the Royal Arch, the double cube of white marble supports the "plate of gold."

Ashlars

1. The Masonic ritual has strong evidence of being underpinned by a chivalric code.
2. The charitable aspects of chivalry are central to Freemasonry.
3. The chivalric devotion to widows and orphans is mirrored within Freemasonry.
4. The Knights Templar excavated below King Solomon's temple.
5. The star symbols within Freemasonry point to the site at Pech Cardou.
6. The star symbols within Freemasonry either contain or are linked to Knight Templar crosses.
7. A Past Master's jewel contains a reference to the Templar cross.
8. Masonic symbolism appears to have roots in Cabalistic symbolism.
9. The "official" explanation of the origins of Freemasonry states that no one knows how Freemasonry originated.
10. There is an ancient tradition, the legend of Enoch, which seems to describe what may lie within Pech Cardou.

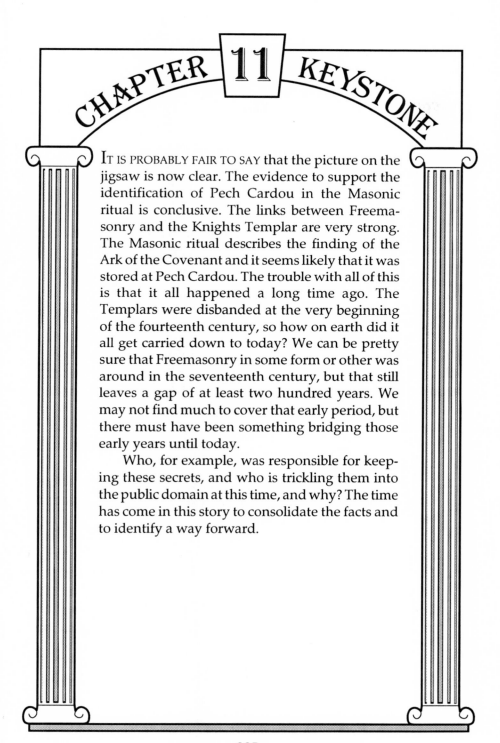

CHAPTER 11 KEYSTONE

I<small>T IS PROBABLY FAIR TO SAY</small> that the picture on the jigsaw is now clear. The evidence to support the identification of Pech Cardou in the Masonic ritual is conclusive. The links between Freemasonry and the Knights Templar are very strong. The Masonic ritual describes the finding of the Ark of the Covenant and it seems likely that it was stored at Pech Cardou. The trouble with all of this is that it all happened a long time ago. The Templars were disbanded at the very beginning of the fourteenth century, so how on earth did it all get carried down to today? We can be pretty sure that Freemasonry in some form or other was around in the seventeenth century, but that still leaves a gap of at least two hundred years. We may not find much to cover that early period, but there must have been something bridging those early years until today.

Who, for example, was responsible for keeping these secrets, and who is trickling them into the public domain at this time, and why? The time has come in this story to consolidate the facts and to identify a way forward.

WAITING

Minds that are to our minds as ours are to those beasts that perish,
intellects vast and cool and unsympathetic, regarded this earth with
envious eyes, and slowly and surely drew their plans.

H. G. Wells, *The War of the Worlds*

S THIS STORY HAS UNFOLDED, I have deliberately concluded each chapter with a summary of the conclusions drawn from that particular chapter. Some of these conclusions are strong assumptions, but many are facts which can be replicated or measured by anyone. They can be summarized as follows.

1. The Royal Arch Masonic ritual contains a coded message based on an angle of 33° which identifies Pech Cardou.
2. The Royal Arch symbol, the triple *tau*, "A place where a precious thing is concealed," fits neatly over the three pillars on the site on Pech Cardou.
3. Close to Pech Cardou is Camp Grand, and the distances between the two and the nearby Château is a 1:2:3 relationship.
4. The Masonic Craft regalia also contain clues that point to Pech Cardou, but using different angles, one of 3°, and another of 60°. Combining the two sets of landmarks, it is possible to identify a circle of 9 miles (14.5 kilometers) diameter almost centered on Pech Cardou.
5. For approximately two hundred years there was only Craft Freemasonry, and it was not until around 1730 that the Holy Royal Arch degree made an appearance.

6. Circa 1750 it was apparent to cartographers that the Paris Meridian did not go through Pech Cardou. Some fifty years later the Order of the Knights Hospitaller came under severe attack from the French authorities.

7. The quarried feature on the side of Pech Cardou resembles the Masonic first degree tracing board.

8. There is a 2-mile (3-kilometer) long snake feature at Peyrolles, which is necessary to locate Pech Cardou.

9. Ignoring the 3° error, had the Paris Meridian gone through the site on Pech Cardou, it would also have split the snake.

10. A variation, for magnetic north, of 3° west of true north existed at the end of the fourteenth century.

11. There is an equal and opposite 3° "error" in the layout of the gardens to the Luxembourg Palace.

12. The 9-mile (14.5 kilometer) diameter circle is clearly marked on the IGN map 2347 Quillan scale 1:25,000 by 33 ordnance survey points exactly on the line of the circle.

13. The nine-mile diameter circle also matches the circular map of Jerusalem held at the Royal Library at The Hague.

14. The Masonic ritual includes a reference to two spheres with maps of the heavens and earth, as an amendment to the Biblical story.

15. Early books of Masonic ritual leave little doubt that early masons found the Ark of the Covenant.

Within these fifteen items, there is more than enough evidence to confirm a link between Freemasonry and Pech Cardou; it is therefore appropriate here to examine the various hypotheses and/or assertions and speculations being put forward. In making a start on this process, I am attracted to a philosophical framework put forward by a Franciscan monk, William of Ockham (1285-1348). "Occams razor," as it is called, asserts that "if there is more than one explanation, the simpler theory is to be preferred."

One thing that must be made clear is that I am only claiming to have satisfied the hypothesis that the Masonic ritual identifies Pech Cardou. The existence of a temple in Pech Cardou can be readily resolved by physical exploration. If a temple is there, the question of whether the Knights Templar or Hospitaller created it can be confirmed or denied by archaeological examination. The available evidence does, however, point to a Templar involvement. Whether the Ark of the Covenant was ever stored in the temple may or may not come to light if the temple is uncovered. If the marble altar is there, it will go a long way to confirm the suggestion. Finally, the existence of a conspiracy to record for posterity the route taken by the Ark of the Covenant by allocating lines of longitude will only be confirmed if someone with the secret knowledge breaks rank and confirms the suggestion. It is probable that in the interim period those in positions of authority on matters of cartography will continue to assert that the whole thing is one big coincidence; this approach will always provide for an element of doubt to remain.

The existence of the IGN, in this investigation, is almost unhelpful for it leads to a possible conclusion that the linkage was created by them. Perhaps that is indeed the intended conclusion which they wish to be drawn. That said, one thing is certain: based on the evidence of the IGN maps, the Masonic ritual identifies Pech Cardou. This claim can confidently be made, with or without the 33 ordnance survey points that describe the nine-mile diameter circle. The weakness in the argument is the IGN maps, and this problem will not go away. We are used to accepting a map produced by a National Cartographer as being something as certain as death and taxes. Can we be as certain with the IGN map? The answer must be no. It has to be no because the data are not consistent through time. I have established that points such as "Pech de Rodès" and "Les Crêtès d'al Pouil" did not exist on the maps published between 1950 and 1970. Either they were there prior to 1950 but then hidden, or they have never existed and are figments of the imagination of staff at the IGN or the relevant local authorities.

Notwithstanding the clear reservations, the facts are that the angles, the ritual, the regalia, that quarried snake feature, and the Masonic symbolism all point to Pech Cardou. From here on, however, we are into the area of speculation. Too many books seem to settle for sensationalism at the expense of rigorous analysis. A hypothesis is speculated, a few supporting bits of information listed, and the matter is accepted as proved only to have yet another supposition built on top. Before long, the whole unstable argument has lost track of where it started, and matters become entrenched as fact simply because enough people have repeated them parrot fashion. I will at least try to avoid this pitfall.

This is, in essence, a historical debate, and because of that, it is particularly difficult to separate fact from fiction. The investigation, thus far, has already identified the subject as a possible secret and, if that conjecture is correct, then it is likely that false trails will have been laid. The contacts, so far made with the IGN and Cypriot Ministry of Antiquities, tend to support the idea that there is something in the knowledge surrounding these matters which these people are reluctant to disseminate. It is a fact of life that the mention of the word "conspiracy" drives people who should know better into prepared bunkers muttering, "I don't believe in conspiracy theory." We are asked to suspend disbelief and accept that there have never been any conspiracies in the whole of recorded history. The reality is that human beings conspire all the time. Secrets are power, even if the power is simply being party to some knowledge that others lack. To be taken into another's confidence and to thus join a select few who know a particular secret performs the same boost to an individual's level of self-esteem as being invited to join a select club. Having accepted the *danegeld*, whether in the form of secret knowledge or matchless membership, any doubts that an individual might have are soon replaced by a warm glow of self-righteousness, generated by the psychological attribute called "cognitive dissonance."

Historical research brings its own intangible problems. There are the uncertainties which surround the quality of any data that might come to hand. What were the motives of the people who created the records which archaeologists or archivists then uncover and assess? How can we know whether anyone, in ages gone by, has sifted through the available records and destroyed any that did not suit his particular cause. In reality, we will never know, and for that reason we must move forward only on the basis of what we can find and what we can measure. In the final analysis, we must collect as much information as possible and then compare it with the other available contemporaneous data. After the due process of critical analytical academic disputation, a consensus of the best assessment of what really happened in the past will hopefully emerge. Let us now turn to some of the other conclusions—or ashlars—that cannot be defined as facts.

1. The 9-mile circle alludes to the Knights Templar.
2. IGN has ties to the Knights Hospitaller.
3. The Royal Arch ritual describes the finding of the Ark.
4. The Templars were rumored to have found the Ark.

In the case of the "9-mile circle alluding to the Templars," it would be hard to find another more plausible explanation for this circle than a reference to the nine founding Templar knights. The region did accommodate some 30% of their total world-wide properties, many of which are still standing today.

The juxtaposition of those strange "beehive" shaped structures, the capitelles, supports the contention that the Pech Cardou location had something to do with Templar activity. Furthermore, it was doubtless a French person who added the nine-mile diameter circle of 33 data points to the map; so why use miles if not to highlight something that predated their own metric system? The red marble *"serpent rouge"* feature must be taken seriously, for no one would build that for a joke. The Templar map at The Hague is almost the icing on the cake. The historical fact that the region around Rennes-le-Château had a strong Templar presence during their years of existence provides a logical explanation. It was most likely that the circular arrangement of local mountains, together with the positional similarity of some of them to those around Jerusalem in Israel, enabled the Templars to identify this area as their New Jerusalem. The close proximity and 1:2:3 locational relationship of Camp Grand to the site on Pech Cardou seems to link the area not only with Templar activity but to further confirm the link with Freemasonry. It would however be necessary to establish the long-term existence of Camp Grand before one could confidently include this particular point in support of the argument.

Questions have been asked about data originating from the IGN, but these data certainly support the premise of a link between the Knights Templar and Freemasonry, rather than to deny it. The question of "links between the IGN and the Knights Hospitaller," and for that matter the Paris Observatory, are there to be seen. It could of course be argued that it is impossible to move in Paris without tripping over a hospital, military or otherwise, and this is to some extent true. That said, although there are indeed more hospitals per square mile than in most cities, the proximity of the two Paris IGN offices to Paris hospitals looks to be more than mere coincidence.

The suggestion that the "Royal Arch ritual describes the finding of the Ark of the Covenant" is necessarily a matter of opinion. What was described in the ritual as having been found, was "a parchment" containing Moses' law, and the "word" engraved on a plate of gold. As a metaphor, the "word" can readily be seen as representing God, from Biblical references.

In the beginning was the Word, and the Word was with God, and the Word was God.

John 1:1

The use of the term "engraved on a plate of gold" can also be pointing towards the Ark of the Covenant which, according to Biblical references, was covered inside and out with gold. We thus have two separate allegorical descriptions, either of which could refer to the Ark with an equal measure of symbolism. Although I am comfortable with this as a reference to the Ark, even without the further evidence of the early ritual, others may not be. My late, in terms of this investigation, acquisition of early books of Masonic ritual does appear to confirm this conclusion, but there is a weakness in this statement. If the apparent "facts" are there to be read by anyone curious enough to purchase the old books of ritual, why haven't the Masonic historians acknowledged this information? There is clearly something suspect in the data which will doubtless surface in time. These caveats imply that it cannot be taken "as read" that the Royal Arch ritual identifies the finding of the Ark, but it is another brick in the wall that may in time constitute a proof. There is anecdotal evidence that the Templars were "rumored to have found the Ark," but so what? This information is of little value other than as perhaps a small piece of mortar in the wall. It is however apparent that within the ranks of Freemasonry—and in the context of this book we must include the Hospitallers—something happened at the beginning of the eighteenth century. Whatever this event was, it brought about the introduction of a new Masonic ritual called the Holy Royal Arch Chapter, and this clearly included the number thirty-three.

The quarried features on the side of Pech Cardou are pillars that closely resemble the first degree tracing board used in a Craft Freemason's lodge, and they have exactly the same orientation as the four cardinal points of a compass. The three pillars that are visible in this quarried feature may, or may not, symbolically represent the three "pillars" who ruled Jerusalem, namely the Patriarch, the Grand Master of the Knights Templar, and the Grand Master of the Hospitallers. The site on Pech Cardou with its pillars at the front seems to be a Knights Templar monument or perhaps even a temple. The inclusion of two Grand Masters *and* the Patriarch of Jerusalem do support the contention of the site being the Third or Grand and Royal Lodge.

The nine-mile diameter circular area has references to *Borde,* a word remarkably close to border, around the circumference. The "Templar map" at The Hague is one "fact" that supports the Knights Templar link independently of the IGN. It also endorses the creation of a circular Jerusalem in the Roussillon, a region historically dominated by the Knights Templar. This circular piece of land could have been the Templars' Jerusalem created by them when the original was lost in 1291. These are all small pieces of conjecture and speculation, but they are all mutually supportive. The evidence is building up and it all points to a Templar "Jerusalem" in the Roussillon. It would be wholly wrong to suggest that this final point has been proved because it clearly has not. What I can, however, claim is to have made a strong case for the proposition. It is at this point, from a less than secure foundation, that we shall springboard to the next supposition. If, and the word "if" is worthy of repetition, if the above were to be true and the Templars did build their Jerusalem in the Roussillon, then it is inconceivable that they did not also build a temple; the idea of a New Jerusalem without the temple is hardly realistic. And if they built a temple it could only have one purpose, and that was to hold the image of God, the Ark of the Covenant. There would be no other reason to build a temple and no Ark, no temple and very little reason for another physical Jerusalem. The term "physical Jerusalem" is deliberate and is intended to distinguish it from the metaphorical concept of a New Jerusalem as a better way of life. The conceptual New Jerusalems exist, *inter alia*, in the form of the various Christian denominations which touch many of our lives. What appears however to have been considered in the Roussillon, and the Templars must be prime candidates to have done the considering, was a physical new Jerusalem with the same layout of mountains, roads and buildings. In fact it does not require any great imagination to identify a reason why they should want their region to resemble Jerusalem from the air. Seven hundred years ago only one individual could look down from the heavens and that was God. Perhaps they felt that because they had moved His mercy seat, by making the surrounding countryside look similar to Jerusalem, God would find it easier to revisit the Ark.

One would be perfectly entitled at this point to suggest that I have just committed every crime that I denigrated at the beginning of the chapter, and you would be absolutely right. But, there is a purpose, albeit a little circuitous. The basis of this part of the book must rest on conjecture, the collection of a number of random facts that point to a conclusion. The difference with this particular investigation is that the conclusion is in fact provable. Either this temple is there or it is not. If it is there, then it is reasonable to accept that the arguments used to get to that conclusion are robust. If it is not there, then it is back to the drawing board for me. Sooner, rather than later, someone is going to break through the wall that prevented David Wood[8] from continuing further. In total, there are four cave entrances on Pech Cardou including the ancient mine to the south. There is a cave indicated on the top of each of the two pillars and another on the north side. It is essential that whoever takes on the task of investigating what is inside of Pech Cardou has good pot-holing or climbing experience because it could be a dangerous journey. If this secret place exists, then notwithstanding any natural and man-made obstructions, there may be other obstacles to deter unwelcome visitors.

If the Templars did build a temple, it would have been at the center of their "New Jerusalem." If the Templars built a temple, it could only have had one purpose, to hold what would have been their most precious possession, the Ark of the Covenant. It might even still be there today. The Knights Templar were rumored to have harbored a desire to build a temple on the plans of the Biblical book of Ezekiel[35], so it is possible that the inside of Pech Cardou has been hollowed out to form just such a temple. Alternatively there may be a series of descending arches on the lines of the Legend of Enoch. Either way, if this is so, then the Ark of the Covenant has rested on a cube of marble for hundreds of years in the Inner Sanctum or the lowest arch. These are conclusions of immense interest, but a question remains.

The Knights Templar were destroyed in 1307 by King Philip IV of France and formally disbanded by papal decree five years later, so who carried this secret information through the years to around 1600 when Freemasonry came into existence?

It has never been suggested that all of the Knights Templar were executed. There is evidence to show that even in France, and few if any executions took place outside of France, it was only the older Templars who were left like "tethered goats," and of these not many more than one hundred were burned alive. There were substantial Templar organizations in England and elsewhere that would have been perfectly capable of establishing a covert organization. These covert orders could have operated from within or outside of the Knights Hospitaller order into which some of the ex-Templars transferred. Other authors have explored this possibility, and it is not a line of argument that this book will develop. There is a story that, just before the arrests in 1307, a hay-wagon left the Paris temple. The story continues that this hay-wagon contained several knights and the treasure. Later, it was confirmed that the Paris temple treasury funded the internment of the Templars awaiting trial. This clearly contradicts any suggestion that the hay-wagon made off with the Temple funds. The question that follows is, what then was the treasure that was referred to? I have already speculated, from an entirely different line of reasoning, that it could have been the Ark of the Covenant, and it is apparent that if it was not, then it was something of similar importance that has also failed to see the light of day. The proposition has already been posed that successive generations have selected a few people as guardians of the secrets of Pech Cardou. These select few appear to have passed the secret down through the ages, and this argument is now quite strong. Presumably from among those select few, some allocated the number thirty-three to the line of longitude that passes through Kolossi castle on the island of Cyprus.

We can now turn our minds back to the Roussillon. Pech Cardou clearly had earlier "mystical" connections, and there are a number of "standing stones" both on it and on the surrounding hills. There was indeed a large Celtic community in the Roussillon at around 2000 B.C. Whatever it may or may not have been before, the indications are that Pech Cardou now contains a Knights Templar temple, and it probably did contain, and may even still contain, the Ark of the Covenant. The contention that this site was chosen by the Templars to realize their ambition to build a temple on Ezekiel's or Enoch's plan is not really surprising. It would have been a perfectly normal decision to build underground: the Templars certainly had the necessary expertise, and Pech Cardou is composed of soft limestone which is a very suitable rock for tunnelling.

It was not until the fourth century that churches were built above ground and Glastonbury lays claim to being the first, albeit of wattle and daub construction. The Templars had skills aplenty in tunnelling because this was one of the techniques used to bring down the walls of besieged cities. They would tunnel underneath the wall and when they were ready they would set fire to the supporting props. When the props burned away, the wall would fall down. This is a technique still used today by some demolition experts to demolish factory chimneys. The Templars had the will, they had the knowledge, they had the site, and they had the manpower. It is certainly easier to argue the case that they did construct their temple at the center of their very own Jerusalem than to find reasons that would have prevented them from so doing. If they did build their temple, then there would be some evidence.

Evidence of the existence of tunnelling work inside of Pech Cardou comes in Wood's *Genisis*[8]. This book recounts Wood's search for the golden numbers, which he thought would identify the site of "the treasure." The poignancy, for Wood, is that in his travels throughout the Roussillon he did climb Pech Cardou. Without realizing the implications, he dropped a ranging rod, a painted pole used in surveying, down a hole on Pech Cardou. Exploring further, to recover his pole, he records:

> *About ten feet into the cave was a vertical shaft, approximately eight feet deep, which led into a chamber.*

David Wood came so close to uncovering the secret that had occupied his life for several years. He encountered a brick wall in the chamber, and that prevented him from looking further. In addition to Wood's encounters with tunnels, the IGN map indicates three cave entrances, plus in the southeast corner of the mountain is an ancient mine. If the ancient mine is the entrance to the temple inside Pech Cardou, then someone has ensured that no one will find a way through. Only some 15 feet (4.5 meters) into the mine entrance, someone has dropped the roof leaving tons of rock as an impenetrable barrier to exploration. There then is the evidence required: Pech Cardou has clear indications of tunnelling work in its interior. Furthermore, it is also possible to perceive signs of control over this whole secret. Just north of the Paris Observatory and also on the Paris Meridian is the French National School of Mining, in the gardens of the Luxembourg Palace. I have already indicated that the Palais du Luxembourg holds some special place in this mystery. No one can make a formal inquiry about this matter without "the guardians" finding out first.

Those writers who have published accounts of their search for the answer to the Roussillon mystery have pursued many clues that can now be seen to have been red herrings. One blind alley was the pentagram or five-pointed star. Some investigators have spent many hours in fruitless attempts to fit a pentagram over something meaningful. They have drawn pentagrams over each and every Templar site in the region to try and find the point where the treasure is buried. Others have gone further, and Rennes-le-

Château is littered with tunnels, to the point where the authorities have banned them. The trailing of this particular red herring was particularly well thought out. We are however now able to construct a more plausible explanation for what Abbé Saunière found during one of his walks around his parish. Perhaps he explored one of the caves on Pech Cardou and discovered the temple and, if so, we can speculate where he went with the knowledge—to the gardens of the Luxembourg Palace. In this eventuality, he was probably paid well to keep quiet. The suggestion that Saunière found the entrance to the temple in Pech Cardou from within a cave is not as outrageous as might at first appear. One of the strange things that Abbé Saunière did, and he did several, was to build a grotto in his garden. It does not appear to lead anywhere, and many have searched. But if we return to the earlier use of puns and language substitution we find that "*grotte*" in French means "cave" in English. As if to make the point well, if we change languages and reverse the process, "*cave*" in Latin means "beware" in English. Was this what the Abbé was trying to tell us?

Abbé Saunière holds a pivotal role in this mystery; indeed it may never have existed without him. No one, then, who undertakes to try to solve the riddle, can avoid wondering exactly what it was that triggered Saunière off. Perhaps my next discovery holds the clue.

I have already shown that the Templars set about the creation of a massive 2-mile (3-kilometer) long caduceus on the ground to tell God that they had moved his "mercy seat" or "Word" to their "New Jerusalem." But in order to complete the structure the Templars needed a supply of rock with which to create the tail of the snake that would coil around the imaginary staff made by the *cardo* or meridian. This provided the opportunity that they needed to send God an even stronger message. On the side of Pech Cardou, the very mountain inside of which they had created their new temple, they decided to recreate Golgotha—at last, an even stronger and very demonstrable link with the Templar map held at The Hague. This map you will recall had Golgotha—which means "skull"—sited in the same relationship as Pech Cardou in the "New Jerusalem" in France.

The Templars carved a massive skull in the side of the mountain which God would be unable to miss as He looked down on the earth below. The skull shape was fairly secure from discovery because there it is not overlooked and so no one could accidentally chance on it. To make doubly sure that it was not discovered, the skull shape was invaginated: that is to say it was carved as a "mold." One might, for example, make such a "mold" by pushing a skull into a bowl of plaster and removing it when the plaster has set. Thus the three pillars are the skull's two eye sockets and the mouth or it may perhaps be the nose opening. These same three pillars would be seized upon later as the basis for the Masonic ritual which would forever incorporate a skull in its ritual. The realization that Pech Cardou was the Templars' new Golgotha, within their New Jerusalem, brought that masonic symbol—the triple tau—back into my mind. Roman crucifixion crosses are generally assumed to have been "T" or tau shaped. Thus the crucifixion of Jesus Christ and the

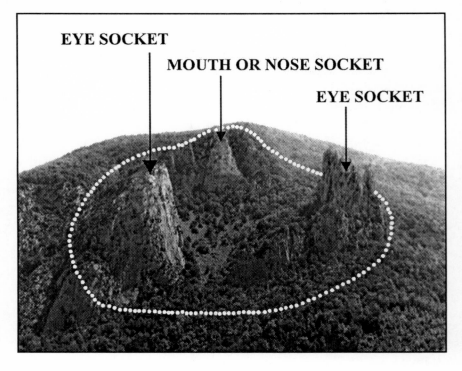

Figure 70
Skull quarry on the side of Pech Cardou

two thieves could be represented by a "triple tau." If this argument is developed, then this site of an invaginated skull, on Pech Cardou, is also the place where the triple tau fits neatly over the three pillars. They were certainly leaving nothing to chance in identifying this site in their "New Jerusalem" as Golgotha—the hill in the original Jerusalem, in Israel, where Jesus Christ was crucified.

It was just when I was flushed with the success of finding another important clue in this mystery, that another, better one came along. It had only been after staring at the picture of the "quarry" on the side of Pech Cardou and trying to make sense of the many references to "mirror images" in this mystery that the inverted skull shape dawned on me. In my endeavor to obtain a picture of the site, as viewed from above, I approached a contributor to the Priory-of-Sion Internet group at http://members.xoom.com/priory_sion, Tim Maidment. He agreed to attempt to create a computer image of the site as viewed from above. Within a day of receiving my high resolution scan of the photographs included in this book and some others that are not, he e-mailed me an astounding message. He wanted to know if I had noticed the carved "head" just in front of the left-hand pillar? Needless to say I had not. But there it is. When you've had it pointed out to you, it is hard to understand how you missed it before. Perhaps here is the explanation regarding Abbé Saunière's remarkable discovery, for, having found the head, the rest follows.

The identification of Pech Cardou within the Masonic ritual has led me to the conclusion that it is within this mountain that the Templars built a temple to house the Ark of the Covenant. This temple, hidden for centuries within the mountain, may very well have been the mysterious cache found by Bérenger Saunière. It may be that the Abbé, known for his long treks through the countryside, stumbled upon yet another treasure, one that some might argue was every bit as amazing as the underground home of the Ark.

The priest may eventually have realized that the surface of Pech Cardou bears a 40-foot (12-meter) high monumental carving of the head of Christ. The man of God would have felt he was witnessing a miracle of immense proportions on the day he first discerned the features of Jesus Christ hewn on the rocky slopes of what must have come to appear as a magic mountain. It is now clear that the

Figure 71
Carved head on the side of Pech Cardou

Figure 72
Carved head with vegetation airbrushed out

challenge to his faith, by contact with the esoteric elite of Paris, was insufficient to divert him from his subsequent actions.

There are two aspects of the sculpture that make its purpose undeniable. First, it is staring at the left-hand pillar indicating that this pillar may be the one called "strength" and where the Ark of the Covenant has lain for seven hundred years. Second, it is placed— where else—but on the temple of the inverted skull, the second Golgotha that requires the presence of the sacrificial lamb. While Pech Cardou bears this remarkable impression of Jesus, viewers can but conjecture on the motivation behind the enormous labor put into creating the carving. Possibly the Order born out of love for the Messiah quite simply wanted to blazon His likeness throughout the second Holy Land they had dedicated to His glory. Or perhaps, in a less sophisticated time, the knights of the Order, creating their haven in the Roussillon, wished to send up an enormous flare to be noticed by the Father, a form of saying, "Your Beloved's features mark the spot where the Ark lies hidden here in the New Jerusalem we've built to Your glory." If the Templars carved the form before 1307, I can appreciate their exquisite line of reasoning. The Ark of the Covenant equals the eternal presence of the Lord: Jesus Christ, Emmanuel, God with us, also represents the living deity. Thus, from a metaphorical stance, the Ark and the Anointed One can stand in each other's place.

From the available evidence it does seem likely that it was the Templars who created the carved head, and this points to it being a representation of Jesus Christ. There is, however, another candidate. The carved head is situated, as has already been mentioned, on the temple of the inverted skull and, if one had a mind to create a pun, one might easily come up with:

"It is the head **on** the Temple."

Which easily becomes

"It is the head **of** the Temple."

This would make the model for the head none other than Jacques de Molay. Those Templar sympathizers of old may alternatively have left a massive memorial to their last Grand Master Jacques de Molay, sitting forever staring at the site of his priceless charge—The Ark of the Covenant—the charge that in the end brought about his most painful death.

The opportunity that the carved head presents to confuse the last Templar Grandmaster and Jesus Christ is not a new idea, viz. *The Second Messiah* by Knight and Lomas. Nonetheless, I choose to see the head as that of Jesus and I believe I am not alone in that decision. The Guardians of the Ark would have an even greater incentive to keep silent about the temple of their spiritual predecessors if the former location of the relic bore an image of the Son of God: with Rennes-le-Chateau becoming a focus of world-wide interest, someone would eventually make out the massive carving hidden beneath the bristly underbrush of Provence.

In light of the above, I'm now inclined to give credence to the rumors about former Priory of Sion Grandmaster Pierre Plantard's having purchased land in the area and having made plans to be buried there. Baigent, Lincoln, and Leigh always saw Plantard as a man with a rich sense of irony. I am sure that he would find satisfaction in knowing he will await the final trump in the "New Jerusalem," the shadow of Pech Cardou. Millions would wonder why he had sought out this obscure site, but to his fellow bearers of the hidden tradition, the choice would be one more secret to be shared among the select. The ultimate candidate for the carved head will have to await scientific analysis. To try and determine whom the head is a "likeness" of will to a large extent necessitate ascertaining when it was carved. The need for privacy carries with it an ability to keep unwanted people away from the site and that would probably place the carving prior to 1307 when the Templars lost their authority to police any site. Thus a pre-1307 date points to the "head" being that of Jesus Christ, if for no other reason than prior to that date Jacques de Molay was just another Grand Master of the Temple. The carved head is there on the side of Pech Cardou; I've indicated whom I believe it to represent, Jesus Christ—the Son of God.

Arguably from the perspective of this book the location of a head, carved many centuries ago, serves to cement the Templar and Masonic ties. The carved head is indicating that the site is that of Golgotha and I argued in Chapter 8 that the fit of the triple tau over the three pillars is also hinting at Golgotha being the likely location being replicated here in this New Jerusalem.

Ashlars

1. Fifteen measurable facts identify Pech Cardou from the Masonic ritual or as a consequence of it.
2. The French cartographers, the IGN, seem to play a central role in this investigation.
3. Conspiracies happen.
4. The region around Rennes-le-Château held some thirty percent of the world-wide Templar property holdings.
5. The three pillars on the side of Pech Cardou might represent the three effective "rulers" of the Holy Land, the Grand Masters of the Templars and the Hospitallers and the Patriarch of Jerusalem.
6. There is a massive skull carved into the side of Pech Cardou, the three pillars being the eye and mouth sockets, representing Golgotha—to let God know that the Templars had moved his "mercy seat" to the New Jerusalem in the south of France.
7. There is a head carved into the site on the side of Pech Cardou which identifies the site as Templar because it is placed on the temple of the inverted skull.
8. The head is staring at the left hand pillar which could be the one called "strength" where the Ark of the Covenant has been stored for 700 years.
9. The head is probably a representation of Jesus Christ.
10. Alternatively the head may represent Jacques de Molay, the last Grand Master of the Templars.
11. If the temple is found to exist within Pech Cardou, it strengthens the argument that it was built to hold the Ark of the Covenant.
12. Previous explorers in search of the Templars' "treasure" have located caves inside of Pech Cardou.

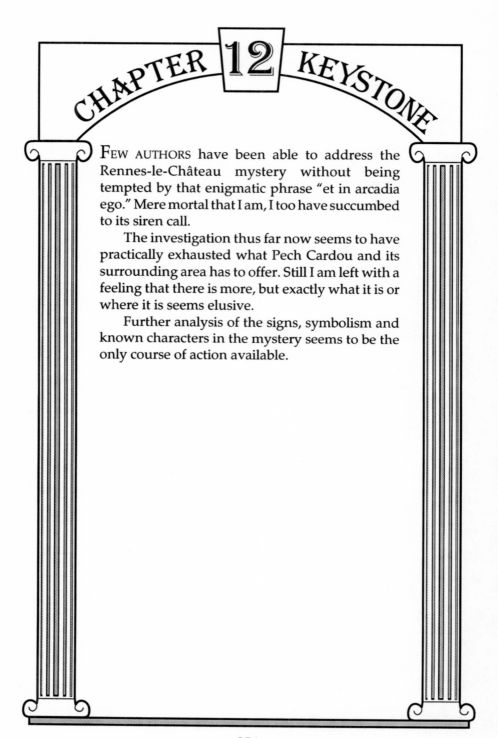

CHAPTER 12 KEYSTONE

FEW AUTHORS have been able to address the Rennes-le-Château mystery without being tempted by that enigmatic phrase "et in arcadia ego." Mere mortal that I am, I too have succumbed to its siren call.

The investigation thus far now seems to have practically exhausted what Pech Cardou and its surrounding area has to offer. Still I am left with a feeling that there is more, but exactly what it is or where it is seems elusive.

Further analysis of the signs, symbolism and known characters in the mystery seems to be the only course of action available.

ET IN ARCADIA EGO

Then she fell on her face, and bowed herself to the ground, and said unto him, Why have I found grace in thine eyes, that thou shouldest take knowledge of me, seeing I am a stranger?

Ruth 2:10

B Y THE TIME the Renaissance painters got to work on the pentagram mystery, scarcely a painting could be commissioned without something leaning against something else at 72°. It was as if the word had gone around that if one did not include the 72° symbol, one was not *in the know*. In reality, those who trailed the clue were pointing to the fact that 72° is the fifth part of a circle and must be multiplied by five, which is the number of arms on the star shape. It is the circle that one is meant to look for. The other attribute of the pentagram is the quarter part of a Templar cross, the unique shape necessary to find the location of the circle. Snezana Lawrence, in the Summer 1998 issue of *Freemasonry Today*, gave a detailed account of the "magical" qualities of the pentagram. Very interestingly for this investigation, she highlighted the fact that all of the angles in a pentagram, 36 and its double 72 and triple 108, all add up to 9 using numerology. $3 + 6 = 9$; $7 + 2 = 9$ and $1 + 8 = 9$. Her further point, that all of the intersections in a pentangle are on the "golden mean," makes it clear why she concluded that:

An imaginative observer of these geometrical phenomena might wonder if he or she hadn't stumbled on one of the Great Geometrician's fundamental building-principles!

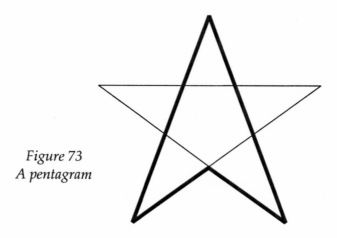

Figure 73
A pentagram

Wood[8], having failed to identify any site of worth, concluded that the significance of 72° lies in the fact that, subtracted from 90°, leaves 18°. He argued that 1 and 8 represented the ancient Egyptian gods from which modern religions derive. Other authors such as Knight and Lomas[6] picked up on this theme and developed the anti-Christian polemic somewhat further. It is not the purpose of this book to question Christian tenets any more than one might question the Christian ideals of those Templar Knights who allowed themselves to be martyred for their cause. Religious belief is a matter for each individual to decide. The only written coded message which I have been able to identify outside of Masonic ritual is:

ET IN ARCADIA EGO

This particular message appears in various paintings by Poussin, also in Guercino's—"Et in Arcadia Ego." Many of the investigators of the Rennes-le-Château legend spent a lot of time analyzing this Latin phrase. Some concluded that the word *sum* should be added to complete the sentence and permit a suitable anagram to evolve. My solution is more simple and, if correct, much more profound. It has already been shown that those who compiled the Masonic ritual and developed all of the allegorical clues were wont to use phonetic exchanges. In this instance, one must try to imagine how a Frenchman might pronounce the words "et in arcadia ego" if he had no knowledge of tutored Latin pronunciation. It would sound rather like

ÉTANT ARC Á DIEU AIGU

Étant is the present participle of the verb *être* and means being or existing. *Arc á Dieu* is quite obviously an allegorical reference to the Ark of God, the Ark of the Covenant. It also explains how the ritual compilers came up with the Royal Arch degree. *Arc* in French means a part of a circle just as in English, in an architectural sense, it means an arch. Arch in French is *Arche*, which, although from a different Latin base, also means Ark as in Ark of the Covenant or Noah's Ark. Using phonetic substitution the phrase above becomes:

Exists - Ark of the Covenant - sharp

Which is readily "fleshed out" to

[It] exists [the] Ark of the Covenant [look] sharp.
Or,
It exists, the Ark of the Covenant, look carefully.

Experience with the work of those ritual compilers of old leads me to conclude that this is not good enough. The first two parts are satisfactory but the *aigu* does not fit well. There is however another solution.

By introducing a new paradigm using two languages within the same phrase, we get as a first stage:

It exists, the Ark of the Covenant EGO

With this new paradigm the word "ego" remains initially in Latin. To complete the decoding using a second language we translate the word "ego" straight from the Latin into English, and we now get:

It exists, the Ark of the Covenant, I

Hardly any better until we revert to the phonetic exchange for the word "I" and it becomes:

It exists, the Ark of the Covenant, eye.

This can be developed one stage further to:

It exists, the Ark of the Covenant, look!

The sheer brilliance of this clue is now clear to see. There is a place where an eye can be seen on its own: it is the most conspicuous place within Freemasonry—between the compasses on the Grand Master's jewel. Further support comes with the Grand Lodge symbol *yôhd*, for although this is generally accepted to represent the English letter "Y," the absence of vowels in Hebrew means that *yôhd* can also represent "I" as in ego. The message, so publicly displayed for so many years, is now clear.

IT EXISTS, THE ARK OF THE COVENANT, LOOK TO THE FREEMASONS.

Now that the message is clear, one may see how cleverly Poussin teased us. He even went so far as to show the Ark of the Covenant in *La Pesta d'Azoth* sitting on the podium in the town-square. This phrase, "**on the** podium in the town-**square**," can easily be shortened to "on the square," a Masonic reference if ever there was one. In Poussin's second painting of *The Arcadian Shepherds*, the academic interpretation of the tomb with the words "et in arcadia ego" engraved on the side is "even in paradise there is death." In the next chapter, the reader will be able to see that in the painting this tomb is placed within the circle of the Templars' Jerusalem in the Roussillon—paradise indeed.

Other intellectuals, painters, writers and philosophers were aware of Pech Cardou as evidenced by the clues that they left behind. The allocation of the 33° line of longitude to Limassol and Kolossi castles on Cyprus is but one apparent example of the invisible hands of people in positions of power who seem to be able to order events to create a permanent record of something important. I have suggested that this important something may be the whereabouts of the Ark of the Covenant. In addition to this level of control over matters geodesic, between 1300 and 1600, some of them wrote books or painted pictures that clearly refer to Pech Cardou. Who were these people and what bound them together? It is difficult to conclude that they anticipated that anyone would be able to solve the riddle on the basis of one or two clues. This leaves egoism, the need to say to the world at large, "I know something that you don't," or some greater plan made up of many small pieces.

Returning to Nicholas Poussin, a French painter who lived from 1594 until 1665, Poussin was from Les Andelys in Normandy and set off for Paris at the age of eighteen in order to develop his painting skills. The next chapter will examine Poussin's paintings in more detail and identify the clues he left behind.

It has already become clear that the Palais du Luxembourg has an important role to play in this investigation. This role will assume even larger proportions in Chapter 15. For this reason I was drawn by the knowledge that Poussin worked with Philippe de Champagne at the Luxembourg Palace. The possibility of a Champagne connection appeared interesting, but on further examination Philippe turned out to be just another Belgian artist. That still left a connection between Nicolas Poussin and the Palais du Luxembourg that needed further examination. While working on the decoration of the Palais, Poussin must have come in contact with the new owner, Marie de Médici, who was the King's mother and had recently returned from exile in Blois. It is, of course, possible that during this exile she gained knowledge of—what is looking rather like—a "Champagne secret" and that she later gossiped about it. We shall never know, and it is apparent that any link between the Luxembourg Palace and the Court of Champagne is far too tenuous to bring into the debate. Poussin finally went to Italy in 1624 and appeared to want to establish himself in the Italian Baroque style. It was from the same area of Italy that the powerful de Medici family had its base. In the 1630s Poussin turned to Arcadian scenes, and it is particularly his work from this period that will be examined in the next chapter.

Law[37] attributes the Medici family with the introduction of Cabalah to the Western world. During the second half of the fifteenth century, Lorenzo de Medici instructed Marcelio Ficini, the head of the Florentine Academy, to cease work on the translation of Plato's dialogues and to set about translating the *Corpus Hermeticum* into Latin. These manuscripts had probably come into Western hands around 1200 during the Fourth Crusade's sacking of Constantinople and had now found their way to Florence. The *Corpus*

Hermeticum is attributed to Hermes Trismegistus and forms the foundation of the Hermetic tradition. Hermes Trismegistus is now believed to be a mythical amalgam of the Greek god Hermes and the Egyptian god Thoth[38].

It was at this time that migrating Jews, fleeing the King of Spain's death threats, descended on Italy as well as other European countries. They brought with them the Cabalah. The Count of Mirandola, Giovanni Pico, commissioned translations of the Cabalah and did much to publicize the results. Another intellectual of the time, Johannes Reuchlin, went so far as to learn Hebrew in order to understand the Cabalah. It was from this heady brew that Hermetic (as opposed to Judaic) Cabalism evolved. A note of caution is necessary here on the question of dates. For although the above comments appear, from Internet entries, to be the perceived wisdom on the origins of Western Hermeticism, the late fifteenth century does seem late for the introduction of Cabalism. There was a well documented[73] and large settlement of Jews, in what is now the South of France, centered on Narbonne, as early as 750 A.D. where they stayed until King Philip IV ejected them from France in 1306. So it is probable that Western knowledge of the Cabalah existed long before the end of the fifteenth century. Perhaps the *Corpus Hermeticum* came into Italian hands from their friends at the Court of Champagne; certainly the French nobility were in the vanguard of the sack of Constantinople.

There is a Champagne connection with Crétien de Troyes (Christian from Troyes), who wrote the original Grail legend with *Le Conte du Graal*. Crétien also worked with the Count of Champagne and with the Count of Flanders. It is Crétien's character, Perceval, in the Grail romances who is referred to as the "son of a widow." Hiram Abif, the architect who, according to Masonic ritual, built King Solomon's temple, was also the "son of a widow." Crétien claimed to have received the outline of the Grail story from Philippe d'Alsace, Compte de Flanders, who had "numerous and close connections with Scotland." From 1124 to 1165 there existed a policy of settling Flemish migrants into Scotland.

The Court of Champagne, and to a lesser extent the Court of Flanders, echo throughout this investigation. Indeed, it was Pope Urban II, himself from Champagne, who proposed the First Crusade to recover Jerusalem. It was also from the Court of Champagne that Hugh de Payens and the Count made their pilgrimage to Jerusalem and set their minds buzzing with plans for the future. It was from the Court of Champagne that the first nine Knights Templar originated. It was the friendship of the Count of Champagne with St. Bernard, also from Champagne, that earned the Templars their early approbation from the Pope. It is therefore appropriate to understand a little about them.

Roger Price[18] provides a source of historical information in this respect. It was Theobald the Bold (940–996 A.D.) who seized control of Blois and founded the line of the Counts of Blois. His successor, Eudes II (996–1037), annexed Sancerre in 1057 and Champagne itself between 1019 and 1023, thus creating a principality that ranked alongside Flanders in strength. The relative strengths of Flanders and the combined Blois Champagne represented a threat to the Capetian Kings, the line to which Philip IV belonged. Blois Champagne achieved its zenith under Theobald IV, also known as the Great (1125–1152), but the lands were divided after his death between his sons, Theobald V (1152–1191) and Henry (1152–1181). The principalities of Champagne and Flanders became close as a result of the famous and successful Champagne fairs that were held from around 1100 until about 1400, where cloth was traded in large quantities. Flanders had a large and prosperous textile industry. In 1284, Joan of Navarre and Champagne married Philip IV's son, Louis X. When Louis became King, the region of Champagne was absorbed into the crown estates of France. The Court of Champagne was abolished along with the rest of the nobility and Royal household during the French revolution (1789–1799).

There is one fact about Champagne that one would not bother to mention other than in the context of this investigation. This concerns the capital city of Champagne, Troyes. It was at Troyes that the Knights Templar received Papal ratification of their order, and it was at Troyes that the Court of Champagne was based. Troyes is pronounced the same as "trois" meaning three, and three is to Freemasonry as grass is to meadow; one cannot go far without touching it. As the academics within the Court of Champagne at Troyes began to translate more of Plato, Pythagoras, and the Cabalah, and uncover the importance of the number three, they must have felt that God Himself had placed them at the center of creation. Looking back, it is easy to understand how they might have come to that conclusion.

There is another possibility. Might it just be that King Philip the Fair's attack, which led to the destruction of the Templars, was simply part of a plan to absorb Champagne into the Capetian Empire? He would doubtless have been aware of the Court of Champagne's "interest" in the Knights Templar, because kings tend to know everything as there are always those who will gain patronage from telling them. Philip, during the period 1293 until 1297, had striven to break his two most dangerous subjects, the King of England and the Count of Flanders. He was less successful with Edward I, but did at least get the King to render homage for Guienne. The commercially and industrially prosperous Flanders was, however, severely punished both militarily and financially. Not a man to fight on two fronts when three were available, Philip clearly had ambitions to bring Champagne into Royal ownership; he did, after all, marry the daughter of the Count of Champagne. It is at least possible that, in order to keep the Counts of Flanders and Champagne apart, he planned the war of words against the Templars. This, he would have known, would preoccupy the Court of Champagne and take their eye off the ball that was to be bowled against Flanders. Once Philip had started the hare running, there was little to prevent him from going all the way and helping himself to a slice of the Templar wealth.

There is another possibility that cannot be discounted but for which any proof is unlikely to surface. The alternative suggestion is that Philip IV was after the Ark of the Covenant all along. He would undoubtedly have known about it, as has already been mentioned, because of his almost unlimited power of patronage. His obsession with ensuring that his grandfather Louis IX was canonized, his continual emphasis of his divine right of rule, and exercise of control over the Pope, all point to an overwhelming compulsion to gain "divine" recognition. There is some support for this proposition from Philip's earlier actions. Only a year or two before his moves to destroy the Templars, he had suggested that the Templars and the Hospitallers be combined into a single unit, with himself as the first Grand Master of the combined organization. The Grand Mastership would thereafter be the hereditary right of the Capetian kings. Philip's actions in this respect do support the idea that the Templars had something which he wanted. If this analysis is correct, then ownership of the Ark of the Covenant would have been irresistibly attractive to him. It may be that Philip somehow felt threatened by the preceding royal lines. The Merovingians and Carolingians both claimed direct descent from the House of David and therefore, according to popular thinking at the time, Jesus Christ.

Returning now to the main theme of this book, it would obviously be wrong to assume that whenever the words *et in arcadia ego* appear, the writer is privy to the underlying meaning. Evelyn Waugh gave the title *Et in Arcadia Ego* to the first book of *Brideshead Revisited*. He was however pointing to the idyllic lifestyle of the two main characters when they were at Oxford. Arcadia was the Greek mythical land of shepherds, made famous by Publius Vergilius Maro, whom we know better as the Roman poet, Virgil. Virgil was in fact drawing on an earlier work by Theocritus, a Greek poet. Based on the notion that Jesus Christ was the shepherd of his flock, Arcadia is therefore an analogy for heaven. A natural interpretation of the phrase *"et in arcadia ego"* is therefore "I am in heaven." The key pointer as to whether the writer or painter is trying to give a message really comes down to its contextual use. If the phrase appears to be unrelated to the rest of the work, then it is at least likely that the writer is pointing to it as a coded message. It is as well to remember that just because a retailer offers a "square deal" does not mean that he is a Freemason.

Any investigation into the early days of Masonic ritual is fraught with disappointment. The apparent lack of documentary evidence makes dating and identification very difficult, not to say controversial. It appears that when the United Grand Lodge of England called for all written copies of the ritual to be sent to them in order that a uniform ritual might be developed, many ancient lodges burned their records. Whether this is true in part or whole is irrelevant to any inquiry. The reality is that, even if there are some worthwhile ancient documents in existence, they are unavailable.

David Stevenson[15] argues that Masonic ritual began to appear around 1600 based around the work of, and particularly the Statutes of, William Schaw, who was the Principal Master of Works to the

Crown. Stevenson maintains that "if . . . the essentials of Freemasonry did emerge around 1600, then chronological considerations alone would make it truly extraordinary for hermetic influences not to be present." Hermeticism, gnosticism and rosicrucianism are all strands of the same esoteric intellectualism that was popular in those times. They would have formed a major part of the curriculum at the School of Esoterica and Cabalism that existed at the Court of Champagne.

Stevenson further quotes that "in the religious literature of the day, 'building the temple' was frequently used as a synonym for building the New Jerusalem, the creation of a truly Godly community." He also explored another interesting aspect of early Freemasonry that might bear on this investigation. In an early Masonic ritual, "The Sloane Manuscript," Stevenson found an ancient password, "mahabyn." His research could find no apparent meaning for this word although he does offer an interpretation involving the splitting of the word into two. *Mahal* was an Indian word, known as early as 1623 in England, and derived from an Arab word meaning "to lodge." Byn or bin is of course still in use and means a receptacle. Stevenson felt that "to lodge" was significant in the sense of to stay. It does however also mean "to place" and when conjoined with "bin" it might signify "to place a container somewhere." Pursuing this theme a little further, we have a lodge as a place where something valuable is lodged or stored. This suggestion takes us immediately back to some Masonic facts established earlier.

- **The First or Holy Lodge was the place where the Ark of the Covenant was stored.**
- **The Second or Sacred Lodge was the place where the Ark of the Covenant was stored.**
- **The Third or Grand and Royal Lodge was the place where the Ark of the Covenant was stored.**

This final statement is arguably correct whether the Third Lodge was in Jerusalem in Israel or France. A further feel for the origins of the ritual comes again from Stevenson's research. He devotes a whole chapter to Sir Robert Mornay who lived from 1607 until 1673.

Mornay was given to writing to his friends about Freemasonry, and some of his letters survive. An interesting detail is that he adopted the pentagram as his personal Masonic sign. Mornay lived an interesting life, becoming involved in various plots to free Charles I and later in supporting Charles II until, with the failure of the Glencairn uprising, he fled to Maastricht in Flanders where he remained from 1657 until 1660. He died penniless, calling himself a philosopher. One of Mornay's surviving letters contains his interpretation of the pentagram using substitute Greek letters, and we have already seen how the use of substitution letters enabled the Masonic code to be broken.

Although most of the references I've read indicate that Freemasonry came down to England from Scotland, it would be wrong to overlook a recent reference that indicates a possible alternative origin. Bauval and Hancock[28] refer to Elias Ashmole, the founder of the Ashmolean Museum in Oxford, as the first man to be initiated into Freemasonry on British soil in 1646. This statement points to an English lodge being the first in the United Kingdom, one predating the first Grand Lodge by some seventy-one years: the facts, however, are less certain. As has already been mentioned, some lodges are unable to date their first meeting, although they are known to be ancient. On the basis of the available information, I stick to the view that Scotland is where the first lodges were formed in the U.K.

Turning now to that mysterious organization that seems forever to be present in this mystery, the *Prieure de Sion* or Priory of Sion. Sion is, of course, Jerusalem, so it does now appear to have a legitimate interest in the Roussillon area. Over recent years, a number of books have been published, some of which seem to be responding to information provided by this secretive organization. The theme of these books is that the Holy Grail is the bloodline descended from Jesus Christ who, it is suggested, married Mary Magdelene and sired at least one son. The introduction of Mary Magdelene, or Madeleine as the French spell her name, is very interesting. As this investigation unfolds, it will be seen that she, or at least her name, is central to the solution. From the perspective of this enquiry perhaps the most important thing about her name is her initials, "MM." For MM in Roman numerals is 2,000—the new millennium. Andrews and Schellenberger[5] develop this argument and conclude that Jesus Christ's remains are interred under Pech Cardou. The honey, in this particular trap, concerns the two coded ciphers supposedly found by Abbé Saunière.

Abbé Saunière lived around the turn of the twentieth century, but the Priory of Sion purportedly made the ciphers available more recently. The legend asserts that some treasure is buried there, and that it is the Knights Templar treasure that was never recovered when the organization was disbanded. The legend gained ground when Saunière suddenly became very wealthy and spent millions of dollars, in today's money terms, on renovating the church and other local monuments. Abbé Saunière had always promised that he would make his secret available before his death, but events dictated that this was not to be.

It is however worth pointing out that the first coded cipher, supposedly found by Abbé Saunière and released by the Priory of Sion in the 1960s, is viewed by many as suspect. I take the view that to use words like "forgery" to describe these documents is misleading. They are probably not the ancient documents which they are alleged to be, but, on the other hand, they do undoubtedly contain information that is relevant to this mystery. Indeed, if one takes a straight line from the s in the first line down to the us of the final *solis sacerdotibus*, it picks out "SATAN IS IN US." Now this may mean "the devil is in us" or "this is mischievous." It may on the other hand simply declare their belief in Catharism. This would be unsurprising because the Roussillon area of France was a major center for a Gnostic sect called Cathars from the Greek *catharos* meaning pure. The Cathars considered themselves to be Christian, but their anti-clericalism and renunciation of many Catholic doctrines brought them into terminal conflict with the Catholic Church who eventually branded them heretics.

The Cathar religion is thought to draw its inspiration from the Iranian prophet, Zoroaster (circa 630–570 B.C.) whose teachings were a major influence in the history of the religions of the world. He is credited with the concept of two opposing forces, good and evil. Zoroaster defined these two forces as Ahriman, the god of darkness or evil, and Ahura Mazda, the god of good or light.

Zoroaster's complete doctrine forecasts a final combat between good and evil which good wins. In the final judgment, therefore, all will be brought to account for the good and bad they have done through life, and punishment or reward follows. The Gnostics developed a synthesis of Christianity, Zoroastrism and Manicheism which was developed by the Persian prophet Manès around 216 A.D. Manès introduced the concept of differentiating spirit and matter and associating good with the former and evil with the latter. The Cathars developed this last theme to identify Jesus with things spiritual or good and Satan with matters material and bad. Their religious services were simple and their priests were known simply as "good men." Some though were female—*perfecta*—and they also sometimes called themselves "good Christians."

Another area of conflict with the Catholic Church was the recognition of only one sacrament, that of the *consolamentum*, which was the making of a "good man." Added to this, were the rejection of the Old Testament of the Bible, a belief in reincarnation and the use of only one prayer—the Pater Noster. St. Bernard tried an evangelical approach to the problem of bringing the Cathars within the Catholic Church, culminating in the Council of Lombers in 1165, which was a complete failure. In 1206 Dominic de Guzman, later St. Dominic, began what was to be an eleven-year mission to convert the "heretics." His mission led to the creation of the Dominican order that was to cause such inquisitional pain to the Knights Templar some hundred years later. In 1208 the murder of the Pope's legate, Pierre de Castelnau, brought forth the papal decree from Pope Innocent III that pronounced the anathema on the Cathars. This offered an indulgence worth two years penance plus the protection of the Church to anyone who killed a Cathar, thus treating this attack on the Cathars just like any other crusade against the Muslim "infidels." In 1209, as a consequence of this papal decree, an army of some 30,000 soldiers from northern Europe descended on the Roussillon and exterminated a major proportion of the population. In fact, only around ten percent of the population of the area were Cathars; however, the arrival of such a large army turned the affair into one of territorial conquest, and the local inhabitants banded together to defend their lands.

If we now return to the two coded ciphers, we can see that the
first one also carried a logotype containing the letters PS or Prieure
de Sion, the same PS as the initials of the leading mason in Royal
Arch ritual, the Principal Sojourner. This may of course be simply
another coincidence, or it could imply an involvement in the preparation of the Royal Arch ritual by the Priory of Sion. The suggestion
that the first coded cipher is a worthless forgery is not born out, as
the existence of pointers to the angle of 33° will later show. The
Prieure de Sion purports to be the forerunners of the Knights
Templar. As the relevant organization, on the spot so to speak, it
may be that they were the ones to draw to the attention of the
intellectuals and academics at the Court of Champagne, the most
likely designers of the Masonic rituals, the surveying errors discovered when Cassini published his map.

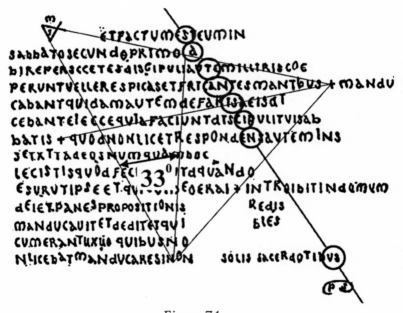

Figure 74
Parchment 1 from Rennes-le-Château showing the "Satan" message
and the 33° angle within the Dalle de Coume Sourde shape
identified by Henry Lincoln

The ritual compilers may have included the Principal Sojourner reference to the Priory of Sion as a simple thank you. The message identified within Parchment 1 by Henry Lincoln from the letters that stand above the lines is:

A DAGOBERT II ROI ET A SION EST CE TRESOR
ET IL EST LA MORT

The absence of accents makes translation somewhat flexible but it is easy to identify a translation that fits this thesis.

A DAGOBERT II	*To Dagobert*, the Merovingian king and direct descendent of the House of David—in other words a Jew.
ROI	*King* (of the Jews), the Fisher King or Jesus Christ or simply God.
ET A SION	*And to Jerusalem*, no further explanation is necessary.
EST CE TRESOR	*Is the treasure*. We have already identified "the treasure" as possibly referring to the Ark of the Covenant.
ET IL EST LA MORT	*And it is there dead*. If this is a reference to the Ark, then it is suggesting that it is "there" (wherever "there" is) and it no longer exhibits its tremendous power or glory. The "glory" was the smoke that manifested itself whenever God was going to speak from the Ark. This reference to the Ark appears in the Pater Noster, "For thine is the Kingdom, the power and the glory," etc.

Based on this premise, the literal translation becomes:

**It belongs to the God, the Jews and to Jerusalem:
it is there, but it is now just a box.**

The suggestion[5] that Jesus Christ or his son is buried in Pech Cardou is difficult to contemplate as the basis for the continued existence of the Priory of Sion. Even if the remains of a person were found, buried in the mountain and carbon-dated to thirty something A.D., what would it prove? We have no genetic material to link the body to Jesus Christ and for that matter precious little contemporaneous documentary evidence of His existence. It is extremely hard to imagine that an organization such as the Priory of Sion could continue to function in the face of these hurdles. The suggestion that the Priory of Sion was, for hundreds of years, the custodian of the Ark of the Covenant makes far more sense. It would also explain the extraordinary eminence and distinction of their Grand Masters throughout the years, who seem to alternate between two groups of individuals. On the one hand there are figures of monumental stature who, through esoterica, the arts or sciences, have produced some impact on Western tradition, history and culture. Alternatively, there are members of a specific and inter-linked network of families, sometimes noble and sometimes royal[12].

1188–1220   Jean de Gisors.
1220–1275   Marie de Saint-Clair.
1275–1307   Guillaume de Gisors.
1307–1336   Edouard de Bar.
1336–1351   Jeanne de Bar.
1351–1366   Jean de Saint-Clair.
1366–1398   Blanche d'Evreux.
1398–1418   Nicholas Flamel—the most famous of the alchemists: he dreamed of an occult book and subsequently found it, he succeeded in deciphering it with the aid of a Jewish scholar learned in the mystic Hebrew writings known as the Cabalah.
1418–1480   Rene d'Anjou—an important force behind the Renaissance.
1483–1510   Sandro Filipepi—better known as Botticelli, the renowned Renaissance painter.
1510–1519   Leonardo da Vinci.
1519–1527   Constable de Bourbon, also known as Charles de Montpensier.
1527–1564   Ferdinand de Gonzaga.
1564–1595   Louis de Nevers, also known as Louis de Gonzaga.

1595–1637   Robert Fludd—England's leading exponent of esoteric thought and the Rosicrucian movement.

1637–1654   Johann Valentin Andrea—the creator of the semi-secret Christian unions and author of the Rosicrucian manifestos.

1654–1691   Robert Boyle—his two closest friends were Isaac Newton and John Locke, who met regularly with him to study alchemical works.

1691–1727   Isaac Newton—conducted alchemical experiments with great secrecy at Trinity College, Cambridge. He learned Hebrew in order to carry out a meticulous exercise on the book of Ezekiel to produce a painstaking reconstruction of the floor plan of the Temple of Solomon.

1727–1746   Charles Radclyffe—personal secretary to Bonnie Prince Charlie. Radclyffe was probably involved with devising the Scottish Rite Freemasonry.

1746 –1780   Charles de Lorraine—the brother of Francois, Duke of Lorraine, who was the Holy Roman emperor who married Maria Theresa of Austria in 1735.

1780–1801   Maximilian de Lorraine.

1801–1844   Charles Nodier—the flamboyant mentor for an entire generation including young Victor Hugo, all of whom drew upon esoteric and Hermetic tradition.

1844–1885   Victor Hugo—prophesied that "in the twentieth century, war would die, frontier boundaries would die, dogma would die . . . and Man would live". . . "He will possess something higher than these . . . a great country, the whole Earth . . . and a great hope, the whole Heaven."

1885–1918   Claude Debussy—an integral member of the symbolist circles which included Oscar Wilde, W. B. Yeats, and Marcel Proust.

1918–1963   Jean Cocteau.

If the Priory of Sion is, or was, the custodian of the Temple in Pech Cardou, why are they drawing attention to the site? There is an explanation that fits the assortment of facts uncovered. If there is a temple in Pech Cardou, which was built for and housed the Ark of the Covenant, then it is inconceivable that the Priory of Sion would draw attention to its location if the Ark were still there. The logical inference, therefore, is that the Ark of the Covenant is no longer in Pech Cardou. What could possibly have prompted the custodians to allow such a fabulous artifact, a treasure indeed, to be moved? The timing of the moves, apparently by the Priory of Sion, to publicize events points to something relatively recent.

Another small detail that was drawn to my attention is the fact that on the published list of Grand Masters of the Priory of Sion, listed above, Rene d'Anjou ceased to be Grand Master in 1480 and Sandro Filipepi did not take over until 1483, a gap of three years. It would be wrong to make too much of this small detail other than to note that this coincides with the period—identified in Chapter 8— when a 3° error existed between magnetic north and true north in the Roussilon region of France. Perhaps whoever created the list of Grand Masters left a small clue.

It is known that during the Second World War Hitler was very keen to gain possession of the Ark. Indeed, his right hand man Himmler helped to finance an investigation of the Roussillon area by Otto Rahn[36]. In 1935, Rahn wrote to his colleague Karl Weisthor to inform him that "he was at a place where he had reason to believe the Grail might be found." That he never found it is evident, for Hitler would not have been able to resist publicizing the fact. It seems likely therefore that the Ark was moved to safety during the war. Which war I do not know, but the arguments given for the Second World War apply fairly equally to the First World War. This still does not explain why the Priory of Sion still seems to be drawing attention to the site of the temple. One explanation is that the whole Priory of Sion business is simply a smoke screen for some other organization. There is some evidence for this if we take the initial letters "P" and "S" and mirror the letters to "S" and "P." Mirroring is something which seems to be popular with whatever group is behind the gradual release of the information surrounding this mystery. Returning again to numerology we can see that "S" is the 19th letter of the alphabet and "P" is the 16th letter, giving us 1916. If the Ark was moved to safety early in the First World War to prevent it falling into the hands of the German invaders, then it is understandable that some memorial would be required, and the Priory of Sion is that allegorical memorial. If this is the case, then the use of Mary Magdelene holds out the promise of a similar date reminder because "M" is the thirteenth letter, therefore, "MM" is 1313, and that is a very credible date for the Ark to have arrived at Pech Cardou. Alternatively, it might be that whoever they sent the Ark to for safety will not give it back. This explanation also answers the question of why no eminent successor to Jean Cocteau appears to have been appointed. No Ark, no need for a Grand Master. In recent years, a M. Plantard has asserted that he is the Grand Master of the Priory of Sion, but in view of his lack of stature by comparison with earlier Grand Masters, it is not unreasonable to discount him.

The list of Grand Masters of the Priory of Sion bears a remarkable resemblance to the quality of the founders and subsequent members of the Royal Society. According to Gardner[1], early Freemasons were men of advanced learning in the fields of philosophy, astronomy, physics, architecture and chemistry. The (Royal) Society was established in 1645 and incorporated by Royal Charter in 1662 by Charles II. Early members included Robert Boyle, Isaac Newton, Robert Hooke, Christopher Wren (who built the observatory at Greenwich) and Samuel Pepys. Gardner also contends that Isaac Newton was also a member of the Priory of Sion. There is a body of opinion that considers the Royal Society to be the channel by which Freemasonry entered England. At the time at least forty members of the Royal Society, amounting to one quarter of the membership, were Freemasons. Just like Adam Smith's "invisible hand" in the affairs of economics, the hands of these men and earlier fellow travellers can be felt all over the data uncovered during this inquiry. I would like, before leaving this particular line of analysis, to show a couple of drawings that are of significance to the solution and point to others who were privy to that solution.

The first is a symbol used by Giordano Bruno, a well-known hermeticist from the sixteenth century, as the endplate to *De triplici minimo et mensura* (Fig. 41).

The equilateral triangle within the circle is tilted at 45° to the vertical. In order to get to 30°, let alone 33°, would require a most tortuous route to be taken. The triangle and circle point to this symbol being probably relevant to the temple in Pech Cardou, if for no other reason than the proximity of other relevant clues from the same source. The most likely explanation, therefore, is that it is pointing to the entrance to the temple in the northwestern pillar on

Pech Cardou. There was an alternative solution to this particular drawing put forward at the end of Chapter 7. This other explanation involved turning the drawing through 135° to disclose the layout of the original landmarks. Time alone will determine which of these explanations is correct, or indeed if both are. This symbol also appears on a page from one of Leonardo da Vinci's sketchbooks, but with Leonardo the canted square was included.

The drawing from Giordano Bruno's *De Triplici Minimo et Mensura* that holds the strongest claim to a viable clue is the hexagram and Plato's canted squares. As has been demonstrated, the concept of canting one figure within another was essential to the solution of the earlier Masonic ritual clues. Bruno's *De Triplici Minimo et Mensura* is dated at 1591, so it is timely in terms of the development of Masonic ritual. The particular interest in this drawing is that it encapsulates every geometric shape necessary for the solution to the location of Pech Cardou, both before and after the discovery of the 3° error.

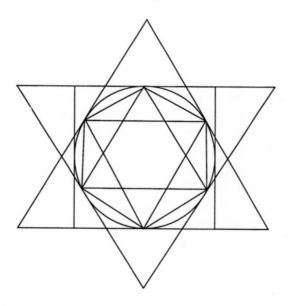

Figure 75
Second drawing from Giordano Bruno's De Triplici

Another alternative was put forward by John Robinson[16], who concluded that Freemasonry was started by fugitive Templars fleeing the wrath of King Philip IV and the Pope. He identified Francis Bacon as another eminent individual who left written clues to the existence of Freemasonry before 1717, when the first Grand Lodge was established and the Order saw the light of day. Robinson's analysis of the links between the Knights Templar and Freemasonry can only be classed as well researched, particularly for someone who was not a Freemason. If we ignore some minor errors that one should expect from a writer unfamiliar with all aspects of the Masonic ritual, we still have to acknowledge that his identification of French roots for most of the Masonic passwords and other unusual Masonic terms is impressive. Robinson builds such an array of speculative links that his thesis must be taken seriously. There are, however, two weaknesses in his final argument.

First, there is very little evidence to support the contention that for a sustained period after the Templar trial ex-Templars would have needed to remain in hiding. There was an open door policy for ex-Templars by the Hospitallers, and even many of those who had been tortured during the trial took that route. In some parts of the world, notably Spain and Portugal, a confrontation with the Church was avoided by the simple expedient of changing the name of the Order and redirecting its allegiance from the papacy to the crown. Other ex-Templars are known to have taken the route which was acceptable under the Templar Rule, that of joining monasteries.

Second, Robinson does not explain how or why a secret organization of ex-Templars was sustained and gained recruits after the original fugitives had died of old age. What possible inducement would anyone have had to join an organization for whom discovery probably meant being burned alive and non-discovery meant being consigned to the furnaces of hell after death?

Dr. Ekaterini Aristidou[41] touches on the "open door" facility offered to the Templars by the Hospitallers, and indeed uncovers evidence of an "organization within an organization" that was created very soon after the Templars were banned and several years before they were finally dissolved.

In the meantime in 1310 the Knights of St. John by the decision of their Commander Foulques de Villaret, transferred their headquarters to Rhodes but continued to keep in Cyprus a Higher Military Force "the Commanderie", with Kolossi as its Headquarters. The status of Kolossi as Headquarters of the Commanderie was confirmed in a ruling of the Chapter of the Hospital dated 1380.

In 1310, the Hospitallers had only just sailed to Rhodes and captured the island from the locals. This act would have required a large force of Hospitallers to be maintained on the island to prevent a counter-attack from one of several interested parties. The most likely explanation for the sudden emergence of sufficient numbers of Hospitallers to maintain a "higher force" on Cyprus is that the resident Templars transferred *en masse* to the Hospitallers. The creation of "the Commanderie" was clearly their solution to the problem of avoiding the Papal decrees against membership of the Templars.

Finally, the introduction into the debate of the body of Jesus Christ requires some explanation. The idea for such a red herring probably came with the evolving nature of languages, in this case the French language. The name "Cardou" is possibly a dialectal development from Cardo into *Corps Dieu*, God's body of men or God's Army. It may be that the Templars referred to themselves, if only in a light-hearted manner, as God's Army, for that is exactly what they were—perhaps not such an unlikely suggestion because the French Foreign Legion refer to themselves as such today. In time the Corps Dieu became Cardou, but there was another development. The word *corps* in French actually means a corpse; its use to describe a military cohort is simply a derivation. It is easy then to imagine how "army of God" slipped back into "corpse of God," particularly when those using the phrase probably had no idea of what was behind it. For purposes of secrecy or allegory, the particular line was developed with the aid of the Bible. John 1:1 states:

In the beginning was the Word, and the Word was with God, and the Word was God.

The actual object of all of the secrecy and the reason for the temple in Pech Cardou, it has been argued, was the Ark of the Covenant. Inside the Ark were/are the Ten Commandments, the Word of God. But the Ark itself, because of its power to speak with God's word, is referred to in the Bible as God. The Word of God and God are the same—the Ark. St. John's opening words allow for a substitution, the body of God for the word of God. This is only a reflection of Jewish belief, that the Ark was the personification of God on earth. When added to the alternative meaning of the word *corps*, the exchange is complete.

Ashlars

1. *Et in arcadia ego* could mean "It exists, the Ark of the Covenant, look to the Freemasons."
2. Poussin left many clues about the Rennes-le-Château mystery in his paintings.
3. Poussin had the necessary French and Italian connections to be aware of the answer to this mystery.
4. Troyes, in the heart of the old region of Champagne, was the seat of the Court of Champagne and is also at the very heart of this mystery.
5. The Templars may have been destroyed because King Philip wanted the Ark of the Covenant.
6. The origins of Freemasonry are shrouded in the mists of history; no one is currently able to define the origins as being from any particular source.
7. The Royal Arch "First or Holy Lodge" held the Ark of the Covenant.
8. The Royal Arch "Second or Sacred Lodge" held the Ark of the Covenant.
9. The Royal Arch "Third or Grand and Royal Lodge" held the Ark of the Covenant.
10. There is an organization which calls itself the Priory of Sion and it appears to be slowly releasing clues about the Rennes-le-Château mystery.
11. One such piece of evidence or clue is a parchment which, when deciphered, may be indicating that

the "treasure" is the Ark of the Covenant, but it no longer acts as a seat for God.

12. The purported membership of the Priory of Sion seems to confirm a link between them and the intelligentsia over the past seven hundred years.

CHAPTER 13 KEYSTONE

THIS MYSTERY IS 700 YEARS OLD and clearly refers to actions by the Knights Templar back in the first third of this millennium. And yet there are indications that it has somehow travelled through time, that it is an ongoing mystery. Certainly the Freemasons are here with us today, although very few members are aware of the full secret. Masonry itself did not appear—if we consider the shrouded time before the first Grand Lodge was formed in 1717—until the seventeenth century, well after the Templars had been destroyed. Somehow the secret knowledge had to have been transferred from one generation to the next and that has to mean that certain people were privy to that special knowledge. The tantalizing question is, who were these people? How or why were they selected? Do they still exist today? Perhaps this last question, do they still exist?, is the most relevant. If, as we can now reasonably assume, they are the guardians of the Ark of the Covenant—where is it now? Is it still in Pech Cardou, or has it been moved? If it's been moved, where to? Then there's the all-important question, is there anything else, apart from guarding the Ark, that these people are doing or trying to achieve? The best place to start is with one individual who fits near to the center of our time-frame and who obviously had something to do with this story.

NICHOLAS POUSSIN

I neglected nothing.

Nicolas Poussin to his fellow painter Abraham Bruegel

THIS CHAPTER DRAWS EXTENSIVELY from Pierre Rosenberg and Véronique Damian's book, *Nicholas Poussin—Masterpieces 1594–1665* (1995) and the Faber Gallery book, *Poussin*.

Nicholas Poussin was born into a poor farming family in a small hamlet near Les Andelys in Normandy in June 1594. Not a lot is known about his early years other than that he appears to have been encouraged to become a painter by Quentin Varin (1570–1634), who stayed in the hamlet during 1612 when he was completing some paintings for the Les Andelys church. From an early age, Poussin was determined to go to Paris to learn to paint. It was when he was still in his teens that Poussin made his first attempt to get to Paris. He was frustrated by his poverty and only made it as far as Rouen, but while he was there, a young nobleman invited him to his château to paint several pictures. The nobleman's mother, however, treated Poussin like a servant, and even at this early age his pride was evident and he stole out and continued on his journey to Paris. Once again poverty intervened, and after enduring a great deal of hardship, Poussin returned home ill and humiliated.

In 1614 Poussin set off again for Paris and this time he was successful, studying for the first month under Georges Lallemant (1575–1636), followed by a further three months under Ferdinand Elle (1580–1649). During this period, he assisted Philippe de Cham-

280

pagne, a Belgian artist, in the decoration of the Luxemboug Palace. Here, he made the acquaintance of the chamberlain to the Queen Mother of France, Marie de Médici. Poussin's biographer— Giovanni Battista Passeri—says that Marie introduced him to the Italian High Renaissance style using reproductions of Raphael, which inspired Poussin to "that light he had longed for." Marie de Médici was born in the Italian City of Florence in 1573. Her father was the Grand Duke of Tuscany and her mother Joanna of Austria. Marie married the King of France, Henry IV, in 1600 and bore him Louis (who would become Louis XIII) and five other children. Henry was assassinated in 1610 and Marie ruled as regent for their son Louis. In 1614, when Louis came of age, Marie continued to rule until some members of the French Court arranged for Marie's confidant and adviser to be murdered. Louis took control and had his mother exiled to Blois, which, with the adjacent region of Champagne, was now part of the Royal kingdom of France.

It was the Counts of Blois who, in the Middle-Ages, established the power base from which the Capetian kings, who included Philip IV, were descended. In 1619, Marie de Médici escaped and raised a rebellion that was settled when her chief adviser, Richelieu, negotiated a peace. She raised a second revolt in 1620, which was also settled peacefully. She was then allowed to build the Luxembourg Palace in Paris that stands to this day; perhaps this was to keep her out of trouble. The Palace is now used for the French Senate. When Marie was not organizing rebellions, her Court was renowned for its glamor and chivalric standards, but by 1628 she had fallen out with Cardinal Richelieu, and in 1631 she was banished from France and died in very reduced circumstances in 1641.

Little is known about the period of Poussin's life between the time he was twenty and twenty-eight (1614–1622). In consequence, they are called "the unknown years." The French *Archives Nationales* throw some light on Poussin's life, recording two deeds. The first a covenant of debt for a sum equivalent to several thousand pounds at today's value to a merchant goldsmith and dated June 10, 1619. The second deed is dated June 23, 1622, and records the fact that Poussin had not repaid the debt. At the time that this debt was incurred, Poussin was living in comfortable style in Paris, near to the Louvre.

It seems likely that Poussin, beguiled by the Court of Marie de Médici, was living above his means—perfectly understandable given his poor upbringing. Perhaps Poussin was attracted to Italy by what Marie had told him, or perhaps he simply felt the need to get away when she began her attempts to regain power. Whichever, he decided to go to Rome where he no doubt hoped that Marie's Italian ancestry would open doors for him. It is also worth noting that the Order of the Knights Hospitaller, into whom many of the Templars were absorbed, has—since 1834 under its later name of the Sovereign Military Order of Malta—had its headquarters in Rome.

Poussin made two unsuccessful attempts to get to Rome, once getting to Florence where there was some sort of trouble, and on the second occasion he got as far as Lyons, where he was arrested over the debt to the Parisian goldsmith and brought back to Paris. Poussin finally made it to Rome in 1624 at the age of thirty, and there he stayed for the next forty years, apart from a short period of four years when he returned to Paris. It was during his third attempt to reach Rome that Giambattista Marino, the Italian poet and friend of Marie de Médici, helped him. This was a period of great building and refurbishment work in Rome. Poussin received a commission in 1628 for *The Martyrdom of St. Erasmus*. This commission was to be for one of the altars in the redecorated St. Peter's. The Pope at that time, Urban VIII, was a francophile who encouraged many French painters to settle in Rome. Poussin's first major work, *The Death of Germanicus* (1627), was commissioned by Cardinal Francesco Barberini, a nephew of the Pope. Although he was carrying out prestigious commissions during his stay in Rome, Poussin appears not to have lived at a very high standard. He suffered from at least one serious illness, thought to have been syphilis, and only recovered with the help of a French confectioner, Jaques Dughet. In 1630, at the age of thirty-six, Poussin married one of Jaques' daughters, Anne-Marie, who was only eighteen, and they set up house together.

From 1631 until 1635 his brother-in-law, Gaspard Dughet, trained with him and shared the marital home in the Via Paolina, an area popular with foreign artists. Poussin was also doing commissions for fellow painters who had returned to Paris. These came to the attention of the French Court, and by 1638 the French King, ably assisted by his Cardinal Richelieu, had tempted a reluctant Poussin back to Paris. Louis XIII gave him a salary equivalent to around $300,000 a year, the title of Painter to the King, and a house in the Tuileries. For his part, Poussin designed the redecoration of the Grande Gallerie in the Louvre. Large-scale paintings were not to Poussin's liking and he had no experience of frescoes. This, however, did not prevent him from painting *The Institution of the Eucharist*, which became a favorite of the king and queen, in the Royal Chapel of St. Germain-en-Laye. The return to Paris was not a happy one for Poussin, and after the death of Marie de Médici and the war against the Protestants, he returned to Rome in November, 1642. He left Paris a lonely and defeated man, convinced that he had not received the praise that was due to him for the works he had completed. The deaths of Richelieu and Louis XIII shortly afterwards influenced Poussin's decision never to return to Paris. Poussin spent the next twenty-three years painting in quiet isolation in his house in Via Paolina, accompanied only by his wife and brother-in-law. Anne-Marie died in 1664 at the age of 52 after a nine-month illness. The loss of his wife drove Poussin deep into the bottle, and he died a year later on November 19, 1665.

It is recognized that he painted "powerful and perfectly balanced compositions." During this second period in Rome, Poussin's self-portraits indicate the assertive and noble persona that he wanted to be remembered for. He was clearly a remote individual not given to joining in with his fellows, somewhat arrogant and with a very high opinion of his own talents. It can now be seen that his paintings carried a powerful message: "I know where the Ark of the Covenant is, and you might find it too, if you look hard enough." This book has but a few examples of the various clues that he sprinkled into his works of art. These clues comprise items such as sprigs of acacia and "falls of water," all of which have Masonic significance, but more importantly, he provides regular pointers to an angle of 60°.

If Poussin's systematic clues were part of some "grand plan" as to the whereabouts of Pech Cardou, then it is now even more apparent why the Masonic ritual compilers and its guardians were thrown into turmoil by the discovery of the error of 3°. The important angle of 60° is the one to be found in an equilateral triangle which should have located Pech Cardou from the Paris Meridian. As has already been amply demonstrated, these landmarks no longer worked because of the 3° error.

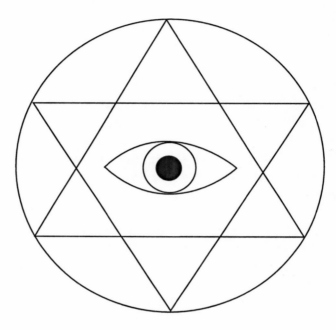

Figure 76
Original landmarks at Pech Cardou

I have been able to identify other clues in other Poussin's paintings, but I will leave it to you to enjoy the pleasure of Poussin's paintings and the satisfaction of seeking them out. You will find many a "fall of water," often from an earthenware jar, and occasionally an ear of corn adjacent to it; these symbols provide a Masonic connection because they are mentioned in the ritual. Nicholas Fouquet was the King's Superintendent of Finance[36], and in 1656 his brother Abbé Louis wrote to him about a meeting that he had enjoyed with Poussin in Rome.

*He and I discussed certain things, which I shall with ease be able
explain to you in detail—things which will give you, through Mon
sieur Poussin, advantages **which even kings would have great
pains to draw from him** and which, according to him, it is possible
that nobody else will ever rediscover in the centuries to come. And
what is more, these are things so difficult to discover that nothing now
on this Earth can prove of better fortune nor be their equal.*

One should not place too high an importance on this letter,
carrying as it does the possibility that Abbé Louis simply wanted to
impress his highly placed brother. That said, however, the contents
of this letter do support in every particular the general thesis of this
book. In his solitary pursuit of excellence, Poussin turned down
many public honors including, in 1657, the prestigious *Prince of the
Academy of St. Luke*. By 1663, at the age of sixty-nine, he wrote:

*It is with great difficulty that I reply to you, due to the weakness of my
shaking hand which no longer obeys my will, as you can see I have laid
aside my brushes forever, and my only thoughts are of dying, death
being the sole cure for the ills which afflict me. May God let it be soon,
as life weighs too heavily upon me.*

His wife Anne-Marie died first, towards the end of 1664, and
after a further year, mostly spent drinking wine, Poussin followed
her. His body was taken to the parish church in San Lorenzo in
Lucina and buried there.

There follows shortly a series of Poussin's paintings on which
various clues to the landmarks leading to Pech Cardou are highlighted. There are, in addition, a number of clearly Masonic references and these too have been highlighted. One of Poussin's most
popular means of signifying that a line is to be drawn is by the use of
a finger, hand or foot. Picknett and Prince[44] identify this technique,
albeit for a different reason, and they refer to it as the "St. John
gesture," because of its very obvious application in Leonardo da
Vinci's (1452-1519) painting of St. John the Baptist (1516) (Fig. 77).

It is also visible in the fresco of *The Last Supper* (1495-97) in the
convent of Santa Maria delle Grazie, Milan (Fig. 78). Picknett and
Prince's "St. John gesture" of an upturned index finger leads to their
particular thesis, that it identifies St. John the Baptist as senior to

Figure 77
St. John the Baptist
by Leonardo Da Vinci
Musée du Louvre

Figure 78
Detail from
the fresco of
The Last Supper by
Leonardo Da Vinci

Jesus Christ. They suggest that this gesture is evident in several other of Leonardo's paintings, including *Virgin and Child with St. Anne* (1501) and *Adoration of the Magi* (1481). They also claim to identify it in Raphael's *The School of Athens* (1509), where it is Plato demonstrating the sign. Picknett and Prince's thesis has no bearing on this investigation; however, it is apparent that the "St. John" gesture does have some significance. In the absence of any contemporary documented explanation, we can explore whether Leonardo was establishing a coding system for later artists to adopt. It is perhaps appropriate to bear in mind that Leonardo da Vinci was considered by some to have been a Grand Master of the Priory of Sion. If such a proposal were to have any merit at all, then one should expect to find some support for the suggestion in his paintings. Such support is there, and it exists in quite an explicit fashion.

Leonardo's first painting of *The Virgin of the Rocks* (1483-86) now hangs in the Musée du Louvre. In it, the outstretched finger and thumb of the Virgin's hand form a perfectly horizontal line. Furthermore, a line drawn from the tip of the Virgin's outstretched thumb to the index finger of the baby St. John the Baptist, which happens to be in the "St. John gesture," is perfectly vertical. A third line from the baby's index finger to the outstretched little finger of the Virgin completes a 30°, 60°, right angle triangle (Fig. 79). What makes this detail even more relevant is the observation that the angel is pointing unmistakably at the 30° angle just described. The triangle mirrored about the vertical axis, the original triangular landmark which would have been essential for locating Pech Cardou, is clear to see. Leonardo painted several versions of this painting, but only in the version hanging in the Louvre is the apparent coded message so clear and precise.

Wood and Campbell[36] record that "the background to his masterpiece, the *Virgin on the Rocks*, has been identified as existing on the heights of Pech Cardou." They do not, however, indicate to which version of the painting this observation applies. The mirroring about the vertical axis of the 30°, 60°, 90° triangle, discernible between the Virgin's finger and thumb and the baby St. John's upturned index finger, provides an explanation for the mirroring of the 3° angle of the gardens at the Luxembourg Palace in Paris. They also provide a possible answer for another puzzle. Wood and Campbell[36] also question why Poussin bisects various staffs in his paintings. For example, the staffs held by both shepherds in *The Arcadian Shepherds* are bisected. The foreground lifting-handle of the Ark, in *The Plague at Ashod*, is similarly bisected by the adjacent column. This technique of indicating a "break" at exactly the half-length may well have been Poussin's method of inviting the viewer to look for one half of a mirror image. In fairness, Wood and Campbell identify a totally different explanation for this eccentricity of Poussin's, if that is what it was.

Figure 79
Detail from The
Virgin of the
Rocks
by Leonardo Da
Vinci
Musée du Louvre

Before I move on to the clues in some of Poussin's paintings, I would like us to pause for a moment and consider the implications of the triangular feature implicit within da Vinci's *Virgin on the Rocks*. If this triangle was da Vinci's method of pointing to his knowledge of Pech Cardou, then we can be sure that plans for the landmarks that would later appear within the Masonic ritual were well advanced as early as 1484 when he painted it. He had curiously "disappeared from public life for several years" around that time[57], and as he was then living in Milan, it was only a short trip across the Alps to take him to the Roussillon.

This begs the question of whether da Vinci had the right "connections," and again the answer must be yes. Da Vinci was born in 1452 and, when he was 30 years old, his first Patron was Lorenzo de Medici in Florence, the "spiritual" home of the Knights Hospitaller. A year later he moved to Milan and began a lifelong fascination with military armaments. Later in life, in 1513, he was again patronized by another de Medici, this time Cardinal Giuliano de Medici, the brother of the Pope. During his time in Milan he had befriended the French king, and in 1516 he moved to his final home, Castle Cloux near Amboise in the Blois region of France. His purported Grand Mastership of the Priory of Sion was around this time, from 1510 until his death in 1519. There can be little doubt that he had close connections with the families that appear to dominate this investigation. Furthermore, his life-style was such that he could easily have accommodated a close association with the Hospitallers or any other similar group. Frère[57] is unequivocal:

> Seldom has so well-documented a historical figure so jealously guarded his intimate life.

This quotation was actually made in the context of his alleged homosexuality. Da Vinci's secrecy is put forward as being his defense against the possibility of such activity becoming known to the authorities. Homosexual practices were the subject of serious punishment at that time.

POUSSIN'S PAINTINGS

The Plague at Ashod

Figure 80
The Plague at Ashod
Musée du Louvre

Painted by Poussin in 1631, *The Plague at Ashod* is now hanging in the Louvre, Paris. Note first the use of fingers and toes to determine the line, the child in the center of the picture with upraised hand and fingers outstretched. The angles are always the same, 30° or 60°, depending from which axis one measures the angle. 30° from the vertical axis is of course 60° from the horizontal axis. This particular painting of Poussin's is especially interesting because of its bold exhibition of the Ark of the Covenant, shown here highlighted in a circle on the town square podium. A note of caution—in these representations, the angles may not be exact because the drawings have been scanned into a computer from reproductions.

The Arcadian Shepherds

Figure 81
The Arcadian Shepherds
Musée du Louvre

This was Poussin's second painting with this title and on the same theme. He painted this one in 1638, and it is also currently hanging in the Louvre. Note once again the use of fingers and toes to demarcate the line that he wishes to draw attention to. In the *Arcadian Shepherds*, we are introduced to "the site" on Pech Cardou, which can be seen highlighted in the rectangle in the top right-hand corner. Also in the rectangle, leaves from an acacia tree can be seen hanging above Pech Cardou, and the acacia has already been identified as the tree from which the Ark of the Covenant was made. At first glance then this might be suggesting that the painter is signalling that Pech Cardou has some connection with the Ark. Matters, however, are not quite that simple. It has been suggested that the sprig of leaves highlighted on this painting is not from the *acacia seyal* or "shittim tree," but rather from the *robina pseudoacacia* or black locust tree. Such comments actually raise more questions than they answer, such as why should anyone take the trouble to study such an obscure, unrelated detail on this painting in such depth? Setting aside the somewhat strange conclusion that, from the 1200 or so species of acacia tree, it is one that is native to southern North America that Poussin appears to have selected, there is an obvious rejoinder. Poussin is not known to have travelled further east than Florence. The *acacia seyal*, on the other hand, is native to Egypt, Sudan and Southern Africa. It is therefore unlikely that Poussin ever saw either of the above species growing naturally and probably worked from sketches provided by others.

The words engraved on the tomb are:

ET IN ARCADIA EGO

And this particular Latin phrase has already been analyzed. However, the kneeling shepherd is pointing to the letter "R" which just happens to be the eighteenth letter of the alphabet and

$$1 + 8 = 9$$

Eliezer and Rebecca

Poussin painted this in 1648 and, like the previous two paintings, it is hanging in the Louvre. It is quite easy to recognize in this painting the depiction of a quarter of a cross patée, the Templar cross. The various water pitchers are placed in such an orderly fashion that they cry out to have a line drawn through them.

Note also the sphere on top of the pillar; indeed, the pillar itself is worthy of a second look. At first sight it appears to be one of a pair of gate pillars, but closer examination shows no sign of another pillar or any gates or hinge brackets. The cisterns to the right of the pillar preclude there being a gate to that side because it would be obstructed. One interpretation might be that this is an allegorical reproduction of one of the pillars from the porch-way or entrance to King Solomon's temple. According to Masonic ritual, each of these two pillars was cylindrical, but with a ball on top.

On which were delineated maps of the terrestrial and celestial worlds,
pointing out Masonry universal.

From the explanation of the second degree tracing board

According to the Bible, no spheres were built on top of the pillars at the entrance to King Solomon's temple. The introduction of these spheres into Masonic symbolism can now be explained by the unusual control that the Hospitallers/Templars exert over the world of astronomy and map making in France. The IGN and the Paris Observatory are in Hospital grounds and the lines of longitude seem to have been predetermined to match a Hospitaller/Templar possession.

Figure 82
Eliezer and Rebecca
Musée du Louvre

The Martyrdom of St. Erasmus

*Figure 83
Martyrdom of
St. Erasmus*

This was painted by Poussin in 1628 and is hanging in the Vatican. Note particularly the two cherubs in the top center of the painting, which could be a symbolical reference to the two cherubim that stood on each side of the Ark of the Covenant in King Solomon's temple. Symbolic they must be, because although the plural of cherub is cherubs or cherubim, the cherubim who guarded the Ark were angels from an entirely different mould. Angelic cherubim have cloven calves feet, as illustrated on the Grand Lodge coat of arms. They also have four sides to their faces: to the front a man, to the sides an ox and a lion, and to the rear an eagle. These four faces are replicated on the four banners in a Royal Arch Chapter room. They have four wings, two to fly with and two wrapped around their bodies, with a hand at each tip. Their duty was to guard the throne of God and to keep man out of the Garden of Eden after he had been expelled. They also guarded the Ark of the Covenant. Satan was a chief cherub before his fall from grace. The man, ox, lion and eagle also happen to be the physical manifestations of the four Islamic angels. The line at 60° is clearly visible by joining the finger of the right hand cherub with the outstretched finger of the priest in the white robes. The two 30° lines can be arrived at using the rod in the hand of the statue in the top right of the painting, which is at 30°, to provide a guide for an identical line just below, based on the finger of the soldier on horseback behind the priest. This technique, of pulling out the intestines of someone whilst they were still alive, is the "drawn," from the punishment of being hung, drawn and quartered.

Tancred and Erminia 1

This is the first of Poussin's paintings of this subject, finished by him in 1630. It now hangs in the Hermitage Museum, St. Petersburg. It is the differences between these two paintings of Tancred and Erminia that draw attention to the points that Poussin appears to wish to make. In both pictures the kneeling soldier is similarly displayed apart from his hat, which in the other version is a fairly clear representation of the symbol on the ceiling in Grand Lodge— yôdh. The two cherubs are missing, as if to emphasize their appearance in the other later picture. In this painting, the 60° angle necessary to complete the triangle is now shown in full. The right-hand line delineated by Erminia's sword is exactly at 30° to the vertical, and the left-hand angled line identified by Erminia's elbow and Tancred's calf and ankle is similarly at 30° to the vertical. An inference that may be drawn from these angles is that the 3° error was either not known to Poussin, or as late as 1630 those who had directed his work did not consider it to be important. Finally, on the right-hand side can be seen what could be Pech Cardou in mirrored image, with what could be an acacia tree appearing to hang over it. Once again, Poussin is drawing the viewer's attention to mirror images, so necessary to unlock the clue in Da Vinci's *Virgin on the Rocks*.

Figure 84
Tancred and Erminia I
The State Hermitage Museum, St. Petersburg

Tancred and Erminia 2

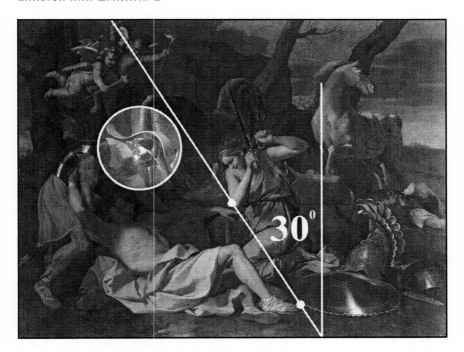

Figure 85
Tancred and Erminia II
© 1635 by Nicholas Poussin (159–1665), The Barber Institute of Fine Arts,
University of Birmingham/Bridgeman Art Library

This was the second painting with this title and subject and was painted by Poussin in 1634. It now hangs in the Barber Institute of Fine Arts, which is at the University of Birmingham, England. Note once more the two cherubs in the top left-hand corner, drawing symbolical attention to the Ark of the Covenant. Tancred's foot and the elbow of Erminia identify the line at 30° to the vertical with the sword. Interestingly, the soldier's hat forms an almost perfect *yôdh*, the Grand Lodge symbol.

The Massacre of the Innocents

Figure 86
The Massacre of the Innocents

The pure simplicity of the 60° line attracted me to this particular painting and decided me to include it. The baby's outstretched fingers and the mother's chin provide one of the clearest examples of the delineation of a line and an angle to which Poussin wishes to draw our attention.

The Death of Germanicus

Figure 87
The Death of Germanicus
The Minneapolis Institute of Arts

Poussin completed this particular painting in 1627, and it now hangs in the Minneapolis Institute of Art. Poussin uses no less than three body parts to identify the angle of 30°: the soldier's index finger (almost in the St. John gesture) and the small child's index finger and left foot complete the markers. It is almost as if he felt the need to over-emphasize the point. Alternatively, Poussin was building into the painting the reference to the number three.

First Self-portrait

Figure 88
First Self-portrait of Poussin

It is perhaps indicative of the man that he reserves the best and most obvious markers for his self-portraits. This, his first, was painted in 1649. The depiction in the background of two cherubs at each end of a box with plaited ropes over their shoulders, highlighted in this copy, cannot be anything other than a symbolic reference to the Ark of the Covenant, the plaited ropes being symbolic wings. The pen that Poussin is holding and the book subtend an angle of 30°, arguably the most obvious reference to this angle among his works.

Second Self-portrait

Figure 89
Second
Self-portrait of
Poussin
Musée du Louvre

In his second self-portrait—painted in 1650 and now hanging in the Louvre—Poussin comes perilously close to shouting his message. Note particularly how the juxtaposition of the two paintings behind Poussin; the overlapping area highlighted with a white line, describes a square. On the little finger of Poussin's right hand is a ring. On this ring is a cross pattern, the highlights of which define a pair of compasses. Thus, in this picture we have symbolically displayed the square and compasses, the badge of a Freemason. In the overlapping area of the rear painting behind Poussin is the picture of a lady wearing a tiara: clearly shown in the center of that tiara is a single eye, the same eye as can be seen on the Grand Master's jewel and on the ceiling of Grand Lodge. The message from the first self-portrait was the Ark of the Covenant, and the message from the second self-portrait is Freemasonry.

Ashlars

1. Between the time, around 1310, when the Templars were destroyed, and today, certain people have been aware of the mystery and acted in such a way as to ensure that the secret is carried forward.
2. Leonardo da Vinci was one such person and Poussin was another.
3. Both Leonardo and Poussin came into contact with the higher reaches of the church as well as the French and Italian upper aristocracy.
4. Both Leonardo and Poussin left clues in the paintings which lead to the landmarks that identify Pech Cardou.
5. Poussin also left clues that link Pech Cardou to the Ark of the Covenant and to Freemasonry.

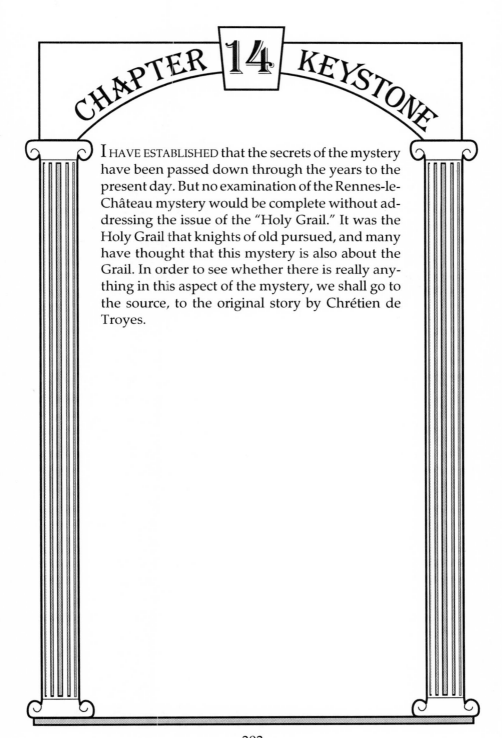

CHAPTER 14 KEYSTONE

I HAVE ESTABLISHED that the secrets of the mystery have been passed down through the years to the present day. But no examination of the Rennes-le-Château mystery would be complete without addressing the issue of the "Holy Grail." It was the Holy Grail that knights of old pursued, and many have thought that this mystery is also about the Grail. In order to see whether there is really anything in this aspect of the mystery, we shall go to the source, to the original story by Chrétien de Troyes.

THE GRAIL LEGEND

But we are more than just an economic or cultural entity, we are a
spiritual force or we are nothing. For hundreds of years our story has
been bound up with Christianity. It is our taproot to the history of
civilisation and our link with the future. From it springs our belief in
the eternal dignity of man and his right to decide his own destiny; our
belief in liberty, responsibility, duty and justice.

Margaret Thatcher to *Les Grandes Conferences Catholiques* 1978

THIS CHAPTER IS BASED ENTIRELY on the translation of *Perceval* by
Nigel Bryant published in 1982. Chrétien de Troyes, literally
"Christian from Troyes," made the first mention of the Grail
in his poem *Perceval*. The fifteen manuscripts of *Perceval*, dated from
around 1260 A.D., that survive in the Bibliothèque Nationale Paris
are the work of no less than five authors. Chrétien is thought to have
written the first poem shortly before his death in 1185. His work was
considered so important that over the next forty years four other
authors continued and developed the theme that Chrétien had
begun. The first continuator is anonymous and the name of the
second is illegible. The third writer only identified himself by the
name Manesier; and finally there is a section interpolated between
the second, the work of an illegible writer, and the third section by
Manesier. This final writer is thought to be Gerbert de Montreuil, the
author of *Roman de la Violette*.

Perceval is the story of a Welsh boy on the brink of manhood who
was brought up by noble parents in a remote area. He is ignorant of
the outside world, and to remedy this he leaves his widowed
mother behind when he sets off on horseback to see the world. The

young man, Perceval, is depicted as gifted athletically but completely ignorant of good manners or for that matter care for his mother. It is clear that this is the metaphorical story of any young man. Early in his travels, Perceval chances on a young girl asleep alone in a richly furnished pavilion, a large tent often circular. Perceval kisses her against her will and steals an emerald ring from her finger. He proceeds to eat of her food and drink his fill before continuing on his way. When the girl's boyfriend returns, he is extremely jealous and angry. He sets off after Perceval vowing vengeance and takes the girl along under the stricture that she cannot wash or change her clothes until he has settled with Perceval. Perceval meanwhile makes his way to King Arthur's castle, Cardoeil.

Cardoeil or probably "Car d'oeil" means something or other of the eye, "car" now means a coach which did not exist in the thirteenth century so it may be a similar phonetic colloquialism as that suggested for Cardou, i.e. corps of the eye. As was explained earlier, the eye is a Cabalistic cipher for God; we therefore arrive at "The Corps of God," or as we know them, the Knights Templar.

Perceval finds Arthur downcast because his kingdom is under threat from the red knight.

Red symbolizes evil

Notwithstanding Perceval's gauche demands to be made a knight, with his statement "just hurry up, then I can go," the king is amused by the young man and says:

Boy, if you live long, I think and feel in my heart that in all the world there will not be, nor will there ever have been known, a finer knight than you; so I think and feel and believe.

Thus knighted, Perceval sets off to find the red knight and, on finding him, demands his surrender to King Arthur. The red knight, angered by the silly demands of the boy, strikes him across his shoulders with his lance. Perceval responds by throwing his javelin, which hits the red knight in the eye and kills him. He then dons the red knight's chain mail, takes his sword, lance and destrier, and sets off on his travels as a knight. In the meantime, word of his prowess has reached Arthur. Arriving at a castle by the sea, he is given lodging and training in the use of his weapons by the nobleman Gorneman de Gorhaut. Gorhaut also teaches Perceval the chivalric code. This new found knowledge prompts Perceval to head home to see how his mother is. When he is part-way home, he takes lodging in a castle where a beautiful lady, Blancheflor, comes to his bed at night and confides that her castle is besieged, and due to lack of food is on the brink of defeat. Perceval behaves honorably towards Blancheflor and the following day defeats the besieger's seneschal, Engyeron, in single combat. He spares Engyeron's life but sends him to King Arthur to be his prisoner.

The besieging lord, Clamadeus, masses his forces for an attack on the castle, but the attack is repulsed. That night, a ship laden with provisions is washed up on the shore near to the castle and the threat of starvation is eliminated. As the siege is no longer a realistic option, Clamadeus challenges Perceval to single combat and, like his seneschal, ends up being dispatched to King Arthur. Although Perceval and Blancheflor are mutually attracted, he insists on continuing his journey to check on the well-being of his mother. Perceval's next lodging is at the castle of the Fisher King.

An obvious reference to Jesus Christ.

At this castle:

They led him to the lodges; and I can tell you a man could have searched as far as Limoges without finding or seeing any so handsome.

The Fisher King gives Perceval a richly decorated sword, saying that there is only one way that it can be broken. During his stay, Perceval witnesses a squire carrying a white lance which has blood oozing from the tip. The squire is followed by two more carrying candlesticks with ten candles in each, and after them follows a maiden carrying the Grail. The Grail is so brilliant that it dims the light from the candles.

There can really be no doubt that the Grail is a metaphor for the Ark of the Covenant. This is substantiated by the contemporaneous pictures that accompany the manuscripts of Perceval and show what is clearly the Ark following the Grail. Just like the "golden" Ark that "breathes" fire, the Grail shines brilliantly.

Hancock[23] refers to Wolfram von Escenbach's *Parzival*:

Where the Holy Grail . . . served as an occult cryptogram for the Holy Ark of the Covenant.

Once the concept that the Grail as a metaphor for the Ark is accepted, everything else drops into place. The Grail is in the castle of the Fisher King, which readily translates into the "Ark of the Covenant is in the temple at Jerusalem." "There are many wonderful lodges at the castle of the Fisher King" translates easily into "there are many wonderful [Templar/Masonic] lodges based on the temple at Jerusalem."

The following morning, Perceval continues his journey home and soon meets a distressed maiden holding the headless body of a knight, her lover. She castigates Perceval for not questioning the sights he has seen: the bleeding lance, the candlesticks, and the Grail. She informs him that he has missed the opportunity to heal the Fisher King's battle-crippled thigh so that he would be able to walk again. The young knight's lack of interest will cost him dearly, for she then informs him that she is his cousin and that his mother died from the grief of losing him. She also tells him that the sword will betray him and will break in battle.

This illustrative simile implies that learning and dedication are prerequisites for an understanding of the Grail, for which we can read the Ark of the Covenant, and this in turn is a representation of God. Perceval was clearly too ignorant to cope with the first test, but hope is held out that he is capable of learning. This is the fundamental Christian message that the kingdom of God is open to all who are prepared to learn its ways.

Perceval turns away from the journey home to his mother and follows the trail of the knight who killed his cousin's love. He overtakes the girl that he had earlier kissed and from whom he had stolen the emerald ring. She is in a dreadful state with her clothes in tatters. Her lover, the proud knight, returns and Perceval confesses that he is the guilty party and affirms the girl's innocence. They fight and, as forecast, the sword breaks on the proud knight's helmet. Notwithstanding this setback, Perceval triumphs and another knight is dispatched to King Arthur, but only after the proud knight has promised to restore his girlfriend to cleanliness and rich attire. At the Court of King Arthur, now at Carlion, the proud knight makes a full confession of his boorish behavior towards his love and is received into Arthur's court. Arthur decides to seek out Perceval and sets off with his barons and knights. One of Arthur's knights, Saigremor, finds Perceval deep in thought and orders him to King Arthur's side. Perceval does not hear him so Saigremor charges him, lance at the ready. At the last moment, Perceval sees the danger and unseats Saigremor, whose horse returns riderless to Arthur. On seeing this, Arthur's seneschal Kay, who upset Perceval at the first meeting, offers to fetch Perceval to Arthur. Kay is likewise unseated from his horse by Perceval, and Kay breaks his arm and collarbone in the process.

The King's nephew, Sir Gawain, then offers to use persuasion to fetch Perceval to the Court. On hearing that he has injured Kay, who had embarrassed him at their first meeting, Perceval is over-joyed and so goes to meet Arthur. After three days of celebration, an ugly hag rides into Carlion and berates Perceval for not taking his chances when he met the Fisher King. She tells Perceval that because of him, the Fisher King's wounds will never heal, the fighting will continue and many knights will die, and it is all Perceval's fault.

Perceval has now become the embodiment of all men.

Before she leaves, the hag tells of a girl besieged in a castle at Montesclaire and foretells that whoever rescues her will win the greatest honor. Sir Gawain and fifty other knights including Perceval immediately undertake to rescue her. Perceval insists, however, that he cannot accept the idea of any knight being raised above another.

Already, he is learning humility and equality.

At that very moment, another knight, Guigambresil, rides into the Court and accuses Sir Gawain of killing his lord without first challenging him. Gawain departs for Escavalon to defend himself against this accusation in trial by mortal combat. Resting over-night at Tintagel, he takes part the next day in a tournament, which he wins.

Although the "real" King Arthur lived in the fifth century, he was "reinvented" in the twelfth century by a Welsh cleric, Geoffrey of Monmouth. Geoffrey's Arthurian stories contain what was probably the first record of chivalric codes of behavior, a new concept at the time. Geoffrey quoted King Arthur's birthplace as being Tintagel.

At the next town, Gawain becomes romantically involved with a local maiden when he is recognized as the knight who killed the maiden's father, the lord of the castle. The townspeople besiege Gawain in the castle until Guigambresil rides in and lifts the siege. The King delays the trial by mortal combat for one year on condition that Gawain seeks the lance that bleeds.

Meanwhile, Perceval has been pursuing adventure for some five years during which time he has completely forgotten God. On Good Friday, he meets three knights who rebuke him for being armed on the day that Jesus died. Perceval is filled with remorse and decides to visit a hermit. He tells the hermit about his visit to the castle of the Fisher King and what he had seen there. The hermit tells him that it is the death of his mother, caused by his leaving home, that has caused his misfortune. Only his mother's prayers for him have kept him alive thus far. The hermit, who turns out to be Perceval's uncle, explains that it is Perceval's father who eats off the Grail; the King who eats off the Grail is also the father of the Fisher King.

A straightforward reference to God the Father of all, as in the Pater Noster, "Our Father, who art in heaven," etc.

The hermit counsels Perceval to go to church every day before anything else.

Love God, believe in God, worship God; honor worthy men and women; and stand up before priests—it's a service that costs little, and God truly loves it as a sign of humility. And if a girl or a widow or an orphan requests your help, grant it, and it'll be the better for you; it's a most worthy charity, so you'll do well to give them your aid; make sure you do so, without fail.

In the meantime, Sir Gawain is tricked into losing his destrier in exchange for a pack-horse. He quickly challenges a passing knight to a duel and wins his charger from him. He is welcomed into what turns out to be an enchanted castle. As he relaxes in bed, seven hundred crossbow bolts fly through the window and embed themselves in his shield. The door then opens and a lion enters which he slays. His host assures him that he has now laid all the enchantment to rest and offers him the lordship of the castle. It is however a trick, and if Gawain had accepted, he would not have been able to leave the castle again. That night, the queen leaves him with two hundred and fifty of her most beautiful girls.

This is a transparent reference to the highest level of the Muslim heaven and an indisputable suggestion that it is a deception.

As Chretien's contribution to the legend ends, Sir Gawain is being rowed across the river to face the girl who was instrumental in his destrier being stolen. She tells him that the lady in the castle, to whom he was attracted, is in fact his sister.

THE FIRST CONTINUATION

King Arthur and his Court visit Arthur's mother's castle where he agrees to the marriage of Gawain's sister Clarissant to Gawain's enemy Guiromelant; after hearing this news Sir Gawain rides off in anger. Gawain comes across the Grail castle where he tries unsuccessfully to mend the broken sword. He returns to Escavalon to report his failure and to find the bleeding lance, but another knight demands that he too wants to fight Gawain, should Gawain survive his forthcoming fight with Guigambresil. King Arthur rides to Escavalon and negotiates a peace between the knights. Meanwhile, an unknown knight is murdered close to the Queen's pavilion and Sir Gawain undertakes to complete the dead knight's mission. Once again he finds himself at the castle of the Fisher King where he again unsuccessfully tries to repair the broken sword. While Gawain is asleep, the Fisher King tells him that the bleeding lance is the one that wounded Jesus Christ on the cross and that it will bleed for ever.

THE SECOND CONTINUATION

Perceval defeats the Lord of the Horn and like the others (some sixty by now) sends him to serve King Arthur. He returns to Beaurepaire (lovely den) and rekindles his love for Blancheflor. After visiting his mother's house, he goes again to his uncle, the hermit, who shows him his mother's tomb and reminds him of his debt to God. In the forest Perceval meets a girl but loses her in the dark. During the night he sees a bright light and finds the girl again the next morning. She tells him that the bright light was the Grail.

> **Further confirmation that the Grail is the Ark by making the point that it shines brightly, as the Ark is reported in the Bible to do.**

The girl gives Perceval a ring and a white mule that will take him to the Grail castle.

> **Perceval has now been elevated to the position of the next messiah who, it is assumed, will arrive in Jerusalem in the same manner as the first: i.e., on a mule. Perhaps an allegorical suggestion that the next Messiah will not come until man behaves in proper holy manner.**

Perceval gets side-tracked into entering a tournament where he meets the girl again and returns the ring and the mule.

Perceval (man) has failed yet again.

Perceval continues on his journey and meets a child holding an apple high in a tree, the significance of which is to make him look upwards towards God. He then arrives at Mount Dolerous where he tethers his horse to the magnificent pillar at the summit. Another lady gives him lodging and shows him the way to the Grail castle. On Perceval's arrival at the Grail castle, the Fisher King tells him that only a chivalrous and loyal knight, free of wickedness, who believes in God, honors him and loves the Holy Church, can properly mend the sword. Perceval mends the sword, but there is a notch on one edge of the blade.

> Because of Perceval's wondrous earthly and knightly deeds, he is able to mend the earthly edge of the sword. The Holy Church's edge is however still broken because Perceval has not met the requirements of the Church. This is a reference to the message of St. Bernard of Clairvaux who said that a knight's sword had two edges, one to enforce earthly justice and one for the defense of the Holy Church.

THE THIRD CONTINUATION

A voice tells Perceval to return to his mother's house and on the way he comes across a circular wall with sounds of rejoicing inside. He is unable to gain access and learns that it was paradise. After various temptations he returns to Beaurepaire and marries Blanche-flor. Travelling again, in unknown lands, he takes a shield that "only the bravest knight can take." He learns that to talk during a church service is comparable to young animals devouring their mother. He also learns that some hermits were beating a cross because of the pain it had inflicted on Jesus Christ.

> Could this be why the Templars were spitting on the cross during their initiation? If so, it is strange that this straightforward explanation was not given at the time of their trial. Perhaps, on the other hand, it is simply the result of intellectual effort to find a plausible explanation for the apparently

strange deviation within the Knights Templar initiation ceremony. For this explanation to be acceptable, however, the attributed date for Chrétien de Troyes work would need to be put back. This is because it predates the destruction of the Templars which was when the details of the initiation ceremony became public. There is of course yet another explanation for the curious action of "spitting on the cross," and that is that the imprisoned Templars concocted a story that they presumed would satisfy the inquisitors and end their torture.

Perceval learns the importance of confession and, after rescuing another maiden in distress, returns to the castle of the Fisher King and mends the sword completely.

THE FOURTH CONTINUATION

The Fisher King explains the secrets to Perceval; the Grail was the vessel in which Joseph of Arimathea collected the blood of Christ whilst he was on the cross. Perceval sets off again and this time defeats the devil with black arms who throws fire; he buries him in the cemetery of three thousand knights.

This appears to be a reference to the Saracens and their naphtha-based Greek fire.

A hermit then advises Perceval against killing knights, but shortly afterwards Perceval's horse is stolen and so he rejects the advice. Perceval is then tempted by the devil, first in the form of a black horse and then in the form of the knight's own wife. A man in a boat with a white sail rescues him and his wounds are healed by the Grail. Perceval returns the Grail to the Fisher King who is healed and bequeaths his kingdom to Perceval. After ruling for seven years, Perceval retires to a hermitage.

A simple enough message, that if the Grail (Ark of the Covenant) is returned to Jerusalem, man will inherit the kingdom of heaven.

Ashlars

1. *Perceval* is a story about every man and his personal quest to find the meaning of life.
2. *Perceval* contains allegorical references which could allude to the Templars or to Freemasonry.
3. The Holy Grail appears to be a coded reference to the Ark of the Covenant.
4. The Templars' crime of spitting on the cross during their initiation may be explained as an action of spite against the structure which held Jesus Christ during his crucifixion and caused Christ so much pain. The Knights' ritual was not in any way meant to be disrespectful or sacriligious.
5. Chrétien de Troyes and those who assisted in the completion of his work suggest that the secret of life is to discover God and to understand his teachings.
6. Not until the Ark of the Covenant is returned to Jerusalem will man inherit the kingdom of heaven.

CHAPTER 15 KEYSTONE

MANY AUTHORS ACKNOWLEDGE some literary angel who guides them when the metaphorical "road ahead" seems to end at a brick wall. I am no exception, but the "angel" came in a more tangible form, the Internet. As part of an ongoing interest in the mystery and aware that there were still some aspects that lay uncovered, I joined an Internet group called Priory-of-Sion, which can be found at http://members.xoom.com/priory_sion/. It was during "off-group" e-mail discussions with a regular contributor, Stella Maris, that matters really moved forward. Stella is a well-known psychic with the apparent ability to "navigate" or fly the astral plain. I confess to starting off completely agnostic on such matters, but this experience has caused me to acknowledge that there may well be something to it after all. Stella pointed me forcibly towards St. Sulpice church in Paris.

As I pondered the enigma that is St. Sulpice church, the solution slowly dawned. It soon became clear that further trips were the order of the day. One visit would be to the "dreaming spires" of Oxford and the other would be to Paris. Paris, for those who have not been there, is a beautiful city and is aptly called the "City of Lights." The thought of visiting Paris brought a shiver as I remembered the problems associated with driving around it in a car. Quite how it is that living among such beauty should bring out the worst of Darwinian driving is a mystery that Milan and Rome also share.

AS ABOVE SO BELOW

Teach us Lord to serve You as You deserve,
*   to give and not to count the cost,*
To fight and not to heed the wounds,
*   to labor and not to ask for reward,*
Save that of knowing that we do Your will.

Prayer most associated with Saint Ignatius

THE PARIS MERIDIAN, it is said, was laid down around 1669. It runs through the east side of the Paris Observatoire which was built at that time and where the telescope itself is located. The Meridian runs due north almost through the center of the Palais du Luxembourg. The garden of the Palais is, you will recall, tilted some 3° to the east. Some 90 meters northwest of the Palais is the church of Saint Sulpice. Saint Sulpicius, as we know him, died in 647; he was born of wealthy parents and became bishop of Bourges in the Aquitaine. Bourges has the cathedral of St. Etienne which also just happens to be on the Paris Meridian. Apart from his distinction in aiding the poor from an early age, he is best known for his defense of his people against the tyranny of the Merovingian "Mayors of the Palace"—particularly during the reign of Dagobert II. Saint Sulpicius resigned his bishopric late in life and devoted himself to the poor.

It was to the church of Saint Sulpice that Abbé Saunière went, in 1892, when he visited Paris, supposedly with his great discovery that would lead to him becoming very wealthy. On the floor of the church is a brass strip which is referred to variously as "the Merid-

316

ian" and "the rose line." It certainly is not the Paris meridian, for that is some 660 feet (200 meters) to the east. The "rose line" is a concept associated with Rosicrucianism, alluding to the stream of blood from Jesus Christ at his crucifixion. It is also associated with Saint Roselin who in turn is linked to the Grail family[60]. It is from the words "rose line," previously written as "roselin" or "rosline," that the name of the famous chapel near Edinburgh, Rosslyn chapel, is thought to have come.

To solve this part of the puzzle, I needed a day out in the Bodleian Library, Oxford. Such is the state of the world today that the Bodleian has found it necessary to employ state-of-the-art digital photographic technology to produce a "reader's" pass with a passport photo on it. This equipment sits incongruously in a room with a high ceiling and fine plaster mouldings. I duly promised that I would not damage any of their property or set fire to it, and I was in. A whole day spent pouring over ancient maps, some drawn before the Templars were thought of, enabled me to establish a number of facts which will be brought into the investigation as appropriate. I was also able to inspect the 178 maps which make up the complete set for France produced by Jacques Cassini and his son during most of the eighteenth century.

On Cassini's map the summit of Pech Cardou is not shown, a fact that some might find significant, although there is some topographical information. In order, therefore, to locate the summit of Pech Cardou on Cassini's map, I had to overlay and align topographical data from the IGN map 2347 OT Quillan 1:25,000 onto the Cassini map (Fig. 90). It was immediately clear that Cassini would have seen that the Meridian was some 660 feet (200 meters) to the east of the summit of Pech Cardou and not through the center as was clearly the intention. We now know from modern surveys that the meridian is actually some 2530 feet (770 meters) to the east of the summit of Pech Cardou but in 1750 they thought that the error was 660 feet (200 meters).

Cassini published the first of his maps of France—showing the primary triangulations which spanned the length and breadth of France—in 1744: *Les principaux Triangles qui fervent de Fondement à la Description Géométrique de la France.* One triangular sight goes from

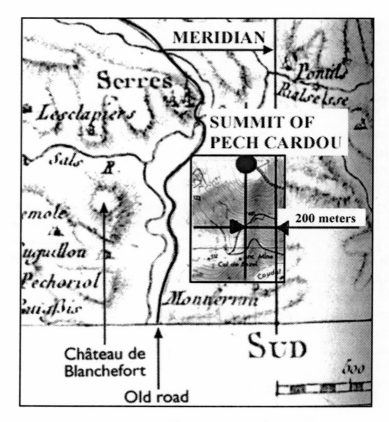

Figure 90
Cassini map circa 1750 of Cardou with IGN topographical data overlain
to show summit of Pech Cardou

Cassini map, Archives de L'Institute Géographique National,
IGN Map No. 2347OT © IGN Paris 1994, Authorization No. 90-0069

the summit of Pech de Bugarach back to a hill just to the west of
Carcassone; this line of sight goes right over Pech Cardou. It would
have been little more than a day's work to drop a triangulation point
onto the top of Pech Cardou and thus determine its relationship
with the Meridian at Paris *en passant*.

It is also now apparent that armed with this knowledge, Cassini,
or whoever was involved in resolving this problem, went to the
Paris church of Saint Sulpice, which is just around the corner from
the Observatory and was still under construction at that time. There

are so many features of St. Sulpice church that are germane to this investigation that the church is almost worthy of a book in itself.

The 108-foot (33-meter) high church of Saint Sulpice was purportedly built during the period 1646 to 1780, although during my visit to the Bodleian I saw a 1630 map with St. Sulpice marked clearly on it. But at some time before 1744 or so, when Cassini discovered the misplacement of the Meridian, his colleagues were able to insert a brass strip in the floor of St. Sulpice. This brass strip is "officially" called a *meridienne* and described as similar to those found in many churches all around France. They were used to define the hour of noon to regulate the church clocks which in those days were not very accurate. Until the end of the nineteenth century, every village of France had its own local time and this was "calibrated" against the gnomon or solar clock in its church.

The facts as just reported are undoubtedly correct, but there is more to St. Sulpice than meets the eye. The new *meridienne* was established in St. Sulpice by the famous English astronomer Henry Sully in 1727. He had a pendulum suspended from the ceiling of the church and swung across the transept at mid-day on the summer *solstice*, a play on words which should not be ignored. The line delineated by the pendulum was set in brass in the floor, ending at the gnomon which is an obelisk or a tall thin piece of carved stone, some 12 feet (6 meters) high. The brass line marking the new *meridienne* continues across the floor of the church and up the face of the obelisk. I have been told that this *meridienne,* if extended south, crosses the Paris Meridian at an angle of 3°. If this is so, then it points to the whole *meridienne* episode having been stage-managed.

The final support for the suggestion that St. Sulpice has somehow been stage-managed comes from the stained glass window at the south end of the transept . It is what one might assume is the logotype of St. Sulpice, two overlapping "S"s. Few people visiting the church would give the window a second glance unless they noticed the enlargement at the top end of each "S" which has the effect of making them look like two overlapping snakes. Here is yet another sign of the awareness of the error at Peyrolles. Assuming one is facing south as in the stained glass window, the first "S" is Saint representing the existing *serpent rouge* and the second "S" from Sulpice representing the actual *cardo* through Pech Cardou and the site where the Meridian should have gone. St. Sulpice church is, as I have already mentioned, worthy of an investigation in its own right, and it was with this realization that I turned my back on it and returned to the main mystery. Whether the lovely old church of St. Sulpice, built on the site of an ancient Merovingian monastery, is ready yet to offer up the many secrets contained within its masonry, only time will tell.

The fact that at some time around 1750 a corrected Roseline or Meridian seems to have been installed in the floor of the church of Saint Sulpice provokes a question: why not simply move the Paris Observatory some 200 meters to the east and reposition the Meridian? This was at a time long before navigation of ships at sea were using the Paris Meridian or any other; therefore, to move the Meridian would have presented a small inconvenience with the rebuilding but that is all. Or, could there have been another reason that prevented such an obvious solution.

This possibility caught my imagination and so I turned my attention to the area around the observatory. It wasn't long before a road, running north west at an angle of 30° to the Meridian, caught my eye. The name of the road is *Rue d'Assas*, which doesn't translate to anything in English but is part of the word "assassin," and it was with the Assassins that the Templars had a relationship in the Holy Land. A little south of but exactly parallel to the Rue d'Assas I noticed two churches: the church of Saint Ignace and the chapel attached to the Ecole Saint Sulpice.

The Saint Sulpice connection has already been dealt with above, and Saint Ignace, or Saint Ignatius of Loyola (1491–1556) as we know him, was the founder of the Jesuits[61]. In an earlier life, Ignatius would undoubtedly have been a Knight Templar or Hospitaller. He was born Inigo Lopez de Loyola, to a family of minor nobles in the Basque region of Spain, not far from the Roussillon. He joined the military, but his career ended when he was struck in the leg by a cannon ball. The pain involved in the rebuilding of his leg, including cutting off surplus bone, can only be imagined at a time before anaesthetic. Having recovered, Ignatius embarked on a life of asceticism, commencing at the monastery which houses the Black Madonna at Montserrat. He was "touched by God" at the age of 32 as he sat on the banks of the river *Cardonas*. Some two years later he entered Jerusalem on a donkey intending to stay and convert Muslims to the Christian faith. His stay in Jerusalem was brought to an end by the local Franciscan monks whose role was to guard the Christian religious sites. They sent him packing because he had become a serious kidnap risk from Muslims angry at his evangelical behavior. Ignatius, who often referred to himself as *il pelegrino*—a pilgrim, returned to Paris where he spent the next seven years studying and working to help the poor before moving to Rome and then Venice. He finally returned to Rome where he settled and formed the "Society of Jesus." The Jesuits, as they became known, received papal approval in 1540 from Pope Paul III. Having formed the Order of Jesuits, Ignatius hardly ever left Rome and died at the age of 65. The Jesuits are most notable for their regime of strict discipline and spiritual exercises. They have one ruler, the Superior-General. The Superior-General had absolute power over the Order and was responsible only to the Pope.

As one reads about the life of Saint Ignatius, it is difficult not to feel that the similarities with the Templars are either remarkable or that history has been "adjusted" to make it seem so. His modestly elevated birth, his army career, the river *Cardonas* and his entry into Jerusalem on a donkey all suggest some sort of a discrete tie with the Templars. You will also recall Loyola's stay at the monastery at Montserrat and observe a rationalization for the spiritual impact of the "Black Madonna" tradition. That such patterns should emerge from historical data is actually not surprising. The suggestion that history might have been "adjusted" is not so outrageous as one might think. In this case, some historians believe that the records of Ignatius' life may have been aggrandized by the Jesuits' own scribes.

> *Superiors and forgers believed innocently that spiritual truth was on their side and the good of souls, so they were justified in the manufacturing or clarifying of evidence where, if by merely material chance, it happened not to exist* [63].

Then, the manner in which the Jesuits were ruled, the strict discipline, and the unusual choice of a single leader answerable only to the Pope reinforce this idea. If one ignores the non-military role of the Jesuits, it is one long story of remarkable coincidences and links to the Templars, and it doesn't end there. The original founders of the Order numbered no less than nine: Ignatius himself, Francis Xavier, Pierre Favre, Diego Laynez, Alfonso Salmeron, Simon Rodriguez, Nicholas Alfonso, Claude le Jay and Paschase Broet. Moreover, in 1773, just like the Templars, the Jesuits were suppressed by the Pope; however, they were able to recover and today are represented throughout the world and are particularly strong in Africa and South America. In addition to the Pope, the Jesuits incurred the wrath of other monastic orders and particularly the Dominicans, who the reader will recall carried out the inquisitional torture on the Templars.

> *They will be among the damned at the last judgement.*
> Melchior Cano, chief theologian of the Dominicans[64]

There is one further, this time pictorial, link between the Jesuits and the Knights Templar and/or Freemasonry. During his evangelizing journeys, Ignatius would hold aloft a board on which were inscribed the letters "IHS," being an abbreviation for the medieval spelling for Jesus of "IHESUS." Later Jesuits added a Christian cross to the horizontal bar of the "H."

Figure 91
Jesuit monogram

It is a simple matter to remove the top spar of the cross—perhaps to represent the removal of the Templars—one of the three ruling bodies over Christian held Jerusalem—to arrive at a triple tau between the "I" and the "S."

When the triple tau is taken out of this monogram we are left with an "I" and an "S" and these when overlain give us the curious, caduceus-like "$" that has intruded several times into my re-

Figure 92
Modified Jesuit monogram to demonstrate Triple Tau

searches. I am beginning to conclude that this symbol stands for "Sol Invictus"—the sun-god—but that is another matter.

After that quick tour of the life of St. Ignatius, it is back, metaphorically, to Paris. Armed with this new information I turned to *L'Indispensible Plan de Paris*. At first I drew a line through the center of the crosses on each of the two churches of Saint Ignace and the chapel of the Ecole Saint Sulpice; it crosses the Meridian just north of the Observatoire. Rotating my ruler through 60° and keeping the bottom end on the intersection of the line through the churches and the Meridian, I drew a second line. This line crossed the cathedral of Notre Dame exactly on the line of the horizontal bar of the crucifixion cross marking Notre Dame; this could not be a coincidence: the cathedral church built to "Our Lady" to whom every Knight Templar swore his initiation oath; the very cathedral where the last Grand Master of the Knights Templar made his impassioned denial of Templar wrongdoing, an act which would immediately consign him to an agonizing death of being roasted alive. This simply could not be a coincidence.

On *L'Indispensible Plan de Paris*, working from the intersection of the cross over Notre Dame, I then drew a horizontal line to meet the line through the two churches and completing an equilateral triangle. What to do next? Of course, just as I had done in the Roussillon, I put a circle inside the triangle just touching the sides. The center of this circle sat exactly on the center of the Palais du Luxembourg, the place where Poussin spent the early part of his career. Another small snippet came out of my informative visit to the Bodleian library and that was the knowledge that the Palais du Luxembourg was called the Palais d'Orleans; certainly up until the eighteenth century only the road in front of the palace had the word

Luxembourg in its name. But a single triangle around the Palais du Luxembourg, even with a circle inside or outside, would not fit with this investigation. We are far more used to seeing a hexagram, the Seal of Solomon, the Masonic symbol of the Holy Royal Arch.

Accordingly, I drew another triangle to complete the hexagram (Fig. 93). The apex sits neatly over the Place de Institut, but that is far from being the most startling thing about this second triangle. The line from the apex to the southwest corner runs down the southern side of a road which is exactly on this line and the name of that road

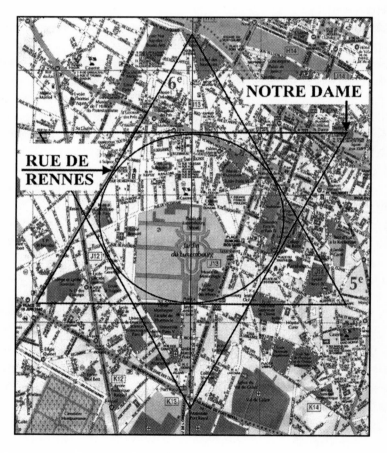

Figure 93
The hexagram in Paris
IGN Map No. 2314OT © IGN Paris 1998, Authorization No. 90-0069

is *Rue de Rennes*. At last the journey is complete and the link is irrevocably made. One side of the hexagram is made by *Rue de Rennes* which takes us neatly back to *Rennes-le-Château*—where it all started. There are of course other *Rennes* in France than *Rennes-le-Château*, but the link with this investigation seems overwhelming. My visit to the Bodleian library provided further help on this matter and I was able to establish that no *Rue de Rennes* existed in Paris as late as 1798, although the beginnings of the eventual line were being created *with Rue de Saint Peres*.

The above drawing, Figure 93, of the hexagram in Paris has been graphically modified to explain the argument being made. In reality, the method of arriving at the hexagram with the northwest side running alongside Rue de Rennes works on the author's map, *L'Indispensable Plan de Paris*. This map comes in book form and the center-fold crosses the map to the right of the Palais du Luxembourg. To provide a clearer picture, I purchased the IGN map of Paris 3615 IGN *Plan de Ville*. Unfortunately from a graphical sense, the arrangement of the hexagram does not work and Rue de Rennes does not sit exactly on the northwest line of the hexagram as shown above. The arrangement does, however, work perfectly, centered on the Palais du Luxembourg and with the northeast point of the star sitting over Notre Dame and with Rue de Rennes sited exactly under the north west line of the hexagram—**only if the Meridian is turned through 3° east of north.**

There was only one way out of this impasse and so I turned to modern technology and ordered a satellite photo of Paris. With the aid of a 1993 "Groupe Spot Image" satellite picture of Paris, as we will see, the picture became clear.

It is now clear why the option of moving the Meridian could not be considered: the Palais du Luxembourg had been built some one hundred and fifty years before the discovery of the 3° error at the *serpent rouge*. The exquisite relationship between the Palais, the Meridian and Notre Dame cathedral simply couldn't be touched. Instead a complex arrangement of geometric lines and a whole new Masonic degree would need to be designed to effect the correction needed to bring the whole arrangement into balance. This knowledge permits us to clear up an area of some confusion, for when the

Palais du Luxembourg was built, Jean Dominique Cassini was not even alive and could not therefore have taken any part in laying down the Paris Meridian.

It is hard to find an explanation for this audacious act other than the desire of a group of "keepers of the Templar flame" to thumb their noses at the French royalty for the actions of Philip IV. The current name of *Palais du Luxembourg* provokes no obvious explanation for the choice of this building as the center of a six-pointed star. The earlier name, however, of *Palais d'Orleans,* does offer a possible motive. The first Bourbon king of France was Henry IV (1589–1610), and he, as was discussed earlier, married Marie de Médici. The House of Orléans is a collateral title with that of the House of Bourbon and is given to the heir presumptive to the French crown. The French monarchy was entirely a male entitlement, bestowed under *primogeniture:* unlike the English monarchy where the title of "Prince of Wales" is only given to the male heir presumptive. It might therefore be that, in drawing a six-pointed star around the *Palais du Luxembourg,* the "Templar sympathizers" simply wished to say—very quietly—"We have the future of the French crown under our sign." In time, these Templar sympathizers would indeed have the last laugh because the Palais du Luxembourg is now the seat of the French Senate, the present day representatives of the same group who had confiscated the French property of the Hospitallers nearly 200 years ago.

The introduction of "As above so below," the motto of various metaphysical movements, such as the Rosicrucians, is now clear. Those hermeticists involved in the creation of this mystery would have been well aware that the early Platonic references to this phrase meant that "true reality exists with the spirit while humans can only experience a reflected facsimile on the earth." They clearly sought, though, to make the phrase come alive at a physical level. The adoption of this saying and its application to the mirroring of landmarks in Rennes-le-Château to Paris has clearly been just another clever use of words, phrases, drawings or geometrical forms to illustrate the secret.

So many facets of this investigation raise questions that it seems almost pedantic to pick on this next one. I refer to the fact that the inverted apex of the first triangle around the Palais du Luxembourg sits exactly over the statue of Francis Garnier.

Garnier was a notable French naval commander who was at the forefront of the exploration and colonization of Indo-China. With the death of the 1866 expedition leader, Garnier took over as commander, exploring as far as Shanghai. In 1871 Garnier was awarded the Medal of Honor by the Geographical Society of France. Returning to Indo-China in 1873 he was decapitated in a minor scuffle with local insurgents in 1875. His ashes were returned to France and placed within the base of his statue in 1983. Without wishing any disrespect to the memory of Francis Garnier, he hardly seems to have made the sort of impact on history that his unique location might appear to warrant. Whilst I have been unable to establish any genealogical link, the name Garnier certainly held a special place in the Holy Land. The Garniers, whether related to Francis Garnier or not, were major landholders in the Frankish kingdom; indeed, one of their fiefs was Jericho, which may just be one of the most ancient cities in the world. Be that as it may, Garnier's statue, laden with

Figure 94
Statue of Francis Garnier

Masonic symbolism in the form of cornucopia, water running from a pitcher and a sprig of acacia being held aloft, does, though, seem eminently in keeping with this mystery. Perhaps it was the manner of his death by beheading that provides a metaphorical link back to St. John the Baptist and thereby the Knights Templar and thus assured Garnier's statue of a special location.

So much of this investigation has centered around matters cartographical and astronomical that it hardly seems surprising that the Statue of Francis Garnier is sited on the Meridian and only 400 feet (120 meters) or so from the front gate of the Paris Observatory. The Paris Observatory is something of a magnet to this investigation. The four sides of the rectangular building which is the Observatory are oriented with the four cardinal points of the compass. In just the same way, but using cryptic language, there is a statue in front of St. Sulpice church called *The Four Cardinals*. In fact, the four individuals depicted were not cardinals but mere bishops. The statue simply ties St. Sulpice to the Paris Observatory. There is something else about the Observatory which deserves a mention. The basement is connected to the catacombs which spread through some 40 miles (65 kilometers) of galleries under Paris. Now, taken on its own, that means little until one becomes aware that the catacombs contain literally millions of skeletons. Might this just be the aspect of the skull and crossed bones symbolism within Freemasonry which is there to bring the researcher back to the Observatory? In Allyn's *Ritual of Freemasonry*[66], a candidate for the Order of Knights Templar is taken first to a "room of reflection" where he finds:

> *The table before him covered with human skulls and "cross bones" of horrible appearances.*

Curiously this is precisely the scene that would have confronted a candidate if he had been initiated in the Paris catacombs under the Paris Observatory. We have already seen how the skull and crossed bones was a Templar symbol and that it may even have been used by them to stand for the Ark of the Covenant. How delicious for the ritual compilers to include it within Freemasonry for yet another, entirely different reason.

Just when you think that the last skin of the onion has been peeled away and you are looking at the whole picture, another skin comes into view. As I viewed my findings with quiet satisfaction, I realized that there was another, even more breath-taking discovery to be made. Once again I turned to my ruler and pencil and drew a line from the southwest point of the hexagram, at Montparnasse, through the center of the Palais du Luxembourg to Notre Dame cathedral. This shape, together with the two lines in the shape of a "V" which join the Palais du Institut and Notre Dame, form one arm of a cross patée or Templar cross. As I completed the full Templar cross based on this single arm, the result was amazing (Fig. 95). Four arms of a cross patée produce eight outward facing points on the star shape and four inverted or inward facing points, a total of twelve points in all. Of the twelve points for the Templar cross drawn over the map of Paris, no less than eight sit exactly over churches, and a ninth is over the site of an ancient chapel. Nine points over existing churches or the sites of ancient churches does, however, offer a fitting tribute to the nine founding members of the Knights Templar.

It was at this point that my wife, Lynne, and I set off for a long weekend in Paris. Few couples can have stayed in this romantic city with a more unusual task in front of them, to photograph whatever sits under each of the points of a large Templar cross that straddles the south side of the city. Commencing with the point on the center of Notre Dame cathedral and working clockwise, we found the following remarkable results. The first point of the eastern arm of the cross is over the church of St. Albert le Grande. The inverted point is not on a church but on an artists enclave comprising a seventeenth-century style terrace of bungalows with a public garden. In the past, such famous names as Gaugin, Jean-Paul Laurens, Rodin, and Modigliani lived here and presumably drew inspiration from the close proximity of like-minded artists.

The third point is over The Reformed Church, Port Royal. The first point of the southern arm is over the church of Notre Dame du Roseaire; the inverted point sits over a clinic on the junction of Rue de l'Harmonie and Rue Labrouste. The third point sits over the church at the junction of Rue Oliver de Serres and Rue Pierre Mille.

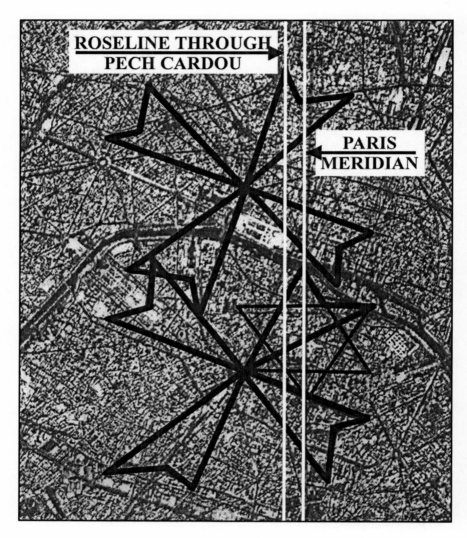

Figure 95
The Templar Crosses over the map of Paris
© CNES/SPOT Image Corp. 2000

The first point of the western arm of the cross sits exactly over the church of Cardinal Amette, the inverted point is over the chapel to the Ecole Militaire (the military school), and the third point is over the church of St. Pierre de Gros Caillou. In the context of this investigation the name of this last church is surprising for two reasons. Firstly St. Pierre was the name of the chapel in Rennes-le-Château which *Abbé Saunière* rebuilt, and secondly it means St. Pierre of the big stone; now *caillou* really means a small stone or pebble and *pierre* also means stone or rock. So we have a church called saint "stone" of the big "small" stone. Caillou is unusual for another reason in that it is one of few French words which take an "x"—perhaps for "x" marks the spot—for the plural and not an "s" like most words ending in "ou." The northern arm of the Templar cross has the first point, not over a church but over the front of the Palais de l'Institut; the inverted point sits in an ancient walkway that once contained a chapel but no longer. The third point is, as has already been mentioned, over the cathedral of Notre Dame.

When taken together with the surrounding of the French Senate with a hexagram, this deliberate siting of churches to create a Templar cross amounts to a staggeringly audacious act. It has presumably been done by Templar sympathizers as a sort of benign revenge for the wrongs imposed on them so many years ago by Pope Clement V. The creation, by using road names and churches, of a Seal of Solomon and a Templar cross, has brought the French Government and the church symbolically under the sign of the Templars. This is clearly not the action of a group wanting to exact revenge in the accepted sense of the word. More likely it is a gentle thumbing of noses that says "we did that."

The link between the six-pointed hexagram star and the Templar cross patée is now evident for all to see. But the matter doesn't end there, for at the center of the cross patée is the modern tower de Montparnasse, the highest building in Paris. The area of Montparnasse was the home for a group of nineteenth-century poets who between them wrote *Le Parnasse Contemorain* from 1866 to around 1870. It was said to be a reaction to Romanticism, but that might now be interpreted as a coded message against the Church of

Rome. The leading contributor, Théophile Gautier, literally "lover of God Gautier," urged that "tears should be replaced with exquisite workmanship." This at around the same time when the floor of a Freemason's lodge stopped being carpeted with a pattern of tears and the black and white mosaic that is now used took over. Other poets in the group, Charles Leconte de Lisle and José Maria de Heredia, introduced an arcadian theme describing a place "peopled only by statues." This strange statement begins to make sense when one stands in front of the Paris Observatory and looks down the tree-lined gardens towards the Palais du Luxembourg. For just over a half of a mile (1 kilometer) is a row of Renaissance statues ending in the Palace gardens which contain tens of similar statues. Yet another contributor, Gerard Manley Hopkins, described Parnassianism as "the kind of verse which genius speaks but does not sing." It is a matter of future scholarship to determine whether this marked the defining moment when the spiritual torch-bearers for the Templars decided to end their grief and set about making a defining statement.

The identification of the hexagram and the Templar cross patée provides a plausible explanation as to why, when a new candidate is brought into Freemasonry, his charitable inclinations are "tested" in the northeast corner of the lodge room. The explanation has always been that foundation stones likewise are always laid at the northeast corner of the building, but no explanation is offered as to why foundation stones are so placed. It is now apparent that sitting at the northeast corner of the hexagram is Notre Dame cathedral where the last Grand master of the Knights Templar made his impassioned speech in defense of his order. It was there that the foundation stones of Freemasonry were laid.

Once again a skin is peeled off the onion to reveal yet another. Centered on the magnificent church of Ste. Marie Madeleine is another Templar cross of very similar size as that just described. This time I started at the church of St. Pierre du Gros Caillou and worked clockwise again. The first point of the western cross sits neatly over the church of St. Germaine. The inverted point is over the church of St. Alexandre Newsky which is opposite the Rue Pierre le Grand and reminds us of the starting point for this cross. The third point is over an absolute eye opener. Contained within three roads, Rue Ampere, Rue Bremontier and Rue Joffrey, are three churches forming a star (Fig. 96); these three roads sit within a near triangle of roads and almost reproduce the layout of the candles in a Royal Arch Chapter (Fig. 39).

These three churches are all named after Francois de Sales, although the one on Rue Joffrey is named Centre Joffrey. Continuing round to the northern arm, the first point sits over Place des Quatre Frères Casadesus, "the four brothers of the house of God," or Jesuits. This may alternatively be an oblique reference to the legend of Christian Rosenkreutz and the three other *Frères Zélés* (brother zealots) who founded the *Rose-Croix*. The inverted point sits over Place Ch. Dullin in the Rue des Trois Frères, the "road of the three

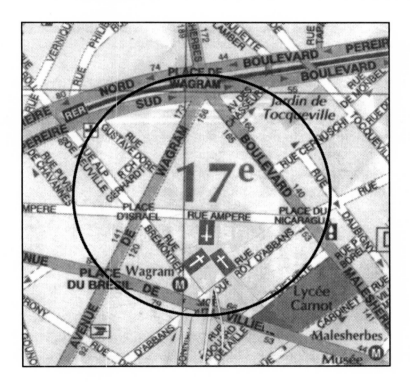

Figure 96
The three roads forming a triangle with churches enclosed
IGN Map No. 2314OT © IGN Paris 1998, Authorization No. 90-0069

brothers." Once again, in the context of this investigation, in the more ancient Masonic Templar ritual, it took three Knights to form an encampment which equates to a present day preceptory. Finally, the third point sits over the church of St. Anne, the mother of John the Baptist. I turned next to the eastern arm. The first point is over the church bounded by the Boulevard de Sebastapol and Rue du Cygne, literally "road of the swan." The inverted point sits over the church of St. Germain Auxerois, and the third point is over the church of St. Chapelle which is beside the cathedral of Notre Dame. Turning now to the southern arm, the first point is over Napoleon's tomb, pulling his remains similarly under the Templar cross as a snub perhaps for turning the Hospitallers out of Malta. The inverted point is over the church of St. Jean, and the last point of the Templar cross is on a line through the church of St. Pierre du Gros Caillou as far as the Place du General Gouraud. This road junction coincidentally has six roads running off it with equal angles between each and this would permit a perfect six-pointed star to be drawn over it. Once again, counting the triplet of churches as one, there are nine churches marking the Templar cross.

It is, though, the first point on the northern arm of the northern cross, the one over the Place des Quatre Frères Casadesus, "the four brothers of the house of God," or Jesuits, which is the most interesting. For the distance from the Paris zero Meridian to this point is 2530 feet (770 meters) or exactly the same distance as that from the summit of Pech Cardou to the Zero meridian. The *cardo* or "Roseline" running through Pech Cardou runs through one of the points on the Templar cross over the North of Paris—not just any point, but the one that is correctly aligned against the same arm in the Southern cross which is tilted through 6°. Once again what at first appears to be an error turns out to be an elaborate method of pulling the "Roseline" through Pech Cardou into the picture. The southern cross has the north-south arm deliberately tilted to tie it to the Paris Meridian and the north-south arm of the northern cross is correctly aligned and picks up the "Roseline."

The discovery of two Templar crosses over Paris leads immediately to their enclosure within two overlapping circles, and this is the hermetic symbol which means "as above so below." The "fish-

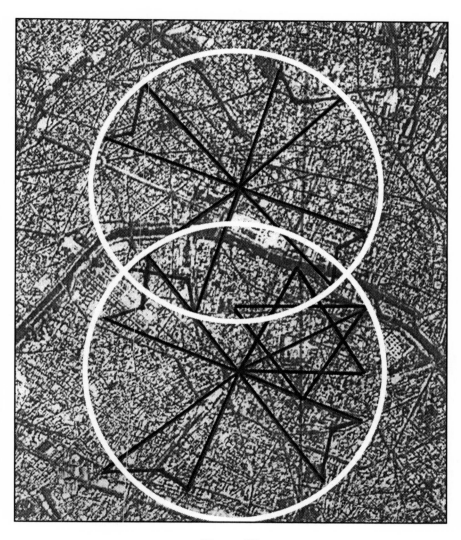

Figure 97
The two Templar Crosses on the map of Paris with circles around them
© CNES/SPOT Image Corp. 2000

ut-a-tail" shape enclosed by the overlap also has a hermetic
icance and it is "the WORD." No clearer evidence can surely be
needed to confirm the findings of my investigation. As in Rennes-le-
Château, so it is here in Paris. The "word" identified and located by
symbolism.

There remains one last question, and that is whether the layout
in Paris can help us to locate the temple in Pech Cardou. Overlaying
the hexagram from Paris onto the map of Rennes-le-Château (Fig.
98), the inverted triangle, an alchemical sign of water, can be seen to
sit over the old mine entrance on the side of Pech Cardou. If there is
a way into the temple it looks as if the old mine is the front door.
Aware that the roof of the mine entrance has been dropped to
prevent anyone gaining access, this final discovery was disappoint-

Figure 98
The Paris hexagram overlain on the hexagram at Pech Cardou
IGN Map No. 2347OT © IGN Paris 1994, Authorization No. 90-0069

ing. But it was at this point that the "literary angels" decided to take a hand yet again.

A contributor to the Priory-of Sion Internet group posted a short comment which was so startlingly obvious I wondered if I had sleep-walked through the whole investigation until this moment. What he said was that if one of the pillars in a Masonic lodge had a name which meant "**in strength**," and if God said "**in strength** I will establish this mine house to stand firm forever," does this mean that we can expect to find the word of God hidden in a pillar? Why didn't I see it earlier? Never mind, the whereabouts of another entrance to the temple within Pech Cardou has been identified. I have already established that the three pillars on the side of Pech Cardou are called "wisdom," "**strength**" and "beauty" after the names of the pillars on the Masonic first degree tracing board. Whichever of the three pillars is called "strength" almost certainly has an entrance to the temple concealed somewhere on it. One pillar, the easterly front pillar, does have a cave entrance at the top marked on the IGN map so this one starts off as favorite. It may just be that the cave, marked on top of the pillar, leads into a series of descending arches. If this were to be the case, then it is possible that the bottom arch will contain a double cube of white marble on which once sat the Ark of the Covenant.

Ashlars

1. The church of St. Sulpice in Paris is on what was thought at around 1727 to be the Meridian that would have passed through Pech Cardou.
2. St. Sulpice was bishop of Bourges where the cathedral also sits on the Paris Meridian.
3. The church of St. Sulpice in Paris seems to have been built to convey another message in addition to a Christian one.
4. Churches have been used in Paris to identify a six-pointed star based on the cathedral of Notre Dame and Rue de Rennes, and their patron saints include St. Ignatius whose life story reminds one of the Templars.

5. This Seal of Solomon is centered around the Palais du Luxembourg.

6. Deriving from this six-pointed star is a Templar cross which has nine churches under the points which it describes over Paris.

7. At the center of this Templar cross is the highest new building in Paris, the Montparnasse Tower.

8. There is a second Templar cross over Paris to the north of the Seine and this one also has nine points over churches, including the chapel within Napoleon's tomb.

9. These Templar crosses are clear evidence of a conspiracy which extends to the present time, and the purpose of that conspiracy seems to be to say that the spirit of the Templars lives.

10. The obvious entrance to the temple within Pech Cardou, through the mine entrance, has been blocked, but another entrance may exist from one of the three pillars quarried into the side of the mountain.

CHAPTER 16 KEYSTONE

ON MORE THAN ONE OCCASION I have made reference to "peeling the skins off an onion." It now seems as if we are either at the heart of the onion or very close indeed. What started out as a bit of detective work into a long-standing mystery in Rennes-le-Château has ended up identifying the most audacious exercise in "thumbing one's nose" at the crown, the state, the Church, and the memory of Napoleon Bonaparte imaginable. It rather looks as if anyone and everyone who has harmed the Knights Templar and Hospitaller over the years has come in for some ridicule.

There are, nevertheless, a few outstanding questions which cry out for answers. Where these answers are not yet available, then conjecture will have to suffice. This next chapter must rely to some extent on speculative reasoning in order to fill in the gaps between the facts already uncovered. I recognize that, in attempting to "second guess" the gaps in this investigation, I am presenting an easy target to anyone wishing to discredit my findings. The soft option would be to leave this particular section out, but that would deprive you, the reader, of an insight into the whole story.

A PRIORI

$$E = mc^2$$

Albert Einstein

ALTHOUGH OFFICIAL RECORDS indicate that millenarianism was not an issue at the turn of the first millennium, it would be surprising if the non-appearance of Jesus Christ did not cause some dismay. Coincidentally, at around that time, the local Muslim ruler destroyed the church of the Holy Sepulchre in Jerusalem. Also around that time, Christian forces had recovered some eastern Mediterranean lands, which had earlier been captured by Muslim forces. This collection of events, coupled with local political pressures, persuaded the Pope to call for the recovery of Jerusalem. In consequence the First Crusade set off to recover the Holy Land for Christendom. Two men from the Court of Champagne—the Count and Hugh de Payens—were either part of that crusade or made a pilgrimage to Jerusalem. On their return to France, the Count instructed a group of temporal and ecclesiastic academics at his Court to prepare a plan. They would design and build an organization like no other before it in the Western world. It would be a brotherhood of warrior monks to fight for the Lord. Their first task would be to locate and seize the Ark of the Covenant.

Whether this plan was an entirely original thought, or whether someone from the Court had visited China and seen one of the monasteries that practiced martial arts, we are unlikely to find out. The Chinese Buddhist monks at the Shao Lin monastery were practising T'ai Chi Ch'uan as early as the fifth century. This is the

340

Chinese form of boxing that may be practiced with or without weapons. T'ai Chi Ch'uan drill may also be carried out on horseback. It is noteworthy that a snake was added later to the five creatures, which form the basis for the different positions.

At the beginning of the twelfth century, the plan of the Champagne courtiers came to fruition and their brainchild was born; we now refer to this organization as the Knights Templar. Within a few years they had realized their first goal and found the Ark of the Covenant, probably in a cave on the site of the Dome of the Rock Mosque where previously King Solomon's temple had once stood. During the thirteenth century, when Jerusalem fell to the Saracens, they were forced to move the Ark to the safety of their fortress in the Holy Land, Castle Pilgrim. At the end of the thirteenth century, when they finally abandoned the Holy Land, they had to find a suitably secure place to keep the Ark. At first they stored it on Ruad, an island just off Tortosa and as near to the Holy Land as they could get. When the Muslims finally dislodged them from Ruad, they moved to Limassol and then Kolossi Castle in Cyprus. It was secure and as close as they could remain to the Holy Land, and it had all of the essentials of life at hand.

When King Philip IV attacked them in 1307 and the Pope followed up with the bull dissolving the Order, many Templars were determined to keep the spirit of the organization alive. They had their "treasure," the Ark of the Covenant, and they would rally around it as their trophy. When the trial was over and those ex-Templars who had survived were released, many joined the Order to which their property was transferred by Papal decree, the Knights Hospitaller. Mutual respect from both sides made the transfer easy and the Templars' trophy was admired greatly by the Hospitallers who welcomed it into their possession. An early act was to find a new home for the Ark. A site existed in one of the regions where the Templars had previously owned large tracts of land, the Roussillon. Working from within the Hospitallers but largely independent of them, maintaining their old lines of discipline, seniority and control, the ex-Templars created here their own Jerusalem. They had already earmarked a potential site within their lands in the Roussillon. There was an almost perfect circle of mountains and hills, although at some nine-miles in diameter it was a lot larger than the Jerusalem in the Holy Land. What made this site so appealing however was that there were mountains there that were in the same geographical arrangement as Mount Zion and the Mount of Olives in the Holy Land. They were even able to replicate the roads and footpaths, which they had known so well, from around the other Jerusalem in the Holy Land. At the center of this site was a mountain that would provide the raw material for a temple to hold their treasure, the Ark of the Covenant.

A temple was accordingly cut into this mountain, which stood at the center of the circle of mountains that now marked out the boundaries of their New Jerusalem. The limestone mountain was ideal for tunnelling, and so they toiled for decades to create their temple inside it, and, using the excavated spoil, they created a location marker in the form of a serpent at Peyrolles. They already had a quarry at Peyrolles as a source of red marble to adorn the many buildings they were involved in constructing. Here, they were able to quarry in such a way as to leave a huge section uncut, which provided the head of what would in time become the massive structure of a snake. The snake feature was intended, together with appropriately sited standing stones, to mark out a "caduceus" so that God would be able to look down and see where the Ark had been relocated. If ever the Templars needed God it was then, in their time of greatest trial. The snake feature was also a massive gesture of defiance toward those authorities who had connived in the destruction of the Templars. The snake sloughing its skin represents rebirth or renewal, and that is exactly what the Templars would achieve by the creation of the Freemasons. The snake devouring itself forms a circle and was thus also the sign of eternity, a fitting tribute to the New Jerusalem. So that there could be no mistake by God, they also excavated a massive skull facing upwards so that God would realize that this was the New Jerusalem and the new temple was next to this new Golgotha. To leave absolutely no room for error, they carved the head of Jesus Christ, as another earthly beacon to God to let him know that his mercy seat was within the mountain. It is, of course, equally likely that the head was a representation of their last Grand Master, Jacques de Molay, on the temple of the inverted skull—

implying that here is the "head of the Temple"—to leave no doubt as to whom were the originators of the site. This site was their religious center. Soon the metaphorical line passing through it, the Cardo, became its name, and in time this drifted into Corps Dieu after themselves—the corps of God. Later the locals knew it from the way the name sounded—Cardou.

With local control over their site as soon as maps began to be published, they changed the name to Cardon to deter anyone from making the connection between Cardou and Corps Dieu. The name Cardon was to remain for some six centuries when it would be changed back to the original Cardou and only then because disclosure was imminent. Cardon was a clever choice that enabled the Scottish friends of the Templar "torch-bearers" to develop a chivalric order with the same initials as the original Knights Templar, namely the Knights of the Order of the Thistle. As with Freemasonry, the thistle would travel back to France, via Scotland, to be incorporated there, this time as a heraldic emblem. Meanwhile, on Pech Cardou, at the entrance to their temple, they formed three pillars to represent the three pillars of the Holy Land: the patriarch, the Grand Master of the Hospitallers, and the Grand Master of the Templars. Because of its association with the two Grand Masters and the Patriarch, it later became known as their Grand and Royal Lodge. It was a secret place, a temple, not for worshippers, and it was the place where they lodged the most important treasure in the world—the Ark of the Covenant.

In relative security, the senior members of the Court of Champagne were not ready to concede defeat for their beloved creation, the Knights Templar. They decided that, when the time was right, they would recreate the Knights Templar as guardians of their most precious treasure. They would bring about a resurrection. The learned members of the School of Esoterica set to work. Their remit was to design an organization, one that would include the standards of chivalry and honor that they had originally built into the Templar order. There was another requirement as well. They had to devise a ritual that would contain landmarks identifying the secret location of Pech Cardou. Their home base at Troyes provided them with the first piece of what would eventually become the design framework. Because Troyes sounded like *trois* or three, they would build the ritual of the new organization around the number three to commemorate their time when the two Grand Masters and the Patriarch had effectively "ruled" the Holy Land. They would ensure that, in memory of their beloved Knights Templar, King Solomon's temple would also figure large. Their work at the Peyrolles quarry provided the key to the nature of this new organization: they would be masons. There was no shortage of other esoteric sources upon which to draw: translations of the Cabalah, Plato and Pythagoreanism had, by then, been around for a number of years.

They proceeded to build into the ritual of the new organization landmarks using the snake feature at Peyrolles pointing to Pech Cardou, plus the great new idea at the time, a Meridian. When the design was finished, the new, very secret brotherhood was tried out in Scotland. It was successful beyond their dreams. The close relationship that they enjoyed with Scottish nobility made Scotland the obvious choice. France was out of the question because the underpinning French word-substitution meant that people might put two and two together. So successful was the new organization that it spread to England and, perhaps from habit, the English claimed it as their own. In 1717 the Grand Lodge of England was formed and the distinct lack of opposition from the Scots indicates that it suited the designers to let the center go to London.

Around 100 years earlier, the painter, Nicholas Poussin, had become aware of the secret. Whether by the command of someone in authority, or from motives of personal aggrandizement, Poussin introduced clues into some of his paintings. Most of the clues were introduced during a specific period of his painting career, his Arcadian period, and this suggests that he was acting under direction. The clues that he introduced into his paintings identify Pech Cardou in the Roussillon region of France. They also hint at what is hidden there and point to the Freemasons as the key-holders. The new order, designed by the Court of Champagne, was called Freemasonry. The ritual was allegorical and symbolical. Layer of symbolism was piled on layer of symbolism and then disguised with allegory. Its underlying purpose was to provide directions to Pech

Cardou and demonstrate what is, or was, hidden there. The layers of allegory were very successful.

For hundreds of years the secret remained hidden from the generations of Freemasons who toiled to break the code. It is debatable whether the ritual compilers ever wanted anyone to break the code and there is an alternative scenario. It is more likely that at some time after the fourteenth century when their order was destroyed, the Templars intended to announce that they had come back as Freemasons. They had the proof because they could point to the ritual, which identifies beyond doubt that they designed it. Whenever they felt that the time was right, they could announce their victory over those who thought that they had destroyed the Templars. They have survived and become, once again, the largest such organization in the world.

However, by 1450, they were aware that there was an error in the landmarks caused by magnetic variation. Then in 1750 something calamitous happened. Jacques Cassini and his son César-François Cassini de Thury completed the first triangulation survey of France and published their first maps. The existence, for the first time, of an accurate map now meant that the magnetic variation error was there for all to see. As if that was not bad enough, it was apparent that the Paris Meridian had missed Pech Cardou, and the Masonic ritual reference,

The sun is always at its Meridian with respect to Freemasonry,

was wrong. The Masonic ritual had been compiled before the full extent of the surveying error was uncovered. The snake had been located using magnetic north, which is constantly moving, so the 3° westerly variation enables us to date when the temple was built in Pech Cardou to around the end of the fourteenth century. No one at that time was aware that magnetic north was not true north; that knowledge was not available until around 1450. At the time magnetic north was all that was available. Action was necessary to correct the error. Whether the intention of those behind the ritual was for Pech Cardou to be found or whether they simply wished to make a point at some time in the future, either alternative was impossible with the wrong landmarks.

Accordingly, the Scottish Rite was modified to include a new higher rank of 33° and the Royal Arch ritual was introduced. To complete the mystery, the appropriate angle was identified on the plate of gold within the Royal Arch ritual. The Royal Arch was now introduced as the completion of the craft degrees. The decision to use an angle of 33° turned out to be remarkably easy. 33° was an obvious cipher for 33%, the one third control that both the Templars and their new hosts, the Hospitallers, had enjoyed in the Holy Land. There was also a fine precedent with the use of Jesus Christ's age at his crucifixion, 33 years of age, to underline His part in the trinity. This single organization now held two of the three pillars on which the Holy Land once stood; there were now two pillars where once there had been three, and this had already been reflected in the Masonic ritual. The ritual compilers were French, and their loyalties remained with the French order, the Templars, not the Italian Hospitallers. They liked 33° for another reason, and that was because three threes are nine, and nine was the number of original Knights Templar.

Over time the French knights, who still carried the flame of the Knights Templar, came to dominate the Hospitallers from within. The organization thrived in the Templars' native land of France and the new role of providing medical care was a satisfying replacement for their much-reduced fighting activity. They knew beyond doubt that they had God's approbation once again. Their extensive property portfolio in France gave them power over the new technologies that were evolving. Astronomers needed land and equipment; mapmakers needed money to fund world trips to mark out new lands. The Hospitaller/Templars had land, money and ships and consequently influence. A bridge here, a road there or a castle could be called nine or its French identical word "new/neuf," or for that matter, anything else to commemorate their beloved Templars. A Meridian to identify Jerusalem with 33°—no sooner requested than granted; a member of the Hospitallers in a senior position, no different to a seat on the Board today. Their influence spread beyond the shores of France. In the small circle of intellectuals responsible for advancing knowledge across the world, the secret was known. They were only too happy to acknowledge the wondrous artifact that the Hospitallers were keeping in trust for the Templars. They found the concept of the Freemasons, as unwitting guardians of the "treasure map," exquisite; they readily joined and moved the organization forward. In time, the line of longitude 33° north would be allocated to Kolossi or Limassol, one of the castles in Cyprus that had once held the Ark of the Covenant.

All seemed to be going well when the legitimate arm of the brotherhood, the Knights Hospitaller, came under attack yet again. This time the attack came from the new French assembly which had come to power when the Revolution had over-thrown the old regime and created the Republic of France. First came the confiscation of the Hospitaller French properties, followed by Napoleon's taking of their island fiefdom—Malta. Revenge for those acts was in the air and in time a series of churches, roads and other monuments would be built, based on Templar, Hospitaller and Masonic patterns which would thumb Hospitaller/Templar noses at each and every authority who had over the years upset them: a six-pointed star around the Palais du Luxembourg which now houses the supreme French legislative body, the senate; two sets of Templar crosses placed over a total of eighteen churches and spanning the length and breadth of Paris; the inclusion of Napoleon's tomb under one of the crosses places his remains under a Templar symbol in perpetuity.

Meanwhile, over the years, Freemasonry grew vigorously until it covered most of the world. It was particularly strong in America where Masonic symbolism was even incorporated into the currency. The eye atop the pyramid on the dollar bill is well known, but what about the dollar sign? It really does resemble the line going through the snake at Peyrolles—the second line being the misplaced Meridian. The new European currency symbol for the Euro is three-quarters of a circle with two lines across it, and, if turned through 90 degrees, is a good representation of the circle around Pech Cardou and the two Meridians.

However, the world is seldom stable for long, and in 1914 the Great War broke out and in due course Germany invaded France.

For the first time since 1307, the guardians of the Ark of the Covenant became fearful about their treasure, for some German intellectuals knew where it was stored. It was not difficult to arrange for the Ark to be transported to safety. Freemasonry has always had a strong representation from the various branches of the armed forces. Indeed, it is to the peripatetic nature of the armed forces that the rapid spread of Freemasonry is sometimes attributed. It is equally unsurprising that an organization, built on the chivalric principles of the Knights Templar, should be attractive to fighting men. Accordingly, trusted Freemasons from within the armed forces were dispatched to the Roussillon, and the Ark of the Covenant was taken to safety, across the sea and out of reach of the German forces. There has long been a rumor that the Ark now resides in the United States of America, supported no doubt by the strong Masonic imagery visible in its bank notes. Only twenty-one years later, Europe was again immersed in war and it was deemed wholly appropriate to leave the Ark in its more secure location. However, in the course of time, peace returned to Europe and by the present day there has even been strong talk of a united federal Europe, well in line with Hermetic principles and thus the aims of the successors to the Knights Templar.

The senior representatives of Freemasonry were now faced with an equally daunting challenge. Whereas previously the ritual had contained open references to the Ark of the Covenant and the role of Freemasonry in preserving it, the myth suddenly became a reality. Furthermore, there was now a very real possibility that a Jewish state might be founded. In that event they would almost certainly demand the return of what they would perceive as their own property. The senior representatives of Freemasonry appear to have decided at that point that it was necessary to delete any overt references to the Ark in the Masonic ritual.

The more recent representatives of the original French guardians of the Ark seem to be the Priory of Sion, and they let it be known that the time had come when the Ark should be returned to Jerusalem—not to the Jerusalem in Israel, for that was seen as far too unstable a location for arguably the most valuable artifact in the world, but to the New Jerusalem in the Roussillon. Such is the control that these long-time guardians are able to exercise that they have even arranged for the National maps to include thirty-three border markers to their nine-mile diameter Jerusalem to acknowledge the Templar connection. The Ark of the Covenant is probably the only artifact that some nations would fight over. For that reason, the guardianship is an onerous responsibility and secrecy has been essential for bickering to be avoided. Unfortunately for the Priory of Sion, the current holders have become quite attached to their treasure. Just like J. R. R. Tolkien's *Gollum*, they could not bear to let "their precious" go back across the sea to France. The Priory of Sion found itself in what chess players call *zugzwang*. There were no moves for them to make that did not make the situation worse. As the new guardians have argued, the Ark is now safer than at any time in the past. No one could possibly steal it now. The Ark is located where particular criteria are met:

1. The Ark needs a location where modern transportation exists to facilitate its immediate emergency evacuation should the need arise.
2. The Ark needs a location where social and political stability would ensure the safety of such a treasure.
3. The Ark needs a location where a long tradition of civil liberties makes the possibility of government intervention impossible or extremely unlikely.
4. The Ark needs a location that for centuries has been free of natural disasters such as floods, hurricanes and earthquakes.
5. The Ark needs a location where, even if anyone knew it was there, uncovering it would be practically impossible.
6. The Ark needs a location where no one, in their wildest dreams, would think of looking.
7. The Ark needs a location within a spiritual milieu, where it will feel at home, where God may just decide to visit.

The present guardians' claim is strong, for they have the Ark. In desperation, the Priory of Sion turned to subtle threats; a story was concocted about the Templar treasure being buried near Rennes-le-Château and hundreds picked up the challenge of the search. When this brought forth nothing, a new twist was added. It was the body of Jesus Christ that was buried near Rennes-le-Château. A clever use of Biblical allegory:

In the beginning was the Word, and the Word was with God, and the Word was God.

John 1:1

All the players know that it is the Ark of the Covenant that is being referred to, the word of God, and God manifest. Eager treasure seekers took the bait and some published their books. In the case of Andrews and Schellenberger[5] they even found the correct site, Pech Cardou in the Roussillon region of France. The puppet masters are, however, becoming impatient with their recalcitrant Pinocchio. They have made it abundantly clear that if they cannot have their treasure back, the whistle is going to be blown. It is one thing to hold the Ark of the Covenant secretly, but it is entirely another matter to hold it when everyone knows that you have it. When the Templars were fighting in battles for their just cause, they knew that capture meant certain death because no ransom money would ever be paid. It is certain that the modern guardians will have seriously considered this possibility, but only they know what conclusion they have come to. It does appear that the clock is running and, in the absence of hard facts, it appears that the alarm may have been set for Mary Magdelene's initials—"MM"—the millennium.

There is now only one tiny matter outstanding. I have suggested that certain Meridians were established for the purpose of marking places where the Ark of the Covenant sojourned for a while. Jerusalem was given the longitude of 33° east by the French who also allocated the zero Meridian to Pech Cardou, or at least as near as they could get to it with the available technology of the time. Kolossi or Limassol Castle was allocated the longitude of 33° east by the British who ended up retaining the international zero Meridian through Greenwich. Of all of these locations, the only one where the Ark appears not to have rested is on the Greenwich Meridian, the internationally recognized zero Meridian. This seems somehow to be at odds with the story so far.

The location of Greenwich has not, though, been overlooked. For in 1999, in Greenwich, was completed the largest dome ever to be built anywhere, and the zero Meridian just about touches its western edge. The new dome is some 1,150 feet (350 meters) in diameter and 165 feet (50 meters) high. It is made of a white Teflon-coated glass-fiber material so that it will light up at night, and it has twelve entrances:

> . . . and shewed me that great city, the Holy Jerusalem, descending out of heaven from God.
> Having the glory of God: and her light was like unto a stone most precious, even like a jasper stone, clear as crystal;
>
> Revelations 21:10-11

> On the east three gates; on the north three gates; on the south three gates; and on the west three gates.
>
> Revelations 21: 13

> And the twelve gates were twelve pearls; every several gate was of one pearl: and the street of the city was pure gold, as it were transparent glass.
>
> Revelations 21:21

The "Millennium Dome" at Greenwich was built at a cost of $1,125,000,000 to celebrate the year 2000 and housed industrial and religious exhibits in a "startling multi-media spectacular on the theme of time." The construction of the dome in the U.K. has not been without controversy and many have argued that the money would be better spent on housing, hospitals and schools. The form of construction is similarly "leading edge"; the white canopy is suspended from twelve towers.

These twelve towers permit a Templar cross to be drawn with the indented end of the arm of the cross created by using the top of a tower, the point where the adjacent tower passes through the canopy and the top of the next adjacent tower. Similarly, six entrances with adjacent globes provide the six points to a "Seal of Solomon" star.

Oooops.

Figure 99
Picture of the Dome at Greenwich

Figure 100
Architect's drawing of the canopy of the Greenwich Millennium Dome
with Masonic and Templar symbolism superimposed

Ashlars

1. There is evidence to support the suggestion that when the Templars were disbanded, some people—ex-Templars among them—wished to keep the spirit alive.
2. Some ex-Templars settled in the area around Pech Cardou and set about creating their own "New Jerusalem."
3. It seems likely that the same people who created the Templars created Freemasonry as a replacement to carry the landmarks for their New Jerusalem.
4. Certain famous people were aware of this arrangement and left subtle clues to show that they were "in on the secret."
5. In around 1450, and later in around 1750, these Templar "standard bearers" discovered two major surveying errors that required the maps and the Masonic ritual to be radically altered.
6. When the First World War broke out, the guardians of the Ark moved it west for safety.
7. When peace returned to Europe, the "guardians" requested the return of their Ark—this request was met with silence.
8. The Greenwich dome bears a remarkable similarity to the Biblical description—in the book of Revelations—of the New Jerusalem.

CHAPTER 17 KEYSTONE

WHAT STARTED OUT as an interest in a mystery in a remote part of southern France has grown to encompass the "long lost secrets of Freemasonry." In the course of solving this extraordinary mystery, a "New Jerusalem" in the south of France has been identified. The realization that the Ark of the Covenant still exists is perhaps startling enough, but the probability that it is still in safe-keeping in the West is truly remarkable. As the layers of obscurity have succumbed to the light, it has become clear that the tentacles of this arcanum spread much wider than the south of France. Indeed, it certainly extends to Paris where two gigantic Templar crosses, marked out by churches and other monuments, were uncovered.

This has been an unusual story to unfold because in carrying out everyday research one becomes accustomed to receiving an accurate response to a reasonable question. In this inquiry I was not the first to meet a wall of obfuscation.

In the face of these difficulties, there was no alternative to getting into my car and driving down to the south of France to try to resolve the few outstanding issues by personal inspection, on the ground, so to speak. There was, however, the small matter of the pillar on the side of Pech Cardou that I dearly wanted to see climbed to find out if there is an entrance in the top. If I could somehow manage to combine these two items into one visit, it would save me quite a lot of time and money. In the late summer of 1999, the fates decided to smile on me.

JOURNEY'S END

And he carried me away in the spirit to a great and high mountain, and shewed me that great city, the holy Jerusalem, descending out of the heaven from God.

Revelation 21:10

IT WAS INEVITABLE that I would have to visit Rennes-le-Château to check whether there is an entrance to the right-hand pillar of rock on the west face of Pech Cardou which would identify it as the pillar called "Strength" in the Masonic ritual. The opportunity came when a colleague, David Ingram, discussed the mystery with his friend, John, who agreed to organize an ascent with one of his climbing companions, Alan. Between them, John and Alan have many years mountaineering experience in the Alps and Himalayas.

It wasn't difficult to plan another tour of Europe with my wife, Lynne, which would include stopping over at Rennes-le-Château to be there when the climb took place. A few days before the date for the climb, which had been dictated by John and Alan's availability, Lynne and I set off by car towards the south of France. Our first stopover was to be a couple of days in Troyes, the ancient capital of the Champagne region and a city central to my investigation. You will recall that Pope Urban II, who called the First Crusade, came from Troyes. It was also from Troyes that the original nine knights and monks, who would create the Templars, set out for the Holy Land, and it was at the Council of Troyes that Hugh de Payens obtained the papal bull establishing the authority of the Knights Templar.

We arrived in the early afternoon and, after unpacking at the hotel, we decided on a walk through the city center to stretch our legs. The seemingly endless supply of timber-framed buildings reminded me very much of those towns in England that still have Elizabethan and Tudor buildings. My first purchase was a local historical guidebook, packed full of wonderful color photographs.

Very soon we were sitting in one of the many picturesque squares, accompanied by a bottle of wine, and I was able to glance through my new guidebook. From it I learned that Troyes is an old town that was developed by the Romans who had called it Augustobona after the Emperor Augustus. In 275 the name reverted back to the original Tricassium Civitas or city of the Tricasses after the Gauls of Tricasse who first established a settlement there. Over the years, Tricasses developed phonetically into its modern name of Troyes. After my many years of research, here indeed was a name to conjure with. "Tri"—Latin for three, when added to the phonetic sound of Troyes—trois—meaning three in French—gave added meaning to the use of three throughout Freemasonry. The second part of this old name "casses" is even more interesting, for, according to my French dictionary, "casses" can mean inter alia "off-white" and "column" or "pillar." As I pictured the three off-white pillars on Pech Cardou, I could immediately see why Pech Cardou had such an attraction for the Templars who had identified it as their next temple. It took them straight back to their early roots in Troyes. I comforted myself with the thought that this trip had started well.

The wine was all the fortification we needed to take us to the cathedral, the first building on my list of "things to see." As cathedrals go, Troyes' is not the most spectacular; indeed as an early center of "operative" as well as "speculative" masonry, it was somewhat surprising to read how often it had fallen down. The first time admittedly was due to fire in 1188 when the local bishop, Garnier de Trainel—oh, how that name keeps cropping up in this investigation—who had been the chaplain of the Fourth Crusade, "lavishly endowed the cathedral with booty from Constantinople." It is in Paris, you may recall, that the inverted apex of the triangle around the Palais du Luxembourg sits exactly over a statue of Francis Garnier.

In 1228 a cyclone caused the collapse of the upper sections of the cathedral which was still under construction at the time. In 1365 another cyclone demolished the belfry; then in 1381 the northern rose window began to lean dangerously. In 1700 lightning caused the great steeple to catch fire and the bells crashed through the vaulting, demolishing the bell-tower on their way down. Many Christian souls may by then have concluded that God did not want this particular cathedral on this particular spot, but the locals were very resilient and never gave up hope, and, with the exception of the bell-tower which was never rebuilt, the cathedral has been completed and maintained. When I finally left the cathedral, it was with the opinion that God still has some doubts because there are glass "tell-tales" on several areas to measure the ever enlarging cracks which can clearly be seen in the stone fabric of the building.

While the cathedral, as a building, was prosaic, its contents were to prove somewhat different. Inside the cathedral Lynne and I visited the treasury where the sacred relics are displayed. Exhibit number two is a finger—or rather the bones of a finger—purported to have once graced the hand of none other than St. John the Baptist. Was this the reason why Leonardo da Vinci had painted such a dramatic gesture with the finger of St. John? To draw attention to Troyes, the heart of Templar country.

The following day was set aside to visit the church dedicated to Sainte Madeleine whose name runs continually through this investigation. Tucked away to one side of the ancient city center, it has a secret which is all but hidden from view. On the south face of the church is a campanile or bell-tower and on the northeast corner is an external staircase just like the one that Abbé Saunière had included on the corner of the Tour Magdala. If the Abbé had wanted to draw attention to the involvement of the Templars in the secret that he was uncovering, then what better way than by pointing unequivocally to Troyes.

It is quite difficult to see why a campanile should have an external staircase, a feature normally reserved for buildings lacking space. The inside of a bell-tower is hardly a place that one might argue lacks the space for a staircase. Inside the church of Ste. Madeleine is an entirely different matter. The carved stone rood screen, which separates the choir from the congregational area of the nave, is but one example of exquisite workmanship, and the stained-glass windows around the transept and apse are of an equally high quality. I have visited hundreds of churches, but few have held the aura of sanctity for me that this particular church possesses. One cannot visit the church of Ste. Madeleine without spending some time admiring those stained glass windows and, in the absence of a brochure, I took several photographs.

All too quickly, though, our visit to Troyes was over and we set off south down the Rue de Soleil. The next item on my agenda was a date with a mountain, where I hoped that we would locate the series of descending arches which would prove conclusively the link between Pech Cardou and the Masonic ritual. At 10:00 A.M. the following morning I met up with David, John and Alan in the square of the small village of Serres underneath Pech Cardou which towered above us. Under a very hot sun the four of us made our way up the south-side forestry road until John and Alan veered off through the undergrowth towards the rock outcrops. David and I continued up the forestry road to secure a better vantage point from which to try and observe their attempt on the rock face.

As we waited, David took several photographs using a telescopic lens. When two of these were developed and examined, they displayed some interesting details. Figure 101 shows a carved eagle on top of Roc Nègre—at the West end of Pech Cardou rather than the East end where the eagle is shown in Figure 18, Chapter 4. This carving of an eagle assumes greater importance with the knowledge that in Rennes-les-Bains—immediately due south of Pech Cardou—opposite the spa and parish church, is a rock foundation which bears the name of Cap de l'Homme which means "head of man." On top of a menhir is sculpted in relief a head. Thus we have on two sides of Pech Cardou carved representations of two of the four heads of the cherubim who guarded the Ark of the Covenant in King Solomon's temple. It remains for someone to locate the remaining two carved figures of a lion and an ox. Figure 102 is less clear, but you may just make out a very weathered representation of the Templar seal of two horsemen on the back of a single horse. This particular feature is to be found behind the left-

*Figure 101
Carved eagle on
top of Roc Nègre*
(photo by
David Ingram)

*Figure 102
The carved
Templar seal on
Pech Cardou*
(photo by
David Ingram)

hand pillar on the west face of Pech Cardou and is fairly conclusive proof of Templar involvement with the site.

The sun quickly reached its highest altitude and it was after what was one of the hottest and longest four hours of my life that John and Alan came down to debrief us. The news was not good. There are in fact three pillars of rock which make up the right hand pillar, as viewed from Roc Nègre. The rear of these three, some 75 feet (23 meters) high, they had surmounted, but there was no sign of any entrance on the top. The two front rock outcrops are both about 150 feet (45 meters) high, but the rock was too loose to permit safe climbing. The rock itself is sedimentary limestone with bedding planes about two or three inches thick, but the cementation between the layers has over the years dissolved. The whole outcrop is thus like a pack of cards leaning at an angle of about 15 degrees from vertical. The problem for John and Alan was that there was nothing on which to gain any purchase or to secure belays—or safety rope ties—which would prevent any long fall in the event that one of them lost their grip. They found that any force which pulled the rock towards them did just that and large and small slabs came away in their hands. In any event, they made three attempts up the three gullies—or indented "V" formations—which can be seen from Roc Nègre. In the interests of safety they had to abandon each as simply too dangerous.

This was almost the worst possible outcome for me as it at first appeared that I could neither rule my theory in or out. Subsequent rational analysis permitted me to rule this rock outcrop out as having any entrance from the top and any descending arches, as foretold in the legend of Enoch which describes the Ark of the Covenant as being concealed in the lowest arch. My reasons for coming to this conclusion are twofold.

First, I was seeking an entrance which the Templars had created and which Abbé Saunière must have found at the turn of the century permitting him to uncover the Templar treasure. The rocks on the south face of Pech Cardou have been unstable for hundreds of thousands of years, so neither Templar nor priest could possibly have climbed them.

Second, the purpose of the hiding place of descending arches was to store the Ark of the Covenant, a wooden box. The whole rock outcrop which John and Alan had so bravely attempted to climb was like a colander. The open lamination layers mean that the rock provides absolutely no protection from the rain which, even now, must be seeping through after every rainfall. This rock outcrop was not what I had been seeking. Somewhat downhearted I bade farewell to the three of them as they returned to their holidays on the coast.

My thoughts returned to the matter in hand. Earlier, as I had waited for my climbing colleagues in the square in Serres, I could not help but notice another outcrop of rocks, this time on the north face of Pech Cardou. They bore a remarkable similarity to the outcrop on the west face that has preoccupied me over recent years in my search for the Ark of the Covenant. I needed a better view than that available from immediately under the rocks, so I now drove back through Serres on the little road towards Peyrolles. From a distance of about a mile I could clearly see that the outcrop on the north face of Pech Cardou described a near perfect triangle made up from a fairly distinct line and a very clear dot (Fig. 103). Even more strangely, this second rock outcrop was at the same level on the mountain as the one on the west face which John and Alan had just attempted to climb.

Figure 103
Rock outcrop on the north face of Pech Cardou

Observing the triangular rock outcrop on the north face of Pech Cardou, I began to realize why the mountain had been so attractive to the Templars as an alternate temple to house their most sacred relics, and around which they could construct their "new" Jerusalem. The three rock outcrops provide a link back to Troyes; plus, the triangle had long been a symbol of the trinity and, as the similar rock outcrop on the west face of Pech Cardou clearly demonstrates, it lends itself readily to being modified into three pillars—three pillars to represent or perhaps contain the three gates to the temple to match the original twelve gates which provided access to King Solomon's temple, three on each of the four faces. It was becoming evident that my earlier speculation in Chapter 11 was probably correct and that the Templars were indeed embarking on the creation of a new temple here in the Roussillon. Had it ever been completed, it would have dwarfed the original; to provide some feeling of scale, Pech Cardou is six times the height of the Great Pyramid at Giza.

My thoughts turned again to the sealed off mine entrance on the south face of Pech Cardou: how appropriate when it was the south entrance of King Solomon's temple that provided the entrance for the ordinary people. In Masonic ritual it is through the south entrance of the temple that the masons went to collect their wages. But, if the west face of Pech Cardou, where John and Alan had just made the attempt on the right hand pillar, was to be the west gates of the new temple and if the north face of Pech Cardou was destined to be quarried into the north gates of the new temple with the workers' entrance as the mine entrance on the south side, then where was the main entrance? The main entrance to King Solomon's temple was at the east end: so it was to the east end of Pech Cardou that I needed to look for some feature that would replicate Boaz and Jachin, the two brass pillars that stood in front of Solomon's temple of the Ark.

And he set up pillars in the porch of the temple: and he set up the right pillar, and called the name thereof Jachin: and he set up the left pillar, and called the name thereof Boaz.

1 Kings 7:21

I turned my car around and headed back through Serres, turning left onto the D613 towards Arques. As I reached the end of Pech Cardou, my heart sank as nothing of consequence came into view. I had little choice but to continue along the narrow road running almost parallel with the smaller ridge of Cardaussel which springs out of the east side of Pech Cardou. Cardaussel has no meaning in French or Occitan but phonetically could mean the "saddle of Cardou," an appropriate name as can be seen from Figure 101, in which Cardaussel is the ridge running off from the left side of Cardou. As I passed the steep valley, the Gorges des Bézis, where Cardaussel ends and La Berco Grando springs upward towards the sky, I looked back again, more in hope than expectation. The shock at what was there caused me nearly to drive off the road into a small ravine. It was not until later that I discovered that the rock on the other side of the ravine was where a stone tomb once stood—the same tomb that was destroyed by the landowner some years ago and which was considered to be the model for Poussin's tomb in the *Arcadian Shepherds*. I drove on a little further until a flat area of verge allowed me to park the car off the narrow and winding road. I got out of my car and stood for some time staring at the two enormous pillars of rock which stand side by side at the east end of Cardaussel (Fig. 104). These two pillars are at the opposite

Figure 104
Boaz and Jachin

end of Pech Cardou to the carved eagle on Roc Nègre exactly as shown in the representation of Ezekiel's temple in Figure 18, Chapter 4. It is also now clear that in Poussin's painting the acacia tree represents these two pillars—to signal the position of the Ark of the Covenant.

I realized immediately why our attempt to find an entrance to the temple had failed—we were looking at the wrong end. Here, in front of me, stood the two pillars, Boaz and Jachin, oriented exactly the same as on King Solomon's temple, at the east end of the temple. Even the shape of Cardaussel added to Pech Cardou mimicked King Solomon's temple. Figure 103 clearly shows Pech Cardou rising up just like the Holy of Holies and Cardaussel to the left, or east, representing the lower porch. As if to finally make the point, there is a smaller rock pillar at the bottom of the valley between the two large pillars just mentioned. Once again they form a triangle but this time inverted against the earlier ones on the west and north faces of Pech Cardou. Adding this triangle to either of the others gives a Seal of Solomon or Star of David.

Only a year earlier I celebrated my thirtieth anniversary of being initiated into Freemasonry. I little thought during all those years that I would one day stand before the very pillars of the Masonic Third or Grand and Royal Lodge and be one of very few who knew that they were doing so. Literally only a few feet away from me the Ark of the Covenant had rested for hundreds of years, probably on a block of white marble.

The next day Lynne joined me to hunt down some of the loose ends which I had, until now, been unable to clear up. The first of these was the Pierre Dressée which had figured in my original investigation but which I now realized was quite close to two rock pillars that I now believed marked the entrance of the temple. Under another cloudless sky we walked up the beautiful hillside that peaks at Mont Redond. I was treading very heavily as I walked, to ensure that no viper basking in the sunshine brought what some might see as a poetic end to my research—on the very edge of le serpent rouge. It was not long before the Pierre Dressée, some ten feet high, stood before us (Fig. 105). It was immediately apparent why it was there, for it is carved in the shape of a finger and it leans over at an angle

Figure 105
The Pierre
Dressée

of around 25° to the vertical, pointing directly towards the two pillars which mark the entrance of the temple.

As some of my earlier speculations start to gain real substance, I feel that I can permit myself one more. The existence of this ancient dolmen suggests that Leonardo da Vinci either visited the site or was made aware of what is there. In his fresco of The Last Supper, da Vinci has St. John's finger pointing directly up towards God. Here on the hillside in the South of France the stone finger was pointing up and forward towards the place where the Ark of the Covenant had been stored. It also pointed towards God.

After the briefest of rests, it was time to continue up the hillside, noticing all around the piles of small rocks; each pile had perhaps a couple of tons of stones which were not local to this hillside. These piles of large stones were randomly spread over the side of the hill. The actual rock from which the stones were made looked similar to some I had noticed in a sort of claystone mixture making up one of the geological bedding layers on Pech Cardou. When we had passed through a small band of fir trees, we came across the remains of an old stone cottage with the date 1900 on the side (Fig. 106).

Figure 106
Derelict stone cottage overlooking Boaz and Jachin

It looked somewhat older and the single window looked out towards the two pillars guarding the entrance of the temple. A little further up the hillside and on the same direct line from the pillars, through the Pierre Dressée and the remains of the cottage, was a hermit's hut with an open side looking down towards the two pillars (Fig. 107).

Figure 107
Hermit's hut
overlooking
Boaz and
Jachin

Both of these, now empty, buildings support my thesis that there is no longer anything left to guard because, as described in Chapter 16, the Ark of the Covenant has been moved to a safe repository further west. More poignant was the realization that the little piles of rock were indeed capitelles and that they had probably provided housing for the hundreds or maybe thousands of Templars who had spent their final days working to hollow out the inside of Pech Cardou while their rest time was spent close to and watching over their treasure, the Ark of the Covenant. It seems that the Templars involved in the construction of the temple in Pech Cardou were using the rocks that they hewed from the inside of the mountain to build the cell-like capitelles in which they lived rather like hermits. The French word *montjoies*—literally "mounts of joy" also means cairns or piles of rock used to mark out a route for pilgrims to follow to a holy site. Perhaps this is what the solid capitelles, referred to earlier, were built for, to mark a route towards Pech Cardou to assist pilgrims from afar to find their way through unknown territory.

Figure 108
Capitelle remains

Time alone and geological examination will confirm or deny my suggestion that the capitelles may have been built from rock hewed from the inside of Pech Cardou. Picknett and Prince[44] support this possibility.

> *Roussillon, to the east of the area [the Languedoc], actually came under the auspices of the Spanish kingdom of Aragon, although the northern parts, which included Carcassonne, were part of France. The Roussillon Templars were arrested and tried—but found innocent— and when the Pope officially disbanded the order they either joined other similar brotherhoods or lived out the remainder of their lives with a pension on their lands.*

The view from the hillside above the Pierre Dressée demonstrated that another of my earlier "proofs" was the result of "artistic license" by the map-makers. The tail of the snake feature runs from the huge head of red marble at Peyrolles down to the river Rialsesse and the D613 road where it turns westward on the IGN map, but the ridge of the actual *serpent rouge*—a ridge of what, from a distance, looked like red sandstone—clearly continues across the river in a straight line. The IGN map-makers have been able to indicate that the tail of the snake feature turns westward because the ridge was cut long ago by the river Rialsesse and more recently by the D613 as well. But the continuation of the ridge was clear to see: it runs right to the foot of the two pillars of rock, Boaz and Jachin, which stand side by side at the east end of Cardaussel (Fig. 109).

The next stop was the village of Cassaignes perched on the top of an escarpment that runs from Couiza to Serres, passing Pech Cardou as it does so. Here I was seeking a bronze pillar that, with the Pierre Dressée, would provide the two pillars reported to have been left by Enoch in his legend to mark where he had constructed a series of descending arches in which was stored the Ark of the Covenant. Despite a careful search of the area where I had estimated that it might be, I was unable to find such a pillar in Cassaignes. With the benefit of hindsight I now realize that this location was calculated using the pillars on the west face of Pech Cardou and that this "loose end" must be revisited based on the pillars at the east end of Cardaussel. During my visit to Cassaignes, however, I did notice

Figure 109
The continuation of the Serpent Rouge

many more piles of stones—collapsed capitelles—similar to those I had seen on the hillside around the Pierre Dressée; indeed they can be seen all along the ridge from Couiza to Arques wherever there is a clear view of Pech Cardou. I also could not help but notice that the church in Cassaignes faces not east but directly towards Pech Cardou. Onwards to Coustaussa, where the church also faces towards Pech Cardou, the little piles of rocks lie eerily around. Why, I asked myself, don't the locals pick them up and use them to build their houses or field walls? But they clearly do not do so and this may very well be out of a sense of respect.

Another self-satisfied night of good food and wine was to be followed the next day by a visit to Rennes-le-Château. Perhaps the biggest secret, which only someone with vertigo would mention, is that the hamlet is built on the top of a mountain. The road, the tarmacadam surface of which Abbé Saunière is purported to have financed, zigzags up the mountainside for the best part of two miles.

This turned out to be yet another beautiful day and it began by taking in the magnificent views over the Roussillon landscape from the top of the mountain. Undeniably the most striking feature of this landscape is the mountain ridge which starts in the south at Pech de Bugarach and sweeps around clockwise and finishes a few miles northeast of Quillan. It is—without doubt—an almost perfect quadrant, the fourth part of a circle. Surely this cannot be the Masonic "square," an angle of 90° or "the fourth part of a circle." I turned my back on this strange geological feature and strolled down, with Lynne, to the church, Abbé Saunière's church. First, a step into the graveyard through the arch with the skull and cross-bones carved into it, immediately I felt at home, and, after all I have read and now seen of the priest's handiwork, I readily confess that I would have liked to have met him.

Turning to the east I could clearly see the peak of Pech Cardou rising above the ridge on which the ruins of the Château de Blanchefort still sit uneasily on a rocky outcrop—the same Château de Blanchefort that links Pech Cardou to Camp Grand in a 1:2:3 relationship. It was immediately noticeable that the church was perfectly aligned with Pech Cardou, just like the churches in Cassaignes and Coustaussa. The variation from east towards Pech Cardou was not as marked as with the other two churches but it was still of the order of 10°. Although the whole church was clearly orientated directly at Pech Cardou, the section of northwest wall between the corner and the campanile was in fact still aligned with the east. It is difficult to argue that the Abbé left this small section of wall facing due east for no other reason than to leave a record of its original orientation.

On the lintel over the front door to the church is carved "TERRIBILIS EST" and underneath in lower case lettering are the two words "locus iste." This has been translated as "this place is terrible" a phrase which has done much to create the aura of mystery that hangs over the building, even though the words could have been culled from the Bible.

> And he was afraid, and said, How dreadful is this place! This is none other but the house of God, and this is the gate of heaven.
>
> Genesis 28:17

I believe that we can now take it that the clergyman was indulging his remarkable sense of humor and that the phrase can more correctly be read as:

Terrible EAST—this place [has]

It is apparent that Bérenger Saunière's renovation of the old 11th-century church went much further than is generally reported, for during this work he had most of the church dismantled and re-erected to align with Pech Cardou. His motivation was quite simple. He had discovered that the Ark of the Covenant—God—was located in Pech Cardou and so he turned his church to face Him. This amazing observation is supported by the alignment of the original presbytery and the adjacent chateau, both of which are aligned with the east. My request for a copy of a map showing the site of the earlier 11th-century chapel to Ste. Madeleine, which Bérenger had rebuilt, brought forth a series of "non monsieur" from each of the locals manning the bookshop or collecting money from tourists.

Stanley James[68] takes the analysis of this phrase even further.

> *"Terribilis est"—"This place is full of dread"—"Que ce lieu est redoutable!"—"redoutable"—"redout a ble"—"a place, structure, containing gold." "Que ce lieu est redoutable!" is an anagram of "et l'est Berque doue au ciel" which means "in the east the Berque is endowed with Heaven—or "will endow of heaven"—meaning not a spiritual shrine but a place of rich material storage and benefit.*

La Berco Grando—the current edition of the IGN map uses a "co" in Berco, whereas James' interpretation requires the use of the near phonetic equivalent "que"—is the mountain, which, with the eastern face of Cardaussel, forms the valley in which stand the two pillars of the new temple, Jachin and Boaz. Saunière's wonderful mind and sense of humor had set it all out for anyone to see. It is a matter for later research, but the question remains as to exactly why the Abbé set about building permanent pointers to the New Jerusalem and the new temple, which seemed so to enthrall him. History may well demonstrate that these clues are exactly what Saunière was paid to do, but it still begs the question—why?

It was not until I had returned to England that I was able to carefully check the alignment of other churches in the area. I was not surprised to find that the IGN map mistakenly had the little church at Rennes-le-Château facing other than towards Pech Cardou; I had half expected it to face due east, but no, those map makers had gone one further and shown it facing due west. Once again the fingerprints of the Parisian mapmakers are found on a "smoking gun."

"Terrible EAST—this place [has]."

Other churches facing Pech Cardou include those at St-Just-et-le-Bézu, St-Louis-et-Parahou, Fourton, St-André, La Serpent and Luc-sur-Aude: a total of nine churches facing the Mountain—nine to commemorate the original nine Knights Templar? The evidence was becoming overwhelming in support of Pech Cardou being at one time the new temple and containing God's seat on earth, the Ark of the Covenant.

The identification of nine churches, all aligned with Pech Cardou, provides further evidence in support of the existence of "guardians"—people who, over hundreds of years, have supported the Templar ideals and passed the knowledge of Pech Cardou and what it contained from generation to generation. These people are clearly able to exercise power or have access to great sums of money, for I have already identified twenty-seven churches in and around Pech Cardou and in Paris which have been built to a pattern that runs counter to the requirements of the Catholic Church.

In just a few days my wife, Lynne, and I would also move on to Renaissance Italy: it was nearly three weeks later that we re-entered France about 200 miles northeast of Rennes-le-Chateau. We were heading for Chambery, the one-time home of the counts of Savoy and the place where the legendary Turin Shroud was first exhibited publicly. As we came out of the Alps with Chambery almost in view, an astonishing site reared slowly up in front of the car: a mountain ridge well over 3,000 feet (1,000 meters) high shaped like a pair of wings and around a mile wide. As far as I could tell this is an entirely natural feature and on altogether far too grand a scale to have been man-made. I could immediately picture a much smaller version of those wings at the top of the caduceus shown in Figure 6. Lynne does all of our "high level" driving because of my vertigo and so she had been driving though the Alps permitting me to look at the map. "Col de Garnier," I thought it said; and now believed that I had, purely by chance, dropped on the reason for Garnier's statue occupying pride of place in the arrangement of triangles in Paris. It was not until I was able to sit quietly with the map in the hotel that night that I realized that the name of the mountain is Granier not Garnier. Oh well—I consoled myself as I drifted into sleep—perhaps there were no famous people in France called Granier. It was only when I had returned to England and made some enquiries that I discovered that such name changes were commonplace via the process of metathesis. Granier had more than likely once been Garnier or vice versa. Perhaps those magnificent "mountain wings" were, after all, intended figuratively to sit underneath the Palace du Luxembourg in Paris mimicking the caduceus further south. During the entire period of researching this mystery, I have become familiar with the way the "guardians" of the secret cannot resist an opportunity for a dramatic gesture. There could be no more dramatic signal than the inclusion within the symbolism of a one-mile wide pair of wings.

Certainly the thesis of Andrews and Schellenberger, that Cardou contains the body of Christ, can now be discounted. It is inconceivable that so many Roman Catholic churches would be built to align with the body of Jesus Christ in denial of His ascension to heaven. There is only one artifact which would prompt people to align their churches towards it: the Ark of the Covenant.

The church at Rennes-le-Château is indeed a fascinating place. But others have analyzed, in great detail, what is there, so I will move on—first to the garden with its circle inside a triangle. This triangle is oriented exactly as the lower triangle shown on page 336, Figure 98, complete with a circle in the center. If Pech Cardou is represented by the central Calvary, then—approximately to the same scale and in approximately the same direction—the Visigoth pillar represents Rennes-le-Château, a village, with a Visigoth ancestry, on top of a pillar of rock. Likewise, the grotto represents the mine entrance of the south face of Cardou.

The visit to the cemetery, followed by a rest in the little church of Sainte Madeleine to soak up the atmosphere, and then the walk around the tiny garden, all merged into one memorable experience. Next, we paid over our francs and took a look around the museum in the old church presbytery. My eyes settled on a sketch drawn by the Abbé. It was of a fleur de lys with a "Seal of Solomon" or six-pointed star above the middle or largest petal. The similarity with the three peaks of Cardaussel, Pech Cardou, and Montferrand was unmistakable, and it was also clear that he was flagging up Pech Cardou as being the temple. It was now becoming likely that Bérenger Saunière had probably visited the church of Ste. Madeleine in Troyes. For the large stained-window in the northeast corner of the larger church was divided into four panels by three stone mullions which unfurled at the top to create an ornate stone fleur de lys (Fig. 111). In the center petal of the fleur is a picture of Jesus Christ

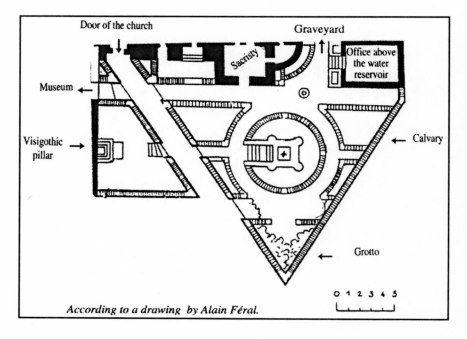

Figure 110
Abbé Saunière's Garden

Figure 111
The stained glass
window in the
church of Sainte
Madeleine at
Troyes.

on the cross; God is in the central leaf—Pech Cardou in Saunière's sketch.

We moved next to the Villa Bethania. The link, in name, between the church, the Tour Magdala and the villa come from the knowledge that "Bethania" was the name of the town where Mary Magdalene and her brother Lazarus lived. Once again, others have analyzed every nook and cranny of Saunière's house, but nowhere have I seen it mentioned that the hall is decorated, above the dado rail or wooden border halfway up the wall, with painted thistles some three feet high, reaching nearly to the ceiling. The more ancient French word for thistle is "cardon," which you will recall is an alternative name for Cardou.

Finally, it was time for a stroll around the belvedere, the Tour Magdala. With the memory of the external staircase to the bell-tower of the church of St. Madeleine in Troyes firmly in mind, I stood in the car-park and admired the outside of the Tour Magdala. If, as now seems highly likely, the clergyman was pointing to the church in Troyes when he built the Tour Magdala, then he was also making the point about mirror images. The turret containing the external staircase on the Tour Magdala is on the southwest corner while the one on the bell-tower at the church of St. Madeleine is on the diametrically opposite northeast corner.

To access the doorway in order to ascend the inside of the Tour Magdala, we had to walk around the adjacent quadrant-shaped terrace with its gallery room below. As we stood on the terrace admiring the view over Couiza and beyond, it was very easy to visualize the layout of the complete little complex as a mirror image of the range of hills running clockwise round from Pech de Bugarach. The concept of a mirror image, once accepted, permits an interesting diagram to be developed.

If the Tour and terrace are mirrored about the north-south axis, a semicircle with two pillars at each end can be seen. A further mirroring of this image produces a circle with four pillars, two at the west end, and two at the east end (Fig. 112)—a near perfect schematic of King Solomon's temple. An "angle of 90° or the fourth part of a circle" from the Masonic ritual that I first introduced in Chapter 6 has been transformed into King Solomon's temple.

After climbing to the top of the Tour Magdala, past an imaginary Saunière sitting by the fire composing his sermons, we stood inside the battlement around the top of the Tour once more taking in the spectacular views, this time including the view back over the Villa Bethania with Pech Cardou in the distance. All too soon it was time to wander back along the terrace to the glasshouse or observatory at the far end from the Tour Magdala.

The heat, the wine, the overwhelming headiness of the success of my visit combined. Before I knew it, I was imagining myself as the Abbé, with his housekeeper Marie Denarnaud and a bottle of the

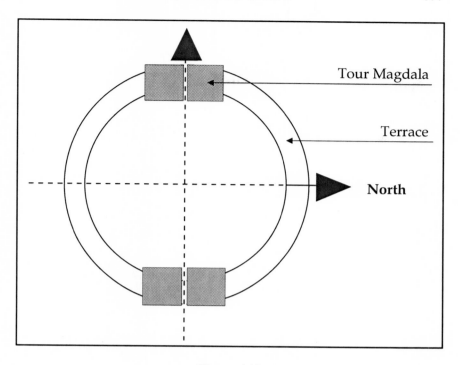

Figure 112
The schematic King Solomon's Temple from the Tour Magdala
and the Terrace Mirrored Twice

local vintage wine. Had the priest been gifted with prescience, he'd have known that soon the relic's guardians would move the Ark of the Covenant to a safe site, a site which would have met with his entire approbation. But, for now, Saunière relaxes in that observatory in the balmy evening air, admiring the mountain he knew so well. Straining his eyes to try to see over the ruins of the Château Blanchefort and the mountain below which obstructed his view, he can almost make out the forty-foot high image of the Savior he loved, the Savior Who had blessed him so lavishly these many years.

POSTSCRIPT

The first wrote,   *Wine is the strongest,*
The second wrote,   *The King is the strongest,*
The third wrote,   *Women are strongest but above all*
        TRUTH beareth away the victory.

From the Canon of the Septuagint

SOME IMPORTANT ISSUES HAVE BEEN RAISED, not least for Free-masons everywhere. Masonic Research lodges have, through the years, overseen the formulation of hundreds if not thousands of research papers expanding on the operative-masonry origins of Freemasonry. It has always been comfortably non-threatening to have a group of stonemasons as one's anteced-ents. It now looks as if that work was misdirected, and that Freema-sonry is in fact the ingenious creation of some remarkably clever people, most likely from the Court of Champagne. These findings, however, should not be a cause for disappointment or any sense of devaluation. The same people who designed Freemasonry prob-ably also devised another successful organization, the Knights Templar. One of the questions that historians, whether Masonic or otherwise, might choose to explore is—just who were these people? What was it that made them able to design such highly-esteemed fraternities? In this modern world of ours, such talents would make them kings of the entertainment business with riches beyond imagi-nation.

This particular book is just a start, as it would be ludicrous for me to submit that all of my conclusions are correct. It is in the nature of

378

research that new evidence will be uncovered that will make some of my assumptions look silly. The facts, however, which underpin this investigation have been double-checked and are there to be re-measured by anyone. As others probe this mystery, new evidence will doubtless emerge to further harden some of the suppositions and move them towards "accepted" status. The very words "fact" and "proof" should be used cautiously when dealing with early history, but it is as well to bear in mind that we lock people up for life on the basis of "beyond reasonable doubt." The most important thing is for the search to continue—the search for the truth. There are still many clues to the links with the Templar cross-patée and other bonds that I have not uncovered; they are sitting there waiting to be found. There are still more clues that I have simply omitted so as to avoid disclosing too much ritual, as the photographs from the castles in Cyprus will testify.

For Freemasons everywhere things will doubtless alter little. For the majority—the *knife and fork masons*—who enjoy the comrade-ship, the fellowship and the fine works—nothing has changed, Lodges will continue to meet and fellowship will be exchanged. Some men will find the idea of a relationship with the Knights Templar attractive; others will simply deny the validity of every-thing in this work and leave matters at that. It is perhaps to be hoped that the majority of the population at large who are not Freemasons can now have a better understanding of the chivalrous nature of the Order. This may go a little way to assuage the generally poor image that Masonry has acquired over recent years. It would be much more helpful if the image of Freemasonry could be shown as that of a group of people with an honorable doctrine who set high stan-dards for themselves, even though many may fail to realize them.

There are other issues raised within these pages that also need to be settled. For example, the position and role of the IGN in this puzzle simply must be resolved. Their explanations to date, for the landmark place-names and the circle of thirty-three points, score very low on any verisimilitude scale. Likewise, the involvement of the Paris and Greenwich Observatories in all of this should be clarified. All three appear to have permitted the Hospitaller authori-ties to exert a level of control over the terrestrial and celestial maps that demands explanation. The difficulties I experienced in obtaining information, the overwhelming number of "coincidences," highlights the problems that future investigators will meet. Sarcophaguses that categorically "don't exist" when photographed are then said to have "no known provenance." If nothing else, there is a good mystery story in this investigation. The author's experiences are, however, nothing new; indeed Henry Lincoln describes in careful detail in his latest book, *The Key to the Sacred Pattern*[40], the curious answers he received to his questions and the obstructive behavior and inexplicable attitude of people and organizations along the way. My grasp of the French language does not permit me to explore the matter further than I have. It is apparent that, thus far, I have been given the brush-off. Others with the necessary skills will need to pick up this particular baton and run with it until the truth is shaken free.

There is also that most tantalizing leftover, the Ark of the Covenant. All of my research has pointed to one conclusion and that is that it still exists. If this assumption is correct, then the fact that the Templars held on to it during their relatively short existence is understandable. Religious bigotry was a way of life; Jews were believed by Christians to have murdered their Messiah, and history is littered with Jewish persecution based on the story of the crucifixion, even into modern times. Measured against contemporary attitudes, the behavior of the Templars was not extraordinary. Indeed, the disappearance from Masonic ritual of any reference to the Ark may be entirely due to the achievement, by the Jews, in 1920 of their own "national home," albeit under a British mandate. Certainly, since they seized self-rule in 1948, they have shown themselves to be a people well able to fight for what they consider to be their own.

Similarly, the behavior of those ex-Templars who carried the torch after the Order was crushed is understandable. They must have felt bruised, and they would have felt an overwhelming sense of wrong. In these circumstances they did what most normal people would do: they clung on to the only tangible artifact they had that bound them to their illustrious past, the Ark of the Covenant. This, however, does not explain the behavior of more recent guardians of the Ark. Perhaps they have continued to hold the Ark of the Covenant secret because that is how it has been kept since its last Biblical mention, and presumably that is how it was passed to them. We are in the end all captives of life's *psychic prisons*[34]. In the meantime the world has changed. In recent times, most of the world has become more stable, and the prospects for peace better than for many a year. More importantly, people are better educated and better informed, more able to handle complex problems and situations. Furthermore, as a consequence of improved education they have become more curious.

Only sixty years ago we were immersed in a savage world war that saw millions of men and women killed. The past fifty years have been spent under the threat of nuclear annihilation, and even now the world is not completely at peace with itself. But we are capable of resolving the fate of this particular "golden treasure." Whether God still speaks from the Ark will quickly become apparent. Whether He ever did might be more difficult to confirm, but at a time when we can look into space and see the origins of the universe we can surely try. However, at the very heart of this conundrum are some questions, and before we can even contemplate issues like "did God speak from the Ark," these must be answered.

1. Does the Ark exist?
2. Who's got it?
3. Is it Moses' original Ark of the Covenant?

None of these questions can be answered until the current guardians put their cards, or rather the Ark, on the table. There must then follow a period of scientific research to authenticate the Ark, to establish whether on the balance of probabilities it is real or a fake. The complicated nature of the negotiations that would precede the establishment of a suitable site for the Ark does not justify not having those negotiations. Three major religions in the world unite around an acceptance of the Ark of the Covenant as being of immense religious and historical importance. It should be available to all of mankind, not a select few no matter how carefully they are selected. The present guardians should, as a matter of urgency, declare their ownership and proffer proof of its authenticity, or put in hand such scientific examination as is necessary.

It is of course possible that those early Knights Templar had an Ark manufactured to provide them with the aura that would lead to their overwhelming prestige. On balance this is unlikely if only because of the intense respect for the power of God that existed in those days, and particularly among men who were pledged to a monastic way of life.

One comment made to me during the research period was to the effect that, "the chances of a wooden box surviving for three and a half thousand years is remote, even if it was covered in bitumen." The interesting aspect of this remark is that the Bible describes the Ark as lined inside and out with gold, and the mercy seat being beaten entirely from gold. The use of the term gold might of course be symbolic to emphasize the importance of the role of the Ark as God's seat. But if not, we are still left with the question of what then is this "Ark" that is or was covered in bitumen? The reference to bitumen may be an error of failing to recognize that some species of acacia contain high levels of tannin and other natural preservatives. It is entirely possible that these preservatives would, over time, have leached out of the wood and deposited on the surface as a layer resembling bitumen. On the assumption that the individual, making the criticism above, was aware of the existence of an "Ark" made entirely from wood, then this does suggest that it is not the one that Moses had manufactured when he descended from Mount Sinai.

Unfortunately for this debate, there is as usual another analysis. The Ark is only reported to have fallen into the hands of "the enemy" once, and that was during the reign of Samuel, i.e., before the construction of Solomon's temple. On that occasion, the Bible reports that the high priest Eli sent the Ark into a battle against the Philistines, a battle which the Israelites lost, and in consequence the Philistines captured the Ark. The Philistines then experienced several months of sickness and, blaming this on the unlawful ownership of the Ark, duly returned it. There was no reported damage to the Ark at that time, but much later, around 587 B.C. when Nebuchadnezzar sacked Jerusalem, he reportedly stripped the temple of its gold sheeting. This act of pillaging the gold sheet might just have included the inside and outside linings to the Ark of the Covenant which, when the gold was stripped away, was viewed as a worthless box and left behind when the temple was destroyed.

There is, of course, another, simpler explanation. As mentioned in Chapter 4, Jewish synagogues all have Arks to hold the copy of their sacred texts, the Torah. If the Templars found anything during their period in the Holy Land it might just have been one of these containers, which would also explain why it could be made from wood without any gold covering. The secretive manner in which they kept it has meant that for hundreds of years it was not subjected to any sort of scientific scrutiny. If this is the explanation, then it also seems likely that quite a number of very eminent men have been misled into thinking that it was the real thing.

The answer to this debate will only begin to emerge after extensive scientific testing, the most important test being that of carbon dating. There will doubtless be a need for a very brave man to cut a piece off the Ark for carbon dating. If the current "Ark" is indeed a Templar fake, then some 2500 years will emerge as the gap between its age and the time that Moses had the real one made. If, alternatively, the tests establish the possible authenticity of the Ark, then the current guardians should open negotiations for a suitable pilgrimage site. It will probably be a site away from centers of population so as to prevent terrorism from spoiling the enjoyment of the many. This would undoubtedly open a major international debate, with the Jewish nation demanding a central role. The fact is, however, that the site of the original temple is in Islamic hands. Any new temple built to display the Ark would need to be as secure as any building in the world but would also need to allow people to pass through and to view this international treasure. This could be the big event of the millennium; there is no shortage of money to fund such an enterprise and surely mankind has earned it. Certainly, only a brave and arguably foolish person would stand up and argue that the world's population is unworthy. If, as I have speculated, the present location of the Ark of the Covenant is shortly to be made public anyway, then any argument over the need for secrecy evaporates. It could be argued that arrogance and a lack of awareness of the reality around them brought the Templars down. It would be a sad reflection on man's propensity for pride if the present guardians allowed themselves to fall into the same trap.

APPENDIX I

YEAR	GRAND MASTERS	KINGS OF JERUSALEM	POPES
1088			Urban II
1099			Paschal II
1100		Baldwin I	
1118	Hugh de Payens	Baldwin II	Gelasius II
1119			Calixtus II
1124			Honorius II
1130			Innocent II
1131		Melisende	
1136	Robert de Craon		
1143		Baldwin III	Celestine II
1144			Lucius II
1145			Eugenius III
1146	Everard des Barres		
1149	Bernard de Trémélai		
1153	André de Montbard		Anastasius IV
1154			Adrian IV
1156	Bertrand de Blanquefort		
1159			Alexander III
1162		Amalric	
1169	Philip de Milly of Nablus		
1171	Odo de Saint-Amand		
1174		Baldwin IV	
1179	Arnold de Toroga		
1181			Lucius III
1185	Gerard de Ridfort	Baldwin V	Urban III
1186		Sibylla	
1187			Gregory VIII & Clement III
1191	Robert de Sable		Celestine III
1192		Isabella & Amalric II	
1193	Gilbert Erail		

1198			Innocent III
1201	Philip de Le Plessiez		
1209	William de Chartres		
1210		Maria	
1216			Honorius III
1219	Pedro de Montaigu		
1226		Yolanda	
1227			Gregory IX
1228		Conrad	
1230	Armand de Périgord		
1241			Celestine IV
1245	Richard de Bures		
1247	William de Sonnac		Innocent IV
1250	Reynald de Vichiers		
1254			Alexander IV
1256	Thomas Bérard		
1261			Urban IV
1265			Clement IV
1268			Hugh III
1271			Gregory X
1273	William de Beaujeu		
1276			Innocent V & John XXI
1277			Nicholas III
1281			Martin IV
1284		John I	
1285		Henry II	Honorius IV
1288			Nicholas IV
1291	Tibald Gaudin		
1294			Celestine V & Boniface VIII
1293	Jacques de Molay		
1303			Benedict XI
1305–1314			Clement

YEAR	KINGS OF FRANCE	KINGS OF ENGLAND	HOLY ROMAN EMPERORS
1056			Henry IV
1060	Philip I		
1087		William II	
1100		Henry I	
1106			Henry V
1108	Louis VI		
1125			Lothar III
1135		Stephen	
1137	Louis VII		
1138			Conrad III
1152			Frederick I
1154		Henry II	
1180	Philip II		
1189		Richard I	
1190			Henry VI
1199		John	
1212			Frederick II
1216		Henry III	
1223	Louis VIII		
1226	Louis IX		
1250			Conrad IV
1257			Alfonso X
1270	Philip III		
1272		Edward I	
1273			Rudolf I
1285	Philip IV		
1292			Adolf
1298			Albert I
1307		Edward II	
1308			Henry VII

APPENDIX II

ANCIENT MEASUREMENTS
(Taken from Reverend F. De Castells – Bibliography reference No. 20 -
and personal Bible)

Finger - Breadth of a finger, about half an inch (1.5 cm.), also known as a
digit.

Handsbreadth - Equal to the distance across the four fingers showing in a
clenched fist, about 2.5 inches (6 cm.). Modern day usage is restricted to
horse heights where a *hand* is 4 inches (10 cm.). Also known as a **palm**.

Span - The distance from the end of the little finger to the end of the thumb
on a spread hand. Equal to 3 handsbreadths or 12 fingers, around 7
inches (18 cm.).

Cubit - The distance from the tip of the middle finger to the elbow, from the
Latin *cubitus* meaning elbow. Equal to 2 spans.

Short cubit - An Egyptian measurement of around 6 handsbreadths.
Babylonian standard scales indicate this to be 14 inches (36 cm.).

Royal cubit - Also Egyptian but around 7 handsbreadths. Similar Babylonian scales put this at 18 inches (45 cm.).

Reed - Supposedly equal to 6 cubits, either 70 feet (21.6 meters) or 102 feet
(27 meters).

Cable - Equal to 120 fathoms or 720 feet (220 meters). In ancient times, a
cable was made from **three** twisted strands, each strand had **three**
ropes and every rope was made of **three** twists. The thicker the cable
required, the thicker was the twist.

Grave - Was—using imperial measures—6 feet by 3 feet wide by 5 feet
deep, totalling 90 cubic feet and 90 degrees is a square.

ANCIENT MONEY

Piece of Silver - Was roughly equivalent to a drachma and very approximately worth about $15 today.

APPENDIX III

SEQUENCE OF IMPORTANT EVENTS AND DATES

614   Persian army captures Jerusalem.

629   Byzantine Emperor Heraclius I recaptures Jerusalem for Christianity.

638   Muslim army captures Jerusalem.

1048 Hospital of St. John founded in Jerusalem.

1096 Peter the Hermit's crusade arrives in Byzantium, but the venture ends in death for most of its participants.

1097 The First Crusade with four European armies under:
Godfrey de Bouillon - Duke of Lower Lorraine,
Bohemond - Norman Prince of Taranto in Italy,
Raymond - Count of Toulouse,
Robert of Normandy, the son of William the Conqueror, arrived in the Holy land.

1099 Jerusalem is back under Christian control.

1118 Formation of Poor Fellow Knights of Christ and the Temple of Jerusalem.

1128 Council of Troyes gives the Knights Templar papal approval.

1129 Christians in the Holy Land attack Damascus and are soundly defeated.

1129 Hugh de Payen returns to the Holy Land with hundreds of knights and secures the Templars' financial future with a huge number of estates in Europe.

1138 Knights Templar engage in their first campaign to retake the town of Teqoa some 8.7 miles (14 kilometers) south of Jerusalem and, although they took the town, the Muslims regrouped and counter-attacked, defeating and killing the Templars.

1140 Around this time, the Hospital of St. John began recruiting knights who became known as the Hospitallers.

1144 Edessa on the northeast frontier is recaptured by the Muslims.

1147 The Second Crusade, initiated by St. Bernard and led by the French King Louis VII and the German King Conrad III, gets under way, but many crusaders are killed on the journey by the Turks.

1148   Christians in the Holy Land again attack Damascus and are again defeated. Some say the Templars were bribed to let the Saracens win.

1153   St. Bernard dies.

1153   Siege of Ascalon during which the Templar Grand Master led his men through a breach in the walls to their deaths because he appeared to want the glory of capture of the city to be credited to the Templars.

1168   King Amalric proposes a third assault on Egypt and the Templars refuse to join because it would breach the existing treaty.

1170   Series of major earthquakes in the Holy Land demolish many towns and castles; six thousand people died.

1172   A Templar, Walter de Mesnil, frustrates King Amalric's alliance with the Assassins by murdering their ambassadors.

1177   Saladin advances on Jerusalem but is defeated by the Christians.

1187   One hundred and thirty-three Templars killed at the Springs of Cresson led by their Grand Master, Gerard de Ridfort, against seven thousand Saracens.

1187   July 4: Christian army, goaded into poor military decisions by Gerard de Ridfort, were destroyed at the Horns of Hattin by Saladin.
        July 5: Tiberias surrendered to Saladin
        July 10: Acre fell to Saladin
        July 14: Nablus - ditto -
        July 20: Jaffa - ditto -
        July 24: Toron - ditto -
        July 29: Sidon - ditto -
        August 6: Beirut - ditto -
        September 4: Ascalon - ditto -
        October 2: Jerusalem - ditto -

1187   Thirteen weeks after the battle of Hattin, only Tyre and a few castles remained in Christian hands.

1189   Guy de Lusignan, the King of Jerusalem, was refused admission to Tyre by Conrad de Montferrat and so Guy set off and laid siege to Acre.

1191   King Richard I of England and King Philip II of France set off for the Holy Land and the Third Crusade.
        May - Richard captures Cyprus.
        June - Richard arrives at Acre.
        July - Acre capitulates and Philip returns to France.
        September - Richard decisively beats Saladin at Arsuf.
        October - Richard turns back in sight of Jerusalem to rebuild the desolated Ascalon.

1192   May - Richard recaptured Daron, the most southerly castle lost to Saladin.

August - Richard retakes Jaffa.

1193   Saladin died and his empire fell apart due to family squabbles.
1194   King Richard leaves the Holy Land.
1209   Pope Innocent III orders the annihilation of the Cathars.
1218   Castle Pilgrim built.
1219   Damietta surrenders to the Fourth Crusade.
1221   Fourth Crusade ends on the Nile when the Muslims open the sluice gates and flood the Christians' position, drowning most crusaders.
1227   Emperor Frederick II excommunicated by Pope Gregory IX.
1228   Frederick's Crusade (fifth) arrives in the Holy Land.
1229   Frederick negotiates the hand-over of Jerusalem to Christianity.
1239   Jerusalem lost again to the Muslim's prince of Kerak.
1241   Hospitallers negotiate the return of Jerusalem to Christian control.
1244   Mongols raze Jerusalem and the Holy Land.
1249   King (St) Louis IX of France's Crusade (sixth) moves up the Nile intent on taking Damietta and then Cairo.
1250   Templars follow Louis' brother Robert of Artois into Mansourah where they were bottled up and slaughtered; sickness forces Louis to surrender.
1252   Templar Grand Master Reynald de Vichiers publicly begged forgiveness from King Louis for negotiating a treaty behind the King's back.
1254   Louis returns to France.
1268   Mameluk Sultan captures Jaffa, Banyas and Beaufort.
1270   King Louis returns with the Seventh Crusade but dies of dysentery shortly after landing in Tunisia.
1271   Hospitaller castle, Krak des Chevaliers, and the Templar castle of Safita fall to Mameluks.
        May - Prince Edward of England arrives with English knights to continue the Seventh Crusade and negotiates a ten-year truce.
1291   Muslims began sweep of Holy Land.
        May - Templar Gibald Gaudin departs from Acre for Sidon with the Templar *treasure*; ten days later the city was razed to the ground.
        May - Tyre surrendered.
        June - Tibald Gaudin elected Grand Master of the Templars and leaves Sidon for Ruad and Cyprus with the *treasure*.
        June - Sidon taken by the Muslims and obliterated.
        July - Haifa and Beirut surrender.
        August - Tortosa and Castle Pilgrim evacuated.
1305   Clement V became Pope.
1307   13 October - Templars in France arrested.
        27 October - Pope orders all Christian Kings to arrest Templars.
1308   February - Clement suspended the inquisition in France.
1309   August - Papal commission got under way.

1310 February - Templar defense began.
April - Philip de Marigny, the brother of King Philip's chief minister of finance, is installed as archbishop of Sens.
May - Provincial church council under Archbishop Marigny orders fifty-four Templars to be burnt alive as relapsed heretics.
May - Papal commission adjourned for five months.
November - Templar defense collapses.

1311 October - Council of Vienne met but Pope Clement was unable to get a decision made on the fate of the Order of the Knights Templar.

1312 April - Council of Vienne reconvened and the Order of the Knights Templar formally dissolved, all Templar property given to the Knights Hospitaller.

1314 March - Templar Grand Master, Jacques de Molay, and the preceptor of Normandy, Geoffrey de Charney, publicly revoked their confessions and were burnt at the stake. The Preceptor of Aquitaine, Geoffrey de Gonneville, and the Treasurer, Hugh de Pairaud, did not revoke their confessions and both died later in prison.
April - Clement V died.
November - Philip IV died.

APPENDIX IV

HEBREW ALPHABET AND CABALISTIC MEANINGS

HEBREW	NAME	ENGLISH	NUMBER	DEFINITION	MEANING	ELEMENT	ASTRO
א	Aleph	'	1	Ox	Power	Air	Uranus
ב	Beth	b	2	House	Attention	Air	Mercury
ג	Gimel	g	3	Camel	Memory	Water	Moon
ד	Daleth	d	4	Door	Imagination	Air	Venus
ה	He	h	5	Window	Reason	Fire	Aries
ו	Vau	v	6	Nail	Intuition	Earth	Taurus
ז	Zayin	z	7	Sword	Discrimination	Air	Gemini
ח	Cheth	ḥ	8	Fence	Receptivity	Water	Cancer
ט	Teth	ṭ	9	Serpent	Suggestion	Fire	Leo
י	Yod	y	10	Open hand	Response	Earth	Virgo
כ	Kaph	k	20 & 500	Closed hand	Rotation	Fire	Jupiter
ל	Lamed	l	30	Ox goad	Equilibrium	Air	Libra
מ	Mem	m	40 & 600	Water	Reversal	Water	Neptune
נ	Nun	n	50 & 700	Fish	Transformation	Water	Scorpio
ס	Samekh	ṣ	60	Prop	Verification	Fire	Saggitarius
ע	Ayin	'	70	Eye	Bondage	Earth	Capricorn
פ	Peh	p	80 & 800	Mouth	Awakening	Fire	Mars
צ	Tzaddi	c	90 & 900	Fish-hook	Revelation	Air	Aquarius
ק	Qoph	q	100	Back of head	Organization	Water	Pisces
ר	Resh	r	200	Head	Regeneration	Fire	Sun
ש	Shin	s	300	Tooth	Realization	Fire	Pluto
ת	Tau	t	400	Mark	Cosmic concious	Earth	Saturn

NOTES

1. Laurence Gardner, *The Bloodline of the Holy Grail* (1996).
2. Zecharia Sitchin, *The Stairway to Heaven* (1993).
3. Leen Ritmeyer, *The Temple and the Rock* (1996).
4. Captain Wilson & Captain Warren, *Recovery of Jerusalem* (1971).
5. Richard Andrews & Paul Schellenberger, *The Tomb of God* (1996).
6. Christopher Knight & Robert Lomas, *The Hiram Key* (1996).
7. John Cohane, *The Key* (1971).
8. David Wood, *Genisis* (1985).
9. Edith Simon, *The Piebald Standard* (1959).
10. Barbara Tuchman, *A Distant Mirror* (1978).
11. Michael Baigent & Henry Leigh, *The Temple and the Lodge* (1989).
12. Michael Baigent, Henry Leigh & Henry Lincoln, *Holy Blood, Holy Grail* (1982).
13. Grant Uden, *A Dictionary of Chivalry* (1968).
14. Joan Evans, *Life in Medieval France* (1925).
15. David Stevenson, *The Origins of Freemasonry* (1988).
16. John Robinson, *Born in Blood* (1990).
17. Henry Lincoln, *The Holy Place* (1991).
18. Roger Price, *Concise History of France* (1993).
19. Edward Burman, *Supremely Abominable Crimes* (1994).
20. Reverend F. De Castells, *Arithmetic in Freemasonry* (1925).
21. Caesar E.Farah, *Islam: Beliefs and Practices* (1970).
22. John Robinson, *Dungeon, Fire and Sword* (1991).
23. Graham Hancock, *The Sign and the Seal* (1992).
24. Chrétien de Troyes, *Perceval* (Translated by Nigel Bryant) (1982).
25. Gérard de Sède, *L'Or de Rennes* (1967).
26. Graham Hancock, *Fingerprints of the Gods* (1995).
27. John West, *Serpent in the Sky* (1979).
28. Robert Bauval & Graham Hancock, *Keeper of Genesis* (1996).
29. Stephen Howarth, *The Knights Templar* (1982).

30. Dava Sobel, *Longitude* (1995).
31. Albert Mackey, *The History of Freemasonry* (1881).
32. Sir Harry Luke, *Cyprus* (1965).
33. Arnold Toynbee, *Mankind and Mother Earth* (1976).
34. Gareth Morgan, *Images of Organisation* (1986).
35. General Albert Pike, *Morals and Dogma* (1977).
36. David Wood & Ian Campbell, *Geneset* (1994).
37. Colin Law, *Kabbalah FAQ (Internet)* (1996).
38. John Greer, *An Introduction to Corpus Hermeticum (Internet)* (1997).
39. Kate Rheeders, *Qabalah, A Beginners Guide* (1996).
40. Henry Lincoln, *The Key to the Sacred Pattern* (1997).
41. Dr. Ekaterini Aristidou, *Kolossi Castle through the Centuries* (1983).
42. Jonathon Riley-Smith (ed.), *The Oxford Illustrated History of the Crusades* (1995).
43. Terry Jones & Alan Ereica, *Crusades* (1994).
44. Lynne Picknett & Clive Prince, *The Templar Revelation* (1997).
45. Godfrey Higgins, *Anacalypsis* (1836).
46. John Hamill, *The Craft* (1986).
47. Kenneth McLeish, *Myth* (1996).
48. John Woodward & George Burnett, *A Treatise on Heraldry* (1892).
49. Arthur Fox-Davies, *A Complete Guide to Heraldry* (1993).
50. Bernard Lewis, *The Middle East* (1995).
51. Brian de Breffny, *The Synagogue* (1978).
52. Louis Jacobs, *The Jewish Religion* (1995).
53. Ed. J. D. Douglas, *The Dictionary of the Christian Church* (1974).
54. Ed. Mircea Eliade, *The Encyclopaedia of Religion* (1987).
55. Ed. John Hinnells, *Penguin Dictionary of Religions* (1984).
56. Jennifer Speake, *The Dent Dictionary of Symbols in Christian Art* (1994).
57. Jean-Claude Frère, *Leonardo* (1995).
58. R. H. Wilenski, *Poussin* (1948).
59. Bernard E. Jones, *Freemasons' Book of the Royal Arch* (1957).
60. I. Begg and D. Begg, *In Search of the Holy Grail and the Precious Book* (1995).
61. Lord Longford, *Saints* (1987).
62. *Paper on shamir*
63. J. C. H. Aveling, *The Jesuits* (1981).
64. Michael Fosse, *The Founding of the Jesuits* (1969).
65. Published by William Reeves, *A Ritual of Freemasonry* (c. 1912).
66. Avery Allyn, *A Ritual of Freemasonry* (1831).

67. ETHRN Federation, *A Brief History of the Knights Templar* (1998).
68. Stanley James, *The Treasure Maps of Rennes-le-Chateau* (1984).
69. Dr. Keith Laidler, *The Head of God* (1998).
70. H. Finke, *Acta Aragonensia Vol. 2* (1923).
71. Steven Runciman, *A History of the Crusades Vols. 1, 2 & 3* (1951-53).
72. Louis Charpentier (transl. Sir Ronald Fraser), *The Mysteries of Chartres Cathedral* (1972).
73. Arthur Zuckerman, *The Jewish Princedom in Feudal France* (1972).
74. Titian, *Arnoldo Mondadori Arte* (1991)
75. Andrew Sinclair, *The Sword and the Grail* (1988).
76. Michelangelo, *Ludwig Goldscheider* (1953).
77. The Pre-Raphaelites, *Tim Barringer* (1988).
78. Ian Wilson, *The Blood and the Shroud* (1998).
79. On Earth as it is in Heaven, *Greg Rigby* (1996).
80. Richard Andrews, *Blood on the Mountain* (1999).

BIBLIOGRAPHY

Allyn, Avery. *A Ritual of Freemasonry*. Philadelphia: John Clarke, 1831.

Andrews, Richard and Schellenberger, Paul. *The Tomb of God. The Body of Jesus and the Solution to a 2,000-Year-Old Mystery*. London: Little Brown & Company, 1996.

Andrews, Richard. *Blood on the Mountain: A History of the Temple Mount from the Ark to the Present*. London: Phoenix, 1999.

Anonymous. *A Ritual of Freemasonry*. William Reeves, c.1912.

Aristidou, Dr. Ekaterini. - *Kolossi Castle through the Centuries*, Nicosia: 1983.

Aveling, J. C. H. *The Jesuits*. London: Blond and Briggs, 1981.

Baigent, Michael & Leigh, Henry. *The Temple and the Lodge*. London: Cape, 1989.

Baigent, Michael, Leigh, Henry & Lincoln, Henry. *Holy Blood, Holy Grail*. London: Cape, 1982.

Barringer, Tim. *The Pre-Raphaelites: Reading the Image*. London: Weidenfeld and Nicholson, 1988.

Barker-Cryer, Rev. Neville. *The Shamir*. Masonic Research Paper.

Bauval, Robert & Hancock, Graham. *Keeper of Genesis: A Quest for the Hidden Legacy of Mankind*. London: Heinemann, 1996.

Begg, E.& Begg, D. *In Search of the Holy Grail and the Precious Blood*. London: Aquarian, 1995.

Breffny, Brian de. *The Synagogue*. 1978.

Burman, Edward. *Supremely Abominable Crimes: The Trial of the Knights Templar*. London: Allison and Busby, 1994.

Captain Wilson & Captain Warren. *Recovery of Jerusalem*. 1971.

Castells, Rev. F. De. *Arithmetic in Freemasonry*. 1925.

Charpentier, Louis (translated by Sir Ronald Fraser). *The Mysteries of Chartres Cathedral*. 1972.

Cohane, John. *The Key*. 1971.

Douglas, J. D. (Ed.). *The New International Dictionary of the Christian Church*. Exeter: Paternoster Press, 1974.

Eliade, Mircea (Ed.). *The Encyclopaedia of Religion.* London: Collier. Macmillan, 1987.

ETHRN Federation. *A Brief History of the Knights Templar.* Internet, 1998.

Evans, Joan, 1893. *Life in Medieval France.* London: Phaidon, 1969.

Farah, Caesar E. *Islam: Beliefs and Practices.* 1970.

Finke, H. *Acta Aragonensia, Vol. 2.* 1923.

Fosse, Michael. *The Founding of the Jesuits.* 1969.

Fox-Davies, Arthur. *A Complete Guide to Heraldry.* London: Bracken Books, 1993.

Frère, Jean-Claude. *Leonardo: Painter, Inventor, Visionary, Mathematician, Philosopher, Engineer.* Paris: Terrail, 1995.

Gardner, Laurence. *The Bloodline of the Holy Grail: The Hidden Lineage of Jesus Revealed.* Shaftesbury: Element, 1996.

Goldscheider, Ludwig. *Michelangelo: Paintings, Sculpture, Architecture.* London: Phaidon, 1975.

Greer, John. *An Introduction to Corpus Hermeticum.* Internet, 1997.

Hamill, John. *The Craft: A History of English Freemasonry.* Wellingborough: Crucible, 1986.

Hancock, Graham. *The Sign and the Seal: A Quest for the Ark of the Covenant.* London: Heinemann, 1992.

Hancock, Graham. *Fingerprints of the Gods: A Quest for the Beginning and the End.* London: Heinemann, 1995.

Higgins, Godfrey. *Anacalypsis.* 1836.

Hinnells, John (Ed.). *Penguin Dictionary of Religions.* London: Allen Lane, 1984.

Howarth, Stephen. *The Knights Templar.* London: Collins 1982.

Jacobs, Louis. *The Jewish Religion: A Companion.* Oxford: Oxford University Press 1995.

James, Stanley. *The Treasure Maps of Rennes-le-Chateau.* London: Maxbow, 1984.

Jones, Bernard E. *Freemasons' Book of the Royal Arch.* London: Harrap, 1957.

Jones, Terry & Ereira, Alan. *Crusades.* London: BBC Books, 1994.

Knight, Christopher & Lomas, Robert. *The Hiram Key: Pharaohs, Freemasons and the Discovery of the Secret Scrolls of Jesus.* London: Century, 1996.

Laidler, Dr. Keith. *The Head of God: The Lost Treasure of the Templars.* London: Weidenfeld, 1998.

Law, Colin. *Kabbalah FAQ.* Internet, 1996.

Lewis, Bernard. *The Middle East: 2000 Years of History from the Rise of Christianity.* London: Weidenfeld, 1995.

Lincoln, Henry. *The Holy Place: The Mystery of Rennes-le-Château: Discovering the Eighth Wonder of the Ancient World*. London: Jonathon Cape, 1991.

Lincoln, Henry. *The Key to the Sacred Pattern: The Untold Story of Rennes-le-Château*. Moreton-in-the-Marsh: Windrush, 1997.

Longford, Frank Pakenham. *Saints*. London: Hutchinson, 1987.

Luke, Sir Harry. *Cyprus: A Portrait and an Appreciation*. London: Harrap, 1973.

Mackey, Albert. *The History of Freemasonry*. 1881.

McLeish, Kenneth. *Myth: Myths and Legends of the World Explored*. London: Bloomsbury, 1996.

Morgan, Gareth. *Images of Organisation*. London: Sage, 1986.

Picknett, Lynne & Prince, Clive. *The Templar Revelation: Secret Guardians of the True Identity of Christ*. London: Bantam, 1997.

Pike, General Albert. *Morals and Dogma*. 1977.

Price, Roger. *Concise History of France (Cambridge Concise Histories)*. Cambridge: Cambridge University Press, 1993.

Read, Piers Paul. *The Templars: The Dramatic History of the Knights Templar, the Most Powerful Military Order of the Crusades*. London: Weidenfeld & Nicholson, 1999.

Rheeders, Kate. *Qabalah: A Beginners Guide*. London: Headway, 1996.

Rigby, Greg. *On Earth As It Is in Heaven*. Belmont: Rhaedus, 1996.

Riley-Smith, Jonathon (Ed). *The Oxford Illustrated History of the Crusades*. Oxford: Oxford University Press, 1995.

Ritmeyer, Leen. *The Temple and the Rock*. York: Ritmeyer Archaeological Design, 1996.

Robinson, John. *Born in Blood: The Lost Secrets of Freemasonry*. London: Century, 1990.

Robinson, John. *Dungeon, Fire and Sword: The Knights Templar in the Crusades*. London: Michael O'Mara, 1994.

Runciman, Steven. *A History of the Crusades Vol. 1: The First Crusade and the Foundation of the Kingdom of Jerusalem*. Harmondsworth: Penguin, 1978.

Runciman, Steven. *A History of the Crusades Vol. 2: The Kingdom of Jerusalem and the Frankish East*. Harmondsworth: Penguin, 1978.

Runciman, Steven. *A History of the Crusades Vol. 3: The Kingdom of Acre and the Later Crusades*. Cambridge: Cambridge University Press, 1954.

Sadleir, Richard (translation). *Titian (1487 – 1575)*. Arnoldo Mondadori (Arte), 1991.

Sède, Gérard de. *L'Or de Rennes.* 1967.

Simon, Edith. *The Piebald Standard: A Biography of the Knights Templar.* London: Cassels, 1959.

Sinclair, Andrew. *The Sword and the Grail.* London: Century, 1988.

Sitchin, Zecharia. *The Stairway to Heaven.* Sante Fe: Bear & Co., 1993.

Sobel, Dava. *Longitude: The True Story of a Lone Genius Who Solved the Greatest Scientific Problem of the Time.* London: Fourth Estate, 1995.

Speake, Jennifer. *The Dent Dictionary of Symbols in Christian Art.* London: Dent, 1994.

Stevenson, David. *The Origins of Freemasonry: Scotland's Century 1590-1710.* Cambridge: Cambridge University Press, 1988.

Toynbee, Arnold. *Mankind and Mother Earth: A Narrative History of the World.* London: Oxford University Press, 1976.

Troyes, Chrétien de (Translated by Nigel Bryant). *Perlesvaus.* Ipswich: Brewer, 1982.

Tuchman, Barbara. *A Distant Mirror: The Calamitous 14th Century.* London: Papermac, 1978.

Uden, Grant. *A Dictionary of Chivalry.* London: Longman, 1968.

West, John. *Serpent in the Sky: The High Wisdom of Ancient Egypt.* London: Wildword, 1979.

Wilenski, R. H. *Poussin (1594–1665).* London: Faber, 1958.

Wilson, Ian. *The Blood and the Shroud: The Passionate Controversy Still Enflaming the World.* London: Weidenfeld, 1998.

Wood, David. *Genisis: The First Book of Revelations.* Tunbridge Wells: Baton, 1985.

Wood, David & Campbell, Ian. *Geneset: Target Earth.* Sunbury- on-Thames: Bellevue, 1994.

Woodward, John & Burnett, George. *A Treatise on Heraldry.* 1892.

Zuckerman, Arthur. *The Jewish Princedom in Feudal France 798–900.* Columbia: Columbia University Press, 1972.

INDEX

Note:
• Page numbers in italic typeface indicate illustrations.
• Page numbers followed by *q* indicate quotations.

400

ABOUT THE AUTHOR

PATRICK BYRNE started work as a structural engineer, moving into major civil engineering project management. Ten years ago he became chairman of a training company. At the age of 49 he took a part-time Masters' degree at De Montfort University Leicester in Human Resource Management.

Patrick is still an active Freemason after thirty years. He lives in Leicestershire, England. He is married with four children and four grandchildren.

Printed in the United States
207058BV00001B/441/A

9 781577 330998